The Least Detrimental Alternative

A Systematic Guide to Case Planning and Decision Making for Children in Care

When children are in distress or at risk in their homes, social service agencies may institute a number of measures. The most drastic entails removing such children from their homes and placing them in foster care. But placement often fails. Many children, some with severe and long-standing psychological, social, and educational handicaps, simply leave one unstable environment for another. In many cases, things just get worse.

Paul Steinhauer, a child psychiatrist at Toronto's Hospital for Sick Children, argues that foster placement has suffered from a lack of proven or generally acceptable models of intervention. It has further been impeded by decreases in the funding of social services and by ambivalence, on the part of both society and the mental health professions, towards the child welfare system. These factors have combined to produce a high failure rate, decreasing morale, and widespread disillusionment and burn-out in both foster parents and child welfare workers.

In this book Steinhauer brings together the fragmented research that has been done in a number of different disciplines. From this body of work he develops a model of intervention based on an understanding of attachment theory, development theory, and the practice of mental health consultation. The model provides a basis for pragmatic decision making and step-by-step guidelines for implementation of many of its components.

Steinhauer provides an important tool in the struggle to protect society's most vulnerable population.

PAUL D. STEINHAUER is Professor of Psychiatry at the University of Toronto's Division of Child Psychiatry and the Hospital for Sick Children.

The Least Detrimental Alternative

A Systematic Guide to Case Planning and Decision Making for Children in Care

PAUL D. STEINHAUER

UNIVERSITY OF TORONTO PRESS
Toronto Buffalo London

© University of Toronto Press 1991
Toronto Buffalo London
Printed in Canada

ISBN 0-8020-2786-5 (cloth)
ISBN 0-8020-6836-7 (paper)

⊖
Printed on acid-free paper

Canadian Cataloguing in Publication Data

Steinhauer, Paul D., 1933-
    The least detrimental alternative

    Includes bibliographical references and index.
    ISBN 0-8020-2786-5 (bound) ISBN 0-8020-6836-7 (pbk.)

    1. Foster home care.   2. Foster children –
Psychology.   3. Attachment behavior in children.
4. Adoption.   5. Social work with children.
I. Title.

HV873.S86 1991   362.7'33   C91-094020-7

This book has been published with the help of a generous grant from the
University of Toronto Women's Association.

To the late Dr John Bowlby and to Dr Gerald Caplan, who gave me the tools; and to the many foster children, foster parents, social workers, and, especially, Miss Jessie Watters, who taught me how to use them; and to my wife and family for their patience, their example, and their unconditional support, this book is dedicated with gratitude and respect.

Contents

viii Contents

Foreword

In the best of all possible worlds, every child would be brought up by his or her biological parents, who would have stable and mutually satisfying relationships with the child and with each other. They would provide the child with loving care and affection throughout childhood, act as role models to exemplify the values and behavioural norms of their culture and the different characteristics of men and women, provide controls and guidance to help him or her internalize the constraints of society, and offer psychosocial support to enable the child to master the stresses of life.

In today's world, although the majority of children receive good-enough parenting of this sort, a substantial and increasing minority do not. In the United States, for instance, every second family is split by divorce, which seriously destabilizes the parental system. If we add to this statistic the many cases of out-of-wedlock births, the families suffering from death or serious bodily or mental illness of a parent or of one of their children, and the large numbers of families burdened by parental psychological or social pathology, we may realize that very large numbers of today's children grow up in a less than optimal home environment, which not infrequently is frankly neglecting, rejecting, or abusive. Happily, only a minority of children react to this family adversity by developing psychopathology or social maladjustment; for instance, only 30 to 40 per cent of children of divorced parents become disordered. Protective factors include constitutional or acquired resilience to adversity in many children, as well as the potential psychosocial support they may receive from one of the parents or from some other key person inside or outside their family, which enables them to overcome their privations in a healthy way.

Nevertheless, the greatly increased risk of illness and maladjustment in children whose needs for loving care and support are not adequately met inside their family has led child welfare services to develop programs to remove such children from their natural homes for shorter or longer periods and to organize alternative facilities for bringing them up. These facilities may take the form of residential institutions and boarding schools that offer a regimented social framework for training and control, which does not involve close personal relationships with adults, or else replacement families, such as foster families or adoptive families, that provide close relationships with parenting adults in place of natural parents.

It is generally assumed, although it has not been proved, that some form of family living for children who must be removed from their natural home is the preferable alternative because it replaces the personal relationships that are lost and that are felt to be desirable, if not essential, in providing the emotional supplies that children need in developing healthy personalities and, particularly, a capacity to relate to others in a satisfying way.

Indeed, an outstanding characteristic of children who grow up in unsuitable homes is their incapacity to maintain mutually satisfying personal relationships, especially those involving trust and intimacy with loved ones; the result is a vicious-circle exacerbation of the problem in the population because such incapacity is a potent cause of marital disharmony when the deprived children become adults and also neglect, reject, or victimize their own children. Thus, the incidence of pathology in the next generation is likely to be increased.

Transfer of children from natural families that are harmful to foster families that offer the promise of satisfying the children's needs for adequate parenting faces three major obstacles. First, the children have to detach themselves psychologically from their biological parents and mourn their loss before they can then proceed to build a meaningful relationship with replacement parents. Such a process of detachment and mourning is often painfully difficult and protracted, especially in older children; paradoxically, it is likely to be the more difficult the more ambivalent the child's original relationship was to the natural parents: the more rejecting and victimizing the behaviour of these parents, the more intense will be the child–parent bond, even though it may be loaded with anxiety and guilt. In consequence it will be harder for the children to leave their home.

Second, children who have suffered from parental neglect, rejection, or victimization, or who have been exposed at home to scenes of violence, are prone as a result to suffer from conduct disorders that take the form of destructiveness and antisocial behaviour, or from oppositional rebelliousness towards adults. They may be too scared of cruel punishment by their natural parents to make much of a nuisance of themselves in their own home, but, once harsh restraints are lifted when they move to a healthy family, they are apt to behave in a particularly hostile and destructive manner that is very hard to curb or to tolerate. Such conduct is not caused just by wilful 'naughtiness' but by lack of a capacity for normal inhibition and self-control rooted in a specific disorder of personality produced by their pathogenic experiences in their natural family. This disorder is often chronic and particularly difficult to remedy, and is not amenable to modification by verbal persuasion and appeals to reason. Of all the forms of psychiatric illness in childhood, it has the worst prognosis as far as continuation into adult life is concerned, and it is the most resistant to treatment by verbal methods of psychotherapy.

The third obstacle is caused by 'transference.' This normal characteristic of individuals, whether adults or children, involves an unconscious compulsion to repeat interactions with figures from earlier life, who had involved them in unresolved emotional conflicts, by symbolically re-enacting these difficulties with people closely associated with them in their current life. Thus, traumatic episodes and relationships with their biological parents may be unconsciously played out by children with foster parents who are cast into identical roles and are expected by the children to be equally untrustworthy and damaging. The repeated re-enactment of these dramas is usually fostered by provocative and manipulative behaviour by the children that is unconsciously aimed at influencing the foster parents to behave badly towards them. The children continually test the foster parents to prove that they are just as untrustworthy as the natural parents, and that they too feel that the children are not deserving of being loved. The children are convinced that basically they are not lovable, and that it was their own badness that caused their natural parents to reject or attack them. Their fantasies of guilt, which remain largely unconscious, drive them to seek relief by provoking parent figures to punish them, while consciously the children pretend to be innocent victims, which in reality was originally the case.

These three expectable psychological obstacles make many foster children very difficult, indeed, to care for in a family setting. Is it not too much to expect of ordinary foster parents, even those of undeniable goodwill, over months or years to put up with the provocative behaviour, the destructive rebelliousness, and the ingratitude of such children, who would not even be accepted by most skilled and experienced clinical specialists as promising candidates for psychotherapy? Before trying to answer this question, let us discuss the community service system that organizes foster care.

This system usually includes five elements: a / a court of law, which determines that a child is psychologically or physically endangered by remaining in the unsupervised care of his biological parents, and orders the temporary or permanent removal of the child to alternative care; b / a child welfare agency that carries out the orders of the court and receives the child into its care, including recruiting and supervising foster parents and accepting responsibility for protecting the child as he moves out of and into his placements; c / a panel of specialist consultants, such as psychiatrists and psychologists, who, on request, advise and support the welfare workers and the foster parents; d / foster parents, who are recruited and paid by the welfare agency; and e / the natural parents, who, under the supervision of the welfare agency, maintain contact with the child while he is being fostered and to whose home he may return temporarily or permanently when the court determines that the danger to the child has subsided. Each element in this system has its own interests and policies. One hopes that communication among them will be sufficiently effective that they will not compete and weaken one another but will coordinate their activities to achieve and implement a mutually agreed-upon plan in respect to each child in care.

This goal is likely to be complicated; but if collaboration is indeed achieved, foster parents will not be left alone in facing the tribulations of caring for these difficult children, and, although they will have to grapple themselves with the day-to-day psychological upheavals, they will do so as part of a cohesive team and with adequate guidance and support by specialists in social work and child psychology, as well as with judicial backing. In particular, there will be effective initial screening to determine the nature and level of personality disturbance in the child taken into care, and if this disturbance is judged too severe for family placement, the child will be referred for institutional care. If he is less disturbed, he will be matched with appropriate foster parents, and both he and they will be helped to adjust to each other. Since crises in this adjustment are inevitable, the program must include the availability, as needed, of expert consultation, whether social work or psychological, to the foster parents, the foster child, or the social workers. This sounds ideal; but the supporters are likely to be constrained by shortage of manpower and of the public funds to pay for consultant or supervisory services. The ever-present danger will be that crises will be mismanaged, and that this will lead to an escalation of tension in the foster home and to the extrusion of the child. Such a situation will add further to the child's poor self-image and to the severity of his conduct disorder. Each time he experiences a failure situation and has to leave his home, his prognosis is likely to deteriorate.

In recent years, ways of reorganizing foster care systems to minimize this danger have been explored. One model that has been developed in several countries, such as Canada, England, the United States, and Israel, has been that of training foster parents in psychotherapeutic techniques, so that they become paraprofessional 'parent counsellors' or 'parent therapists' and organize their foster home as a kind of therapeutic milieu. They are trained to maintain objectivity and distance between themselves and their foster children and to learn to investigate and understand the causes and implications of disturbed behaviour, and how best to handle it, much as do the workers in a therapeutic institution for disturbed children. The training is partly theoretical: it covers child development; the phenomena of attachment, detachment, and mourning; and the manifestations of personality disorders and of transference reactions; and it is partly practical, through regular ongoing supervision of a group of foster parents by a social worker and a psychologist. Some of these foster parent–therapists are specially recruited and remunerated as career paraprofessionals, in addition to receiving the usual child welfare payments for board and lodging of their foster children; some are drawn from the ranks of ordinary foster parents and receive no additional remuneration. In most such experiments, the members of a group of foster families organized for joint supervision develop personal relationships with each other and form a kind of extended family of 'foster uncles' and 'foster aunts' for their children. The children visit in each other's homes and occasionally stay overnight to give their own foster parents a rest. In most such cases, members of the group also help each other out in crisis situations.

The evaluations of these models have shown positive results in terms of increased stability of placements and expressed satisfaction of foster parents and children. The program raises questions of both theoretical and practical interest. The unique contribution of foster parenting would seem to be that the personalized role of the inadequate biological parents has been replaced by a healthy couple who are non-professional and provide what the foster child feels to be close and authentic loving care. It is the very closeness of the attachment that he needs, but, at the same time, unconsciously feels to be so dangerous because it stimulates the re-emergence of his old conflicted feelings towards his natural parents. Institutional placement avoids this danger, but at the psychological cost of cutting off the supplies of needed personalized love, and focusing mainly on satisfying material needs and on behaviour training.

Foster parents who are successful in helping foster children to work through their detachment from and mourning for their lost natural parents, and to discover that they are basically lovable and worthy persons, probably accomplish this by the closeness and the authenticity of their spontaneous personalized relationship; they energize a 'corrective emotional experience' that withstands the provocations and the testing of the child. For this reason, foster parenting succeeds in cases where the verbal interpretations of traditional psychotherapy fail. The *professional* techniques of the therapist, based on maintaining objectivity and professional distance, are not powerful enough to withstand the doubts and suspicions of the traumatized child; and if they succeed they do so only after the child has repeatedly acted out through his provocations and has discovered that his therapist does not in fact reject him despite all his experience of the child's 'badness' – and probably not because the therapist has interpreted and brought into consciousness the child's unconscious fantasies. Words do not impress such children because of their past experience of being repeatedly deceived by the words of their natural parents. Deeds and their own awareness of the real feelings of others are the only facts that may eventually convince them to modify their attitude to themselves.

How then may we understand the apparent success of the subprofessional training in psychology given to foster parent–therapists, whose treatment results seem so much better than those achieved by their mentors when functioning as traditional professionals? The answer may lie in the possibility that this training is not powerful enough to damage unduly the non-professional style of the foster parents, which is based on their spontaneous use of themselves and their subjective feelings that

are experienced by the children as being 'authentic.' Of even more importance may be that it is the supervisory group as a *mutual support
group* that is the potent factor. This support frees members to be more
natural and spontaneous in their interactions with the children, since
they are assured of continuing protection by the group and its leaders,
as well as of the availability of practical help with tasks in emergencies,
and with relief when they are too fatigued to function effectively.

This does not mean that the educational component in these experimental programs is irrelevant. Insofar as it provides the foster parents
with information about the psychology of children who have been traumatized and who have been separated from their natural parents, it
helps the foster parents understand more fully why the children behave
as they do. Such understanding enables the adults to express their loving
care more effectively, much as similar understanding helps natural parents perform better; but spontaneous parenting is the model with which
they identify, and not that of the objective professional who maintains
professional distance from his clients and uses standardized techniques
to treat them.

In the light of these considerations, it may be that, if the true potency
of foster parenting derives from the very closeness and personalized
nature of the relationship between foster parents and foster children,
then services to obviate the inevitable risks of the associated non-professional vulnerability and burn-out should take the form of providing
foster parents with adequate psychological support that promotes and
protects this closeness and spontaneity and avoids trying to profession-
alize them.

This book, written by an outstanding leader in the field, a skilled
psychiatrist who is equally well trained and experienced in family diagnosis and therapy, in preventive psychiatry, in systems theory, and
in mental health education and consultation, discusses in clear language
the complex details of foster care and of the services designed to provide
and support it. It covers the relevant essentials of child development,
attachment theory, and the psychology of mourning. It analyses the roles
of the courts, the child welfare services, and the mental health specialists,
and discusses their interaction with foster parents, natural parents, and
those disturbed children who have been so badly damaged that they
must be taken into care. It deals with complicated issues without
oversimplification or idealization, and it confronts the problems of the
field in a forthright manner; it is an exciting book, and is a fitting tribute
to the thousands of men and women of goodwill who have, with selfless

devotion, spent many years in the service of a particularly needy population of children, whose lives have, in consequence, been greatly enriched.

Gerald Caplan

Preface

Since the Second World War there has been general agreement as to the presence of a major and continuing change in the nature of foster care throughout the Western world. This evolution has resulted from the interacting effects of many factors, including alterations in social conditions and in the pattern of social service delivery, additions to available knowledge of the effects on children of separation from attachment figures, and an upswing in incidence of family breakdown and intrafamilial violence. The result has been that an increasing number of society's most vulnerable, disturbed, and disruptive children are being managed within the foster care system, instead of within the residential treatment and correctional facilities that, until recently, were expected to contain and manage them. The foster care system, in marked contrast with adoptive and residential treatment services, continues in its traditional role as the 'poor relation' of children's and family services. Nevertheless, it has been forced by these various factors to adapt in order to cope with ever greater numbers of older and seriously disturbed children and adolescents who are more and more refractory to management by what was once considered standard foster care.

As this trend has continued over time, those working in the field have found themselves increasingly in a bind. On the one hand, they are forced to accommodate and to deal with growing numbers of disturbed and disruptive older children and adolescents in care, children who, in the past, would have been considered non-adoptable. On the other, widespread emphasis on such factors as children's need for continuity, their responses to separation from major attachment figures, the instability of foster care as it now exists, planned permanence, drift, and children's right to a home of their own have led to a widespread questioning of the efficacy – or even the validity – of long-term foster care. Faced with this inherent contradiction, which is compounded by society's and the mental health professions' traditional ambivalence towards the child welfare system, the decreased funds available for social services, the relatively low status of child welfare services in competition for generally inadequate resources, and the lack of proved or even accepted theories and models with which to explain and cope with the problems at hand, it is not surprising that mounting role confusion, disillusionment, and diminished morale in both foster parents and social workers have become endemic. These tendencies, in turn, have been reflected in the widespread burn-out of both foster parents and child welfare workers, thus further undermining the efficiency and integrity of the foster care system. This burn-out has doubly undermined the continuity of children's relationships with their major attachment figures. Breakdown rates of up to 40 per cent annually in some agencies have directly disrupted continuity for many children. At the same time, the shortage of foster families able to take on the large numbers of disruptive youngsters requiring service has caused chronic overloading of available resources, predisposing to further breakdowns, and thus further compromising, the nature and quality of existing services.

But what is the status of existing knowledge and ongoing research in the foster care field? Because of the many overlapping variables involved, well-designed and controlled studies of foster care are few and far between. Many researchers are loath to commit to study an area in which it is difficult, if not impossible, to design a research protocol sufficiently rigorous to separate the effects of the various input variables and intervening variables. Much of the data now available lack controls, and are inconclusive, and, often, contradictory. As a result, it is not yet possible to be sure whether the damage that is attributed to long-term care is an inevitable result of fostering per se, of inadequate and inconsistent casework services, or even of myths perpetuated by disillusioned workers and clinicians to rationalize their own feelings of frustration, disappointment, and failure. It is also unknown how many young people who develop successfully in long-term care disappear from the system and are therefore not available for follow-up studies.

As discouraging as the picture seems at times, advances in knowledge over the last twenty-five years could, if generally understood, integrated, and effectively applied, lead to improved service delivery. There are three basic areas of knowledge – one might call them the 'basic sciences' of foster care – that, complementing one another, can provide an improved understanding of the complex behavioural and emotional phenomena observed and some potential ways of increasing the effectiveness of systematic intervention. These three areas are: 1 / recent advances regarding normal and pathological aspects of development and, in particular, the applications of attachment theory to the situation of the child in care; 2 / the theory and practice of mental health consultation, as originally formulated by Gerald Caplan; 3 / more recent work on the effectiveness of mutual support groups.

The author contends that the knowledge and integration of what is known of the three areas outlined above make possible a workable, internally consistent, and effective approach to understanding, planning, and undertaking ongoing case management. From this, one can develop guidelines providing a consistent rationale for decision making, case planning, and casework services. These guidelines offer a framework for systematically approaching such vexing, but none the less crucial, questions as whether or not to take a child into care; how and when to decide to restore a child to the natural family; whether to free a child for adoption or to plan for that child to remain permanently in foster care with ongoing access to the natural parents; the significance of assisting a child with the work of mourning, and techniques for facilitating a mourning process that is blocked; the effects of foster care and adoption on the process of a child's identity formation; the respective roles of natural parents, foster parents, social workers, and foster children within the child care system; the ways of enhancing the efficacy of foster care; the effects of the family court system and the child-advocacy process on management; the role of mediation in child welfare; and the role and limitations of psychotherapy and residential treatment for the child in care.

Not only do the rationale and the guidelines it generates enable the systematic addressing of the issues noted above but, possibly even more important in the long run, they invite an experimental testing of the theory on which they are based. They challenge a number of myths that continue to undermine the quality of existing foster care by selecting and organizing the clinical applications of attachment theory into a potentially researchable series of guidelines that can be tested empirically. This approach has been shaped by what was learned through a critical review of the literature as interpreted using more than twenty-five years of continuous experience as a consultant to Children's Aid societies, primarily in Canada but also in the United States and Israel. By testing the validity of such guidelines, we can move beyond a theoretical rationale to develop the empirically based knowledge needed to minimize damage to children in care and to recognize the complex interrelationships among prevention programs, foster care, adoption, and restoration. Perhaps this knowledge will provide more precise indications for the selective utilization of each of these interventions within a comprehensive system of child care services. Until these questions have been definitively answered, however, the application of such guidelines offers a pragmatic basis for decision making and for focusing our efforts to minimize risks and protect the growth potential of one of society's most vulnerable groups of children – those who must grow up in families other than their own.

P.S.

Acknowledgments

This book would never have been completed but for the dedication and hard work of a number of very special people.

Ryna Langer, Brad Park, Annie Steinhauer, and Nancy Steinhauer all contributed to the review of the literature, part of which was supported by the Department of Psychiatry of the Hospital for Sick Children. Pat Follet, who typed the drafts of the early chapters, and Angela Pramberger, who then took over and delivered the manuscript in its final form, were unfailingly willing and helpful, even in the face of those repeated demands for 'Just one more draft!.'

I am very grateful to my colleague, Margaret Snowden, who enriched the two chapters on adoption as an alternative to foster care through the knowledge and perspective she brought from her experiences both as an adoption worker and as an adoptive mother.

The professionalism of my editor from the University of Toronto Press, Beverley Beetham Endersby, which contributed greatly to the clarity of the finished text, and the steadfast support of the Press's managing editor, Virgil Duff, are much appreciated.

Finally, and most of all, I am indebted to my wife, Estelle, not just for the thankless job of typing the references, but for her abundant patience, goodwill, and the encouragement she always managed to find when it was needed, even on those long nights and weekends when I barely emerged from my struggle with the manuscript.

An earlier version of chapter 2 appeared as 'Issues of attachment and separation: Foster care and adoption,' in P.D. Steinhauer and Q. Rae-

Grant, eds., *Psychological Problems of the Child in the Family* (New York: Basic Books 1983), 69–101.

An earlier version of chapter 5 appeared as 'Assessing parenting capacity,' *Am. J. Orthopsychiatry* 53 (3): 468–81. It appears here with permission from the *American Journal of Orthopsychiatry*. Copyright 1983 by the American Orthopsychiatric Association, Inc.

The original statements from which chapter 11 was developed were included in 'The Laidlaw Workshop on the "impossible" child: An overview,' *Can. Psych. Assoc. J.*, Special Supplement 23 (SS): SS61–74, and 'The management of children admitted to child welfare services in Ontario: A review and discussion of current problems and practices,' *Can. J. Psychiat.* 29 (6): 473–83.

Chapter 15 is an expansion of material initially published as 'The Foster Care Research Project: Summary and analysis' (with M. Johnston, M. Snowden, J. Santa-Barbara, B. Kane, P. Barker, and J.P. Hornick), *Can. J. Psychiat.* 33 (August): 509–16, and 'The Foster Care Research Project: Clinical impressions' (with M. Johnston, J.P. Hornick, P. Barker, M. Snowden, J. Santa-Barbara, B. Kane), *Am. J. Orthopsychiatry* 59 (3): 430–41. The latter is used with permission from the *American Journal of Orthopsychiatry*.

Chapter 16 expands on material in 'Criteria and methodology for assessing credibility of sexual abuse allegation' (with W. Wehrspann and H. Klajner-Diamond), *Can. J. Psychiat.* 32 (October): 615–23.

Chapter 17 expands on material in 'Adoption,' in B. Garfinkel, G. Carlson, and E. Weller, eds., *The Medical Basis of Child and Adolescent Psychiatry* (Philadelphia: W.B. Saunders, 1990), 428–40.

Chapter 19 expands on 'The preventive utilization of foster care,' *Can. J. Psychiat.* 33 (August): 459–67.

PART ONE

The Historical Context
of Foster Care and Adoption

Chapter One

The History of Adoption and Foster Care

The problem of how to deal with orphaned and homeless children is known to have existed for at least forty-eight centuries. The earliest recorded adoption was that of Sargon I, the founder king of Babylon, in the twenty-eighth century BC. His story, told in an ancient inscription, resembles that of Moses: Sargon was placed in a vessel made of reeds and floated down a river, where he was found by a simple water carrier who, out of the 'kindness of his heart ... raised me as his own son' (Rank 1914, quoted in Clothier 1939).

Originally, reasons for adoption had less to do with the welfare of the adoptees than with that of the adopters. Reasons for adoption included ensuring the continuation of the male line or the religion (for example, The Essenes), guaranteeing the financial and political power of an individual or family, or even political assimilation, as in the early eighteenth century when the Iroquois adopted the Delawares. Adoptive practices of a nation often reflected its cultural values. For example, the Roman Code of Justinian of AD 534 showed the Romans' preoccupation with war. Under this code, 'a child took the name of a person who adopted him but did not gain property rights, although he agreed to bear arms on behalf of his adopted father' (Clothier 1939).

With the establishment of Christianity and its emphasis on the sanctity of human life, infanticide and abortion, methods previously used to dispose of unwanted children, began to be considered crimes. The humanitarian ideology of the Enlightenment established a secular basis for protecting the rights of the child. However, even with these newfound attitudes, adoption was a rare solution for the problem of a growing population of orphaned and abandoned children. Instead, care for the masses of homeless children was relegated to institutions. In Western Europe, 'as a corollary of legislation against infanticide, institutions to care for foundlings came into existence' (Summer 1959).

The first sign of an organized child welfare society in medieval Europe was an asylum for abandoned infants, founded in Milan in AD 787. Next, in 1160, Guy de Montpelier established the Order of the Holy Spirit for the care of foundlings and orphans. Foundling homes attempted to provide an alternative to infanticide and haphazard abandonment, offering temporary care for children, but not proper parenting. In 1741, the London Foundling Home was founded in order to 'prevent the murders of poor, miserable children at their births, to suppress the inhuman custom of exposing newborn infants to perils in the streets, and to take in children dropped in churchyards or in the streets or left at night at the doors of church wardens or overseers of the poor' (Kadushin 1980).

Such hospitals, however, were less than successful. In the foundling hospitals, the number of abandoned children dying 'probably varied at the frightful rate of 50 to 80%' from city to city (Kadushin 1980). From what Spitz described (1945) as the effects of extreme emotional deprivation, which he termed 'hospitalism,' this death rate, as high as it is, should not be surprising to the reader.

The first sign of legal consideration of the welfare of the adoptee came in 1300, when Alphonso V of Castille established the 'great code.' In it, he defined adoption and stated that children under age seven could not be adopted, since they were not sufficiently developed to give an informed consent. Children age seven to fifteen could be adopted only with the king's permission, following an investigation to ensure that the adoption would be advantageous to the child (Clements 1971).

Meanwhile, with the decline of feudalism and the start of the industrial revolution, more and more children were being used for child labour and industrial slavery. Finally, in the nineteenth century, laws were passed to aid these children. In 1869, in England, the National Children's Home and Orphanage was founded, and legislation was passed to govern the education and labour of children (Clements 1971). In France, by 1830, there were some 230 'tours,' revolving boxes in front of churches, into which abandoned children were being dropped to ensure protection by the church, and between 1824 and 1833, 297 infants were legally abandoned (Kadushin 1980). In the United States, in 1984, Yates, the Secretary of New York, established almshouses, which were to instruct children in trade and moral training. Unfortunately, these almshouses also became the homes of social misfits, paupers, drunkards, drug addicts, and perverts, with no segregation of the sexes. These were the companions of the children in these institutions. In 1868, New York State banished these almshouses, recommending instead 'segregation of the dependent child in congregate orphan asylums' (Clothier 1939).

In the mid-nineteenth century, Massachusetts passed the first adoption law in the United States; it aimed at making a provision for the dependent child, and required: the written consent of the child's parents; the joint petition of the adoptive parents; a decree by the judge if satisfied that the adoption is 'fit and proper'; and complete severance of relations between the child and his or her natural parents (Clothier 1939).

Charles Britwell of the Boston Children's Aid Society, concerned with the needs of the individual child, brought about the institution of supervised boarding homes rather than asylums or unsupervised homes as a placement resource for dependent children. Foster care developed as an attempt to rescue 'good' children from 'bad' parents (Maluccio et al 1980). Foster parents provided room, board, and training for good citizenship in exchange for the child's helping out in the family's home, farm, or business. It wasn't until the 1930s that the process of assessing and approving foster homes was introduced. At about this time, foster parents began to be paid a basic per diem to cover the cost of the child's room and board, and, for the first time, an attempt to match children and foster homes was undertaken. Foster homes continued to be regarded as the placement choice for homeless and unadoptable children – that is, older children, children with handicaps, and children still in contact with their natural families – until the 1960s. Foster care remained, however, much less socially acceptable than adoption (Cooper 1978). Although there are virtually no adequately controlled follow-up studies, the overwhelming general impression is that few foster children made successful adjustments as adults, although those cases most accessible to review were the ones with multiple problems. Those foster children who had married and made at least an apparently successful social adjustment usually broke contact with agencies, and were less accessible for follow-up research. During this period, there were few clear guidelines for decision making, and, as to the role of foster parents themselves, it was often unclear whether they were clients of the agency, substitute parents, surrogate therapists for psychosocially handicapped children, or all of the above (Cooper 1978; Eastman 1979; Katz 1976; Wiltse 1979).

The Changing Nature of Children Who Are
Being Fostered and Adopted

Since the Second World War, there has been a marked change in the type of children in the foster care system and those available for adoption. Traditionally, many foster children were normal healthy infants being observed for their first three months prior to being placed on adoption. Currently, infants are placed on adoption immediately upon discharge from the hospital nursery, that is, within the first week of life, and so there no longer exists a large pool of normal, healthy infants in foster care. Another traditional use of foster care was to provide temporary caretaking for children whose parents were ill or for families in financial distress. Because of the development of other community resources, such as homemaker services, mother's allowance, and day-care services, such problems are now usually dealt with without removing children from their families.

Those children who do come into care these days usually do so as a result of abuse or chronic neglect, both of which are generally symptomatic of a family system in the process of breaking down and chronically unsatisfactory parent–child relationship. Many of these children have been repeatedly exposed to violent conflict in their families prior to coming into care. As a result, they are commonly both disturbing to their foster families and emotionally disturbed (Rutter 1979c). The majority of them are older or 'special needs' children who, at the point of entry into the foster care system, already display a variety of mental, physical, emotional, and behavioural problems. They require not just basic care and surrogate parenting, but some form of active remedial intervention according to a management plan worked out between the agency and the foster parents. Because such 'special needs' children often have a considerable disrupting effect on the life-style of the foster family, some foster parents receive, along with a boarding and maintenance allowance, an increment related to the special – that is, treatment – services they provide. Such foster parents require ongoing training, support, and supervision in order to ensure that they understand the children's complex needs and the meaning of their behaviour well enough to provide the necessary therapeutic milieu (Darnell 1987; Hochstadt et al 1987; Allison and Kufeldt 1987; Steinhauer 1983b; Cooper 1978; Hawkins et al 1985; Chamberlain 1988; Friedman 1987; Webb 1988).

In the 1960s, group homes began to challenge foster homes as the placement of choice for the increased number of disturbed adolescents coming into care. Group-home placements demand less intensity of relationship than do those in foster families. Thus group homes were considered less likely to arouse loyalty conflicts and a need for distancing. Also, in the 1970s, long-term fostering came to be challenged generally on the grounds that it is inherently unstable (Cooper 1978; Finkelstein 1980; Prosser 1978). The result was an increased pressure to place in adoption homes, in the name of 'permanency planning,' many children who would once have been considered unadoptable because of age, racial background, and/or multiple physical, social, and emotional handicaps.

In the twentieth century, two events have been responsible for great increases in the number of adoptions: the world wars, which produced large numbers of orphaned children requiring care; and research on children forcibly separated from their parents (Freud and Burlingham 1943; Robertson and Robertson 1971), which focused attention on the importance of maintaining the continuity of relationship with major attachment figures in order to protect successful development (Clements 1971). This new awareness led to the legalization of adoption in England and Wales in 1926, and the passing of new legislation in the United States that increased emphasis on the need for investigation into whether or not a home is indeed 'fit and proper' before permitting adoption.

Following the Second World War, there was an increase in the number of total adoptions, which reached a peak in the late 1960s (Hepworth 1980; Hersov 1985). Since then, although the total number of adoptions still exceeds pre-1960 levels, an increasing percentage – estimated in Great Britain as 70 per cent and in Canada as over 50 per cent – of total adoptions consist of intrafamilial adoptions by step-parents, reflecting the steep rise in divorce and remarriage rates (Office of Population Censuses and Surveys Monitor 1976; Hepworth 1980). Thus, although the total number of adoptions has decreased slightly, both the number and the percentage of extrafamilial adoptions have fallen off sharply. Two main factors seem to have contributed to this decline.

First, most adoptees are the offspring of unmarried mothers, especially of mothers under age twenty (Guyatt 1980; Hepworth 1980; Hersov 1985). Second, although the number of illegitimate children remains significantly above that of the early 1960s, the number of healthy infants available for adoption has decreased sharply. Since there has been no corresponding decrease in the popularity of adoption, there are now too many applicants for too few babies. Reasons for this situation include: 1 / new legislation permitting dissemination of birth-control information and sale of contraceptives, although these may be used more effectively by older women than by those under age twenty (traditionally the largest source of babies for adoption) (Guyatt 1980); 2 / the legalization of abortion, which shortly preceded the sharp decrease in illegitimate births; and 3 / the fact that significantly more unmarried mothers are now keeping their babies. This last cited trend presumably results from changing community attitudes towards illegitimacy and the increased availability of social benefits (e.g., mother's allowance and day care) (Guyatt 1980; Hepworth 1980; Hersov 1985).

One of the most striking results of these changes is a convergence and overlapping of foster care and adoption (Cooper 1978; Kadushin 1980; Gill and Amadio 1983). With fewer healthy normal infants available for adoption, more and more special-needs children who would once have been considered unadoptable are being placed in adoptive homes. There is great pressure to find adoptive homes for all children whose relationships with their biological parents have been permanently severed. The motives for this exertion of pressure are mixed. To some extent, of course, agencies are trying to find each child a permanent substitute home in order to avoid allowing children to drift into unplanned permanent foster care, neglected by their biological parents, their foster parents, and the agencies supposedly responsible for their care. Adoption is viewed, at times naïvely, as generically better (that is, as a consistently more permanent and better placement) than foster care. Because such children, once adopted, are supported by their adoptive parents and are no longer a financial drain on the state, it is not difficult to see why government social-service departments press for adoption wherever possible.

But just as the children who are becoming available for adoption resemble more and more the typical long-term foster child, other forms of long-term placement, which take up a position somewhere between foster care and adoption, are emerging. These include subsidized adoption – that is, adoption that continues to receive financial support, presumably because of the special needs of the child – and adoption with access, in which a child is placed in a home with adoptive parents who are able to tolerate the child's retaining contact with significant attachment figures from the past, such as previous foster parents or even biological parents. At the same time, forms of foster care are evolving that are much closer to adoption, such as planned permanent foster care and foster care with tenure. These types of placements are usually reserved for children who have formed an attachment and who are developing well in caring foster families. Such foster parents, for a number of reasons, including marginal financial status and a fear of taking full emotional and financial responsibility for a child who is already acting out and is likely to need multiple remedial services in adolescence, are not prepared to adopt. Thus, there are a number of forms of both foster care and adoption that fall somewhere in between the traditional definition of these two forms of placement.

Often, one of the major factors determining whether children will remain in foster care or proceed to adoption is the age at which they are removed permanently from their biological parents. If the removal is complete at an age where the child is young enough not to retain an attachment to the biological parents, the chances of that child's being adopted are significantly greater than for a child old enough to retain a strong, even if ambivalent, attachment to the biological parents.

There are many variants of attachment, all of which affect children's responses to separation and placement. Because of the importance that issues related to attachment and separation have in determining children's adjustment to and development in foster care, the research on attachment and separation will be reviewed in chapter 2. Then, chapter 3 will provide a clinical illustration of one child's response to the loss of her parents.

PART TWO

Background Issues

Chapter Two

Issues of Attachment
and Separation:
Mourning and Loss
in Children

Definition of and Influences on the Process of Mourning

Among the most important psychological and developmental hazards
faced by children within the child welfare system are those related to
problems of attachment and separation, and to children's difficulty in
successfully mourning their losses. This chapter reviews in some detail
the literature on attachment, separation, and mourning, demonstrating
how problems in any one of these areas may spill over to undermine,
first, the others and, ultimately, the child's overall development.

For optimal development, all children ideally should grow up in a
family that is caring and able to provide both high-quality and continuity
of parenting. The infant's first basic need, a prerequisite for optimal
development, is for a secure attachment to a primary caregiver, usually,
but not necessarily, the mother. 'Attachment' refers to the bond of caring
and craving that ties child and caregiver to each other. Once formed,
the attachment persists, even in the absence of the primary caregiver.
Initially, in response to separation, the pull towards the other increases,
like the tension in a stretched rubber band. As children get older, they
willingly separate, and 'good-enough' parents appropriately encourage
this separation. The initial forays into independence are tentative ones,
with the child checking back frequently to gain reassurance from the
attachment figure who remains available as a secure base for the child.
With aging, increased confidence and security on the part of both parents
and child allow further taking and granting of independent and exploratory behaviours.

Children form multiple attachments, but usually the strongest and most significant are those to the parents, usually the mother (Ainsworth 1967), even if the child is raised by a substitute caregiver or in day care (Ricciuti 1974; Farran and Ramey 1977; Cummings 1980). In such cases, the need for a successful attachment to parents is, if anything, intensified. The bond to this primary attachment figure is stronger than those the child forms with others; therefore, the mother is preferred over other figures to whom the child is attached when comfort or reassurance is needed. This capacity for selective bonding to a primary attachment figure is crucial to normal development, since a failure to develop the capacity for selective bonding in the early years – as occurs, for example, when a child is raised in an institution with multiple and changing caretakers, none of whom takes a particular and continuing interest in the child – has been associated with permanent and uncorrectable problems in social behaviour (Rutter 1979c).

The strength of an attachment depends less on the amount of time that adult and child spend together than on the quality of the parents' involvement and the extent to which they are able to respond sensitively and consistently to the needs of the child. A secure attachment is crucial to the development of trust and the capacity for intimacy (Ainsworth 1969; Tizard and Hodges 1978; Tizard and Rees 1974; Tizard and Tizard 1971). It also plays a critical role in the process of socialization and in preparing children to give up what, to them, are perfectly acceptable behaviours in order to safeguard their major attachments (Bowlby 1969). A secure primary attachment evokes protest and distress from the young child in response to separation from the attachment figure. It also reduces anxiety and encourages exploration in strange situations, and prompts proximity-seeking behaviour in the infant when the parent leaves or returns.

In 1951, Bowlby published a detailed description of three stages by which children react to separation from – that is, disruption of the selective bond to – their primary attachment figures. He outlined a number of serious and long-term sequelae occurring in children whom he considered had not mourned successfully the parents from whom they had been separated. Rutter, reviewing the topic in 1972, confirmed Bowlby's claim that experiences in infancy and early childhood might have serious and persistent effects on development, but suggested that Bowlby's formulation of the harmful effects of separation per se was overstated. In his repeat (1979c) review of the topic, Rutter again surveyed the experimental evidence, coming to the following conclusions.

The *acute distress syndrome*, Rutter demonstrated, was a result of interference with attachment behaviour, rather than of the act of separation per se. The work of the Robertsons (1971) with young children admitted to hospitals and residential nurseries demonstrated that infants cared for in a family following separation showed less acute distress than did those placed in an institution. Hinde and McGinnis (1977), studying young rhesus monkeys and their mothers, related much of the infants' emotional disturbance following reunion to tensions in the mother–child relationship. Both these studies suggested that, while the reaction was precipitated by a separation, factors in addition to the act of separation itself, probably including conditions preceding or following it, had more effect on subsequent attachment behaviour than did the separation per se (Rutter 1972, 1979c).

Rutter (1971) had earlier shown a strong association between *conduct disorders* and family conflict, even in the absence of separation. Epidemiological research conducted in the mid-1970s (Rutter et al 1975; West and Farrington 1973, 1977) and Robins's (1966) longitudinal study have confirmed this close association. Lambert, Essen, and Head (1977) demonstrated that, in most children removed from their homes because of behavioural problems, the disturbed behaviour preceded the removal, so that, while the separation may have been an additional source of stress, it was not the cause of the antisocial behaviour. The dysfunctional behaviour common to such children has been shown to be related more to the chronic discord and disharmony typical of their natural families prior to separation than to the act of separation (Hulsey and White 1989; Pianta, Egeland, and Hyatt 1986; Wadsworth 1984). Rogeness et al (1986) have demonstrated that conduct disorders are seen more commonly in abused and neglected boys and abused girls than in neglected girls.

The *intellectual deficits* described by Bowlby were shown by Rutter (1979c) to result more from a lack of early linguistic and perceptual stimulation than from the process of separation. This finding is also clear from Tizard's studies of institutionally reared children who, despite major discontinuity in child–caretaker relationships – with some having been cared for by up to eighty parent surrogates – were shown at age eight to be of normal intelligence (Tizard and Joseph 1970; Tizard and Rees 1974; Tizard and Hodges 1978). Thus, continuity in relationships with major attachment figures is less crucial to intellectual development than to social development. However, the poor task involvement of institutionally reared children in the classroom, demonstrated by the same studies, would probably affect their school performance and, possibly, their later cognitive development. The association between systematic measures of home stimulation and children's IQ has been clearly demonstrated (Bradley and Caldwell 1976, 1980; Clarke-Stewart 1973; McCall, Appelbaum, and Hagarty 1973). Neglected boys have a lower verbal IQ than do abused or well-parented boys. In contrast to boys, both abused and neglected girls show decreases in performance and in verbal IQ (Rogeness et al 1986).

Similarly, *disturbances in socialization* were shown to be related less to the act of separation than to a disturbance in the original selective bonding process. Rutter (1979a, 1979c) suggests that a failure to bond selectively in infancy is later associated with a series of socially inappropriate behaviours. At age four, Tizard's institutionally reared children were more clinging, overly friendly with strangers, more attention-seeking, and less likely to form deep attachments (Tizard and Rees 1975; Tizard and Tizard 1971). At age eight, the same children were still more attention-seeking, more restless, more disobedient, and more unpopular. Fewer than half of them were considered closely attached to their housemothers, and they remained more demanding of affection than did other children (Tizard 1977; Tizard and Hodges 1978). Tizard and Hodges's (1978) study showed that children adopted after age four usually did bond selectively to their adoptive parents. In school, they continued to show the same social and attentional problems as those who had remained in institutions. Rutter (1979a) concluded that, while children are capable of forming attachments after age four, early selective bonding is a prerequisite for normal social development.

We must acknowledge our debt to Rutter for this comprehensive review of the literature. However, in demonstrating that factors other than separation per se are also major determinants of the sequelae described above, he seemed to minimize the importance of separation from the major attachment figures. Rutter concedes that separation can be an important precipitant of and an additional stress exacerbating pre-existing vulnerabilities. But, it is Rutter who has done so much to demonstrate the cumulative effects of simultaneously existing stresses (Rutter et al 1975; Quinton and Rutter 1976). Surely the literature on children's responses to marital separation (Hetherington et al 1986; Robson 1987; Tessman 1978; Wallerstein and Kelly 1982; Wallerstein and Blakeslee 1989; Rae-Grant and Robson 1988) demonstrates that children's responses to separation, even when not preceded by conflict and discord, are by no means benign. Typically, they show signs of both acute and chronic distress, conduct and emotional disorders, learning problems, and a deterioration of social behaviour and relationships. This finding is not surprising, since separation cannot occur without disrupting a selective bond.

At least in those areas discussed above, Rutter's contribution complements and expands on Bowlby's original formulation of children's responses to separation. In other areas – for example, his conclusion that the child's major bond to the mother does not differ in quality from those to other attachment figures – the two formulations are clearly incompatible. But Rutter, like Bowlby, agrees that the lack of selective bonding in the very young child seriously compromises later social adjustment and cannot be entirely overcome by subsequently placing the child in a more advantageous environment. The significance of this conclusion for children over the age of six months who have to be separated from inadequate parents is crucial. How can one effect such a separation when necessary while still protecting the child's capacity for selective bonding throughout those critical early years?

As we have seen, many of the long-term effects that Bowlby ascribed to separation, Rutter and others have demonstrated were largely attributable to family discord and disharmony preceding the separation. Most foster children experience considerable and prolonged family discord, neglect, and/or violence with or without abuse prior to separation from their families (Pianta, Egeland, and Hyatt 1986; Schaughency and Lahey 1985). While individual children's reactions to separation may vary, there is little doubt that the traumatic effects of separation will be intensified by conflict and discord that have preceded it. Rutter et al (1975) and Quinton and Rutter (1976) have shown that two or more interacting stresses have a total effect much greater than the mere sum of these same stresses occurring separately. Thus, the risk of psychological disturbance in response to family discord or abusive or violent behaviour followed by separation is multiplied, often many times over (Rutter 1979b; Brown and Harris 1978). The extent of this disturbance is likely to undermine the child's acceptability to and integration within the substitute family provided. Substitute parents committed enough to persist in spite of severe and chronic distancing and provocation can sometimes succeed in helping such a child form a selective and secure reattachment (Tizard 1977). Less committed surrogates, however, are often put off by children's repeated provocations and rejections. All too often, they respond with increasing frustration and insensitivity, leading, in time, to withdrawal, rejection, or even renewed abuse. This is one example of how children's disturbances of personality and behaviour resulting from earlier adverse experiences invite a repetition of the noxious environmental response (Littner 1960; Bowlby 1982; Rutter 1979c).

The rejection of the substitute parents is yet another hazard that, added to the existing stresses of parental discord and separation, adversely affects the child's behaviour, thus increasing the risk of further placement breakdowns. Such a child, by this stage, shows the cumulative effects of disturbance within the natural family, one or more separations, and secondary rejection within several foster families – all negatively interacting with one another (see figure 2.1).

Rutter (1971) was also one of the first to demonstrate that not all children respond similarly to separation from their major attachment figures. A number of factors will affect the intensity of a particular child's response to separation. Each of these factors interacts with the others in an ongoing way, either intensifying or undermining one another's effects. These factors are considered below.

1 / *The age of the child.* Studies of infant development demonstrate that an infant can remember and respond differently to the smell, voice, and face of the mother as early as the first few weeks of life. Infants are not, however, thought to have the integrated concept of another person to whom they are selectively attached until, according to the best available evidence, early in the second half of the first year of life. Separating a child younger than six months from the primary attachment figure frequently causes a brief disruption of eating and sleeping, and may temporarily increase irritability. It is doubtful, however, whether the child removed from parental figures before age six months will experience the full force of the acute distress precipitated by disruption of an existing selective attachment (Yarrow 1967). The intensity of an initial separation is likely to be greatest when it occurs between ages six months and four years (Quinton and Rutter 1976). During these years, children are, because of their stage of cognitive and emotional development, particularly vulnerable to separation, as they are intensely dependent, physically and emotionally, on the primary caretaker. In addition, their cognitive development at this age is insufficient to allow them to understand the reasons for the separation or to be reassured of the temporary nature of even a necessary and clearly explained separation. Nor will it allow them to express easily or to work through successfully at a symbolic (i.e., verbal or play) level the acute distress generated by the disruption of their primary attachment.

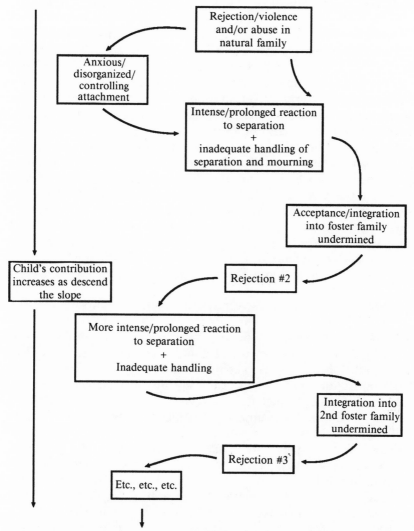

Figure 2.1   The slippery slope: cumulative effect of unresolved separation

2 / *Previous mother–child relationships.* Stayton and Ainsworth (1973) have demonstrated that children with a secure attachment show less short-term distress following separation than those whose attachment

is insecure and ambivalent. Thus, children of sensitive, responsive mothers are less upset following separation than are those whose mothers are insensitive and inconsistently responsive. This finding is consistent with the theory that one of the 'purposes' of bonding is to provide the sense of security – the availability, when needed, of a secure base – to prepare the child for exploratory behaviour and eventual independence (Bowlby 1979). It is also supported by a number of studies of separation of primate infants from their mothers (Harlow et al 1966; Hinde Spencer-Booth, and Bruce 1966; Mineka and Suomi 1978). Abusive or inconsistent parents, who are less able to provide security when the infant is stressed, could be predicted to have children who show a more insecure attachment and, therefore, greater anxiety and clinging than do those parents who are consistently indifferent. In animal experiments, at least, anxiety seems to increase the intensity of the primary attachment, regardless of the response of the attachment figure (Rosenblum and Harlow 1963; Seay, Alexander, and Harlow 1964). From systematic data on humans now available, there is little doubt that the same is true (Lamb et al 1982; Ross and Goldman 1977; Rutter, Quinton, and Liddle 1983).

A number of observers have noted how one- and two-year-olds responded to reunion with their parents after two weeks or more in an institutional setting without the support of special caregivers (Robertson 1953; Robertson and Bowlby 1952; Heinicke and Westheimer 1965; Robertson and Robertson 1971). Their observations have confirmed that a major separation from parents at this age modifies the behaviour of a child towards the parent following reunion. Children reunited after a relatively short separation appeared anxious, clinging, and irritable, and alternated proximity-seeking with avoidant behaviours. Those who had been away from the parent for a longer time actively avoided the parent on reunion or, at best, alternated moving away with unpredictable outbursts of hostility.

The Ainsworth Strange Situation (Ainsworth et al 1978) is a laboratory observation of a standardized paradigm involving infants and their mothers. The infant is first introduced to a room and the toys it contains, and later to a stranger who enters the room. This having been done, the mother leaves the room for a set period of several minutes and then returns, only to repeat this procedure a few minutes later. The infant's responses to the mother's leaving and to her return are carefully noted. Using these reactions, Stayton and Ainsworth (1973) classified infants' responses to separation from their primary caretakers. Three major patterns of response, which are consistent with home behaviour, were noted:

- *Group A babies* – termed 'insecure-avoidant' by Ainsworth – showed little upset when the mother left, and ignored or actively avoided her on her return, often paying more attention to the stranger.
- *Group B babies* were 'securely attached' to their mothers. They were moderately distressed when the mother left and when she returned, but sought comfort from her. After a brief cuddle, they gradually and comfortably returned to playing with toys. Their responses contrasted markedly from those of the two other groups of children who were insecurely attached.
- *Group C babies* – termed 'insecure-ambivalent' – showed much more upset than either of the other groups when the mother left. When she returned, they remained upset and clinging, their distress often punctuated by interspersed outbursts of anger for much longer, before being ready to return to play.

In summary, it appears that separations from major attachment figures evoke a change in infants' behaviour towards them. This change shows particularly in their responses to reunion with the parents. From the proximity-seeking of the securely attached infants, through the clinging but angry responses of the intermediate-ambivalent group, to the avoidant behaviour of those longest separated, we see a progression of disruption of children's responses to their relationship with their caregivers. Proximity, over time, is replaced, first, by ambivalence and, eventually, by indifference. These responses strongly parallel those described by Ainsworth as insecure-ambivalent (Group C) and insecure-avoidant (Group A) in the 'Strange Situation.'

Schneider-Rosen and colleagues (1985), Lamb and colleagues (1985), and Erickson, Sroufe, and Egeland (1985) have demonstrated that significantly larger numbers of maltreated infants whose attachments were measured at twelve, eighteen, and twenty-four months were insecurely attached than was true for a control group of adequately cared-for infants, although it was surprising how many of the high-risk infants seemed securely attached. Furthermore, while the attachment patterns of the infants who were not maltreated remained stable over time, those of the infants who were maltreated did not. Further analysis demonstrated that maltreated infants who had been insecurely attached retained their insecure attachments, whereas those maltreated infants who seemed initially securely attached tended to drift into the insecurely attached groups.

In some ways, the increase in Insecure/Avoidant (Group A) attachments – from 29 per cent at twelve months to 46 per cent at eighteen months, and to 46.5 per cent at twenty-four months – may represent an increasingly organized and adaptive attempt by the maltreated infants to cope with an excessively frustrating relationship with their primary caretakers. Such a solution, however, decreases the usefulness of the primary caretaker as a partner in the learning process. Thus it is not surprising that the Group A toddlers, so highly represented in the maltreated group, showed lower communication skills, including linguistic performance levels (Schneider-Rosen and Cicchetti 1984; Gersten et al 1986). Schneider-Rosen and colleagues (1985) demonstrated that subsequent interactions can help compensate for an earlier insecure attachment to abusive parents. They concluded that the child who is insecurely attached as a result of parental maltreatment is more vulnerable to difficulties in accomplishing subsequent developmental tasks in a competent and adaptive manner.

In their extremely comprehensive recent review of the more recent attachment literature, Main and Solomon (1990) drew attention to a significant number of children who cannot be reliably classified as belonging to group A, B, or C. Two independent studies of high-risk populations (Lyons-Ruth et al 1987; Carlson et al 1989) have reported that the great majority of infants of maltreating parents are best classified in a fourth category – Group D, or 'Disorganized/Disoriented.' (This category also includes a minority of infants from a control, low-risk, population). By attempting to force such disorganized infants into the traditional A, B, and C classification – as was done routinely until the Group D category was suggested by Main and Solomon (1986) – one ended up with excessive numbers of infants who appeared 'secure' (Group B), even though many were known to have had an insecure attachment and/or to have been maltreated (Egeland and Sroufe 1981a; Crittenden 1985, 1987; Spieker and Booth 1985).

Prior to Main and Solomon's description of the 'Disorganized/Disoriented' category in 1986, a number of attempts were made to develop new classification systems to describe infants whose attachment behaviours were so disrupted as to place them beyond the original A, B, and C categories. Egeland and Sroufe 1981b developed another D category for many of the known abused and neglected infants in their sample. In their original classification, these insecurely attached infants had been forced into the B (insecure) category because their behaviour was apathetic and disorganized, rather than avoidant or resistant. Crittenden (1985, 1987) had found that those known abused or neglected infants in her sample originally classified within the B group were better described by what she termed an A/C, that is 'Avoidant/Ambivalent,' grouping. These infants sought proximity with the returning parent, but in a manner suggesting high avoidance or resistance. They approached their caregiver on reunion without the expected evidence of strong pleasure, often obliquely and in a whining and petulant manner. In addition, these infants showed a number of unusual behaviours indicative of a high stress level, such as head covering, head cocking, huddling on the floor, and rocking or wetting.

In the 'Strange Situation,' the infants in Main and Solomon's (1986) 'Disorganized/Disoriented' (Group D) classification typically showed episodes of behaviour that seemed to lack any clearly observable goal, intention, or explanation, in addition to one or more of the following behaviours: expected temporal sequences were frequently disorganized; they showed simultaneously contradictory behaviour patterns; their movements or expressions were often incomplete or lacking in direction, and at times included stereotypes; direct signs of confusion or apprehension of the parent were common, as were behavioural stilling or freezing. (For a more extensive and well-illustrated description of this category, see Main and Solomon's excellent 1990 review.)

Main and Hesse (1989, 1990) explained the behaviours so typical of 'Disorganized/Disoriented' infants as their response to the frightened or frightening behaviour of their caregivers. These behaviours, they hypothesized, were in response to the caregivers' own unresolved attachment-related traumas, which interfered with their ability to respond to their infants supportively in times of stress. The parents' behaviours were not necessarily neglectful or abusive; at times, their own anxiety and distress led to conflicting signals or displays of anxiety that disorganized and disoriented their infants. Infants showing D behaviour with a parent can be differentiated from other children at age six by their highly pathological controlling and parental – that is, either punitive or controlling – behaviour towards that parent (Main and Cassidy 1988).

As Goldberg (1990) has demonstrated in her excellent review of attachment in infants at risk, most but not all studies have shown that securely attached infants are more competent, intellectually and socially, than those whose attachments are insecure or disorganized up to age eight while conduct disorders are frequently associated with an insecure (or disorganized) attachment. This evidence is not yet conclusive, however, particularly since standardized measures for use with pre-schoolers, children five to seven years, and adults paralleling those of the 'Strange Situation' have only much more recently been developed and are just now being standardized and validated. Thus, it is premature to draw definite conclusions regarding attachments in infancy and the nature of children's subsequent behavioural patterns and competence.

While attachment is only one aspect of the parent–child relationship, it seems safe to conclude from the above that serious disturbances in a child's attachment relationships in infancy are likely to increase the risk for that infant or child in subsequent separations.

3 / *Temperament (genetic predispositions) of the child.* Not all children are equally vulnerable to stress. Infants' responses to stress are increased by a number of temperamental traits, including a predisposition to withdrawal rather than approach in new situations, low physiological regularity, low threshold and high intensity of responses to stimuli, persistence of physiological reactions, negative mood, and low adaptability (Thomas, Chess, and Birch 1968). Studies on this topic indicate that these factors probably affect vulnerability to separation in three ways. First, they influence the intensity and nature of the primary attachment – Crockenberg (1981) predicted insecure attachments at one year from neonatal irritability, but only for mothers who were relatively unresponsive and lacking in social supports. Second, children who are temperamentally more reactive to stress (Kagan, Reznick, and Snidman 1987; Kagan et al 1988) will show a higher intensity and duration of the initial acute distress in response to separation. A highly reactive temperament will also affect the child's potential for adapting to the new situation following placement (Bates, Maslin, and Frankel 1985). The work of Bohman (1970) suggests that children's reactions to separation are also sex-linked, with boys reacting more intensely than girls.

4 / *Previous separation experiences.* While a number of authors suggest that the effect of multiple separations is cumulative (Eisenberg 1961; Maas and Engler 1959; Fein et al 1983), no straight-line relationship exists (Quinton and Rutter 1976). Some studies surprisingly have not found a significant correlation between the number of previous separations and subsequent adjustment (Lahti et al 1978). Possibly a better predictor than the exact number of placements is the quality of the child's ad-

justment in the longest previous placement. Certainly the weight of clinical evidence suggests that multiple placements are likely to increase vulnerability to subsequent separations. Those studies that dispute this finding suggest that other simultaneously active factors, among them the quality of the placement following separation, tend to mask and/or distort the effect of the repeated separations. Recently, Bowlby has suggested that the effects of adverse childhood experiences, including repeated separations, are of two kinds. Some act, first, by sensitizing the individual to later adverse experiences. Second, as a result of attitudes and behaviour stemming from personality disturbances caused by the earlier separations, the child is more likely to elicit other adverse experiences (Bowlby 1982). Children sensitized by multiple rejections and separations are prone to behave in ways that invite further rejections (Littner 1960). These behaviours can include extreme and sustained distancing, an inability to trust others, an unwillingness or inability to modify their behaviour in order to remain acceptable to others, and an excessive demand for attention and poorly controlled anger outbursts.

5 / *Duration of separation.* Several authors have shown that a longer separation is more likely to prove traumatic than one lasting a few days (Douglas 1975; Quinton and Rutter 1976). This factor clearly is influenced by several others. For example, after a child is capable of selective bonding at or about age eight months, the younger the child, the shorter the separation that can be tolerated without precipitating acute distress. The child previously sensitized to separations, the temperamentally vulnerable child, or the child with an insecure or disorganized attachment could be expected to respond more acutely to even a moderate separation than could a securely attached or a relatively invulnerable child.

6 / *Effects of strange environment.* Distress and long-term ill effects of separation are significantly reduced if the child remains in familiar surroundings, presumably at least partly because of the continuing presence of others, including siblings, to whom the child is also attached (Heinicke and Westheimer 1965; Schwartz 1972; Rutter 1978). That this is so suggests the potential mediating effect of multiple attachment figures, and the desirability of keeping siblings together whenever possible (Cutler 1984; Ward 1984).

7 / *Nature of the child's situation subsequent to separations.* Rutter (1972, 1979c) has demonstrated how the capacity of the post-separation envi-

ronment to provide security and stability can buffer the child's response to the separation and support his subsequent adjustment and behaviour. Anna Freud has hypothesized (1960) that the sooner an adequate parent substitute is provided, that is, the shorter the time that the child remains in limbo, the sooner reattachment to a parent substitute will begin and the less risk there is of serious long-term sequelae. Children need the active assistance and tolerance of the surrogate parents or other available adults to mourn the loss (Furman 1974), and thus to protect the capacity for selective bonding (Bowlby 1951).

Some children's parenting has been so neglectful, insensitive, and unresponsive that they never form a selective bond to either parent during the critical first year or two of life. When this happens, it results in the major and lasting effects on social behaviour described by Rutter (1979a, 1979c). If the child has selectively bonded, this attachment will be disrupted by separation, and may not be replaced by an equally selective bonding to the parental surrogate.

One might hypothesize that one of the major 'purposes' of the work of mourning as described by Bowlby (1951) is to protect the capacity to bond selectively, since the absence of such a bond in the early years is associated with such important and persistent emotional and behavioural sequelae. These will seriously impair the child's developing the capacity for normal socialization, even if the child is placed subsequently in a satisfactory and nurturing environment. Thus, the completion of mourning protects the capacity for selective bonding and may avoid the long-term consequences of disruption of the selective attachment. Should these consequences develop, they will invite further rejection by parental surrogates and others. The degree and quality of the substitute parents' commitment, their sensitivity and responsiveness, and their ability to tolerate the acute distress precipitated by separation will help determine whether or not the child retains the capacity to bond selectively in time to avoid such serious consequences (Tizard 1977; Raphael 1982).

No one who has worked with children who have been taken into care can doubt that children miss their parents and mourn for them. These reactions are overdetermined and are not just a response to the separation itself. Certainly the discordant nature of the natural family prior to coming into care, the child's temperament, the insecure and avoidant attachments typical of many of these children, the disruption of the selective bond to the primary caretaker and other family members, persisting behaviour patterns, and a substitute family that may be far from ideal, especially in its response to the child's initial distress, may compound each other to escalate the child's upset. This distress has been precipitated by the loss of the parents, and it is usually perceived by children, foster parents, and child welfare workers as a response to separation. For these reasons, even though the response is overdetermined, it is clinically useful to understand Bowlby's model of how children mourn in response to separation, and to apply that model to minimize children's distress, thereby facilitating their adjustment to the new family that will play such a key role in their subsequent development. Thus, from this point, whenever the term 'separation reaction' is used, it will refer to the sum total of the reaction precipitated by the child's separation from the parents.

DEFINITION OF MOURNING

Mourning is the psychological process initiated by the loss of a loved one, through which a long-standing selective attachment to that person is gradually undone. The 'purpose' of mourning is the giving up of the lost person. To mourn successfully, the mourner must accept the fact that someone to whom he or she was attached is gone and must make a corresponding change in his or her inner (i.e., psychological) world. This change is achieved by allowing the gradual withdrawal of interest, caring, and feelings invested in the child's introject (memory and mental image) of the lost attachment figure. This process, which Bowlby terms *detachment*, must be completed before the child can accept the finality of the loss and be freed to transfer those feelings to a parent substitute (that is, to form a selective reattachment). Such detachment is a prerequisite for normal development. This process of gradual detachment, often referred to as *the work of mourning*, is accompanied by periodic experiencing of *grief*, a normal response to loss that includes signs of anger, pining, sadness, and preoccupation with memories and fantasies of the lost person.

Mourning is precipitated when children are separated from attachment figures to whom they are selectively bonded. The more distressed the parent–child relationship – that is, the more insecure the attachment – the more intensely the child is likely to resist a separation, and the harder it will be for that child to mourn successfully (Stayton and Ainsworth 1973; Ainsworth 1982). Yet, according to Bowlby (1973), unless

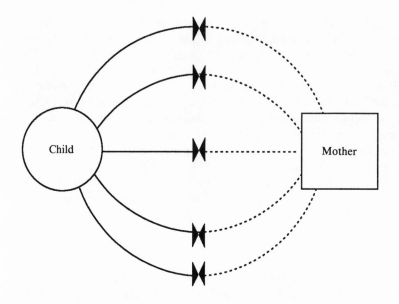

Figure 2.2   Relationship prior to separation
Source: Steinhauer (1983b)

detachment occurs, the child may not be sufficiently free to form the new selective attachments necessary for the resumption of normal development.

STAGES OF MOURNING

Figure 2.2 represents diagrammatically the selective attachment between a child and the primary caretaker. The arrows between the mother and the child represent the bonds of craving and caring that hold them together in the attachment relationship.

Bowlby (1951) described three stages of mourning in children.

The stage of protest, illustrated in figure 2.3, persists as long as the child still hopes for reunion with the lost parent. During this stage, the child typically cries, kicks, threatens, bargains, pleads, or behaves in any way that he or she hopes may force the return of the absent parent.

In *the stage of despair*, also illustrated in figure 2.3, the child appears listless, apathetic, lethargic, and withdrawn. Adults, noting this state, often take the end of the protest to mean that the child has lost interest

1. Stage of protest
2. Stage of despair

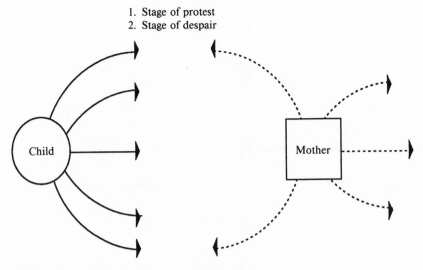

Figure 2.3   Initial reactions to separation
Source: Steinhauer (1983b)

in the absent parent(s). Such is not the case. Having given up all hope, the child has stopped trying to force a reunion, but remains passively pining for the parent(s). While willing to accept care from others at this stage, the child has not detached from the lost parent sufficiently to be ready for a selective reattachment to even an adequate and available substitute.

The stage of detachment. Figure 2.4 illustrates the result of a successful selective reattachment. Bowlby states that children can reattach successfully if they have mourned sufficiently to detach themselves from the lost parents and are provided with adequate parental substitutes. Anna Freud (1960) has emphasized the importance of the critical period during which the child remains in limbo between the loss of the primary attachment figure and the provision of adequate and permanent parent substitutes. The longer this period, the greater the risk of permanent detachment. Age is also a factor here. There have been varying estimates as to how long a time a given child can tolerate in limbo without experiencing psychological abandonment (Goldstein, Freud, and Solnit 1973, 1979). Generally speaking, the younger the child (above a lower limit of six months) the shorter the period that can be tolerated before

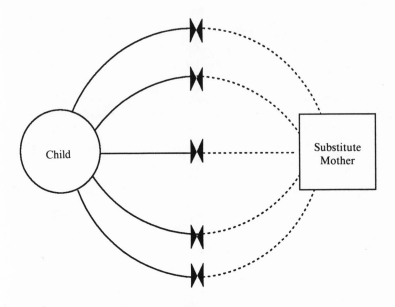

Figure 2.4   Successful resolution
Source: Steinhauer (1983b)

the child feels psychologically abandoned. As soon as this sense of abandonment occurs, the work of mourning and/or superficial reattachment
is precipitated.

In *Beyond the Best Interests of the Child*, Goldstein, Freud, and Solnit
(1973) estimated that infants and toddlers could be without contact with
absent parents for only a few days before being overwhelmed by anxiety
and loss. They also suggested that only rarely can children under age
five tolerate an absence of more than two months without experiencing
their loss as permanent, a situation that would precipitate a separation
reaction. In their more legally oriented sequel, *Before the Best Interests
of the Child* (1979), they propose that one year for a child younger than
three, and two years for a child older than three, represent a conservative
estimate of how long a child can maintain an attachment to absent
parents.

The author believes that, in their second book, Goldstein, Freud, and
Solnit were too generous in estimating how long the average young child
can remain in limbo without risking severe and possibly permanent

damage. However, for every child, some point exists where the transfer of attachment away from the absent parents and towards the substitute caretaker is made, so that the new attachment has the potential to develop into a selective bonding. From that point, as long as the surrogate caretakers are meeting the child's developmental needs and are committed to doing so on a long-term basis, Goldstein, Freud, and Solnit suggest, the child's need for continuity of the attachment should be recognized and protected. Those needs should not be undermined by moving the child from a known successful placement to an unknown one, even one with a potential for being better.

Example 1. Andrew had just turned four when his status in his foster family since birth was challenged after his foster parents sought to adopt him. Since Andrew was a treaty Indian, the band to which his natural parents had belonged claimed, under the constitution, its right to demand that he be returned to the band to be raised as an Indian. In doing so, it ignored the facts that his foster parents were the only parents he had ever known, that he was securely attached to them, and that they were his psychological parents. Cases like this have, in at least some jurisdictions (Alberta and Ontario), ended by forcing a court to determine which takes priority, the psychological needs (i.e., best interests) of a child or the rights of an Indian band to have an infant member returned to it in order to satisfy its constitutional rights.

Example 2. In the late 1960s and throughout much of the 1970s, great pressure was put on Children's Aid societies either to restore all permanent wards to their natural families or to place them on adoption. This policy was almost universally taken by provincial and state welfare authorities to decrease the number of children permanently drifting in minimally supervised long-term foster homes of often inferior quality. In taking this position, the authorities were undoubtedly well-intentioned; however, applied in a blanket way, this policy left no room to consider the needs of a number of older children who had grown up in excellent foster homes since infancy. For them, the only parents they knew were their foster parents. They were secure in their foster homes and developing well. It made no sense to remove them from their families to put them through an unnecessary separation in order to place them on adoption probation in a family of strangers, all in the name of trying to protect the continuity of their major attachment relationships. Nevertheless, again and again this was done. If such a child had a caseworker who appreciated the importance to the child of an existing placement, that worker could often protect that child by strenuously and repeatedly arguing the case for maintaining the child's ties to the foster family. However, the pressure exerted on both child and foster parents by the fact that the placement can be challenged every few months often interfered markedly with the ability of each to form an attachment to the other. If, however, that child's worker was inexperienced, uncommitted, or unsure of herself, the importance of the foster family to that child would be overlooked, the placement would be disrupted, and the child would be transferred to an adoption home. Many children and many foster families were badly hurt by the well-intentioned but misguided attempt to place every permanent ward on adoption. (This topic will be discussed in more depth in chapter 12.)

The long-term result of failure to reattach selectively is likely to include the following sequelae.

1 / *Permanent detachment* (see figure 2.5): While Bowlby (1973) attributes permanent detachment to failure to complete the work of mourning, Rutter considers it less a response to the act of separation than to the lack of a satisfactory selective attachment prior to the separation, especially following chronic neglect (Rutter 1979c; Tizard and Rees 1975).

It is possible, of course, that Bowlby and Rutter are describing different populations. If so, the former would be expected to have the better prognosis and the latter, while still possibly capable of later selective bonding, might continue to show the inept social behaviours described earlier as an inevitable result of the lack of a selective bond within the critical period.

Other factors contributing to persistent detachment include too long in limbo (A. Freud 1960; Wilkes 1989), lack of continuity of parent substitutes, inadequate or inconsistently available parent substitutes (e.g., multiple placements) (Eisenberg 1962; Maas and Engler 1959; Winnicott 1957), and a child too disturbed prior to placement to relate to or be tolerated in any but the most exceptional surrogate family. Should permanent detachment occur, instead of forming a new selective bond with the surrogate parents, the child will turn and reinvest the energy and love withdrawn from the original mother into himself, thus undermining the capacity to trust and to relate to others.

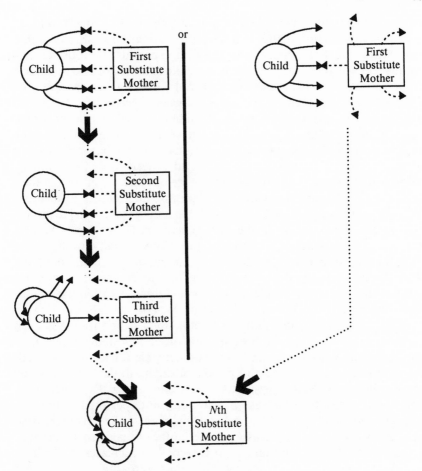

Figure 2.5   Permanent detachment
Source: Steinhauer (1983b)

As toddlers, such children are often overly and indiscriminately friendly (Tizard 1977; Rutter 1979a), though, when older, they typically appear cold and aloof, shallow, superficial, demanding, manipulative, and narcissistic in their dealings with others. They frequently develop the kind of adult personality described by Winnicott (1960) as 'false self' or by Kohut (1971) and Kernberg (1975) as 'narcissistic.' Rutter considers this personality development a long-term result of the absence of selective bonding during the critical period. Clinical experience supports Bowlby's 1982 hypothesis that this results from the child having developed a 'defensive exclusion' – that is, a selective inattention to stimuli, either from within or from others, that would, if experienced, arouse attachment-seeking behaviour. As a result, the child is unwilling and/or unable either to love or to experience being loved. Others, therefore, are used for what they can provide, valued only when they satisfy the child's often inappropriate needs of the moment, only to be discarded or turned upon whenever they fail to do so. Alternatively, such children may combine exaggerated demands for attention and immediate gratification with an inability to tolerate intimacy and a need to distance others. These attitudes and behaviours can have serious delayed effects on their subsequent parenting behaviour, undermining their ability to form selective bonds with their children, thus perpetuating personality disorders and parenting incapacity in the next generation (Ilfeld 1970; Quinton and Rutter 1985; Rutter, Quinton, and Liddle 1983). Many mothers who have themselves experienced deprivation as children unconsciously act so as to deprive – and thus encourage the development of anxious attachments and other problems in – their children (Rutter and Madge 1976; Frommer and O'Shea 1973a, 1983b; Wolkind, Hall, and Pawlby 1977; Ricks 1985). Chronic and severe childhood deprivation has been correlated with later marital breakdown (Rutter and Madge 1976; Meier 1965, 1966) and with numerous forms of parent–child pathology, including excessive anxiety, guilt, and phobic disorders in the child (Bowlby 1973), child abuse (Smith 1975; Parke and Collmer 1975; DeLozier 1982), and subsequent disturbances of children's interpersonal behaviour (George and Main 1979). Two mechanisms seem to be involved: first, the childhood adversity predisposes the mother to poor social circumstances and a lack of marital support; second, it increases her vulnerability and undermines her coping skills, thus increasing the risk of her succumbing to the social disadvantage (Rutter, Quinton, and Liddle 1984).

Should permanent detachment occur, Bowlby has suggested that the energy withdrawn into the self and unavailable to others can be:

a *Reinvested in the child's own body.* Initially, this reinvestment results in excessive self-stimulation and auto-eroticism (extremes of thumb-sucking, rocking, masturbation, head-banging). Such children remain vulnerable to somatoform disorders and psychosomatic complaints when stressed in later life.

b *Reinvested in fantasy*, which then becomes more important to the child than external reality. This reinvestment leads to a progressive withdrawal and an increased turning to fantasy rather than to real experience or relationships for gratification (Freud 1960). It also encourages the idealization in fantasy of the lost attachment figures, as described by Furman (1974). Since no real parent surrogate can compete with the idealized fantasy of the lost parent, the preference for fantasy over reality as a source of pleasure is continually reinforced, which undermines the relationship with the surrogate parent.

c *Reinvested in self-concept.* The character structure of these children becomes increasingly narcissistic as the result of the child's investing in his or her self-concept the energy withdrawn from and unavailable for relating to others. The substitute parents' eventual frustration and subsequent rejection, in response to the child's emotional inaccessibility, further reinforces such children's conviction that getting involved with others will eventually prove disappointing and hurtful. Pseudo-independent behaviour – an inability to get involved with, to rely on, or to use the help of others, since any involvement leaves the child vulnerable to abandonment – can thus be encouraged. Fantasied involvements are more under the child's control and, therefore, safer as well as more satisfying. This may limit such a child's accessibility to individual psychotherapy, since successful therapy requires that the child be free to form a relationship with a therapist, while the child's whole defensive pattern is based on the avoidance of relationships to limit vulnerability to rejection (see also chapter 14).

2 / *Persistent, diffuse rage.* Bowlby (1960) attributes this rage to the deprivation resulting from the loss of the parent. Rutter (1979c), however, emphasizes its strong association with chronic conflict experienced within the disturbed family prior to separation. Undoubtedly disturbed and conflicted family experiences both prior to and following separation contribute greatly to the rage so prominent in many of these children later in life. It would, however, be unwise to underestimate the extent or persistence of the rage generated in the child who has – or who feels he or she has – been abandoned. (See Staynton and Ainsworth's description [1973] of the reaction to separation of children with a Type C [anxious-ambivalent] attachment.) For those children who have difficulty controlling their feelings, the cumulative rage, its expression blocked and distorted by the defences developed against it, may become dammed up, repressed, generalized, diffused, and displaced. This process stresses the developing personality, undermines and destroys potential relation-

ships, and can dominate both mood and behaviour. Anger, like love, can be internalized and turned against the self, in which case it will contribute to the depression commonly seen in such children.

3 / *Chronic depression.* Bowlby (1980) considers a sense of hopelessness and helplessness, to him the predominant characteristics of clinical depression, as stemming from three types of experience in childhood: from the child's never having attained a stable and secure relationship with the parents; from the child's having been assured repeatedly, especially by the parents, that he or she is unlovable, inadequate, and incompetent (that is, emotional abuse); and from the child's having experienced the loss of a parent, the sequelae of which have not been successfully resolved. These result in persistent 'cognitive biases' that predispose the child to a sense of personal failure and to a tendency to internalize anger. At times, one sees frank depression in the adult sense – overwhelming sadness, loneliness, hopelessness, self-destructive behaviour (including drug abuse), or suicidal thoughts or attempts (Adam 1982). At others, the depression takes the form of a pervasive apathy, lethargy, giving up of former interests, lack of drive or available energy, deteriorating school attitude and performance, loss of initiative and/or persistence, or global and persistent pessimism. These sequelae may alternate with bouts of acting-out, antisocial behaviour, or somatic complaints, which serve dynamically as depressive equivalents.

4 / *Asocial and antisocial behaviour.* Rutter has associated the asocial and antisocial behaviour that continues on into later life as a response less to the separation itself than to the family discord and disruption experienced prior and subsequent to it. Three sets of factors that commonly compound one another account for the frequent asocial and antisocial behaviour seen in abused and neglected boys and abused girls. These include:

a *The inability to empathize with others,* presumably a consequence of the failure and/or disruption of selective attachment, so that the child never develops the capacity to appreciate empathically the effects of his or her behaviour on potential victims.

b *Defects in conscience* (superego), resulting primarily from disruption and discontinuity of attachment relationships. The lack of stable relationships keeps these youngsters from forming the identifications needed for effective conscience formation. As a result, while frequently demonstrating diffuse feelings of shame and worthlessness, they lack the mature conscience's capacity for experiencing guilt appropriately.

c *Defects in impulse control* (ego defects), which manifest as a lack of ability to bind or tolerate emotional tensions which must therefore be discharged immediately through behaviour. Thus, such children are prone to sudden explosive behavioural outbursts to relieve the sweeps of rage to which they are so vulnerable.

5 / *Low self-concept* originates in the child's never having felt sufficiently loved or cared about to feel a valued and worthwhile person. This original lack is exacerbated by the child's compulsive, though unrecognized, need to set herself up for repeated rejections, thus proving again and again that there is nothing worthwhile or lovable about her (Littner 1960; Bowlby 1979; Adam 1982; Ney 1989; see also chapter 4).

6 / *Chronic dependency.* Many such children never become emotionally self-sufficient or autonomous. Because of the disruptions in their attachments, they fail to develop an internalized 'secure base' – that is, the capacity to soothe themselves and to replenish their own sense of security and the inner confidence needed to support exploratory behaviour (Bowlby 1979). In turn, both their progression towards autonomy and their development of the social skills necessary for successful relationships with others are limited. These lacks further undermine and frustrate both independent and social behaviour. Another consequence of the failure to achieve autonomy is a continued reliance on the approval of others (i.e., social approval) rather than on themselves (i.e., psychological [self] approval) to provide a secure base, to maintain self-esteem, and to ward off depression (Winnicott 1976; Steinhauer and Tisdall 1984). Thus, the need for dependency on others is perpetuated.

These long-term sequelae of failure to mourn successfully in response to separation are schematically summarized in figure 2.6.

At What Age Are Children Able to Mourn?

The literature disagrees as to when children are developmentally capable of mourning. Some authors have questioned whether children are capable of mourning the loss of a parental figure, arguing on theoretical grounds that it is not until adolescence that a child's personality structure is sufficiently developed to permit mourning as described by Bowlby.

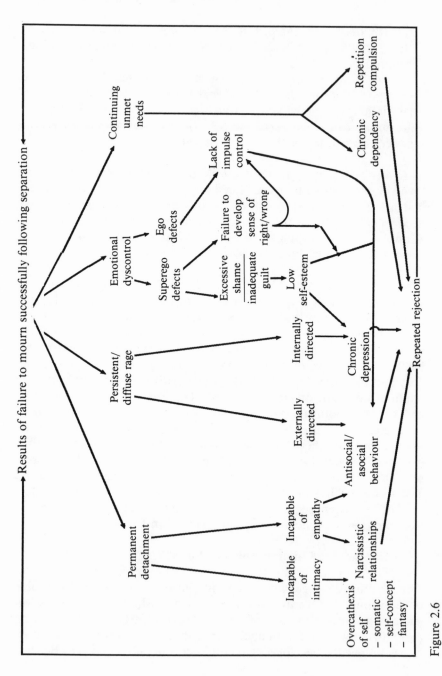

Figure 2.6

Source: 'The preventive utilization of foster care,' *Can. J. Psychiat.* 33 (August 1988): 462

Wolfenstein 1966; and Nagera 1970 argue that, although children appear to adapt following parental loss, they are psychologically unable to tolerate lasting grief or to pursue active mourning until well on into adolescence. These authors see the young child as so dependent on the parents to maintain his security and self-esteem (i.e., narcissistic supplies) that he is incapable of tolerating the anxiety generated by parental loss. They argue further that the fear of being overwhelmed by the intense helplessness, rage, and despair generated by parental loss is so great that the child has no alternative but to repress it. As he does so, they hypothesize, he loses the capacity for gradual decathexis (that is, withdrawal and detachment by stages from the child's internalized [psychological] image of the lost attachment figure). As a result, the child remains vulnerable to having feelings explode into uncontrolled discharge unless the repression is maintained. It is this fear of loss of control and of being overwhelmed by chaotic feelings generated by intolerable loss that leads to those feelings being repressed. Consequently, these authors maintain, the child experiences no real grief, no preoccupation with the lost parent, no prevailing sadness, no general loss of interests. Instead, he relies upon self-protection through the repression of the resulting helplessness, rage, and despair. This repression is supported by two additional defence mechanisms: the child tends to *idealize* the absent parent; any negative feelings held towards the lost parent are *split off* and displaced onto some available surrogate person, such as a foster parent or social worker (S. Freud 1946; Klein 1946).

Furman (1974), however, argues, and the studies of Lifschitz and colleagues (1977) and Raphael (1982) agree, that, under the right conditions, even very young children can be helped to mourn enough to free them to form meaningful and selective attachments to parent substitutes. Furman suggests that, under optimal conditions, children are quite capable of mourning by about age four. She outlines three prerequisites for successful mourning in younger children:

a The child must have achieved 'libidinal object constancy.' This means that the child cannot mourn successfully until he or she is cognitively and emotionally mature enough to remember the lost parent(s) and of how he or she felt about them.
b The child must be able to understand the meaning, extent, and permanence of the loss. Furman, writing about children's reactions to the death of a parent, was referring to the child's ability to conceptualize the permanence of death. For purposes of this discussion, we

will need to explore how the experience differs for the child whose loss of the parent through separation and placement may be more ambiguous, less complete, and not necessarily permanent. This discussion will be expanded upon towards the end of chapter 3.

c The child must be able to tolerate experiencing some continuing sadness. According to Furman, this is possible under three conditions: the child's ongoing need for security is continually met; the key adults in the child's life directly and repeatedly confront the child with the reality of the loss, even when he or she attempts to deny it; and these key adults can tolerate the child's expressions of helplessness, rage, and despair generated by the loss.

In the author's experience, if the key adults in the child's life are unable to meet Furman's conditions for guiding the child through the process of mourning, the situation will turn out much as Wolfenstein and Nagera have predicted: there will be failure to detach from, or decathect, the lost parent; there will be idealization of the absent parent; there will remain an excessive reliance on splitting as a defence; one will see many of the long-term results of aborted or pathological mourning referred to above. If, however, substitute parents are able and available, with or without professional help, to meet the prerequisites listed above, the author agrees with Bowlby (1980) and Furman (1974) that even very young children can mourn sufficiently to be freed to form the stable and selective reattachments needed for a resumption of normal development. The more vulnerable the child prior to the loss of the parent – either because of organic liability, difficult temperament, past deprivation or parental discord, previous separations, insecure attachment (especially those remaining incompletely resolved) or because of a highly strained and/or ambivalent relationship to the parent who was lost – the less likely the child is to mourn successfully even under optimal conditions.

Furman's work emphasizes the crucial importance of the substitute caretaker or other significant adults (e.g., child welfare workers) in actively supporting and leading the child towards the completion of the work of mourning. Yet several studies have shown that foster parents and social workers frequently collude with children in avoiding mourning and suppressing grief (Palmer 1974, 1982). Because of their difficulty in tolerating the child's distress, they often block attempts at mourning through selective inattention, denial, or even active distraction. All these responses collude with the child in avoiding the work of mourning.

In summary, this chapter has reviewed the effects on children of separation from their major attachment figures. We have seen how children's responses to separation are modified by a history of chronic conflict and repeated violence in the natural family prior to their removal, by a failure or abnormality of the child's selective bonding to the parent(s), and by the nature of the family situation in which the child is placed. The chapter has reviewed a number of factors that, through their interaction, will influence a specific child's vulnerability and responses to separation. Finally, it has described Bowlby's formulation of how children mourn, the controversy around the age at which they are first capable of mourning, and the conditions that clinicians have considered prerequisites for even very young children to mourn successfully.

Many of the processes referred to above will be illustrated in the description of the psychotherapy of a young girl who suddenly and unexpectedly lost both her parents, presented in the next chapter.

Chapter Three

The Child Who Could Not Mourn

In the early 1960s, shortly after having become interested in Bowlby's description of children's typical responses to separation, I was asked to see in consultation a five-year-old girl who, just two days earlier, had lost both her parents. Charlene had been riding with her parents in the family car when it collided head on with a tractor-trailer. Both parents were killed instantly, but Charlene was left without a scratch. Immediately following the accident, she was removed from the wrecked car by the police, who described her as 'stunned' and 'in shock.' The officers correctly suspected that she didn't fully grasp what had happened. Not knowing how to deal with her, they called upon the local Children's Aid Society to provide immediate interim care for Charlene as well as to devise a more permanent plan for her long-term management.

The assigned social worker immediately placed Charlene in an experienced emergency receiving home, then began to attempt to find out what she could about the extended family. She learned very little. Charlene was an only child, and her parents had only recently moved to the area. The family had made no close friends, either currently or in their previous neighbourhood, although they got along without difficulty with the neighbours in each location. The only relatives who could be located were the maternal grandparents, who were in their sixties. They were strangers to Charlene, as they lived several thousand miles away and had had no contact with her for several years. However, they expressed an immediate interest in her, and in taking over her care. They were adamant, however, that they could not do so for at least three weeks, since the grandmother was recovering from recent abdominal surgery.

For the interim period of two-and-a-half weeks, the agency would hold Charlene in the receiving home.

When her worker first met her at the police station within hours of the accident, Charlene showed no sign of acute distress. Passively, but cooperatively, she allowed the worker to take her to the receiving home and obediently, without obvious upset, she accepted the stranger who was to be her interim foster mother. The foster mother, aware of what Charlene had been through, showered her with attention and affection. Initially, she was pleased with how Charlene seemed to respond. The child did not cry, brood, or seem upset. She did not talk about the accident or her parents, and showed no severe tension. After a day or so, however, the foster mother began to sense that something was unnatural or 'weird' about Charlene's passivity and automatic compliance. She wondered why Charlene gave no overt sign of missing the parents, and began to see her as 'too good.' The only time Charlene showed any feeling at all was on those occasions when they travelled in the car. Then she would become very tense, and would silently shiver. It was the foster parents' reporting these observations to their social worker that led to the request for consultation.

After discussing Charlene with the social worker and foster mother, I decided to meet with her in the presence of her social worker five times over the two-and-a-half weeks that she would be remaining in her interim placement. I made this decision for a number of reasons. If, as I suspected, Bowlby's formulation of the process by which children mourn was valid, something was clearly blocking the work of mourning in Charlene's case. The enormity and unexpectedness of the loss, I hypothesized, had overwhelmed Charlene, causing her to repress the event and abort the mourning process. If Bowlby were to be believed, unless something could be done to activate the work of mourning, Charlene would remain unable to mourn successfully. Should that occur, according to Bowlby, she was unlikely to detach herself emotionally from the parents she had lost. But without such a detachment, Charlene would not be free to reinvest her energies in a selective attachment to her grandparents. Thus the major goal of her therapy was to activate the aborted mourning process in order to free Charlene to form a strong and, one hoped, secure attachment to the grandparents who would be her long-term substitute caretakers.

At the same time, I recognized that I had been given a unique opportunity to observe directly one child's immediate responses to dramatically sudden parental loss. This opportunity would allow me not only to compare my clinical observations with Bowlby's theory, but to obtain clinical data on such important questions as: Are even very young children able to mourn or, as Wolfenstein (1966) and Nagera (1970) have suggested, does mourning become possible only well on into adolescence? What forms do the work of mourning – and the defences against the pain of loss – take in the very young child? What role, if any, can a sensitive and concerned adult take in assisting the work of mourning?

I had decided in advance to limit myself to what could be done within the two-and-one-half weeks prior to Charlene's move to the grandparents' home. I had no illusions about her being able to complete the work of mourning in such a short time, but to extend her therapy would mean prolonging her time in the interim placement, which would increase the risk of Charlene's forming an attachment to the receiving-home foster parents, thereby exposing her to a second, and unnecessary, separation when it came time for her to join her grandparents. Thus, to maintain the limit on the time Charlene would spend in the interim placement, I was determined to avoid, for any reason, extending the duration of her therapy. My hope was that, if it proved possible to activate the mourning that presumably had been repressed, Charlene would be able to complete the process on her own, with the assistance of the grandparents.

Rightly or wrongly, I decided against seeing Charlene more than twice a week, because I did not want her to become too dependent on me, since she would lose me, too, in less than three weeks. The social worker was included in the sessions to demonstrate – to her and, through her, to her colleagues in the agency – both the work of mourning and the ways in which adults might assist this process.

In preparation for my first therapy hour with Charlene, I purposely bought two additional toys for the playroom. One was a police car, a friction toy that sounded a siren and flashed a light when its wheels were rubbed across the carpet. The second was a tow-truck. I bought these, thinking that they might serve both as a useful stimulus and as a vehicle for helping Charlene express in play her feelings about the accident. They were there among the other toys in a cupboard prior to each therapy session.

Session 1

I intended to use the first session largely to allow Charlene to get acquainted with the playroom and with me.

Charlene readily entered my office with her social worker and, after a few moments, separated easily from the worker when I indicated that there were toys in the cupboard that she might like to play with. She showed appropriate initial shyness, indicated by mild behavioural and verbal inhibition, but within just a few minutes seemed at home and was able to speak to, or otherwise involve, me as she wished. The social worker sat quietly in a far corner of the room. After the first ten minutes of this session, Charlene rarely directly involved her, although she would, from time to time, look at her, as if to re-establish the contact. Since my main goal in this first session was to familiarize Charlene with her new surroundings, I took a passive role throughout, responding to her invitations for interaction but not intruding or trying to shape the course of the interview or play in any way.

As soon as she opened the cupboard, Charlene was fascinated by the police cruiser. It would be the first toy she would select in each of the five sessions. She picked it up and asked if the light flashed on and off. I replied that it did and that there was a siren, too, if she rubbed the wheels of the cruiser against the rug. Gingerly, she did so, her face registering a mixture of fascination and, I thought, horror as the light and siren began to work. Abruptly she pulled her hands off, as if the car had suddenly become too hot, and she abandoned it. Several times later in the session, however, she returned to it, either by looking at it from a safe distance or by picking it up briefly only to leave it again, equally abruptly. She did not, however, activate the siren or the flashing light again until the final session. My thought, as I watched her, was that she was gripped by the memories and feelings that the police car stirred in her, but that she found them too hot (that is, too upsetting and painful) to handle directly.

During this first session, Charlene played with many things, but with none of them did she engage in any real depth. I merely observed her and tried to understand what I could from the content and process of her play. After a while, I gradually became aware that it didn't seem to matter what Charlene chose to play with – whether she had an imaginary tea party with a china tea service, engaged with a family of dolls, made up a puppet play from a selection of human and animal puppets, or arranged a collection of farm animals. No matter what she did, two themes repeated themselves in every medium. First, there were always lots of accidents, ranging from people at the tea party falling off their chairs to family members falling downstairs or owls flying blindly into trees. But, second, all these accidents had something in common: either no one got hurt in them or else the characters died but were quickly brought back to life, rejoining the story as if nothing had happened.

As I tried to make sense of the session after Charlene had left, a number of thoughts occurred to me. There were obviously some things that Charlene was avoiding. She had made no mention of the car crash, the sudden disappearance of her parents, or the plan to move her to a new home. She showed no outward evidence of either sadness or anxiety. Yet her play showed that she was preoccupied with the theme of accidents. They occurred one after another, but each ended up with no one being hurt.

In her play, Charlene was demonstrating two defence mechanisms commonly used by children her age in her attempt to master the feelings stirred up by the accident and the loss of her parents. First, she would repeat the traumatic situation (i.e., accidents) again and again in her play, but with one important difference: whereas in real life Charlene had been the helpless victim who had no control over what was happening, in her play she took a much more active and controlling stance. It was she who made the accidents happen, and she could decide whether the victims had been hurt. She could even reverse the process and make them well and alive again! The constant repetition of the accidents in play seemed integrally related to the anxiety that I assumed Charlene must feel as a result of the recent event. Also, again and again throughout her play, Charlene repeated a common theme: people don't die in accidents, or, if they do, they don't stay dead. Thus, in her fantasy, Charlene was able to deny that the results of accidents can be devastating and permanent. Both of these defence mechanisms, commonly used by children reacting to a sudden and severe trauma, are well described by Anna Freud (1946).

Session 2

I had decided to take a much more active role in this session. I did so because I knew that Charlene and I would have only four more sessions together and I would have to be active to achieve the goals I had set, those of helping Charlene face the loss that had been so overwhelming that she was avoiding dealing with it and of assisting her to begin the work of mourning, which had, for that reason, been blocked.

Charlene seemed relaxed and pleased to see me when she arrived. After picking up and rapidly discarding the police car as in the first session, she announced that she was going to draw. I supplied her with paper, a pencil, and crayons, and sat down beside her at the table. As she drew, I questioned her about what she was drawing.

Charlene drew a house. When I asked who lived in the house, she replied that nobody did. I asked where the people who used to live in the house were. She replied that they were gone, after a brief but significant pause adding that they had gone to the store. When asked how long they had been gone, Charlene responded that they took too long coming back. Then the following dialogue took place:

Therapist: Do you want them to come back?
Charlene: Yes.
Therapist: Are they going to come back?
Charlene: I don't know. [She hesitated, looking upset, then continued spontaneously.] Yes, they will.

As she spoke these words, Charlene suddenly looked very sad. In response, I picked up a pencil, took another sheet of paper, and began to draw beside her. She soon stopped her drawing and began to watch and listen to me as I talked while I drew.

Therapist (drawing a little girl): This is the little girl who used to live in that house. She keeps looking out the window for her mommy and daddy. She hasn't seen them for a long time. She pretends that they've gone to the store, and that they will be back soon. But inside, she's really afraid that they will never come back.

We were both silent. Charlene continued to look very sad. She then came very close to me and stood beside me, with her body touching my side. I put my arm around her. She stood there for what seemed like a very long moment and then, suddenly, ran over to the toy cupboard and picked up two hand puppets, an alligator and a whale. As she played with them, she told me, partly spontaneously and partly in response to short questions, what they were doing.

Charlene: The alligator is mad at the whale. The whale talks too much.
   [The alligator meanwhile was fighting with and biting at the whale.]
Therapist: The alligator is fighting with the whale.
Charlene: Oh, no. The alligator is just *pretending* to fight with the whale. They're really just playing.

Therapist: The alligator is angry at the whale because the whale says things that make the alligator sad.
Charlene: The alligator isn't angry. See? It's just playing. It's smiling. [Meanwhile, the alligator continued to bite and fight the whale ferociously and repeatedly.]

At this point, as she often did when the therapy got too hot – that is, when the meaning of her play or what we were talking about got too close to consciousness for comfort – Charlene abruptly broke off the play, immediately shifting to something else. In this case, she soon returned to the table and again began to draw.

Charlene drew a picture of another little girl, who, she said, wanted to go to a party. Then, on another page, she drew a second little girl, this one with the corners of her mouth definitely turning down.

Therapist: She looks sad.
Charlene: Oh no. She's happy.
Therapist: You've drawn two girls. You say they're both happy. But each of them is all alone.
Charlene: That's not true. I'm going to draw their mommy and daddy. [She proceeded to do so, but, as she did, she appeared near tears.]
Therapist: You look very sad.
Charlene: I'm not.
Therapist: You say you're not sad, but you still look very sad to me.
Charlene: I'm not crying. [She left the table and crossed the room to the doll house, where she rapidly began rearranging the furniture.]
Therapist: If a girl is feeling sad, is it all right for her to cry, or is it better for her to pretend she's not sad?
Charlene: She shouldn't cry if she's drawing.
Therapist: Why not?
Charlene: Because if she did, it would splash all over the paper. No, it's better to pretend you're happy. Even when you're sad, you pretend you're happy.

In this second session, my suggestion that the little girl I had drawn was missing her parents and was afraid that they would not come back but was handling her fear by pretending they'd soon come home clearly made contact with Charlene's feelings of abandonment and loneliness. Evidence for this contact was, first, the change in mood as she softened and stood so close to me and, later, the anger she expressed by having the alligator (i.e., herself) attack the whale (i.e., the therapist) who 'talks too much' and 'says things that make the alligator sad.' In this, Charlene showed that she had to deny not just her sadness at the loss but also the anger stirred up when I confronted her with it. Therefore, she denied that the alligator was fighting and insisted that it was 'really just playing ... just pretending.' When this defence proved insufficient, and she felt threatened by the feelings she was trying to avoid, Charlene again changed the play and drew a second girl. Both were alone, but the first had a happy face, and the second a sad one. I chose to confront her with the denial, choosing at that point to remain at the level of the metaphor – that is, not drawing the parallel between the theme of her play and what Charlene herself was feeling – by commenting that, even though she said that both girls were happy, each was all alone. She again attempted to deny her loss by announcing that she would draw a mother and father. As she did so, however, she looked even sadder, because, I thought, she was thinking of her own mother and father. I commented on the obvious sadness. Still remaining in the metaphor of the play, Charlene let me know that, when a girl was sad, it was better that she pretend to be really happy. In my final comment of the session, for the first time I drew a connection between Charlene's play and her reality.

Session 3

Happily entering the room, Charlene first picked up, but immediately rejected, the police car and then rapidly returned to the metaphor she had used the session before. She picked up the alligator and whale puppets, announcing while she played that they were 'swimming to-gether ... playing together.' She left me an opening when she told me that the alligator caught enough food for both himself and the whale.

Therapist: But suppose something happened to the alligator? The alli-gator wouldn't be there any more to care for the whale. Who would there be to get food for the whale?

Charlene: That wouldn't matter. The whale would just climb up on the shore and eat the grass. She'd be okay. [There was a pause, during which Charlene continued to play; afterward, she continued sponta-neously.] The whale is pretending that the alligator isn't gone. That's why she acts happy. She pretends that there's nothing to be sad about. As long as she thinks the alligator isn't gone, she doesn't have to feel sad.

Therapist: She's just like you. As long as you pretend your mother and father are coming back, you don't feel so sad and lonely.

In response, Charlene broke off the puppet play. Running to the cupboard, she took out some Tinkertoys, which she brought to the table. She played quietly with these for almost fifteen minutes, during which time neither of us said a word. At first, I didn't understand what was happening. As I continued to watch, attempting to understand what she was doing and why, it became increasingly clear that Charlene wasn't really very involved in her play. Her mind seemed to be on something other than the activity. As I continued to observe her, I became increasingly convinced that this was, indeed, what was happening. Therefore, I decided to intervene once more.

Therapist: You're making a truck, but you're thinking about something else.
Charlene: That's right. I'm thinking about my mommy.
Therapist: You miss her so much that you think about her even when you're trying to play.
Charlene: Yes.

Charlene continued playing silently with the truck for another few minutes, but then, leaving the Tinkertoys, she began to play with the doll figures. Taking two grey-haired dolls, she announced that they were the grandmother and the grandfather. She then took a little-girl doll and had the grandparents bathe the little girl, watch TV with her, and feed her.

Charlene: She lives with her grandparents.
Therapist: I see. Her grandparents take care of her. They do for her the things that her mother and father used to do.
Charlene: Her mother and father are at the store.
Therapist: She *pretends* that her mother and father are at the store and that they'll come back soon. That way, she doesn't have to miss them so much.

Instead of breaking off the play as she had so many times in the past, this time Charlene was able to let it continue. She had the grandparents put the little girl to bed. Then she announced that the girl was having a dream. In the dream, the parents were just asleep and could be woken up; but, she announced in apparent contradiction, her grandparents were looking after her now. One could almost feel the struggle between the part of Charlene trying to deny the loss by pretending that her parents could come back and that increasingly strong part of her that was beginning to accept the inevitability of the loss and, with it, the fact that she would be cared for, instead, by her grandparents.

Suddenly, Charlene's play became quite agitated. There was much running in and out of the house by the little girl, who finally left in a truck that Charlene had fetched from the toy cupboard for the purpose.

Therapist: She seems upset. What's going on?

Charlene: She's asking her mommy if it's okay for her to get in the car with her grandmother and grandfather so she can go and live with them.

Therapist: What does her mommy say?

Charlene: She says it's all right.

Therapist: She doesn't know her grandmother and grandfather very well. Is she scared?

Charlene: Yes. She doesn't know what they'll be like. Or the house. [Then, she drove the truck in a huge circle, ending up under the diagonally opposite corner of the table.] There's the house. It looks nice.

Note the progression occurring during the course of this third interview. At the beginning, Charlene returned to the metaphor of the previous session (i.e., the alligator and the whale), continuing to deny the loss (i.e., the whale was self-sufficient and wouldn't miss the alligator). Spontaneously, however, she could state that the whale was only pretending not to miss the alligator in order to avoid being overwhelmed by feelings of sadness. When I drew the parallel between her play and her reality, she experienced some of the sadness she had been trying to avoid, first, within herself (i.e., when she was building the truck) and, later, quite openly (when she acknowledged that she was thinking about and missing her mother). It was only then, only after she was able to let herself face and begin to mourn her loss, that she was free to begin to accept her new reality. As she introduced into her play the grandparent dolls who were taking care of her instead of the absent parents, one could see the struggle between the part of her that persisted in trying to deny the loss (i.e., the mother and father were at the store; they were just sleeping and could be woken up) and the part of her that was beginning to accept the permanence of the loss and, with it, the idea of being cared for by the grandparents. Some of this struggle seemed to be eased when she asked her mother for permission to go and live with the grandparents. Having received it, she played out the move to the new home by incorporating the truck in her play. After a brief acknowledgment of anxiety about what her grandparents and the new surroundings would be like, she began to overcome the anxiety by announcing that the new home was nice.

Session 4

In this interview, Charlene introduced a new theme, one commonly experienced by children who have lost their parents. She connected feelings derived from parental loss with the theme of badness on the part of the abandoned child. She did this in two ways. First, during her brief initial touching of the police car, Charlene announced that the police car had been set on fire by a bad boy who had disobeyed his mother. Then she shifted rapidly to the puppets, again choosing the alligator and the whale. At first, they seemed friendly and playful, but rapidly they became increasingly aggressive and began to fight.

Therapist: They're acting really mean. They must be pretty upset to act that way.
Charlene: They're naughty. Their mother is angry at them. She doesn't like them.

As she said this, Charlene, as if taking the part of the angry, rejecting mother, repeatedly and violently smashed the puppets on the rug and against a chair. As they were punished, they, at times, showed anger, but this was never directed against her, although she (i.e., the mother) was the one punishing them. Always it was something (i.e., someone) else in the environment (e.g., the rug, the leg of the chair) onto whom the anger was displaced.

Therapist: Why do they bite the rug and the chair? Their mother's the one who's punishing them.
Charlene: Because they don't want her to know they're so angry. If she knew, she'd hit them.

Charlene was expressing in her play two themes commonly experienced by children in foster care. The first was that it was her own badness that had resulted in her being abandoned. The second was that it is safer to try to hide anger from adults (such as foster parents or other parent surrogates) since, if they realize how angry a child is, they will become punitive and/or rejecting.

At this point, Charlene shifted and began to tell me of a cartoon she had seen on TV. Of all those she had seen during the preceding week, she chose to tell me about one in which Popeye had been mad at the man who had abducted Olive Oyl. I responded:

Therapist: Popeye was mad at the man who took Olive Oyl away from him. You are mad that your parents were taken away from you.
Charlene: Olive Oyl comes back in the end.
Therapist: But your parents didn't.
Charlene: No, they're dead. And when you're dead, you can't come back.
Therapist: Popeye is angry at the man who took his woman. You are angry because your parents have been taken away. But you feel you have to pretend not to be angry because, if you showed how angry you were, you'd get into trouble.

At this point, Charlene broke off this play. Going to the cupboard, she took out the little-girl doll and, placing it in the truck, she began the long journey around the table. Pausing only briefly at the far corner, which, during the previous meeting, had represented her new home, she completed the circle, arriving back at the point from which she had started. I announced that Charlene was pretending that she wouldn't really have to move to a new home, and that she was going back to live in the same home she had lived in with her daddy and mommy. She responded by putting the girl doll back in the truck and taking a second trip, ending this time at the 'new home' corner of the table. There, using a number of wooden doll figures, she showed a group of children playing while the 'Charlene' doll stood outside the circle, watching. Eventually, one of the 'new' children made an overture, which the 'Charlene' doll accepted and, joining in, played comfortably with the other dolls for the few minutes remaining in the session.

Just prior to terminating the hour, I reminded Charlene that the next session would be our last one. She responded by going to the cupboard, taking out a gun – the first time she had used it in any of the sessions so far – and shooting me in the face before she left.

Session 5

The final session began with the alligator and whale fighting. When I asked why they were fighting, Charlene replied that the whale was angry because the alligator wouldn't leave him alone. I interpreted this as a reaction to this session's being our final time together, and I suggested to her that it was the other way around. Maybe the whale was angry because the alligator would not see her any more after today. In response, the play immediately became violent, as Charlene repeatedly smashed the alligator, took the gun and shot him, announced she was ripping his teeth out, punched him, and so on. As she did so, I took an owl puppet from the cupboard and announced: 'This is the owl. He lives in a tree. He met the whale and the alligator just five times.'

In response, whale and alligator joined forces and, together, turned on the owl, repeatedly biting, smashing, and shooting him.

Charlene: He sees too much. He says bad words.
Therapist: The owl says things that the whale doesn't want to hear. That upsets the whale and makes her angry. But also, the whale is angry because, after today, the owl won't see her anymore. The owl is leaving her, just as the alligator once left her. It's just like you and me: today is the last time we'll see each other.

Charlene hotly denied that this was our last meeting and also that she was at all angry, but meanwhile the attacks on the owl increased in intensity. Then, suddenly, as if under great pressure, she went to the cupboard and took out the police car and, for the first time, really played with it. This was her only direct reference in play to the fatal accident.

Again and again, she crashed the police car against the leg of the chair. This activity was followed, first, by much searching in the back seat and, then, by an announcement that they had been in the back seat but now they were gone because they were dead.

Unfortunately, at this time I did not realize that the impact of the accident had thrown her dead parents into the back seat with her. I learned only later, after this final session, that, after she had been taken from the scene of the accident, she had kept insisting that her parents were in the back seat of the car. Unable to persuade her otherwise, the police had returned her to the car briefly to demonstrate that her parents were no longer there, prior to taking her to the receiving home.

Charlene then took a man doll, one that she had briefly used to represent me on one other occasion. Having this doll turn over the car, she announced that the accident was his fault. It was because of him that her mommy and daddy had died. There followed another short period of frantic searching in the back seat.

Therapist: If she's so sad and angry, why doesn't she cry?
Charlene: You're not supposed to cry when your mother and father are killed.

And Charlene did *not* cry. Instead, she tipped over the car and smashed it repeatedly with my reflex hammer, announcing that she hated cars. Then she killed the 'doctor' doll and threw it away. As soon as she had done this, however, she picked him up and put all the dolls and puppets she had used, including the recovered 'doctor' doll, in the truck and drove them to the corner of the table that twice before had represented her new home.

Therapist: You took the doll that was me with you to your new home. You can't take me with you. But you can take one toy with you if you'd like to.

Confused, Charlene chose three and started to leave the room with all of them.

Therapist: Look at the three things you'd like to take with you. First, you chose the whale, the puppet that was you when you made up stories about the alligator leaving you all alone. Then you chose the police car. That was the car you played with when you were thinking about the accident in which your mommy and daddy were killed. And, finally, you chose the truck, the truck you used when you were playing at moving to your new home with your grandparents. But I'm afraid you can't have all three. But you can choose one.

With reluctance, Charlene put down the whale and the truck, but continued to hold tightly to the police car as if that, too, was in danger of being taken from her.

Therapist: You can take the police car with you. You used to play with the police car when you were feeling sad, frightened, and angry about the accident. You still have a lot of those feelings. So, you can take the police car and play with it in your grandparents' home.

Notice how much rage was expressed in the early part of this session, rage at the parents for leaving and rage that, in the absence of the parents, had to be blamed on (i.e., displaced to) something else (e.g., the leg of a chair, the doctor doll) that was tangible and available. Often foster parents, as the adults who are substituting for the abandoning parents at whom the foster child is really so angry, are the recipients of much of these rages. It is worth remembering, however, that, in the previous session, some of the anger and badness had been directed against herself, when Charlene had been preoccupied with the role that children's badness plays in their being punished and rejected. This, of course, has major implications both for the child's self-concept and, in many cases, for the child's behaviour while in care.

As we saw in chapter 2, several authors have questioned whether a pre-adolescent is sufficiently developed psychologically to mourn a loss, even the loss of a parent (Wolfenstein 1966; Nagera 1970). Note how much Charlene remembered, and how much sadness, rage, and fear she was capable of expressing, even though it took quite active intervention by a therapist to make possible the re-experiencing of these feelings and the initiation of the work of mourning. Note, also, that the eliciting of these feelings caused considerable pain, not just for Charlene but for her therapist and the social worker who observed the sessions as well. Although Charlene did not cry at any point during the session, each of us did on several occasions. I mention this fact both to emphasize how hard it is to assist a child through the work of mourning and because of the frequency with which those adults whose assistance the child needs to mourn successfully protect themselves – while rationalizing that they are protecting the child – by colluding with her in avoiding the subject (Palmer 1974; Aldridge and Cautley 1975). But note how, repeatedly during these sessions, each move towards an acceptance of reality was preceded by some indication that the work of mourning was proceeding. Thus, by helping Charlene experience and deal with the mourning process that she was in danger of repressing, the therapy seemed to allow her to assimilate, in digestible doses, the feelings stirred up by the parental loss. This assimilation, in turn, was considered a prerequisite for her being freed sufficiently to proceed with her development and to come to grips with the future.

One might reasonably ask whether it was necessary to put Charlene through such a painful experience, and whether it would not have been wiser to avoid challenging her defences. There is a difference between an experience that is upsetting and one that is destructive. There was considerable evidence that Charlene's therapy, while upsetting, was not traumatic. Her foster mother reported that Charlene seemed happy and excited prior to all sessions except the first. She would stand near the door, waiting for the social worker to come and drive her to her therapy. After each session, she would return home, seeming relaxed but, according to the foster mother, 'her mind was a million miles away.' The social worker compared her mood while in the car after each session to that of her own children after they had had their bath and were being powdered prior to getting ready for bed. Charlene's fear of driving in cars disappeared over the sessions, and her foster mother described her behaviour in the foster home as 'more like that of other children': 'she doesn't act too good, the way she used to.' She even began to mention the accident and missing her parents within the foster home, in contrast with the period prior to therapy during which she had acted as if nothing had happened.

From contact with a child welfare worker in her new community, who, at our request, enquired periodically about Charlene's progress following her placement with her grandparents, superficially at least she seemed to adjust well. Follow-up continued until approximately three years after the placement. At that point, Charlene seemed to have formed a secure attachment to the grandparents, and was relating well to peers, neighbours, and teachers. She was doing well in school. Her development seemed to be proceeding satisfactorily and she showed no grossly apparent neurotic or behavioural problems. It was reported that, for almost four months following the move to her grandparents' home, she played with the police car at least once a day. Suddenly, at that point, she announced that she no longer wanted the police car in the home and, with the help of the grandparents, disposed of it in the garbage can. My hypothesis would be that this point coincided with that at which she no longer needed the police car as a prop to facilitate the work of mourning.

This brings us, then, to the final question to be explored in this chapter: how similar was the process Charlene went through to that of a child who is separated from her parents by being taken into care? For the average foster child, many of the same feelings and means of defending against them exist, but usually not in a form as clear-cut or accessible to intervention.

A previously abused and neglected child, or one from a home rife with family discord, would generally have much more difficulty trusting and relating to a therapist, so that communication with the therapist would probably be more guarded. Thus, it would be more difficult for the therapist to see as clearly what the child was saying in his or her play, and to provide successfully the support needed to assist the work of mourning. Also, the many feelings and conflicts resulting from the child's chronic exposure to violence, neglect, and abuse while still in the natural family would confuse and intensify the child's feelings – and the need to defend against them. It would also greatly compound the number and complexity of the issues needing to be resolved in treatment, which would therefore be longer, more difficult, and, probably, somewhat less successful.

After all, Charlene had come from a previously intact family, and, in contrast with the situations of many children separated from parents by coming into care, there was no known history of family conflict, rejection, neglect, or abuse. She lost her parents suddenly, dramatically, and permanently, unlike many children in care for whom the parental loss is much more ambiguous; usually one or both parents are still alive, and the child may have regular or irregular contact with them. There is often the realistic possibility of the courts returning the foster child to the natural parents at a later date. Often the reason for the child's leaving the natural parents is extremely ambiguous, with even neglectful or abusive parents protesting that they love the child, accusing the protection worker of taking her from them, or blaming the child for the family breakdown. All these factors tend to confuse, mask, and diffuse at least the expression and probably the experiencing of the foster child's sense of loss. But the work of mourning, though often at least partially aborted, is generally reactivated from time to time, when naturally occurring environmental stimuli trigger new periods of grief. The child's emotional and behavioural life often shows signs of bursts of mourning alternating with evidence of incomplete mourning and the defences against it, as were described in the discussion of the long-term effects of incomplete mourning in chapter 2.

Chapter Four

Identity Formation and the Influence of Life History and Special Status of the Foster and Adopted Child

Before discussing the effects of being a foster child on the identity and life history of the child who grows up in a family other than his or her own, let us review briefly some aspects of normal development particularly relevant to foster children.

The term 'self-concept' refers to the one's cognitive understanding of what one is like. One aspect of it is one's self-esteem, the feeling about oneself that reflects the kind of person one thinks one is. A child's identity is a combination of these; it describes what children would say if they could supply complete answers to the questions 'Who are you?,' 'What are you like?,' 'How do you feel about yourself?'

Development of the Biological (Average) Child's Sense of Identity

The development of self-concept and self-esteem begins as early as the first year of life. If the fit between child and parents is a good one (Thomas 1981), and if the child experiences 'good-enough' parenting – that is, if the parents are able to perceive accurately and respond adequately to the child's needs – the child is likely to experience what Erikson (1950) has called 'basic trust' and Ainsworth (1974) has termed 'a secure attachment.' Such a child is likely to feel loved, confident, and secure. This, Harter suggests, predisposes to later success in peer relationships. In contrast, children whose parents are consistently unable to perceive and respond to their needs are likely to lack a sense of basic trust. Theirs is more likely, especially over time, to be an anxious, avoidant or disorganized attachment, since much of the time they are left feeling insecure, helpless, and uncontrollably tense, lacking in confidence and control over events and the environment (Fenichel 1945: Harter 1983, 1985a; Connell 1981; Harter and Connell 1984; R.W. White 1959, 1960, 1963).

Since no parents are perfectly able to perceive and respond to all their infant's needs, no infant goes without experiencing some frustration. Infants can tolerate a reasonable amount of frustration without suffering ill effects; in fact, learning to soothe themselves when frustrated is an important aspect of emotional development (Brazelton, Koslowski, and Main 1974; Greenspan 1981; Kohut 1971; Tolpin 1971). If the infant receives adequate satisfaction and is spared intolerable levels of frustration, the parenting is said to be 'good enough.' If, however, the satisfaction received is consistently insufficient, and the infant is regularly frustrated beyond the limit of tolerance, development of basic trust and a secure attachment is likely to be undermined (Thomas 1981).

The origins of self-concept and self-esteem begin soon after the child has developed the awareness that someone out there, the primary caregiver, exists apart from her and has the ability either to satisfy her needs (i.e., bringing comfort and security) or to frustrate them (i.e., leaving her unsatisfied and tense) (Ferenczi 1926). In time, children internalize a picture of themselves that directly reflects their perception of how they feel valued by their major attachment figures (Cooley 1902; Harter 1983). If they feel loved, they picture themselves as worthwhile and attractive. As Epstein has put it, the person with high self-esteem 'in effect carries within him a loving parent, one who is proud of his successes and accepting of his failures.' In contrast, 'the person with low self-esteem carries within him a disapproving parent who is harshly critical of his failures' (S. Epstein 1980, p. 106). If children are frequently neglected, they will regard themselves as unlovable and unattractive (Rosenberg 1979; Bowlby 1979; Adam 1982). If the primary attachment figure is grossly inconsistent (e.g., sometimes nurturing and loving, and, at other times, unavailable, frustrating, punitive, or rejecting), or if several important attachment figures respond differently to the child (e.g., if the mother is nurturing and loving, but the father uninterested, harsh, or rejecting), the child's self-concept will be confused: Is she lovable (as she seems to the mother) or unlovable and unattractive (as she seems to the father, or the day-care attendant)?

The origins of the child's self-concept are laid in the first two years of life, as she internalizes a picture of herself that reflects how she thinks she is perceived by her major attachment figures (Fenichel 1945; Harter

1983). The child who has experienced good-enough parenting and formed a secure attachment will derive from it a confidence, both in herself and in the continued availability of the parents, to encourage initial exploratory behaviour (Bowlby 1979; Ainsworth 1974; Sroufe and Waters 1977). The confidence with which the child begins to explore her competence at mastering the environment, the availability and supportiveness of a secure base (the attachment figure) there to provide reassurance whenever needed, will all contribute to the ratio of successes to failures during these early forays into independence. A predominantly successful pattern will encourage confidence, especially if the parents and others are supportive (Fenichel 1945). Such a child is likely to view herself as competent and effective, and this image may remain relatively stable despite passing phases of praise or blame (Cooley 1902), bolstering confidence for further explorations, broadening experiences, and assisting in the development of physical and social skills, thus further reinforcing the child's view of herself as competent and effective (Ainsworth 1974; Harter 1983).

In contrast, the child with an insecure primary attachment will lack much of the confidence and support needed to explore the environment boldly (Harter 1985b). This lack can be particularly limiting for a child whose basic temperament predisposes to anxiety (e.g., tendency to withdraw from new persons and situations; low physiological threshold and greater than average reactivity and persistence of response; lower than average attention span and perseverance; or, relatively poor manual dexterity and coordination) (Kagan et al 1984, 1987, 1988; Garcia-Coll, Kagan, and Reznick 1984; Suomi 1989). Repeated failures are likely further to undermine confidence, especially if the caregivers are inconsistently available or unable to provide the encouragement and support needed to overcome unavoidable sporadic defeats. Such a child is likely to learn to see herself as a loser – incompetent, ineffective, unattractive, and, more often than not, unsuccessful. Such a perception will discourage subsequent risk-taking, further restricting the range of experience and limiting even further the development of physical competence, confidence, social skills, and the capacity for mastery of the environment (Harter and Pike 1981; Harter 1983; Kagan et al 1988).

Throughout the pre-school years, the self-concept continues to develop (Sarbin 1962). Through play, and particularly through the cognitive processes of ordering and grouping objects into categories, the toddler develops an increased understanding of what he is (that is, what categories he belongs to) and what he is not (Mussen, Conger, and Kagan

1981). In the process, he increasingly identifies with his family and its attitudes, values, and characteristics (Fenichel 1945). Typically this identification, which could alternately be described as 'role modelling' or (predominantly unconscious) 'imitation,' is primarily with the same-sexed parent. Lacking a parent of the same sex, the child may choose substitute identification models: a member of the extended family, a neighbour, a teacher or group leader, a respected peer and so on (Rosenberg 1979). Some children use fantasies of an absent and/or idealized parent as model for identification. Through identification, the child takes on attributes, characteristics, values, and mannerisms of the role model, which then become part of his internalized self-concept and identity.

There are both positive and negative aspects to the identification process. The child's behaviour and values may, in some areas, closely resemble those of the role model; in other areas, they may be markedly different. These identifications and contra-identifications can be measured directly. The greater their product, the more conflict or confusion over competing internalized values and goals – that is, identity diffusion – there will be (Weinreich 1979).

When the child enters school, the primary reference group extends beyond the family to include the peer group. While the six-year-old judges the correctness of her friends' behaviour and views others critically, the seven-year-old begins to worry about what others might think of her. The average eight-year-old increasingly compares herself to others, determining how she is the same and how she differs (Gesell and Ilg 1946). This new awareness is soon organized within the newly developing ability to think logically and organize thoughts hierarchically. Concomitantly, for the first time, a global – as opposed to a particular – sense of self-esteem based on hierarchical arrangements of personal traits develops (Rosenberg 1979; Epstein 1973; Coopersmith 1967; Harter 1983). Particular characteristics assume less importance once the self-concept is organized hierarchically. For example, the child may recognize that she is good at most things but bad at sports or at academics. Any particular incompetence will be less disturbing if the child's general sense of self is positive. Once formed, the child's global self-esteem will do more than any individual success or failure to determine the overall self-concept (Harter 1985a).

School entry introduces a period of acute comparison with peers, even for children who, defensively, deny it. Children are very much aware of how they match up to their peers in scholastic ability, athletic skills, attractiveness, courage, and popularity (Minton 1979). Through their continuing comparison of themselves to others, their self-concept and self-esteem are reassessed and adjusted (Harter 1985a), particularly children who carry any handicap or stigma that has been taken for granted and accepted by their family and previous circle of acquaintances but that conspicuously sets them apart from other children exposed to them for the first time (Le Febvre 1983). During adolescence, when formal operational thought and an increasing ability to abstract and reason develop, these capacities allow the values of others, particularly those of peer group, to challenge or even displace those of the parents in the individuating teenager's personal value system (Harter 1983; Rosenberg 1979; Main, Kaplan, and Cassidy 1985).

One of the compelling developmental tasks of adolescence is the achievement of unity and coherence in this sense of identity (S. Epstein 1981; Lecky 1945; Erikson 1950, 1959, 1968). When accomplished, this task results in a sense of self that unifies and integrates the competing self-perceptions, remains relatively stable over time, and achieves some correspondence between the teenager's own sense of self and significant others' sense of him. In this way, adolescents integrate different aspects of the self into an all-encompassing view of their personality. To do so, however, they must deal with inconsistencies within the self, which many find troubling and confusing (Monsour and Harter 1984; Lecky 1945). The more conflict and the less integration they achieve, the lower their sense of self-regard (Harter 1985b). Also, adolescents' perception of their global attractiveness – more so than their perception of partial competence in the scholastic, sociability, or behavioural areas (Harter 1985a) – is the crucial factor in defining self-esteem.

In some cases, identity can change long after adolescence, but by the end of the teenage years, or at least the mid-twenties, some sort of closure and stability in self-concept are normally achieved. After adolescence, a longer and stronger impact is needed to shift significantly the sense of identity (i.e., self-concept and self-esteem) than would have been required earlier. Nevertheless, even at this relative point of closure, identity is not written in stone (Fenichel 1945). A good or bad marriage, extreme or sustained work success or failure, a successful experience in therapy, a religious or semi-religious conversion, a severe illness or injury can still affect, for better or worse, one's identity, self-concept, and self-esteem (Harter 1985a; Ricks 1985).

One other psychological factor affecting the individual's sense of her own identity is the completeness of the boundary that separates the self from the non-self (i.e., the outer world). If this boundary is complete, individuation will have progressed to the point where the individual rarely confuses her own thoughts, feelings, values, and motives with those of others (A. Freud 1946; Harter and Barnes 1981; Harter 1983). Such individuals can usually tolerate ambivalence, and are able to recognize both desirable and undesirable qualities both in themselves and in others. Those whose boundary remains incomplete, however, will have difficulty relating to others, and are likely to have difficulty sustaining long-term relationships, since relatedness to others threatens to overwhelm their own sense of self. Such individuals may either restrict themselves to highly stereotyped interpersonal relationships or distance themselves from others, leading to further estrangement (Laing 1960; Harter 1983; Steinhauer and Tisdall 1984).

When the process of individuation stops short of being able to distinguish self from non-self reliably and consistently, this interpersonal boundary remains incomplete. This allows disowned thoughts, feelings, and motives to be projected onto others, while only desirable attributes continue to be attributed to the self (A. Freud 1946; Harter and Barnes 1981; Harter 1983; Steinhauer and Tisdall 1984). In the attempt to achieve a unified sense of self (S. Epstein 1981; Lecky 1945), the individual tries to expel or project inconsistencies in his self-perception through the defective self–other boundary (Lecky 1945). The inability to tolerate ambivalence associated with major boundary defects predisposes to the widespread use of the defence of splitting. Through splitting, individuals deal with powerful but intolerable ambivalence towards key attachment figures by unconsciously displacing the negative feelings towards the ambivalently loved person onto someone else. This displacement allows them to avoid the conflict inherent in the ambivalence: the key figure is now idealized and totally loved, whereas whoever has projected onto them that person's 'bad' qualities is vilified and hated (A. Freud 1946; S. Freud 1946; Klein 1946).

These, then are the normal processes that together contribute to a child's developing a sense of identity. How are these modified by the special situation of the foster child or the adoptee?

Development of the Foster Child's Sense of Identity

Most children entering foster care do so following a long period of privation, neglect, and/or abuse within a seriously disorganized and conflicted natural family. Such children lack the 'good-enough' parenting needed to develop basic trust and a secure attachment (Ricks 1985). However, some foster children, for most of their first year of life, have mothers who meet their needs adequately, but once their motor and cognitive development allows them to crawl about, they no longer function as living dolls to be played with or ignored by their mothers at will. Instead of providing the secure base they so badly need, their mothers respond to their early exploratory behaviour as a source of frustration and defiance rather than as a normal stage of developmental progress. Such mothers, who have usually been extremely deprived and frustrated in their own formative early years, are unconsciously dealing with residual feelings of deprivation by trying to re-create with the infant the ideal mother–child relationship of their fantasies. As long as parenting remains gratifying, they are loving and, altruistically identifying with the infant, they experience the feeling of being cared for and loved that they missed in their own upbringing (A. Freud 1946). But once the baby becomes a source of frequent frustration, the relationship rapidly breaks down. From this point, what may have begun as 'good-enough' mothering rapidly becomes a conflicted relationship with a mother whose own needs keep her from tolerating even normal and necessary frustration and demands by the baby (Quinton, Rutter, and Liddle 1984). The resulting hostile interaction can progressively undermine the attachment (Schneider-Rosen el al 1985).

As a result of family chaos, conflict, and inconsistency, many foster children form a negative initial picture, seeing themselves as unlovable and deserving of rejection. At the very least, their self-image is confused, reflecting the inconsistency of parents who are ambivalent and who constantly fluctuate in their ability to meet their child's needs. Toddlers have an egocentric world-view – that is, they assume that everything that occurs happens because of them. When separated from their parents, especially during the toddler years, they are likely to believe that their badness caused their rejection, their removal from the family, and the difficulties preceding the family breakdown. Such thinking merely reinforces the child's initial image of himself as unwanted and unlovable.

Temperamentally more passive and withdrawn toddlers may respond to the inadequate nurturing and the failure to encourage early attempts at exploration by a progressive undermining of their trust in others and their confidence in themselves. The result can be a generalized withdrawal from and avoidance of unfamiliar situations, peers, and activities. Such avoidance will interfere with the development of motor, athletic, and social skills and ultimately, of the child's sense of mastery, and, in turn, will undermine the child's confidence, further disadvantaging him or her in relating to other children.

In contrast, children with a more determined and approach-oriented temperament will not give up so easily. While continuing to struggle against the mother and against the adversities of the environment, they will soon learn not to depend upon others for satisfaction of their emotional needs. Giving up any hope of having these met in reality, they withdraw into themselves behind a pseudo-independent façade. Becoming increasingly narcissistic, they look more and more to fantasies than to other adults who, they have learned, cannot be relied upon for understanding and support.

The self-concepts of young children separated from their families at an early age are at considerable developmental risk, even though, for some, the risk would have been even greater had they remained in chronically rejecting families consistently unable to meet their minimal emotional needs. A common reaction of young children to any severe and especially chronic emotional turmoil is interference with normal development. Thus, it is not unusual for toddlers coming into care to be far behind the norms for their age in many aspects of development. Given a timely placement in an adequate substitute environment, many such children, after an initial period of distress, settle in and rapidly catch up in those areas of development in which they lagged. Those whose placements are not successful, however, or those who bounce in and out of care repeatedly after premature restoration to families that are rejecting or ambivalent, will make much less satisfactory developmental progress (Fanshel and Shinn 1978; Quinton and Rutter 1985; Tizard 1977). Such children are likely to remain well below the norms for their age at the point of school entry, and to have a high incidence of psychosocial problems in adolescence (Rutter 1982).

On entering school, foster children too begin to compare themselves with their peers. As we have seen, many of them because of insufficient stimulation in their natural families and developmental interference both before and after removal, may, by the time they attend school, already lack many of the basic skills required for academic and social success. The child who has had multiple placements will have been exposed to multiple separations and parental figures. With each such separation, the child's sense of lovability, security, and stability will have been further undermined. Such children are often confused by the contrasting expectations of a succession of families whose definitions of what is acceptable differ considerably. Since these children egocentrically assume that each such breakdown is their fault, it is not hard to see how their conviction of their inadequacy and unacceptability could be reinforced, so that they might be preoccupied with emotional turmoil rather than being motivated to attend, concentrate, risk, and achieve at school. Then, when they begin to fall behind academically, their growing conviction of their own inadequacy is once again confirmed. If, in frustration, they lash out, the resulting immaturity, badness, or aggressiveness become other negative labels compounding their sense of inherent inferiority.

In the early grades of school, names are particularly important. It is not long before the foster child becomes painfully aware that, unlike other children, her name differs from that of the family with whom she lives. Already sensitized to rejection, she soon learns that there is a strong stigma attached to being a foster child, one that reflects the low esteem in which the poor, the failures, and the illegitimate have traditionally been held in our society. The child may seek to avert this stigma by trying to 'pass,' pretending that her surname is the same as that of the foster family. Even if she succeeds at first, within herself she knows she isn't really a full member of that family, and sooner or later someone – a classmate, a teacher, the foster parents themselves – will confront her with the fraud. The subsequent embarrassment will further emphasize her difference and the vulnerability of her position.

With each separation, the foster child must cope not only with his increased sense of failure and unacceptability, but also with the rage and helplessness stirred up by his feelings of loss. Often, assuming that his anger has caused his rejection in the first place, he tries to conceal it from the foster parents to avoid yet another rejection. This assumption may be realistic, since not all foster parents will tolerate for long the repeated expression of such a child's distress. Often, particularly if he lacks ongoing contact with the birth parents, he attempts to handle this rage through 'splitting.' He can do this easily since, because of developmental interference, his individuation has not progressed enough to allow him to separate clearly self from non-self. As a result, he is encouraged to idealize the absent parents, protecting this idealization by projecting the rage stemming from their inadequate parenting and rejection onto currently available adults, such as foster parents, social workers, or teachers.

A lack of regular contact with the natural parents makes it easier for the child to idealize them in fantasy. Meanwhile, those onto whom he has projected the rage displaced from the natural parents cannot compete with the latter's idealization in fantasy as providers of satisfaction. As the child increasingly turns to fantasy rather than to others for gratification, they are likely to experience his distancing of them as a rejection. At the same time, the initial period of empathy and tolerance of his hostile or oppositional behaviour begins to wear thin, further straining their relationship with him. They increasingly begin to resent receiving only anger, distancing, and rejection in exchange for their attempts at understanding and caring. If they respond to his misbehaviour with growing frustration, his stereotyped view of them as uncaring and rejecting is reinforced, thus confirming for him their unreliability and further undermining the placement. At the same time, his feelings of being unwanted, alone, and rejected – except in his fantasies – is again confirmed, since he fails to appreciate how much his defensive behaviour has contributed to the self-fulfilling prophecy coming true. Ricks (1985) argues that the child who sees himself as unworthy and unlovable can at least use his perception as an organizing principle to make some sense out of his life experience. He will, therefore, interpret the behaviour of others in accordance with this belief, possibly even provoking others to confirm it. He will also resist contrary evidence (see also Bowlby 1979). As he retreats increasingly to the more controllable world of his fantasies, the likelihood both of a successful integration into the foster home and of satisfying relationships with others his own age is further undermined

The above sequence is likely to occur unless the child is assisted successfully through the work of mourning and reattachment as described in chapter 7. Should the child, with the help of foster parents and social work, mourn sufficiently to permit successful integration and secure reattachment within the foster family, development will once again be free to proceed. The stronger and more positive the child's relationship with the foster parents, the more likely he will be to internalize new images of himself based on how he believes he is seen by them. The nature and intensity of these images will depend on the strength and duration of his attachment to them. By this time, the foster child is likely to have internalized two conflicting images of himself: a negative one that remains from his experiences with his natural parents, reinforced by separation from them and by any subsequent unsuccessful placements; and a newer and, initially, more tentative but positive one that begins to develop as he starts to internalize his foster parents' picture of him as worthwhile and valued. Frequently foster children describe being torn between partial and conflicting views they have of themselves, and equally conflicting identifications with two sets of very different parents.

It can be a real struggle for a child to come to grips with having two sets of parents. The foster parents, whom she may be beginning to love and trust, are often very different from both the biological parents, whom she sees on visits, and the idealized natural parents of her fantasies. The result can be real confusion, as she vacillates between an identification with the natural parents and one with the foster parents, leading to a clash between two incompatible internalized images of what and who she is. Especially if she begins to prefer the foster parents, she may experience real guilt and a sense of betrayal of the natural parents, to whom she feels her first loyalties are due (Blum 1976; Schwam and Tuskan 1979; Weinstein 1960). This loyalty conflict, stemming from her confused identity, will be exacerbated if either set of parents criticizes the other, in which case the child often finds herself identifying with and springing to the defence of whichever parents are under attack. This situation can create serious problems for her, especially if the foster parents are critical of and competitive with the natural parent. If so, they will resent her continuing attachment to the natural parents, seeing it as a failure to appreciate them, in spite of all they have put up with, how much they have done for her, and so on.

Adolescence is a time during which even the most normal of children are acutely and painfully sensitive to ways in which they differ from their peers – witness the frantic search for conformity in dress, behaviour, hair styles, tastes in music, and so on. For this reason, as the foster child enters adolescence, the stigma associated with being in care is further intensified. Since they may, by now, be having serious difficulties in several major areas of life, it is not surprising that they feel an increasing sense of failure, which further undermines their self-esteem. The resulting depression further drains energies desperately needed for academic achievement and social growth, again undermining developmental progress and increasing the sense of failure and of having missed out.

The failure, over the years, to satisfy exaggerated needs for affection and security now begins to interfere with the foster child's successfully negotiating a major task of adolescence – the completion of individuation. If he is already so passive, restricted, and/or depressed that he has given up hope, he may stop trying at this point. If so, instead of achieving mastery, he may develop a pattern of manipulating others into doing or caring for him, as if to obtain compensation for past deprivations.

Those who go this route are very vulnerable to being used and abused by others who appear to offer the approval they so desperately crave. The foster adolescent's fantasy that some day he will achieve the love and acceptance he has always dreamed about leaves him or her vulnerable to unscrupulous exploitation, including sexual abuse, by others. For a time they go along, fitting their exploiter into their fantasies of the idealized caring parent, only inevitably to end up feeling betrayed, abused, and abandoned once more (see the example of Ken in chapter 14).

Other, more resourceful foster teenagers aspire to independence but lack the inner resources to achieve it. They may go through the motions of individuating via exaggerated but unconvincing or self-defeating pseudo-independent posturing. In so doing, they end up alienating others and demonstrating, to others and to themselves, their lack of readiness for any real assumption of independence. At times, such foster adolescents may live together or even occasionally marry during their teens, hoping, through the union, to find the caring that has eluded them all their lives. Unfortunately, however, underneath a façade of emotional competence, their partner is often just a mirror image of themselves. Instead of providing the dependency gratification and support they crave, they turn out to be equally needy, a further drain on even the inadequate emotional resources on which the teenager has been struggling to subsist. Hope soon sours into disillusionment and resentment. The majority of such unions are short-lived (Hepworth 1980), although many do not break up until after the birth of one or more children. These offspring even further strain the limited resources of the couple, whose unresolved neediness make it almost impossible for them to provide the 'good-enough' parenting their infants need (Hall and Pawlby 1981; Hall, Pawlby, and Wolkind 1979; Pawlby and Hall 1980; Wolkind, Hall, and Pawlby 1977). As a result, all too frequently, their children are doomed to repeat the cycle of neglect, abuse, rejection, separation, and deprivation in the next generation (see also Fromer and O'Shea 1973a, 1973b; Ney 1989).

Some foster children, despite a similar history, manage to overcome their disadvantages and to mature into productive, mature, and independent individuals with realistic self-concept and reasonable self-esteem (Zimmerman 1982; Festinger 1983; Fanshel, Finch, and Grundy 1990). Why this occurs is not always clear, but a number of factors, alone or in combination, probably contribute. These factors may include: temperamental invulnerability; a prolonged stay in a caring foster family that provided the 'good-enough' parenting and the effective role models they needed; a pattern of defences favouring acceptance rather than rejection by others; a long-term relationship with a committed and experienced social worker who remains continuously available over a period of years; a successful – and usually prolonged – experience in psychotherapy; a stable and gratifying marriage. Unfortunately, there are few follow-up studies to provide an accurate estimate of how many foster children eventually reach such a positive solution, although Fanshel, Finch, and Grundy (1990) found that 60 per cent do. Most 'successful' graduates of foster care sever their ties with the agencies that raised them. As a result, the sample available for the few follow-up studies that have been done is not necessarily representative. Most experienced workers in the child welfare field know some such cases, however. They are mentioned here just to underscore the fact that the identity and self-concept of the long-term foster child are not always major problems.

Development of the Adopted Child's Sense of Identity

The sense of identity of the child adopted in infancy generally parallels that of the biological child but, because of several important differences, is at greater risk (Frisk 1964; Schoenberg 1974; Sorosky, Baran, and Pannor 1975; Hoopes 1982). It is primarily these differences that will be highlighted in this brief account.

As with the biological child, the fit between adoptee and adoptive parents and the success of both the infant's attachment and the adoptive parents' bonding are important in the subsequent development of the child's self-esteem. A number of factors contribute to an increased risk of attachment failure in an adopted population. Since the adopted child genetically bears less resemblance to the adoptive parents, one would expect that she is somewhat less likely to experience a 'goodness of fit' (Sants 1964; Weider 1978). As well, the adoptee enters the family with an unknown but generally disapproved-of (often illegitimate) parentage (Blum 1976; Schwam and Tuskan 1979). Also, many adoptive parents have not yet resolved the feelings of inadequacy and resentment that often attend infertility, which can increase the likelihood of struggles with their adopted child (Rickarby and Egan 1980). These and other factors, singly or in combination, are hurdles to be overcome before a secure attachment can be achieved. They leave adoptive adolescents more prone to loss, rejection, and abandonment than are non-adoptive adolescents (Esson 1973; Sorosky, Baran, and Pannor 1977; Hoopes 1982).

Where a secure attachment is achieved, the early development of basic trust and its internalization as a sense of being loved and valued will proceed for the adoptee as it does in the biological child. If, however, the attachment process is impaired, the adoptee is particularly liable to feel that she does not really belong in the adoptive family. Also, more than a few adoptive parents, fearing that their child will someday be drawn to re-establish contact with her biological roots, hold back so that they are unable to invest themselves fully in bonding to their newly placed child. This holding back may be followed by rejection, as they begin to wall off the child emotionally as a foreign body that does not belong within their family. The risk of withholding may be greater if a supposedly infertile family conceives a natural child subsequent to the adoption (McWhinnie 1967; Hoopes 1982). A natural child is not only a product of their own flesh, blood, and genetic material, but also proof of their fertility. The adopted child, meanwhile, remains as an unwanted reminder of the stigma of their reproductive inadequacy.

Of course, not all adopted children and parents experience these difficulties. When they do occur, however, they interfere with the parent–child relationship and can contribute to undermining the attachment/bonding process, which, in turn, can lead to an internalization by the affected child of a sense of herself as an unwanted and/or devalued intruder.

Where attachment and bonding are weak, there are several likely results. The weaker the attachment, the less the child will be motivated to please the adoptive parents, and the greater interference there may be with the ongoing process of socialization and social relationships. Also, the more insecure the bonding, the more problems the adoptive parents are likely to have in resolving their normal ambivalence towards the child whom they fear they may some day lose. This insecurity may undermine their ability to take and hold a consistent (parental) stand for fear of alienating the child. The absence of such a stand will favour non-compliant behaviour in the child, further eroding the tolerance of both adoptee and adoptive parents for the hostile component of the ambivalence normal to all parent–child relationships and perhaps leaving both with more than average difficulty in dealing with anger occurring between them (Steinhauer 1983b). It can deteriorate into a vicious circle of escalating hostility and alienation, masked at times by excessive parental permissiveness, which is a reaction formation (defence) disguising unrecognized rejection. This increased conflict can significantly undermine the normal pre-adolescent identification with the parents, further exaggerating dependence/independence conflicts, especially in adolescents (Sokoloff 1977; Sorosky, Baran, and Pannor 1977). Should this occur, the child will incorporate an image of herself as unworthy, unloved, and unlovable. Note that it is the quality of the parenting and not the adoption per se that is the primary cause of these difficulties (Ricarby and Egan 1980; Sabalis and Burch 1980).

Mention should be made here of the controversy over the age at which children should be told that they are adopted, and how this knowledge will affect their sense of their own identity. The literature is divided on this issue. Most authors (e.g., Triseliotis 1973; Eldred et al 1976; Kirk 1964; Sorosky, Baran, and Pannor 1975; Sokoloff 1977; Blum 1976; Brodzinsky, Braff, and Singer 1981; Stein and Hoopes 1985) hold that the topic of adoption should be introduced early, even before the child can fully understand what the term means. Most clinicians have advised parents to answer questions about a child's origins as the child asks them, clearly and directly, during the pre-school and childhood years. The questions will reflect different understanding and fantasies about adoption at different ages. But more important than the timing of these discussions is the emotional climate and the quality of the relationship in which they occur. Disclosure is more likely to be traumatic because family relationships are disturbed than because of the age at which it occurred (Lawton and Gross 1964; Sorosky, Baran, and Pannor 1977; Steinhauer 1983b; Stein and Hoopes 1985). The rationale for this position is that, sooner or later, the child will learn that her situation differs from that of children raised in their natural families. Since adopted children *are* different, these authors argue, they should learn of that difference gradually and naturally from loving parents in what Schoenberg (1974) has termed 'a climate of social comfort' so that they can feel different but not devalued. If the parents do not introduce their adopted status early and naturally, such children run the risk of learning of their adoption unexpectedly and traumatically from curious or hostile peers or from insensitive adults (Triseliotis 1973). In either case, both the unexpected shock and the fact that the truth was kept from them will increase the chance of their feeling deceived, which, in turn, increases the risk of the revelation seeming shameful and stigmatic rather than merely different (Eldred et al 1976; Sants 1964; McWhinnie 1969).

Schechter (1960), Schechter and colleagues (1964), Goodman and

Magno-Nora (1975), and Wieder (1977a, 1977b, 1978), drawing their conclusions about adoptions in general from their experience with their
patients, warn against telling adoptees of their adoption at an early age,
arguing that doing so will intensify the 'family romance.' This fantasy,
almost universal, and experienced by most children at some point in
their development, is that they were born into another, usually much
more desirable, family, only to be plucked away from their 'real' parents
after birth and deposited in the family in which they find themselves.
Telling children of their adoption early, Schechter suggests, risks exaggerating this fantasy, which could result in alienation between parents
and child as well as the undermining of the adopted child's sense of her
own identity. However, others (Triseliotis 1973; Kirk 1964) argue that
adoptive parents who cannot or will not comfortably and openly discuss
a child's birth parents – whether because of lack of specific information,
a more general inhibition of communication, or discomfort with their
adoptive status – will increase the child's chance of becoming preoccupied with romanticized or idealized fantasies of the birth parents
(Blum 1976; Brodzinsky, Braff, and Singer 1981; Schoenberg 1974; Sokoloff 1977; Sorosky, Baran, and Pannor 1977; Stein and Hoopes 1985).

Although most authors favour telling children they are adopted early,
identity formation for adopted children is more complicated than for
the average child, since each adoptive child, in consolidating her own
identity, must somehow reconcile her knowledge of being biologically
connected to unknown birth parents (Sants 1964; Frisk 1964). She must
reconcile having two sets of parents: birth parents who gave her up and
adoptive parents who took her in. She may also have to come to grips
with an obvious lack of similarity to members of the adoptive family
(Wieder 1978; Stein and Hoopes 1985). This risk is not entirely separate
from that of difficulties in attachment, since the more secure the child's
sense of belonging in the adoptive family, the more she will identify
herself as a member of that family. The consolidation of such a child's
sense of her own identity during adolescence may be only slightly more
complicated – but not necessarily more stressful – than that of the average child (Stein and Hoopes 1985). If, however, that sense of belonging
within the adoptive family is seriously undermined, there will be more
centrifugal force towards a competing identification with the birth family, with all the fantasies and feelings that have been invested in it over
the years (Clothier 1943; McWhinnie 1969; Triseliotis 1973). For these
reasons, the development of a stable sense of identity is more complex
for the adoptee than for the average child (Hoopes 1982). However, at

least for white, middle-class adolescent adoptees placed by agencies before age two, it need not be unsuccessful or more than normally stressful. In spite of the additional difficulties to be overcome, many adopted children develop a stable sense of their own identity, even in jurisdictions in which access to information about the natural parents is available on request (Triseliotis 1973; Sachdev 1989). Factors that have been associated with unsuccessful adoption include a higher number of previous placements; a high level of aggression and previous diagnosis of conduct disorder; a strong attachment to the biological mother; total time in placement prior to the first adoptive placement; adoptive parents whose self-esteem, flexibility, relationship with their own parents, and comfort in the handling of their own anger were low (Kagan and Reid 1986; Rae-Grant 1978). All of these would be expected to interfere primarily by undermining the relationship with the adoptive parents, thus blocking identification with the adoptive parents and the development of a stable sense of identity and self-esteem.

Development of the High-risk Adopted Child's Sense of Identity

Because of both the dearth of healthy, normal infants available for adoption and current pressures to eliminate long-term foster care by placing as many foster children as possible in adoptive homes, many older children who were once considered unadoptable following a series of foster-home placements end up on adoption. Another group of 'unadoptables' now frequently placed on adoption are children with one or more severe physical and/or mental handicaps. Both of these groups will have their sense of identity and self-esteem affected by factors related to both their history (e.g., multiple foster placements) and their special status.

The greater the number of foster placements that have preceded the placement on adoption, the more likely a child is to have his sense of identity and self-esteem compromised by those complications common to both foster and adoptive children. Children with multiple handicaps who are adopted will also have to cope with those complications common to both adoptive and handicapped children (Lefebvre 1983).

Chapter Five

Assessing for Parenting Capacity

This chapter deals with the central dilemma faced by child welfare agencies and family courts, that of when to remove children permanently from their natural families. It is a dilemma because failure to remove a child from a sufficiently destructive family soon enough can lead to serious and lasting damage, but premature or unnecessary removal will violate parental rights while proving no less damaging to the child in the long run (Tooley 1978). Intended as a guide to gathering and assessing the information needed for appropriate decision making, this chapter consists of three major sections. The first briefly reviews children's basic developmental needs; the second deals with determining parents' ability to meet these needs; and the third addresses the question of assessment and prediction of parenting capacity.

What Are Children's Basic Developmental Needs?

For optimal development, all children need a family that is both caring and able to provide not just for basic physical needs, but for high-quality and continuity of parenting and adequate parental stimulation. In determining the quality of the parent–child relationship, five main dimensions need examination.

1 / *Quality of attachment.* A secure attachment to a primary caretaker, usually but not necessarily the mother, is a prerequisite for optimal development. The nature and varieties of attachment, the responses of children to separation from their attachment figures, and the factors

governing a particular child's vulnerability to separation are described in detail in chapter 2.

Generally speaking, children with anxious attachments have more difficulty tolerating separation (Ainsworth 1969; Bowlby 1969). Nevertheless, grossly inadequate and/or abusive parenting may leave no choice but to remove some such children to placement in order to minimize the physical and developmental risks to them. Rutter (1979c) has shown that such children develop better in adequate substitute families than in chronically inadequate biological ones. Although taking anxiously attached children into care, even from such families, has its hazards, leaving them exposed to abusive or chronically inadequate parenting can be even more destructive. Quinton and Rutter (1985), Bohman and Sigvardsson (1981), Tizard and Rees (1974), and Wolf, Braukmann, and Ramp (1987) have shown that the damage done to children by moving them back and forth between foster care and parents who are rejecting, ambivalent, and/or unlikely to provide adequate care repeatedly interferes with their attachments and plays havoc with their emotional development and social attitudes and behaviours (Tizard 1977; Tizard and Hodges 1978; Rzepnicki 1987; Hawkins et al 1985; Bank, Patterson, and Reid 1987; Wolf, Braukmann, and Ramp 1987). Rutter (1979a, 1979c) noted that such children have a high incidence of social problems, including problems in control and in the parent–child relationships (see also Quinton and Rutter 1984), and also parenting problems when they became adults (see also Quinton and Rutter 1985). However; Fein and colleagues (1983) found that children who had been returned to their biological homes from foster care at least once in the past were adjusting better than those who had not, even if they were no longer with the natural family. This suggests that there can be some justification for returning a child home as a time-limited trial, either to test the bonding or to undermine the child's idealized fantasies of what the natural parents were like, as long as a realistic evaluation of a return to family is the least detrimental alternative for that particular child. This suggestion does not condone allowing children to drift, more through inertia than according to plan, back and forth between foster care – often a different placement each time – and parents whose incompetence and/or rejection are clear to all. Nor is it in children's best interests to remain indefinitely in limbo, nursing the forlorn hope that someday the parents who abandoned them, and who visit only sporadically, may take them back (Wilkes 1989).

Adoption is the early-childhood intervention most likely to produce an environmental change of long-term benefit to the child (Bohman and Sigvardsson 1981). To avoid deciding to free a child for adoption may have the effect of letting that child slip into limbo. It is, therefore, critical to determine as soon as possible whether a child's parents have the potential for learning to parent adequately, so that, if they don't, that child can be freed for adoption. This decision is a difficult one, since children's varying vulnerability to chronic stress makes it hard to predict with certainty how any given child will be damaged by various types and degrees of inadequate parenting. Nevertheless, the earlier one can identify families clearly unable to meet their children's emotional needs in the foreseeable future, the sooner one can begin to protect their children by freeing and preparing them for permanent placement in adequate substitute families.

2 / *Ability of parents to perceive and respond to the needs of the child.* As well as providing a secure attachment, parents need to be able to perceive accurately and respond appropriately to their child's needs, in order to protect the child's attachment and emotional development. Significant mental retardation, severe depression, acute or chronic schizophrenia, or alcohol or substance abuse may impair parents' ability to perceive children's needs for stimulation and security (Anthony 1970; Chandler 1978; McLean 1976; Roth 1972; Salomon 1981; Speers and Lansing 1965). Parents so psychologically immature or so preoccupied with their own needs that those of their children are consistently eclipsed are likely to undermine their children's development (Anthony 1970; Roth 1972; Salomon 1981; Speers 1965). As children grow older, their needs will change. Parents must be able to perceive this change and to adjust their parenting accordingly. The same devotion that meets an infant's need for a secure attachment can lead to overprotection, infantalization, and interference with normal individuation if the parents cannot modify their involvement to allow the child scope for independent behaviour. Parents dominated by internalized conflicts remaining from their own pasts that lead them to misperceive their child's behaviour – like those of a three-week-old who misinterpreted his colic as wilful disobedience and provocation – will have trouble responding appropriately to that child's behaviour (Anthony and Benedek 1970; Anthony, Koupernik, and Chiland 1978).

Earlier, it was suggested that mental retardation, depression, and schizophrenia could potentially undermine parenting capacity. None of these conditions, in itself, necessarily results in poor parenting. The psychiatric disturbance of a parent is relevant to parenting capacity only insofar as it affects that parent's availability to meet a child's needs. Such a determination can be made only when one knows the nature, extent, and duration of the parental condition; its effects on parental responsiveness and behaviour; whether or not there are remissions; whether another unaffected parent is in the home; how both parents parent during both remissions and exacerbations; and child's age; the extent of the child's needs and ability to understand the unresponsiveness and/or unusual behaviour of the parent; and the availability of other family members to compensate for the indisposed parent's incapacity by supporting the child in the face of bizarre or unresponsive behaviour. Anthony (1970) has suggested that children can cope better with bizarre psychotic behaviour (especially if their reality testing is confirmed by other family members) than they can with either symbiotic/enmeshed (smothering) or autistic/disengaged (extremely withdrawn) behaviour. Thus, severe and chronic depression can prove more damaging, especially to the young child, than some forms of parental schizophrenia, since the former diminishes responsiveness, thus causing more deprivation than the latter. Anthony also distinguishes the child who is expected to conform to the psychotic parent's expectations from other children who, while still participating in parental delusions, are capable of a double reality testing through which they escape from the delusional system when away from that parent. In such cases, whether the other parent supports the delusional system or, alternatively, the child's reality testing, is crucial. Several authors have demonstrated how much the other parent can compensate for the disturbing behaviour of a psychotic parent (Anthony 1970; Lander et al 1978; Rutter 1971, 1978b).

While discussing the influence of specific conditions on parenting capacity, consider the likely effect of parenting by a homosexual parent. In his excellent review, Leverette (1981) concluded that the lack of long-term studies makes definite predictions impossible. Those studying the matter, however, agree that the quality of the relationship and care of the child probably matters more than the parent's sexual orientation (R. Epstein 1979; R. Green 1979; Kaplan 1979; Marmor 1977; Money 1977; Harris and Turner 1986; Golombok, Spencer, and Rutter 1983). Green's short-term study agrees that a child does better with a loving and competent homosexual parent than with one who is heterosexual but uncaring, rejecting, or uninterested.

One should mention those parents who, having been deprived or abused as children, can accept their children only as providers of the gratification and sense of adequacy that they (the parents) never achieved when young. Such a parent–child relationship is vulnerable, indeed, to potential abuse (Galdston 1965; Ilfiend 1970; Lystad 1975; Silver, Dublin, and Lourie 1969; Quinton and Rutter 1984; Steele and Pollock 1968; Wright 1976).

3 / *Ability to transmit the values of the culture.* A third task of parents is to transmit to their children the values of the culture. Beginning even before the end of the first year, what parents say and the examples they set will influence their children's perceptions of good and bad, right and wrong. Ideally, prior to adolescence, the child will have begun to internalize her own concepts of 'right' and 'wrong' modelled primarily on those of the parents, and will have developed sufficient impulse control to meet those standards. These personal standards and values will be revised during adolescence as the teenager compares her family's values with those of her peers, but the child who enters adolescence without any internalized values or capacity to bind tension – that is, without the ability to contain the urge to act first and ask questions later – will likely have continuing difficulty respecting the rights of others and living in harmony with society (Steinhauer 1984). What aspects of parenting contribute to the development of these capacities?

First, the parental values must fit with those of the culture. If, for example, the family belongs to a subgroup whose values are incompatible with those of society at large, their child may be acculturated to their family but not to the broader community. Examples include the lack of a work ethic in a child growing up in a family on welfare for three generations or the delinquency of a child many of whose relatives have been in open conflict with the law.

A more difficult problem occurs in the children of recent immigrants. Immigrant parents often try to impose on their children the values of the old country, while the children, rejecting these as foreign, strive to adopt the values, attitudes, and behaviour they encounter at school. Examples include the daughter of Portuguese or Greek immigrants who refused to be chaperoned and demanded the freedom to date typically granted North American teenagers; the Orthodox Jew or Latvian who marries outside the cultural group; the use of physical punishment by West Indian parents. The values of the parent culture are not necessarily deviant, but they differ from North American norms. The clash of cultures can lead to extreme family conflict, which, if sufficiently violent, can spill over into the community. How far should the community accept behaviour that is deviant by North American standards but appropriate within the parent culture? How do we balance respect for the family's cultural traditions and its right to freedom from societal interference against society's duty to provide protection when needed by youngsters caught between two cultures?

Under what conditions can parents transmit values to their children? The child must be exposed to consistent expectations, as when husband and wife agree upon what is acceptable, so that neither colludes with or ignores behaviour that would not be tolerated by the other. Effective socialization requires minimal discrepancy between stated values and observable parental behaviour, since much internalization of values results from identification with parental behaviour (i.e., role modelling). Children are more likely to identify with what parents *do* than with what they *say*. Parents will distort the values of a child whom they unconsciously utilize to discharge their own unrecognized antisocial impulses, especially when these values contrast directly with their manifest behaviour and stated expectations (Johnson 1949). Unless treatment removes such parents' need to act out through the child or the child is protected by separation from the parents, such a child will internalize the parents' view of him. In time, what started as a projection onto the child of unrecognized parental psychopathology may become a self-fulfilled prophecy (Tizard and Hodges 1978). Finally, the parents must be regularly available – physically and emotionally – to meet the child's needs, to serve as identification figures or role models, and to enforce the expectations referred to above. Youngsters learn to control their impulses and bind tension only with continual consistent parental availability and follow-through. Without it, they remain essentially unsocialized.

4 / *Quality of relationship – rejection, overt and covert.* Severe and chronic rejection seriously distorts emotional and personality development. This distortion is easily recognized when overt, or when neglect or abuse is obvious. It is harder to detect when convert, or when masked by extreme indulgence, overprotection, or constant excuse making that help the child avoid the consequences of her behaviour. Parents often repress or try to conceal their rejection to avoid the attached stigma, or because to acknowledge it would evoke intolerable guilt or a major threat to their own already fragile self-esteem. Some recurrently battle for custody or access, even though, if they win, they remain as uninterested, neglectful, or abusive as before. The road to many a child's psychological

hell is paved by the naïve acceptance of parents' verbalizations of good intentions in court, despite repeated behavioural evidence to the contrary.

5 / *Continuity of relationship.* Children's next basic need is for continuous relationships with their primary attachment figures, their psychological parents (Goldstein, Freud, and Solnit 1973, 1979). Yet, judges all too often allow natural parents custody or access as a biological right, unaware that psychological abandonment may already have occurred. Children's Aid societies, too, sometimes violate the principle of continuity by separating children from foster parents to whom they are securely attached and with whom they are developing satisfactorily, often on the questionable grounds that they are better served by being placed on adoption probation, although this means exposing them to yet another unnecessary separation. The child's sense of permanence, rather than the legal status of the placement, is what is most closely related to the child's sense of well-being (Lahti et al 1978; Bush and Goldman 1982).

Children between six months and four years are particularly vulnerable to separation because of their time sense and their inability to tolerate an emotional vacuum (Goldstein, Freud, and Solnit 1973, 1979). At this age, dependency is maximal, while the capacity to mourn the feelings stirred up by separation is particularly limited. Toddlers have little ability to tolerate anxiety without having to repress it, and can rarely conceptualize and articulate their feelings symbolically enough to allow concerned adults to help them mourn successfully (Furman 1974). Generally speaking, the more continuity is disrupted, be it through multiple moves or through being left too long in limbo while wardship and future plans are being contested, the greater the risk of severe and lasting personality damage (Derdeyn 1977; A. Freud 1960; Goldstein, Freud, and Solnit 1973, 1979; Madison and Schapiro 1970; Pike 1976; Steinhauer 1980a; Tizard 1977; Wiltse 1979; Wilkes 1989). Many juvenile-court judges, lawyers, and even Children's Aid Society workers still do not fully appreciate how damaging it is for a child to be left in limbo while his case is adjourned again and again to suit the convenience of the parents or the legal system.

Some parents leave their children in the care of grandparents or other extended-family members, either repeatedly or for a prolonged period of months or even years. The effect on the child will depend on a number of factors, including the age of the child, the nature of the continuing relationship and contact between parent and child during the placement, the quality of the care supplied by the substitute caretaker, and how well the substitute parent was known to the child prior to the placement. The reason for the placement may also be significant: it may signify rejection and, therefore, be potentially pathogenic, or it might be temporary and occasioned by financial, health, or other short-term family stresses. In some such cases, especially when the child is an infant or toddler, the caretaking relative with whom the child spends most time will soon become the psychological parent, which may cause problems after the child returns home.

Literature Review

Simmons and colleagues (1981) developed a Parent Treatability Inventory (PTI) designed to study the effects of parental involvement on their children's improvement in a residential treatment program. The authors identified twenty-seven variables derived from a study of ninety-seven children treated over a ten-year period. A number of these variables seem related more to socio-economic status than to the therapeutic process per se, but this work did suggest that reliable ratings of parent treatability can be derived from a careful social history.

Steinhauer (1983a) approached this topic by defining children's basic developmental needs and discussing the contributions of history taking and psychological and/or psychiatric examination to assessments of parenting capacity. This led to his proposing a framework for sufficient and systematic assessments of parenting capacity. He then discussed frequent problems in the relative weighting of the history of past parenting and responses to intervention as opposed to current expert assessments in determining parenting capacity, stressing courts' prevalent bias towards overrating experts' assessments at the expense of the historical 'track record.' The paper then considered the prediction of future parenting capacity and the prognosis for change in response to intervention. By contrasting the data obtained for eight key variables, it defined three clinical profiles that could serve as guidelines for permanency planning. This paper served as the take-off point for the work of the Toronto Parenting Capacity Assessment Project, to be described later in this chapter.

Grisso (1986) has critically reviewed a series of self-report instruments relevant to parenting capacity that have been considered potentially useful in the determination of child custody. None of them involves any direct observation or rating of parent–child interaction, and most are irrelevant to assessing parenting capacity in a child welfare population. Two of them, for example, the 'Child-Rearing Style Scale' (CRS) and the 'Problem-solving Test Child-Related Stories,' of Shure and Spivack (1978), basically test the mother's ability to encourage her children to problem-solve effectively, while 'The Children's Reports of Parental Behaviour,' developed by Schaefer in 1965, attempts to define parenting style in terms of two basic dimensions (Love/Hate and Freedom/Possessiveness). The relationship of these dimensions to parenting capacity has not been established, and this test does not provide a direct and valid assessment of parenting abilities.

Most of these tests are poorly standardized and the nature of the non-clinical group from which their norms are derived is frequently not described, so that their validity – and often their reliability as well – has yet to be demonstrated.

Three of these tests, however, are relevant to assessments of parenting capacity within child welfare, as they are intended to identify parents at risk for abusing their children. The authors of the tests make it clear that the tests are not intended to replace a thorough clinical investigation, although they may serve as adjuncts that may either confirm or challenge a clinical assessment.

The 'Child Abuse Potential (CAP) Inventory' (Milner 1980) is an attempt to screen parents at high risk for abusing their children. The CAP contains 160 items, each stating a psychological condition or opinion with which the parent must agree or disagree. These items identify personality traits or background variables that the literature associates with abusive parents, such as feelings of loneliness and isolation or negative childhood experiences with or without abuse.

The test can be answered by anyone reading at a grade-three level, and contains a lie-scale. Its norms, established from 132 largely rural and lower-class white females in North Carolina, obscure the validity of predictions of its usefulness with fathers, with mothers from other ethnic groups, or with members of the middle and upper classes. Milner is reported to have tried to establish new norms on a broader population base, using parents of various ages from a variety of locations and clearly specified socio-economic levels. In spite of this limitation, reliability and, even more, construct and concurrent validity have been well established. A high score on the CAP correlates positively with expectations of lacking a feeling of personal control on Rotter's Locus of Control, and inversely with a measure of ego-strength in the MMPI. Predictive validity is encouraging; the CAP identified 125 out of 130 subjects (65 abusers; 65 non-abusers), thus achieving 96 per cent accuracy with no false positives. Haddock and McQueen (1983) achieved 93 per cent accuracy in identifying 18 of 21 abusers with only three false negatives. These results need replication by samples with different socio-demographic characteristics.

The 'Adult–Adolescent Parenting Inventory' (AAPI) of Bavolek (1984) is designed to assess teenagers' attitudes towards parenting and child-rearing practices in order to identify pregnant teenagers who need to develop more appropriate child-rearing and parenting skills since they are at risk for abusing their children.

Its thirty-two items, which state opinions or beliefs about children's abilities, behaviour, relations to parents, and parenting duties, are rated on a five-point scale (from strongly agree to strongly disagree). From these items, four parenting scales are derived: appropriate expectations, lack of empathy for children's needs, belief in the value of physical punishment, and parent–child role reversal. A grade-five or -six reading level is required. Two forms of the test exist. They differ in that those positive items correlated with good parenting potential in Test A would be negatively keyed in Test B. The AAPI is one of the better standardized and more reliable of the parenting instruments reviewed. Its construct validity is impressive, and its concurrent and predictive validity are promising. Since, however, the AAPI surveys abusive attitudes and risks of physical abuse, one cannot responsibly use it to predict whether families are likely to prove neglectful or emotionally and sexually abusive.

The third of the relevant tests reviewed by Grisso is the 'Michigan Screening Profile of Parenting' (MSPP) devised by Helfer, Hoffmeister, and Schneider in 1978. Also intended as a screening instrument for potentially abusive parents, it alone of these three tests seeks information about how the parents feel about their own childhood experiences as well as tapping their attitudes about relationships between children and parents and their current interactions.

The authors specifically discourage the use of the MSPP for clinical or forensic purposes, but although they intended to create merely a research instrument, the MSPP has been used for decision making against the authors' advice. Like the CAP, this test incorporates etiological and personality characteristics that the literature considers typical of abusing parents, but, unlike the former, it has a number of scales, which make it advantageous for research, but less so for custody determination. Since there are no published norms, the use of the MSPP in a child-custody action could not be supported. Also its failure to distinguish consistently abusive from non-abusive parents raises question as to the conceptual relationship of the MSPP to what is known about abusive parents.

Muir and colleagues (1989) made an intuitive checklist of 10 items from 173 risk factors drawn from the literature and used it to predict who would relinquish care or have major parenting difficulties (i.e., neglect or abuse) in two different samples separated by a four-year interval and a major socio-cultural change in the community being studied. By using statistical techniques rather than intuition to maximize the predictive ability of the checklist, they produced a new list of 9 items, which they then validated in a random sample of pregnant mothers. While they found this effective enough to recommend for routine use for predicting parenting difficulty in the two years after childbirth, they make the point that its usefulness in cultural settings other than New Zealand, where the study was carried out, is unknown.

All of the tests noted above may help identify caretakers at risk for physically abusing their children, but they were not designed to identify caretakers who are chronically neglectful or emotionally or sexually abusive. Also, their norms are very limited, as is their validation, and *none of them involves any direct observation of caretaker and child in interaction.*

An instrument of a very different sort is the 'Objective Parenting Profile,' developed by Oldershaw, Walters, and Hall in 1989. It provides a three-dimensional profile of one parent's interaction with a child in a thirty-minute structured observation. A child and parent are introduced to a room, at one end of which is a snack (cookies and juice). Near the other end is a set of shelves, well equipped with a variety of toys. The parent is instructed to give the child a snack and keep him away from the toys for the first ten minutes. For the next ten minutes, the child is allowed to play freely with the toys. For the final ten minutes, the parent is to have the child put the toys away and leave them alone.

This interaction is videotaped, and the tape is then rated using a sophisticated standardized technique to provide scores for three domains of parenting. *Behavioural/social interaction* consists of what parent and child actually do. How they do it is rated on a scale of *affective style/attitudes.* How child and caretaker see each other is rated in terms of *cognitive/perceptual cues.* The profile obtained by combining the three is a structured analysis of a standardized interaction. Norms have been obtained for children between age two and eight.

These scores are used in combination with a structured interview, a standardized mood-state questionnaire (POMS), the Adult–Adolescent Parenting Inventory (AAPI) described earlier, a test of the child's socio-emotional development (TOEDS), and a test obtaining the child's symbolic conceptualization of the parent to derive the Objective Parenting Profile.

Currently the author and colleagues from two Children's Aid societies and the local family court clinic are working together as the Toronto Parenting Capacity Assessment Project to develop a set of comprehensive guidelines to be used for assessing current parenting ability and predicting future (potential) parenting capacity. No matter how precisely such criteria may be defined, any assessment using them will be at best semi-objective, dependent, as it must be, on the skills, beliefs, attitudes, and biases of the assessor. Nevertheless, since many front-line workers have had little training and experience in normal child development or in recognizing and understanding distorted and pathological developmental variants, it makes sense to define the major parameters relevant to assessing parenting capacity and predicting future parenting ability. To this end, the guidelines explore, via clear, easily observable questions, many complex and abstract concepts that an inexperienced worker would have trouble understanding and assessing.

The research group has identified nine basic parameters relevant to parenting capacity, and has developed for each clinical guidelines that define its critical characteristics. These are listed in table 5.1, and then briefly described.

Guideline 1 – Current stressors. This guideline provides an environmental scan, documenting major sources of stress in the larger social environmental, such as problems of poverty, housing, unemployment, public assistance, a history of violence or criminality, substance abuse, recent immigrant status, or severe chronic illness in any family member.

Guideline 2 – Child's developmental progress. Developmental delay can be a major indicator of chronic parental neglect, especially in infants and younger children. Often such children respond dramatically to even a relatively brief period in a nurturing environment. This response may be diagnostic, but unless a baseline was achieved when the child first entered care, much of the significance of these changes may be lost for court purposes. Many child-welfare workers and other health and mental-health professionals lack a comprehensive model (and, often, the training and experience) for conducting a developmental assessment. This guideline will outline and simplify the process for doing so briefly and comprehensively for infants and children of various ages, and will help

TABLE 5.1
Guidelines for assessing parenting capacity

A. *Focus on the context*
Guideline 1. Current stressors

B. *Focus on the child*
Guideline 2. Child's developmental progress

C. *Focus on parent–child interrelationships*
Guideline 3. Attachment status
Guideline 4. Observations of current parenting ability

D. *Focus on the parent*
Guideline 5. Impulse control
Guideline 6. Parental acceptance of responsibility
Guideline 7. Behaviours affecting parenting ability and capacity
Guideline 8. Parent's manner of relating to society
Guideline 9. Parent's use of clinical interventions

---

select those cases where formal developmental testing by a multidisciplinary team is indicated.

Guideline 3 – Attachment status. This guideline is about attachment, relationship, and feelings of belonging, separation, and loss. It provides a map for the assessment of attachment status for children of various ages. It suggests what to ask and what to look for to assess attachment status, while providing a guide to explore how the caretaker's memory of his or her own early parenting may influence his or her ability to meet the child's attachment needs.

Guideline 4 – Observations of current parenting ability. This guideline shows what to look for and how to use the observations of caretaker–child interactions as a guide to the caretaker's parenting capacity. It helps assess such factors as the depth and quality of the observed relationship; the emotional availability and the appropriateness of the caretaker's expectations; the effectiveness and constructiveness of the caretaker's limit-setting; the child's response to limits; how child and caretaker influence each other's behaviour.

Guideline 5 – Capacity to contain tension. This guideline provides a framework for analysing the caretaker's ability to bind or internalize tension. This ability, if adequate, will allow for internal (symbolic) or negotiated problem solving, instead of frequent explosive and poorly controlled behavioural responses to pressure.

Guideline 6 – Ability to accept responsibility. The determination of a caretaker's acceptance of responsibility can be a subtle yet extremely important task. Often, even if the caretaker is trying to cooperate, which is not always the case, there are inconsistencies among what is said, what is meant, and what is done. This guideline presents a format for helping even relatively inexperienced professionals assess this important aspect of parenting capacity.

Guideline 7 – Behaviours affecting parenting ability and capacity. This guideline helps the non-psychiatrist identify probable signs and symptoms of psychiatric disorder in a caretaker and, even more important, assess how these behaviours are affecting that person's parenting.

Guideline 8 – Parent's manner of relating to society. This guideline determines whether there is a history of criminality or violence outside the home. It also assesses the availability of and the caretaker's ability to use social and community supports, and charts his or her history of relating to social agencies and authority figures in the community.

Guideline 9 – Parent's use of clinical interventions. This guideline documents the historical dimension, which is so often overlooked – the caregiver's track record of working with professionals and agencies, which may or may not correspond with promises for future willingness to accept treatment. If the caregiver has been involved with a professional, clinic, or agency in the past, the results of the intervention (as seen by all participants), the caregiver's attendance record, and the ability to form a therapeutic alliance are assessed. A framework is presented to simplify and help objectify the key question of whether or not the caregiver is capable of entering into a therapeutic alliance. The guideline also directs attention to the possibility that failure to benefit from past involvements has resulted from inadequate service. Even if there have been no previous agency involvements, this guideline can also be used to evaluate the cooperation obtained during the current assessment. A provisional form of this guideline is included in the appendix to this chapter.

Following field-testing of the guidelines, the research group will next attempt to develop *subscales* whose validity and reliability can then be established, leading, it is hoped, to a practical research instrument. After the subscales have been developed, their relationship to each other, to socio-economic status, to other measures of parenting ability, and to the judgments of experienced clinicians will be assessed.

This type of rigorous approach to the assessing of parenting capacity should prove extremely useful for case planning and effective case management. These guidelines should prove useful for teaching a broad range of mental-health and child welfare professionals both in universities and in community colleges. They are also intended for orientation and ongoing in-service training of workers, supervisors, consulting psychologists and psychiatrists in child welfare agencies, as well as for other professionals within the child welfare system, including lawyers and judges in the family court system. In clinical practice, such guidelines should help front-line workers and their consultants gather and organize, both for clinical purposes and for more effective presentation to court, the kinds of clinical data relevant to parenting capacity. A systematic investigation of all relevant parameters should help avoid premature closure, thus minimizing avoidable errors in decision making. Such guidelines should decrease the number of decisions distorted by the lack of sufficient necessary information or by unrecognized assessor bias (countertransference), always problems to be guarded against in such highly polarized assessments.

A manual amplifying the guidelines has been prepared. The discussion of the guidelines will include indications for when to refer the case for consultation with experts in a related area, and which experts – for example, infant or child psychiatrist, clinical psychologist, child neurologist, paediatric specialist in child development, speech therapist, general psychiatrist (for the parent) – would be most likely to supply the balance needed for a full assessment. The factors described below are simplified and organized within the guidelines.

Assessing Parents Ability to Meet Children's Developmental Needs

There are basically two components in an assessment of parenting capacity. The first is a proper history of the child's development and of the parent–child relationship. The second is an observation of the child relating to other members of the family. The latter involves at least four and possibly more components, including: a developmental assessment of the child; a psychiatric/psychological assessment of the child's current mental status; a systematic assessment of the current family situation, particularly of the parents' ability to meet the child's developmental needs; and further psychiatric and/or psychological assessment of either or both parents, if indicated.

Let us examine what each of these can contribute to assessing parenting capacity and consider its role in evaluation parenting capacity.

1 / *Contribution of the history to an assessment of parenting capacity.* To assess parenting capacity, one requires a systematic history of the child's development, focusing particularly on parent–child relationships and attitudes towards the particular child. Did the child result from a planned pregnancy? What prenatal care did the mother receive throughout the pregnancy, and did she use or abuse cigarettes, alcohol, or street drugs while pregnant? How did each parent react during pregnancy and following the birth? One would obtain an ongoing chronological record of the child's physical, cognitive, emotional, and social development, with particular reference to:

a any emotional, behavioural, language, or academic problems noted; attitudes towards the child in general, and towards any problems noted in particular; the reasons for and apparent effects of disruptions in continuity of the parent–child relationship;
b a history suggestive of avoidant, anxious, or disorganized/disoriented attachment, including: persistent detachment, distancing, and isolation; marked over- or underreactions when temporarily left by the parent during the toddler years; constant attention-seeking; multiple separations; multiple shallow relationships that fail to distinguish between casual acquaintances and long-term caregivers; parental violence or antisocial behaviour; excessive parental harshness, insensitivity, or rigidity; overindulgence and extreme permissiveness combined with a lack of appropriate expectations; excessively controlling or parentified behaviour;
c a detailed description of any psychiatric or major social problems affecting the parents or other family members, including the psychiatric diagnosis, if available; and the severity and duration of the illness; whether it consisted of a single circumscribed episode, a repetition of apparently time-limited episodes, or a pattern of chronic disturbance; whether it fluctuated in severity or continued to deteriorate; what treatments were tried, along with the reported success of each.

One should routinely attempt to verify key information obtained from the parents, of course, with their knowledge and consent. Should they refuse, their reasons for doing so should be explored and noted, as should previous attempts at intervention. For the latter, one would explore: the reasons for the intervention; the referral source; whether the involvement was voluntary or imposed; whether each referral was acted upon; the response to each referral; the number of attempts at each form of remediation; the nature, duration, and result of each.

One should routinely attempt to determine and record in concrete terms the best level of functioning achieved by child and family over the past year and over the past five years. Doing so forces one to evaluate and compare current and past functioning, and to document otherwise vague statements as to how much – or how little – improvement has occurred.

Respected colleagues approached in preparing this chapter confirmed the author's impression that courts, generally speaking, undervalue the importance of the historical record and overvalue cross-sectional assessments by psychologists or psychiatrists. Courts frequently consider historical data unreliable, especially since it is often obtained from unwilling, hostile, or manipulative clients who tolerate the agency's involvement only under duress. Workers' testimony is further undermined by the ambiguous nature of the child welfare agency's involvement with its client. The same worker assigned to 'help' can, at any point, unilaterally decide to use information volunteered or observed during the helping process as evidence against the family in court. Presumably for this reason, lawyers frequently explicitly advise clients not to cooperate with Children's Aid Society workers since, should today's worker become tomorrow's witness, anything said could be used against them.

Certainly for some clients, especially those who rely heavily on paranoid defences and on splitting – though not all who use these defences are incompetent parents – the worker's double role will complicate attempts to assess accurately or to achieve a meaningful worker/client relationship. The fact that a meaningful worker/client relationship, and therefore trust, is not always possible again underlines the importance of routinely obtaining corroborating information from secondary sources, such as day-care centres and schools, whenever possible.

In spite of the rich potential for mistrust inherent in the double role of the Children's Aid Society worker, many parents form alliances and work effectively with their worker. One should not routinely dismiss a family's inability to do so as a normal or inevitable response to the agency's ambiguous role or its potential use of authority. The inability to trust or to form a therapeutic alliance often stems from the character structure and defensive style of the parents. Despite their initial and understandable suspicion, many families learn, in time, that the agency may be just as eager as they are to avoid taking a child into care. It is not just welfare agencies whom difficult families cannot trust; many have a long history of mistrust or conflict with school principals, psychiatrists, family doctors, other social agencies, neighbours, extended family, police, and so on. Despite the strain placed on both client and worker by the worker's double role, the more evidence there is of an inability to form a working alliance in a variety of situations, the more likely that family pathology and not just agency involvement is a major contributor to the mistrust and inability to work together.

All too often, court-room promises by distraught parents to seek professional help are unrealistically seized upon by judges looking for a way to avoid taking children into care, in spite of a long and well-documented history of that same family's repeated failure to attend, complete, or benefit from similar services in the past. Many parents repeatedly consult clinics of professionals for assessment but avoid treatment. Some who do temporarily enter treatment defensively ignore any attempt to explore their own attitudes or behaviours, in order to protect their precarious psychological equilibrium. A preliminary version of the guidelines, which has since been improved upon, has already proved helpful for workers organizing their data for presentation in court. Both the agency and its legal representatives have found that it helps workers organize and emphasize the importance of parents' track record in a way that helps judges remain realistic in determining how much credence to give to court promises to seek professional help (see appendix).

When a family's defensive style has repeatedly constituted an impenetrable barrier against the formation of a working alliance in the past, the chance of future intervention effecting substantial change is slight.

2 / *Contribution of the psychological or psychiatric assessment of child and family to determining parenting capacity.* An adequate assessment consists partly of a relatively passive observation but also of a more active, directed seeking-out of information not spontaneously revealed, such as fantasy material and how a child responds when the parents set limits. Active intervention allows the examiner to test the truth of hypotheses derived from earlier observations. In general, it is risky to rely too much on the validity of impressions derived from a single assessment session. A second observation may support or, even more important, may contradict, conclusions derived from the first. It is dangerous to make authoritative statements based on only a few minutes' observation, but, unfortunately, this practice is adopted far too often by less cautious or less conscientious colleagues. Highly anxious

or resistant children may appear quite different on a second visit, when the examiner is no longer a stranger and the child trusts that he will return home after the interview is over.

Jimmy, age nine, was very inhibited and constricted during his first interview with the author. He had been brought for assessment by the same social worker who had placed him in his present foster home after his previous one had broken down. During the first meeting, he sat with his hands folded in his lap, looking down and avoiding eye contact. An attempt to determine what he saw as the reason for the assessment and how he felt about taking part in it got nowhere; Jimmy either refused to answer, said, 'I dunno,' or replied in noncommittal monosyllables. Any attempt to reassure him or put him at ease was unsuccessful. Invited to play freely with a broad selection of toys, he declined. He just sat there, looking miserable. On the basis of that interview, the author was unable to determine whether he was retarded, depressed, angry and passive-aggressive, anxious, electively mute, or any combination of the above.

On a second interview a week later, however, Jimmy was transformed. In marked contrast to the first session, he was spontaneous and involved, relating well and making good eye contact. After several minutes of initial shyness, he asked if he could play with the toys. He then got quite involved, making several puppet plays and playing with soldiers, barn animals, Play-Doh, and Lego pieces. His play suggested intelligence and creativity, a preoccupation with themes of violence in the environment, and feelings of deprivation. He responded readily to factual questions or to ones designed to tap his fantasy. Near the end of the interview, I asked what had been bothering him during the first interview. He replied that he had been afraid that I was planning to remove him from his new foster home, which he enjoyed and did not want to leave. Since he had considered the interview a threat to his placement, he had been angry and afraid, hence his non-cooperation. When he had confided his fears to the foster mother after that meeting, she had reassured him that he would stay with them. (This had been told him by the social worker, but he had not believed her.) Since he trusted the foster mother, his attitude and involvement the second time were entirely different.

During an assessment, it is important to compare the child's physical, intellectual, cognitive, emotional, and social development to the norms for the age. While a developmental delay is not in itself proof of inadequate parenting, significant developmental delays, particularly if associated with a history or evidence of inadequate parenting and other signs of a disturbed parent–child relationship, are at least suggestive. Such is especially the case in infants and toddlers in whom developmental delay coexists with signs of obvious normal intelligence. Marked change in developmental level in response to an improved environment strongly suggests that the environment of the natural family was not meeting a child's developmental needs.

One will observe how child and parent(s) relate to each other during the assessment. Here, again, the interpretation of observed behaviour depends on a knowledge of age-appropriate norms. For example, for a toddler, separation anxiety is normal, while a total absence of stranger anxiety and a pattern of going to strangers as if they were old friends strongly suggests a failure to bond selectively, implying severe personality damage. For the older child, however, the situation is reversed; marked stranger anxiety suggests maladjustment, while its absence is more age-appropriate.

In observing parents with children, one notes the nature and extent of their relatedness. Do they ignore each other? Does either constantly and obtrusively demand the other's attention? To what extent do they talk, listen, and make eye contact? Are the parents intuitively empathic; do they tune in and respond appropriately to the child's verbal or behavioural demands for attention, or do they appear distracted, uninterested, or annoyed when the child tries to engage them? Is their need for control or to express affection so intrusive that they cannot allow the child to explore freely or to play independently? Are the parents' expectations reasonable, clearly inappropriate to the child's needs, or excessive? Can they let the child speak for herself, or must they always answer for her, expressing what she is feeling, directing and intruding into her play, and so on? Do they limit inappropriate behaviour, or pretend to ignore it? If asked to set appropriate limits, can they do so effectively, avoiding confrontation where possible and without excessive harshness? If one comments on clearly observable behaviour, can the parents acknowledge it and modify it if indicated? Can they discuss how they feel about the assessment, reflect on their interaction with the child and on the observations of the examiner? Can the parents relate to the examiner in a way that suggests a base on which to build a potential therapeutic alliance?

> Robert, age ten, was suspected by his teacher and principal of having been physically abused. The parents denied any evidence of either abuse or excessive discipline. They also denied that Robert had any problems, although he was already two years behind academically, and frequently in trouble for fighting in the school yard. Several mothers in the neighbourhood had refused to let their children play with him. Whatever question the examiner asked, the father would deny as a problem, or would claim that the teacher or neighbour had it in for his son. When asked about the principal's report, the father dismissed him as a 'damn liar.' On several occasions during the interview, husband and wife argued with considerable heat about their different approaches to raising Robert. After the third such clash, the examiner commented that they seemed to have trouble agreeing on how to deal with their son. They both hotly denied this, insisting that they had no trouble reaching agreement with each other, even though a few minutes later they were clashing and belittling each other again. This interview, for obvious reasons, did not bode well for the formation of a therapeutic alliance.

Many children cannot directly express much of what they feel, especially if they have been told not to or threatened for having done so. Others feel guilty for making a parent look bad, or are afraid to say anything that could lead to their removal from even a highly destructive family. The ability to trust, relate, and communicate, especially around highly conflicted and emotionally charged areas, is decreased in deprived or abused children. Such children may suggest through their play and fantasy much that they could never verbalize in response to direct questions, and their play often stands in striking contrast to their verbal content. Drawings and doll or puppet plays and dreams may tell more about how a child feels about biological and foster families or about who are seen as the psychological parents than the guarded and conventional responses obtained by direct questioning. For this reason, an adequate assessment should always move beyond direct questioning to explore, via several different parameters, the child's fantasy life. One cannot conclude from a single episode of puppet play that parents were abusive or unresponsive. However, the more the same theme is spontaneously repeated using a variety of media, the more one would suspect that a true picture of the child's perception of the family is emerging.

Carol, age five, came to her foster home when she was two, far behind in all areas of development and extremely withdrawn and mistrustful of adults, especially men. For three years she had been living in her foster home but visiting her biological parents every other week. Just recently, in view of the dramatic social and psychological gains she had made, the Children's Aid Society sought psychiatric consultation about whether to remove her from her foster home to place her on adoption, a plan with which Carol was reported to have agreed.

In a psychiatric assessment, Carol's fantasy and play suggested, that, beneath the surface, in spite of her improved functioning, memories of past distress and continuing confusion persisted. These she handled without allowing serious disruption of her current functioning and behaviour. In her puppet play, a little girl was left crying while one set of parents violently fought, only to be rescued and comforted by a second set, presumably the foster parents. She described herself as having two mothers and two fathers, and stated that soon she would be adopted and would then have three mothers and three fathers. Thus, adoption to Carol meant adding yet another set of parents, not separating from either of those she already had. This preoccupation with family relationships spilled over into her 'three wishes', in which she wondered what had happened to a cat's kittens, and speculated on the relationship between a puppy and its mother. Finally, when asked to draw a picture of her family, she very carefully drew just one little girl. The examiner interpreted this as reflecting some confusion as to just who did constitute her family.

A psychological examination, especially one administered by a psychologist skilled in interpreting projective tests, can provide another independent assessment and may either support or contradict clinical hypotheses about the child's true thoughts, feelings, fantasies, or needs.

Although hypotheses drawn from puppet play and drawings alone would be inconclusive, such data can contribute much to the total picture. It would be equally misguided to rely exclusively on a young child's responses to direct questions about her relationship with her parents or her preferences for placement, whether these are obtained in a clinic, in open court, or in chambers. What a child wants and what a child needs may be very different. Failure of mental health professionals or judges to recognize the limited utility of responses to direct questioning, or their confusion of a child's wants with needs, frequently contributes to well-meaning but destructive planning.

Carol [see above] had said that she wanted to be adopted. She said so because her worker and her foster mother, believing adoption to be in her best interests, had both painted a rosy picture of what life after adoption would be like. Had a judge responded only to what Carol said she wanted, he would never have realized that Carol had no idea of what adoption really meant for her, or the losses it would entail. Carol said she wanted to be adopted, but adoption – at least if it involved separating and placing her with strangers while she expected that adoption just meant adding a third set of parents to the two she already had – was not what she was requesting.

In assessing for parenting capacity, one learns more from combining an assessment of the child with an observation and assessment of the family than from either component alone. A well-documented history is often more helpful and reliable in assessing parenting capacity than even the most meticulous psychiatric or psychological assessment. One-shot (cross-sectional) psychiatric or psychological assessments exploring complex family relationships, often over the resistance of a highly defensive family, are frequently less reliable than a well-documented pattern of chronic parental inadequacy that emerges from a carefully taken and well-organized historical record. Such is particularly the case since many of the parents in a child welfare population suffer from personality disorders, and people with this diagnosis can appear quite normal at any single occasion. It is only by following them over time and noting the contrast between what they say when assessed and how they actually function over a longer period that the chaotic relationships and erratic coping style so characteristic of their long-term functioning become apparent.

3 / *In-patient assessments of parenting capacity.* How effective are in-patient assessments in determining parenting capacity? They allow trained staff more chances to observe the child over an extended period, in interaction with a variety of other children and staff as well as with his own family during visits. The picture of child and family obtained

is more extensive and, therefore, potentially more reliable than that obtained in a cross-sectional assessment. Differences in behaviour in the absence of the parents may clarify how much the child's symptoms are reactive to family rather than the result of an internalized disorder. Prolonged observation may suggest whether all siblings are equally at risk, or why a particular child has developed symptoms, by revealing soft neurological signs, hyperactivity and poorly controlled impulsivity, evidence of sado-masochistic tendencies, and so on. Through an extended assessment of the family's defensiveness and accessibility to involvement, to confrontation, to direct suggestions, and to other forms of input, one can assess the family's likely response to ongoing intervention. At times, short-term admissions can offer a badly needed cooling-off period, a chance to help child and parents learn and practise new ways of binding tension and of understanding and relating to each other. Although such admissions are often accepted only under external pressure, some initially highly resistant families can cooperate with and learn from them, while others, especially those relying heavily on denial and paranoid and splitting defences, never overcome their distrust sufficiently to form a working alliance with milieu staff. In summary, while in-patient assessments of parenting capacity often fail to live up to excessive expectations, they do permit extended observation of the child interacting with the family and others, and can offer a preview of both child's and parents' ability to enter into working alliances and to change in response to initial interventions (Carr 1982).

Many Children's Aid Society workers believe that courts generally undervalue social workers' evidence and overrate cross-sectional assessments by psychiatrists and psychologists. Frequently, a society, having worked with a family for many years, has amassed a wealth of historical data, often supported by independent secondary assessments, which consistently suggest an established pattern of inadequate parenting highly resistant to change, despite numerous attempts at intervention. Yet judges will often give less credence to social workers' historical evidence than to embarrassingly speculative one-shot psychological or psychiatric opinions.

The author suggests that courts have a bias, largely unrecognized, against caseworkers' longitudinal (historical) data as opposed to cross-sectional (current assessment) data of a psychologist or psychiatrist (Steinhauer 1984). This bias is partly traceable to the tendency of the courts to respect the social workers' degree and expertise less than those of psychologists and psychiatrists. If mental health professionals, recognizing this tendency, merely play the game – that is, if psychologists and psychiatrists continue to provide unnecessary assessments merely to satisfy the courts' bias when, in reality, the agency has more convincing historical data to establish its case – are we merely colluding with the system and reinforcing courts' overvaluation of clinicians' evidence? But, if we refuse to collude, are we placing the welfare of innocent children in jeopardy (Steinhauer 1978a)?

But if a bias against workers' evidence exists, where did it originate? Children's Aid Society workers vary enormously in both training and experience. Workers often approach courts not expecting to be heard, so that, when they testify, instead of effectively selecting, focusing, and organizing their evidence so that it stands on its own merits, they err either by being rambling, overinclusive, poorly focused, vague, and tentative, or by going to the other extreme and appearing arrogant or dogmatic, as if to say, 'How dare you demand supporting facts? It's enough that I've given you my professional opinion.' Courts have every right to demand that *all* professionals lay out the evidence on which their conclusions and recommendations are based. Not all the information important for casework purposes is relevant to the issues considered by the court. Workers need to learn how to select and organize only those data relevant to the purposes of the court. Both facts and opinion should be included but carefully distinguished, and, wherever possible, the facts, and how they were used to lead to conclusions on which opinions are based, should be provided.

Biological parents, however neglectful, rejecting, or abusive, are usually hit hard by any decision to terminate their parental rights by taking their child into care. Wherever possible, they should be allowed some part in the decision (Cooper 1978). Biological parents not infrequently withdraw their opposition to permanent wardship if assured that the agency recognizes that they care about their children even though they are unable to care adequately for them, and that by supporting the child's admission to care they are helping provide developmental assistance that they, themselves, could not deliver. They are more likely to cooperate if they sense that the agency is non-judgmental, and that it will protect their importance to the child via continued access, which, especially for many older children, is frequently reasonable. Whether or not planned permanent foster care with access is indicated for a particular child, the agency has a responsibility to attempt to deal with the depression and anger generated in biological parents by termination of their parental rights. This can best be done by avoiding unnecessary criticism or condemnation, by acknowledging that neglectful or abusive behaviour may not have been intended, by responding empathically and providing help in working through the distress precipitated by the loss of parental rights, rather than by abandoning the parents when they feel most impotent and depleted.

Predicting Parenting Capacity

Except when evidence of severe and repeated physical abuse is obvious, one relies in child welfare less on such hard evidence as broken bones and bruises etc. than on the carefully developed picture obtained with painstaking regard for supportive detail of a pattern of ongoing inter-action between parents and children considered at risk. This pattern will emerge mainly from the history, but will be supported – or at times contradicted – by the results of direct observations and of psychiatric and psychological assessments performed at key points along the way. Whoever gathers and integrates the data should, in addition to giving an opinion on the parents' adequacy, provide the evidence on which that opinion is based, as well as indicating other possible conclusions that have been considered and why these have been rejected. In this way, one can ensure that the judge, with whom the final decision rests, is aware that alternative dispositions have not been left unexplored because of clinician bias, unrecognized overidentification, or superfi-ciality or premature closure. After drawing together the data obtained, one can usually fit cases into one of three categories:

Group A. The child's development is not, and never has been, seriously at risk. The parents are adequately meeting the child's developmental needs. Either no further intervention is needed or the decision of whether to seek further intervention should be left to the family.

Group B. The child's current adjustment shows serious problems, al-though, until recently, the parenting and development seemed adequate. With prompt and adequate intervention, the prognosis for these parents once again meeting their child's needs so that development can again proceed is reasonable. Cases in this group would generally approximate the following profile:
– evidence of basically good developmental progress with minimal or no developmental interference;

- recent onset of problem, leading to decompensation in family functioning and in the parents' meeting the child's developmental needs, as opposed to a chronic inability to parent;
- the presence of at least one parent who does not show signs of a major psychiatric illness;
- evidence of cooperation, openness (as shown by their willingness to discuss even events, thoughts, and feelings that might prove incriminating; openness to the examiner's observations, impressions, and suggestions); a history of being able to accept and benefit from help for psychological or family problems;
- ability of parents to accept responsibility for their role in the problem and/or the failure of past attempts to overcome it. It is not required that they assume total responsibility, but that they be open to exploring how they may have contributed to the problem's development or perpetuation, and that they have some capacity to internalize conflict, of which reasonable guilt is one indicator;
- the family members have maintained adequate relationships with extended family, friends, neighbours, and/or community agencies, from whom they can accept and utilize advice and support.

The closer the family's profile resembles that of Group B parents, the better the prognosis that adequate and timely therapeutic intervention can significantly improve parenting capacity.

Group C. The child's development and adjustment have chronically been significantly impaired. The parents have long been unable to meet their children's developmental needs, and there is little to suggest this will change significantly, even given realistically available intervention. Cases in this group would generally approximate the following profile:

- evidence of chronic and widespread impairment in physical, cognitive, language, academic, emotional, and/or social development and adjustment;
- the single parent or both parents have a psychiatric illness that significantly impairs parenting capacity and has a poor prognosis;
- repeated referrals for help or attempts to provide help in the past have proved unsuccessful. A lack of parental cooperation and openness, irregular attendance, strong resistance to involvement in the therapeutic process, unilateral and poorly (if at all) discussed decisions to terminate treatment in the past are characteristic;
- parents in this group cannot accept any responsibility for their role

TABLE 5.2
Use of profiles to predict potential for change in parenting capacity

	GROUP B Significant improvement in parenting capacity possible with successful intervention	GROUP C Significant change in parenting capacity extremely unlikely in spite of attempted intervention
1. Developmental progress	Not impaired	Severely impaired
2. Onset of problems	Recent	Chronic
3. Parental psychiatric disorder decreasing parenting capacity	Absent, or good prognosis	Present, and poor prognosis
4. Past history of using help successfully	– sought it – formed alliance – significant benefit	– refused it, or multiple unsuccessful involvements – no alliance formed – no real benefit
5. Assessment of present parenting capacity	Impaired	Impaired
6. Openness, willingness to seek/utilize help at present	Present	Absent
7. Parents accept some responsibility	Present	Absent
8. Capacity to internalize tension	Present	Absent
9. External supports and ability to use them	Present	Absent

SOURCE: 'The preventive utilization of foster care,' *Can. J. Psychiat.* 33 (August 1988): 463

either in the genesis or in the perpetuation of the problem, or for their failure to benefit from past treatment;

– the family is isolated from and unable to accept help or emotional support from friends, neighbours, extended family, or appropriate mental health professionals.

The closer the family's profile approximates to that of Group C, the poorer the prognosis that therapeutic intervention can significantly improve that family's parenting capacity.

These issues are summarized in table 5.2.

This chapter began by summarizing children's emotional needs. The subsequent discussion of the relative roles of history and psychiatric or psychological examination in assessing parenting capacity is based on the literature, as interpreted through more than twenty-five years of uninterrupted experience within the child-welfare field. Apart from certain circumscribed areas (e.g., child abuse; autism; children of retarded, psychotic, or homosexual partners), there is little in the literature that draws together and integrates what is known to provide general guidelines for assessing parenting capacity, hence the final section containing the 'prognostic profiles.' The profiles, at this stage, are clinically derived, but not yet proved, although the author and colleagues are currently working in the Toronto Parenting Capacity Assessment Project to prepare scales derived from these guidelines for experimental validation. When carefully applied, even in their present form, however, the guidelines offer a useful framework for gathering and organizing the information needed for systematic assessments of parenting capacity. This process one hopes, will lead to fewer children unnecessarily being left in limbo, drifting in and out of care, being inappropriately placed, or exposed to unnecessary damage by malfunctioning of the foster care service system. Pending the completion of further studies, one will have to select on an individual basis which placement is least detrimental for each individual child, either delaying decisions until evidence for removal is overwhelming (despite the risk of leaving children in limbo) or deciding to act promptly on the basis of a continuing pattern even in the absence of hard evidence of extreme neglect or abuse. Because no guidelines can predict the risk to an individual child with 100 per cent accuracy, one will always be dealing with calculated risks. The guidelines are suggested as one way of focusing the data gathering and minimizing the truly horrendous risks involved in deciding whether or not to terminate parental rights.

APPENDIX
**Assessment of Parents' Past Utilization of
Health/Mental-Health Services**

SECTION A
Evidence That Parents Utilized Mental Health Services Successfully in the Past. (Please circle answer.)

I. Sought help in past   Yes   No
    (If YES, proceed to II. If NO, proceed to Section B)

II. Evidence that alliance with professional/agency was achieved.

1. Regular, reasonably punctual attendance	Yes	No
2. Openness within helping relationship	Yes	No
3. Ability to consider/utilize therapist's/worker's input	Yes	No
4. Motivation & cooperation	Yes	No
5. Evidence of follow-through on tasks, suggestions, etc.	Yes	No
6. Accepted responsibility for providing material	Yes	No
7. Some insight or, at least, some ability to accept responsibility for situation	Yes	No

CUMULATIVE: WAS ALLIANCE ACHIEVED?   Yes   No

III. Evidence that the previous contact actually helped.

1. Opinion of parents	Yes	No
2. Opinion of professional/agency	Yes	No
3. Confirmed (by at least 2 sources) evidence of substantive behavioural change	Yes	No

    e.g., stealing stopped;
    e.g., child stopped vomiting, began to gain weight
    (confirmed by family doctor)
    e.g., truancy stopped, child started doing
    assignments on regular basis (confirmed)
    e.g., other (specify)

CUMULATIVE: DID PREVIOUS CONTACT HELP?   Yes   No

SECTION B

Evidence That Help Was Unable to Be Used in the Past

I. Refusal to accept an appropriate referral from an   Yes   No
involved professional/close friend or relative
    e.g., grandparent
    e.g., school principal
    e.g., public-health nurse
    e.g., family doctor

CUMULATIVE: Yes   No

II. Referral accepted, but alliance never achieved shown by:

Critical variable	Evidence for/against		
a. Poor attendance	multiple 'fail to show'/	Yes	No
	multiple late cancellations (esp. without a request for alternative time)	Yes	No
	male partner regularly present and participating	Yes	No
	spotty pattern of attendance	Yes	No
	CUMULATIVE:	Yes	No
b. Extreme defensiveness	withholding of known information	Yes	No
	refusal to let professional/ agency contact colleagues/agencies involved in past	Yes	No
	denial of information known from other sources; lying	Yes	No
	CUMULATIVE:	Yes	No
c. failure to accept responsibilities that are prerequisites for successful involvement in treatment	unwillingness/inability to bring in material for sessions	Yes	No
	unwillingness/inability to follow through on recommendations/ therapeutic tasks/on continuing to work on specific assignments between sessions	Yes	No
	CUMULATIVE:	Yes	No

d. hostility and mistrust	repeated evidences of hostility, unwarranted suspicion, attacks upon, threats towards, or accusations against therapist or worker	Yes	No
	multiple changes of therapist/worker/agency e.g., the honey-bee syndrome, with subsequent degradation of the previous therapist worker/agency and/or the service offered	Yes	No
	number of professionals or agencies with whom there has been an unsuccessful involvement in the past	☐	
	CUMULATIVE:	Yes	No
e. manipulative behaviour	multiple simultaneous involvements of professionals or agencies in a manipulative and/or self-defeating manner	Yes	No
	extreme and/or repeated manipulation of one or more therapists or agencies	Yes	No
	pattern of avoiding any direct expression of satisfaction or anger with a professional/agency, even if such expression is directly encouraged, combined with pattern of repeatedly complaining to agency 'Y' about professional 'X' and 'W' and v.v.	Yes	No
	CUMULATIVE:	Yes	No

f. premature/unilateral termination	unilateral termination by the parent(s) of their involvement against professional advice and especially, without prior discussion	Yes	No
	CUMULATIVE:	Yes	No
g. lack of tangible results	– as seen by parent(s)	Yes	No
	– as seen by professionals	Yes	No
	– as demonstrated by lack of demonstrable behavioural change		
	CUMULATIVE:	Yes	No

SECTION C

Evidence That Inadequate Service Was Provided (see Note, below): Should be considered as a potentially mitigating factor before concluding that inability to use help is, primarily, related to patient rather than to helper variables.

I. Scheduling of sessions	Irregular and inappropriately infrequent in view of conditions prevalent at the time	Yes	No
	CUMULATIVE:	Yes	No
II. Therapist/worker cancellations	Frequent cancellations by therapist/worker, esp. at last moment; esp. without an alternative time being given; esp. with failure of advance notification for non-emergency cancellations	Yes	No
	CUMULATIVE:	Yes	No

III. Failure to face key issues	Obvious failure during past contacts to tackle obvious but contentious major issues	Yes	No
	CUMULATIVE:	Yes	No

Notes

1 The more professionals/agencies with whom a given client was involved unsatisfactorily, the less likely it would be that the agency/professional involved was primarily responsible for the failure of any given involvement.

2 The more professionals/agencies with whom a given client had worked successfully, the more likely it would be that failure to work successfully with a given agency/professional would not be primarily the responsibility of the client.

PART THREE

Client-Related Issues

Chapter Six

Guidelines for Removal
and Placement of Children

This chapter, first, discusses factors that should be considered in deciding the key question of where to set the threshold between the level of parenting that, while far from ideal, is at least tolerable and that which is sufficiently inadequate to demand removal and placement despite the risks involved. It then reviews a number of ways of avoiding placement, even in some situations where parenting is inadequate, including mediation and preventive interventions. The chapter concludes by presenting a number of ways to protect children from some of the more harmful effects of removal and placement through active and informed planning assisted by systemic case work.

Setting a Threshold Beyond Which the
Level of Parenting Is Unacceptable

Let us consider first how high a threshold to set and what guidelines to use in deciding whether to remove a child from an adverse family situation.

The question of whether to remove a child is one of determining the lesser of two risks. Except for children in immediate danger of abuse, one must weigh the relative hazards of leaving the child in an often far from satisfactory family against those of a separation from major attachment figures, when there are no guarantees that such a separation will provide the desired quality and permanence within the new placement so necessary for normal development. In view of the risks involved, removal should be utilized only when all alternatives short of separation have been adequately tried and found wanting (Bush 1980; Bush and Goldman 1982).

While the decision to apprehend a child can be made only by those actually involved in that particular case, the following guidelines can inform such a decision:

a / *Is there imminent danger of repeated or severe abuse?* If so, there may be no choice but to remove either the child or the abuser. But, remember, removing the abuser may not resolve the threat to the child. Many chronically abusive families continue to scapegoat and reject the abused child, blaming her for breaking up the family by revealing the abuse.

b / *How inadequate* (in its inability to meet minimal developmental needs) *or damaging* (as a result of recurrent discord, conflict, or violence) *is the family?* To evaluate this, one must estimate which is likely to be least detrimental: maintaining the status quo or removing and placing the child, often under far from optimal conditions.

c / *How likely is supportive intervention to change the currently inadequate family?* Ways of estimating the prognosis for change are discussed in chapter 5. A more detailed discussion of preventive interventions occurs later in this chapter.

d / *What factors will affect a child's response to removal from the family?* Except for children in limbo so long that they are incapable of forming meaningful relationships with any parental figure, the more separations a child has already experienced, the more she is likely to be upset by a subsequent one. The patter of multiple acute stresses occurring in the context of chronic disadvantage and, often, insecure attachment constitutes the sequence most likely to produce a long-term disorder (Rutter et al 1975; Rutter 1979b). A given child's reaction to previous placements – for example, whether by withdrawing and internalization or by becoming aggressive and acting out – can help predict the likely reaction to a subsequent one. The longer the child has been trapped in a deteriorating family situation, the more intensely she is likely to react to its loss. Children from chronically deprived homes are more prone to adverse reactions to hospital admission (Quinton and Rutter 1976). Admission to care from a similar family seems analogous, so that one would expect such children to react more intensely to separation from their families than do those from less depriving and discordant homes.

e / *What concrete evidence is there that a particular child is vulnerable to an adverse family environment?* Some children may show remarkable resilience to even a highly conflicted and rejecting family. Before deciding that a child requires removal, her particular personality and adjustment should be assessed. What are that child's temperament and status within the family system? It is known that genetic factors generally increase vulnerability to environmental adversities (Block and Block 1980; Crockenberg 1981; Garmezy 1981; Rutter 1979), and that in discordant homes, the child's temperament can either diminish or increase the risk of parental criticism, rejection, or verbal and physical abuse (Rutter 1978a). Also, what mitigating factors, such as a good relationship with one parent in the home, a highly resilient temperament, or evidence of protective relationships within the extended family or the school, may serve to protect the child in question, even within a highly pathological family situation (Rutter 1978)?

f / *What, and how adequate, are the alternatives available to meet the child's needs if the child is removed?* The more extreme, long-standing, and pervasive a child's disturbed behaviour and the less adequate the choice of available alternatives, the more one would try to avoid removal and placement (Berridge and Cleaver 1987, p. 198). When a foster-care system is in crisis – underfunded, overextended, undersupervised, and overstressed, as many are currently across much of North America – one must be less inclined to remove a child than if a ready supply of adequate and well-supervised foster homes from which to choose and match exists.

A first placement with a competent and caring relative whom the child already knows may present distinct advantages, since children who have been in temporary care with relatives have been noted to do better in subsequent placements (Grinnell and Jung 1981; Fein et al 1983; Rowe et al 1984).

g / *How does age relate to the decision for or against removal and placement?* This factor is extremely complex. A number of age-related considerations exist.

– The younger an infant or child, the greater the risk of serious physical abuse, and the less that child can avoid or protect himself from that abuse.

- Environmental improvements, even as late as early adolescence, can still assist a lagging child's intellectual development. However, such changes in the early years are probably more effective than those occurring in later childhood (see Rutter's review 1979c).
- Studies of late-adopted and foster children demonstrate that, while environmental changes as late as middle childhood can produce marked social and behavioural improvements, these are greater if instituted earlier. This finding is consistent with a sensitive period for early socialization, since normal social development seems dependent on early selective bonding (see Tizard and Hodges 1978; Rutter's review 1979c).
- Since younger children are more likely to respond adversely to hospital admission (Rutter 1972), one would expect younger children to find it more difficult to come into care. This finding has been confirmed by Rowe and colleagues (1984). (Chapter 2 defined the period between ages six months and four years as a stage of maximum vulnerability to separation and placement [Quinton and Rutter 1976].) Difficulty on the part of children who are highly dependent on their major attachment figures in understanding why they are in care has been associated with an increased incidence of placement breakdown (Berridge and Cleaver 1987; see also Thorpe 1980).
- Younger children admitted to care are more likely to be permanently separated from their natural families than are older children (Fanshel 1976).
- Attempts to correlate frequency of breakdown with the age of entering care have been contradictory, both in North America and in Great Britain. For example, R. Parker (1966) and George (1970) found that the older the child, the higher the breakdown rate. Rowe and colleagues (1984) not only agreed but found that most children placed after the age of five have already fallen by the wayside. However, Berridge and Cleaver (1987) Meier (1966), Murphy (1964), and S.E. Palmer (1979) did not find the expected association between age of entry and breakdown. Since factors listed thus far act simultaneously, it is not surprising that the effect of any one will at times be obscured by the combined influence of others.

In summary, then, age alone can have differing and, at times, ambiguous effects on the indications for placement of a given child. One should note which of these factors seem most applicable to that specific child's situation before deciding whether that child's age favours or contradicts placement.

h / *Is a placement intended to be of short or intermediate duration* – with the expectation that the child will soon return to an improved family situation – *or is it planned to sever the child's ties to the natural family?* The more permanent the removal is intended to be – especially for older children strongly identified with the natural family and already disturbed – the stronger the need to justify apprehending a child. In determining 'how bad is bad enough,' one must always consider that even a separation intended to be temporary may, in spite of everyone's best intentions, drift into a permanent rupture of that child's relationship with the natural family.

From the preceding chapters, it should be clear that taking children into care always involves a considerable risk that should only be considered when: the family environment is so inadequate and/or damaging that the child is in immediate physical danger, or ongoing development and future adjustment are seriously and chronically at risk; or all possibility of improving the family situation, either through direct work with child and family without removal, or through the provision of appropriate support services such as homemakers, enrolment in a therapeutic nursery school, attempting to empower the parents by involving them in appropriate and (to them) acceptable mutual support or self-help group, and so on, have been adequately tried without success.

Ways of Avoiding Unnecessary Placements

1 / HAVE ALL OTHER POSSIBLE ALTERNATIVES BEEN CONSIDERED?

A demand to take a child into care indicates a family crisis, a declaration of psychosocial bankruptcy. The family or community – or, at times, the child – may insist that the only possible solution is removal and placement. Other quite workable alternatives may exist, although the family, in its distress, cannot imagine them. If less extreme but workable and concrete alternatives – such as immediate involvement in a crisis-intervention program, a therapeutic day nursery, or immediate provision of an appropriate family-support service – are made available, some families are willing and able to use them. The worker who overreacts to a crisis by prematurely removing a child may have lost the opportunity to explore whether less drastic but equally or more effective alternatives exist (Burt and Balyeat 1977).

Mrs James, an excellent and experienced foster mother, had, temporarily, had it with Donny, a stubbornly oppositional ten-year-old who had been her foster child for almost three years. On a day that she had undergone painful gum surgery, he so frustrated her that she called the agency and demanded to speak to her worker, adding that it was urgent because she'd had all she could take. She was told that her regular worker was on holidays but that Mr Blake, a new staff member, would return her call. Mrs James asked that he be told that Donny was driving her crazy, and requested a call as soon as possible. Several hours later, when she had not heard from him, she called again, repeating the message. An hour later, without having called, Mr Blake arrived at the house. Briefly introducing himself and without explanation, he told Donny to get in the car and come with him. When Mrs James asked where he was taking Donny, he replied that, since Donny's behaviour had upset her so, he had arranged another placement for him on an emergency basis; he would take Donny now and be back for his things in the morning. Mrs James was dumbfounded. She had had no intention of asking that Donny be moved, as she was solidly committed to working things through with him. She had called the agency not to eject him, but for some help in venting her frustration and anger in order to help her again begin to deal with Donny rationally. By the time she could think and speak clearly, Mr Blake's care was half-way down the block.

2 / CAN PRESSURE ON THE WORKER BE REDUCED?

Workers are, at times, exposed to great pressure – from parents, children, police, or the community – to take a child immediately into care. The worker's initial anxiety level, attitude, conviction, negotiating skills, and response style may either escalate the crisis or gradually and safely focus and relieve tensions, allowing more orderly and less damaging solutions to be explored. When workers are stampeded by family or community pressures into taking immediate action instead of proceeding according to an appropriate plan, children are liable to end up out of the frying pan but deep in the fire. Such pressures can often be withstood by workers convinced of the value of determining a course before rushing into action (S. Palmer 1974; Littner 1970), especially if adequate back-up from flexible and responsive mental health professionals is available to them (Bush and Goldman 1982).

3 / CAN MEDIATION IN CHILD WELFARE AVOID PLACEMENT?

Mediation, if appropriately utilized, may significantly decrease the damaging effects on foster children of continued conflict and non-cooperation among the key adults on whom their security depends (Gardner 1989; Palmer 1989).

The Child Protection Mediation Project utilized mediation by a trained neutral third party to help caseworkers, parents, lawyers, and others reach a mutually agreeable solution in more than 187 child-protection cases. The intention was to remove the necessity for the child-protection worker to act simultaneously in two conflicting roles. On the one hand, protection workers are expected to be supportive counsellors and advocates for natural parents. On the other, they must simultaneously function as limit setters, enforcers, and, if the case comes to court, witnesses 'for the prosecution,' since what parents tell them in confidence can be used by the worker as evidence against them. The net result of these contradictory roles can be the undermining of workers' effectiveness and also of their credibility and trustworthiness in the eyes of their clients. Frequently the result is a polarization between protection workers and natural parents who, upset, defensive, and antagonistic in response to allegations of neglect, abuse, or having had a child taken into care, are unable to cooperate with their worker.

Though it is often first suggested by the court, mediation is a voluntary attempt to defuse and depolarize such a situation. It is one way to encourage constructive problem solving focused on the best interests of the child, in spite of the necessary and appropriate use of authority by the responsible agency. While long used in the field of marital breakdown, mediation has only recently – and in the face of considerable initial resistance – been used broadly in child welfare, where traditionally disputes were settled on an adversarial basis through the legal system. Yet, over 70 per cent of such cases can be resolved through pretrial negotiation, if the interaction between the natural family and the agency can be shifted from a court-ordered to a negotiated one. The goal of mediation is to help caseworkers and parents find mutually acceptable solutions in spite of their, at times, competing interests. Also, a neutral third party can often make the caseworker's role more understandable to the parents. Mediation should serve as an adjunct rather than an alternative to the legal system where abuse and severe, chronic neglect have occurred. Also the mediators, acting as a neutral third party, can at times interpret the caseworker's role sympathetically, making it more acceptable to the parents.

Cases involving the termination of parental rights, conflicts over custody, parent–child (or adolescent) conflict, the natural family's intention of moving beyond the jurisdiction of the agency, supervision of children (including techniques of discipline), failure to thrive, educational neglect, and child placement and parenting standards can be assisted by mediation in achieving a consensus on future planning for a child. Such a consensus might involve an agreement to close a case, a joint recommendation to court, or a voluntary service contract.

All but four of sixty-seven (94 per cent) in one study (Mayer and Golten 1987) worked out a written statement concerning some aspects vital to case planning agreed upon by all parties. While 60 per cent of workers feel that agreements obtained through mediation involve more compromise than those achieved by litigation alone, attorneys and outside reviewers see them as differing little from those achieved through the courts. Caseworkers were also more likely to view mediation as a good use of their time and a time saver than were attorneys. Compliance was best achieved when custody and visitation arrangements, conditions for a child returning home, changes in household rules, therapy, or parenting classes were the subject of the mediation. All groups, but especially parents, tend to prefer mediation to direct casework alone (Jaffe et al 1987; Maresca, Paulseth, and Rivers 1989).

4 / HAS THERE REALLY BEEN AN ADEQUATE ATTEMPT TO RESOLVE THE CRISIS WITHOUT REMOVING THE CHILD?

In spite of the risks, children are often admitted to care even though there is little indication of immediate danger and alternatives to placement have received only token exploration. Two possible scenarios come to mind. In the first, a child is apprehended by a worker who lacks any real understanding of the family dynamics, the factors predisposing to and precipitating the crisis, or the likely effects on child and family of the apprehension. In the second, a worker who has 'worked' with the family for some time has consistently avoided the crucial but loaded issues that should have been the focus of the casework. Often, in such cases, one finds a long history of cancelled or failed appointments, frequent and very late arrivals for appointments, indirect complaints, agitated phone calls, increasing financial demands, or avoided issues that were never openly and directly followed through.

Mrs Brown was assigned to the Duchesne family, who had contacted the Children's Aid Society voluntarily because, they said, their fourteen-year-old daughter, Margaret, was out of control. She refused to come home when expected. She regularly avoided her share of family chores. She was increasingly sullen and non-communicative, spending most of her time either locked in her room or monopolizing the telephone, another source of friction. Margaret, after initially refusing to talk, complained that her parents were too bossy and too strict. She considered some of their expectations unfair for a girl her age, and said that her parents treated her as if she were 'just a child.' By the end of the initial meeting, she and her parents were beginning to talk, not just to Mrs Brown but to each other. The tension between them seemed relieved, and they accepted a follow-up appointment for the following week.

At the last moment Mrs Duchesne called to cancel their appointment, but gave no reason why. Mrs Brown offered her another for the following week. Mrs Duchesne was not sure if her husband would come in again. Asked to discuss this with him, she failed to confirm the appointment as requested, and none of the Duchesnes showed up. Mrs Brown, already pressured by too large a caseload, was annoyed but did not follow through.

Two nights later, the psychiatrist on call at Children's Hospital was called to Emergency at 11:15 p.m. The Duchesnes had brought Margaret, who had swallowed an unknown number of aspirin tablets, she claimed in response to being grounded for arriving home half an hour past her curfew. The parent demanded her hospitalization as a suicidal risk. They refused to have her home, as they had 'had it.'

The psychiatrist first talked with all three as a family, and then with Margaret alone. Clearly more angry than depressed, she had intended to scare her parents, not to harm herself. Alone, she admitted that she had taken only three aspirins, spilling others down the toilet to alarm her parents. A blood test confirmed that she was in no danger.

The psychiatrist then met with the family again. She agreed that they had major problems resolving disagreements and dealing with their anger at each other. She suggested that Margaret go back home and that the family return to Mrs Brown for further counselling. Mr Duchesne retorted that Mrs Brown was useless, citing the suicidal gesture as proof of her ineffectiveness. When the psychiatrist explored the regularity of their contacts with Mrs Brown, learning about the two missed appointments, she suggested that they hadn't given Mrs Brown a chance; by cancelling twice in a row, they had, without realizing it, undermined the therapy. She stated, and all three agreed, that both with Mrs Brown and with her, the presence of a neutral professional had enabled them to communicate with each other, but that tension escalated and communication broke down without a therapist to act as a catalyst. The family acknowledged the importance of regular meetings for therapy to succeed. The psychiatrist suggested that they call Mrs Brown to set up an appointment the next day, obtaining their permission to speak to her herself. The next morning, she described to Mrs. Brown the encounter in Emergency, emphasizing the importance of actively following through after any cancelled or missed appointment, until the family learned to communicate and negotiate verbally rather than through defiant and provocative behaviour.

5 / CAN PREVENTIVE INTERVENTION HELP?

Various types of preventive services have been suggested to resolve family problems enough to avoid taking children into care (Miller 1987; Burt and Balyeat 1977). But several studies show that avoiding placement is not always possible. In M.A. Jones's (1985) controlled study, only 12 per cent fewer children ended up in care, so that the major effect of the preventive service was to delay the apprehension, especially of younger children. The question is therefore raised as to whether postponement is worthwhile, or whether it increases the risk of abuse or of further family deterioration. Jones found that preventive services that postpone entry into care neither increase nor decrease the likelihood of abuse, but the study was not designed to monitor and detect forms of family deterioration other than admission to care. The most tangible benefit of preventive service was that each day for which entry into care was delayed saved a day's costs. Moreover, Jones's data suggested that children of parents receiving preventative services remained longer in care.

Such an extension of care may not be as disadvantageous as it at first appears, since many of the benefits of foster care appear to be lost if children who are doing well are returned home (Block 1981; Rzepnicki 1987; Wald, Carlsmith, and Leiderman 1988; Wolf, Braukmann, and Ramp 1987). But, despite demonstrable positive results of the Jones study, the energy and enthusiasm expended on it, the enhanced resources available to the study population, and the influence of the Hawthorne effect,* one-third of the children who were expected to enter care did so eventually. Jones could not determine whether this finding represented an irreducible minimum, or whether a better or more appropriate preventive service could have further decreased the apprehension rate.

In the Jones study, the continuous presence of both parents – regardless of the quality of their parenting as long as the mother remained the primary caretaker – was the key to whether a child remained at home. Preventive services that ignore what the mothers see as their needs while attempting to enhance parenting capacity may improve the quality of family life, but, in this study at least, did little to decrease the rate of entry into care. Both M.A. Jones (1985) and Geismar (1979 p. 464) suggest that, unless the needs of vulnerable and insecure parents are being met by someone 'just being there' for them, other services provided are unlikely to prove effective. Jones also found that problems in the children's behaviour and school performance, especially for children from age six to thirteen, did more to determine that a child would come into care than did problems experienced by the parents (see also Cautley and Plane 1983). The suggestion is that preventive services designed, among other things, to improve the child's developmental deficits and functioning might be more effective (see also Cohn 1979; Wald et al 1988).

Finally, Jones concluded that fewer children might have entered care if the preventive service had been offered *before* placement had been requested, instead of after, as in this study; if intervention is delayed too long, is one locking the barn door after the horse is out? There is a suggestion, also previously noted by Jones and Halper (1981), that premature withdrawal of the preventive service because of agency limits on its duration may contribute to the failure to keep children out of

---

* At times, merely the interest and enthusiasm of those conducting an experiment can influence the results in the expected direction, thus contaminating the study. The contamination is called the 'Hawthorne effect.'

care. Nearly half of those entering care from families receiving preventive service did so after the service had been withdrawn, while two-thirds of those interviewed on follow-up wished that they were still involved. Also, a lack of premature withdrawal of the preventive service, the completeness of the service provided, and the experience level of the family's worker were three predictors of children *not* entering care. Jones concluded that preventive services that augment a family's back-up resources and keep parents 'on the job' as caretakers should be given high priority, via a broad range of services, including:

- providing improved access to financial, housing, and medical care;
- making services available longer, in the form of educational/vocational/marital/personal assistance, as well as helping the family deal with extended family and outside resources;
- directly working to improve the functioning of dysfunctional children;
- the use of experienced workers who are given the time to address the multiple needs of a multiproblem family through access to a broad range of services, as in the Homebuilders Program, in Tacoma, Washington (Kinney et al 1977); and
- advocacy and coalition-building to improve the resources of poor minority families in general (M.A. Jones 1985, pp. 138–52; Kieffer 1984; Hegar and Hunzeker 1988).

Other studies of regular visits by public-health nurses, at times combined with a variety of services directed towards other family needs, suggest that home-visiting can be partially effective in reducing the incidence of child abuse (Gray et al 1979; Olds et al 1986; Cohn 1980; Siegel et al 1980; Ten Broek and Barth 1986; Schmitt 1980). Several studies suggest that the visits must continue long enough, and Olds and colleagues (1986), who began providing home supports for high-risk mothers during their pregnancy and continued through the first two years of the child's life, succeeded in reducing the rate of abuse from 19 per cent in the control group to 4 per cent in the visited group. A study by Siegel and colleagues (1980) on the influence of hospital and home support during infancy on maternal attachment, abuse, neglect, and health care utilization reported some benefits in mother–child interaction but no differences between experimental and control groups in the incidence of abuse. In this study, the home visits were confined to the first three months after birth, and data were collected only at four and twelve months. One wonders whether an earlier intervention that was continued longer and followed for a longer period would have reduced the incidence of abuse.

In her excellent review of these studies, MacMillan (1987) stresses the importance of visits being made to the client rather than merely having services available in a hospital setting. Schorr (1989) has noted how frequently physical facilities, administrative procedures, and staff attitudes of hospital-based preventive services combine to intimidate and antagonize the very clients most requiring them. Schmitt (1980) suggests that visiting nurses may be less threatening – and therefore more acceptable and potentially successful – with high-risk mothers than workers from a child-protection agency.

Arguably the most successful prevention initiative in the child welfare area is the Homebuilders program, which, in its first six years of operation, rendered placement unnecessary for over 90 per cent of the client families, which, among them, had 849 children originally considered for an out-of-home placement (Kinney et al 1977; Schorr 1989). Accepting only families in crisis for whom removal of one or more children was actively being considered, the program provides a prompt, intensive, and home-based service designed to meet the needs of all family members and the family as a unit. In order to ensure that participating families receive the attention they need, more than a hundred hours may be spent by one or several workers during the crisis period. To ensure that they have the time and energy to provide an adequate intervention, workers have a caseload of only three, and can draw upon a wide range of practical and professional resources and community services offered by cooperating agencies. On call around the clock, they are frequently required to juggle their personal schedules to meet their clients', at times, overwhelming needs. Workers serve as advocates and brokers for the families in their dealing with agencies and institutions as part of their attempts to help previously overwhelmed clients regain control of their lives. A cost-effectiveness component has suggested that, in spite of the high initial outlay, the long-term saving for the community is in the vicinity of five or six dollars for every dollar invested in the program.

In their review of the Homebuilders Model, however, Cameron and Bidgood (1990) draw attention to how few outcome studies of the model were able to provide reasonable estimates of the program's effectiveness and cost. They quote Frankel (1988) who notes that Homebuilders are, in fact, screening out the more serious cases of child abuse, neglect, and family disorganization through their criterion of demanding at least one family member willing to participate – with none opposing the goal of placement aversion – even though such families could potentially benefit from such a program (Schwartz, Auclaire, and Harris 1990). Frankel notes that physically abusive families, who constitute only 10 per cent Homebuilders' clientele, have considerably lower placement aversion rates than do non-abusive families. This finding suggests that the Homebuilders' results could be less impressive within a typical child welfare caseload with a higher percentage of abusive families.

The same reviewers stress that, in the absence of a control/comparison group, one cannot accurately estimate the percentage of placements averted, since, even in a high-risk child welfare caseload, only a portion of those children considered very high risk – only 44 per cent in one study quoted – are taken into care (see also Frankel 1988; Pecora, Fraser, and Haapala 1990).

There is also evidence that placement aversion rates vary from site to site, and tend to decline after program involvement ends; Pecora, Fraser, and Haapala (1990) found that placement aversions declined from 93 to 70 per cent in one year. Of course, if the family were eligible for re-entry into the program during subsequent crises, the higher aversion rates might be retained, though at increased cost.

None of the above studies or reviews questions that the Homebuilders program, and other intensive in-home family support programs, can help to avert impending placements, though they do suggest that the extent to which they are effective has not yet been credibly established. In summary, however, they emphasize that:

– a control group is needed to accurately assess the effectiveness of any such program;
– earlier intervention increases program effectiveness;
– documented physical abuse decreases program effectiveness;
– following discharge from the program, placement aversion rates decline;
– even with high-risk adolescents, such programs can decrease both entry rates and time spent in care;
– the level of support and the range of services available increase program effectiveness;
– the potential for rapid response to crisis adds to program effectiveness.

But even with vigorous attempts at outreach, not all abuse can be eliminated. Cohn (1980), in a national evaluation of the pediatrician's role in the treatment of child abuse, found that, while the program appeared to protect 42 per cent of the children studied, 30 per cent of the parents continued to abuse their children during the study. Since this was an uncontrolled study relying on case-manager reports rather than on direct contact with the mothers and children involved, no firm conclusions can be drawn. One notes, however, that these figures are remarkably similar to those of Jones quoted above. However, even in the more carefully designed Olds and colleagues' (1986) study, one finds that 4 per cent of the nurse-visited group still abuse or neglected their children. These findings suggest that one essential component of an adequate preventive service is a constant awareness that neglect and/ or abuse could be continuing, so that the decision as to whether continuing the preventive intervention or taking a child into care is least detrimental will require ongoing monitoring and evaluation.

Ways of Minimizing the Harmful Effects of Removal and Placement

When removal and placement are unavoidable, how can one minimize the potential hazards of separation and placement in order to safeguard the child's developmental potential and future adjustment?

1 / HOW CAN CHILDREN BE ASSISTED THROUGH
THE WORK OF MOURNING?

It is crucial that supervising agencies help children actively deal with the often overwhelming feelings stirred up by separation from the natural family. This issue will be discussed in chapter 7.

2 / THE IMPORTANCE OF AN OVERALL PLAN

Sometimes, despite a worker's best efforts, children must be brought into care. Except in dire emergencies, such a decision should be part of an overall pro-active plan rather than an isolated act whose long-term implications have not been carefully considered (Levitt 1981). Admission to care is too often seen, especially by minimally trained and overloaded workers or by the community, as an end in itself, as if to say, 'There now. He's out of that terrible situation. Now I can relax,' rather than as a means to an end, as in 'How will this admission contribute to the overall welfare of this child?' The time to think of where a child should go *after* placement is *before* he is placed. One should always be working towards clearly defined goals derived from at least a provisional understanding of the child's needs. Whenever possible and realistic – in the best interests of the child – this consideration of needs should include reuniting the family. As one proceeds, it may be necessary to change the initial plan. However, without clearly defined and explicit goals towards which both client and worker are working, one risks aimless drifting or jolting from crisis to crisis without any real sense of direction (Chappell 1975; Berridge and Cleaver 1987; Kagan and Schlosberg 1989; Katz 1990; Miller et al 1984; Seaberg 1986; Steinhauer 1983b, 1984; Wiltse 1978). Agencies should always have a realistic, up-to-date, comprehensive long-range plan for each child. In view of the frequency of racial and cultural bias in decision making (O'Toole, Turbett, and Nalepka 1983; Hampton and Newberger 1985; Katz et al 1986), members of class and racial minorities should be included in all decisions. Examples of two such plans, one of Sarah, age ten and a half, and the other for Danny, age twenty-four months, will be given and then discussed.

Example 1. Sarah, age ten and a half, will require a permanent substitute family, since the following factors suggest that there is no realistic prospect of her family ever being able to provide adequate ongoing care, and since several attempts to restore her to her natural family have failed.
(List factors derived from assessment of the case leading to this conclusion here.)
Nevertheless, Sarah remains strongly attached to her family. This fact, as well as her age, points towards planned permanent foster care in the Stephenson home with regular ongoing contact at a frequency to be negotiated with the natural parents under the supervision of the foster parents or agency. Over the next six months, the goals of the work with (a) Sarah, (b) her foster parents, and (c) her natural parents are as follows:
(All three sets of goals should be clearly listed.)
The case will be reviewed in six months to ensure that progress towards these goals is being made. At that time, goals for all of those involved will be reformulated for the following six-month period.

Example 2. It is crucial to determine promptly the prospect of rehabilitating two-year-old Danny's family sufficiently to determine whether restoration to them is in Danny's best interests. Factors supporting restoration as realistic include:

(List factors here.)

The following factors would suggest that it is unrealistic and potentially harmful to work towards restoration. Should this be so, the agency should move, instead, towards a permanent placement, which, because of Danny's age would involve freeing him for adoption.

(List factors arguing against restoration here.)

Until that is decided, the agency will do the following, in order to minimize damage from the separation and to help Danny settle within his foster home while, at the same time, maintaining his attachment to his natural parents.

(List ways that agency is intending to meet this goal, including details of timing and supervision of visits.)

Should the court rule against restoration, the reasons favouring adoption over planned permanent foster care as long-term plan are:

(List evidence in favour of adoption.)

Since, in view of Danny's age, a permanent decision should be arrived at as soon as possible, the case will be reviewed in three months.

Table 6.1 lists and compares the elements common to these two plans.

One might argue that such a procedure is unrealistic, since circumstances might change, necessitating major revisions. It is important to define in advance what information needs to be collected to monitor and revise the plan if necessary, and to gather those data systematically. Regular periodic reviews should be scheduled in advance, at intervals determined in advance and stated in the plan. Even though such a formalized document will require periodic review and updating, it provides the best protection against unnecessary drift, and the best guarantee of active and appropriate intervention (Pike et al 1977; Chappell 1975; Berridge and Cleaver 1987, pp. 77–80).

Danny's plan demonstrates that, although the possibility of his separation becoming permanent was clearly considered, the supporting of his attachment to his natural parents was a major goal. At the same time, the agency gathered the information needed to evaluate, correctly and as soon as possible, his family's potential for changing enough to meet his developmental needs in the foreseeable future. Such a prediction involves a program of regular visits with the natural parents at a

TABLE 6.1
Elements common to plan of management

	Sarah (age 10½ years)	Danny (age 24 months)
Primary goal(s)	Prepare for permanent substitute family	1. Determine whether or not realistic prospect of family rehabilitation exists. 2. Determine for or against restoration.
Factors on which goal is based	Factors suggesting that there is no realistic prospect of rehabilitating the family include (list)	1. Factors indicating that rehabilitation and restoration *are* realistic (list) 2. Factors indicating that rehabilitation and restoration *are not* realistic (list)
State of attachment to natural family	Remains attached	Remains attached
Provisional plan	Planned permanent foster care in present foster family *and* regular (biweekly) supervised access	1. Protect attachment to natural parents via at least twice-weekly visits until a decision for either restoration or adoption is made. 2. Minimize sequelae of separation through casework. 3. If restoration not realistic, determine relative merits of adoption vs planned permanent foster care with or without access.
Goals of casework until next review	1. With Sarah (list) 2. With foster parents (list) 3. With natural parents (list)	1. Protect attachment to natural parents via visits: list details of timing of visits. 2. Obtain/document evidence for/against restoration. 3. If restoration decided against, obtain/document evidence for/against planned permanent foster care and adoption.
Date of next review	Six months	Three months
Agenda for next review	1. Assess progress towards each of the goals listed above.	1. Review evidence for/against the practicality of restoration towards the

2. Reconsider provisional plan, and either confirm or modify.
3. Update goals for ongoing casework with:
   a / Sarah (list)
   b / foster parents (list)
   c / natural parents (list)
4. Set date for next conference.

aim of reaching a decision for/against restoration.

2. If restoration decided against, review evidence for and against:
   a / freeing the child for adoption
   b / planned permanent foster care
   towards the aim of reaching a decision for/against freeing the child for adoption.
3. If either 1 or 2 cannot be decided, list factors that will be used to reach a decision at time of next conference.
4. Set goals of casework prior to next conference (list).
5. Set date for next conference.

frequency that depends on the child's age. For an infant, these visits should be scheduled daily, or as frequently as possible; during them, the natural mother should take an active part in parenting the infant, possibly with the support and help of the foster mother. For toddlers like Danny, visits ideally should occur two or three times a week. Whenever possible, those natural parents who can acknowledge the need for placement should be encouraged to help their child understand why he is in care and that they support the placement. Natural parents who can do so should be encouraged to facilitate understanding with older children during weekly or every-other-weekly visits, since their sanctioning rather than criticizing or undermining the placement may ease the transition and increase the effectiveness of foster care. While not all parents can assist their child in reaching such understanding, active and committed casework can frequently help develop mutual acceptance and a good working relationship between foster and natural parents, which, when achieved, can be so helpful to all involved, but especially to the child (Steinhauer et al 1989). A boy of Danny's age, especially one whose attachment to his parents was an anxious one, might well, like a toddler in hospital, find such visits upsetting. Why, then, continue them for as long as the ultimate disposition remains unclear?

Toddlers cannot long remain in limbo without assuming they have been abandoned and beginning to form a substitute attachment. Detachment from his own mother would favour Danny's developing a substitute attachment to his foster mother. In the absence of regular, sufficient contact with his natural parents until a decision was reached, Danny would have been encouraged by their absence to separate from them and to attach himself, instead, to his foster parents, who would soon become his psychological parents. If, then, the court were to restore Danny to the natural parents, he would be forced into a second, and, this time, artificially created separation from his new psychological parents in order to reattach to his natural parents. They, in not visiting Danny, would have been allowed by the agency to become strangers to him psychologically. To avoid the possibility of such 'agency-created abandonment,' especially in younger children, and in the absence of a specific contra-indication, the highest priority should be given to maintaining regular contact with natural parents as long as restoration remains a possibility (see chapter 9 for a more comprehensive discussion of the various roles that visits can play within an effective plan of management.)

The foster parents' perception of their own place in a child's life is crucial in this regard. Temporary foster parents who compete with the natural parents by presenting themselves to the child as the new mommy and daddy – especially for a child who may return home – will greatly compound confusion and distress. If, however, they care to present themselves as temporary caretakers, they will help preserve the bond to the natural parents by minimizing the loyalty conflicts and the inevitable confusion to which the child is exposed (Goldstein, Freud, and Solnit 1973; Berridge and Cleaver 1987; Burk and Dawson 1987; Kufeldt, Armstrong, and Dorosh 1991).

Cooper (1978) suggests that a maximal push towards restoration to the natural family immediately following placement minimizes the risk of unplanned and unnecessary drift, since only one in four children remaining in the care for six months ever returns home (Rowe and Lambert 1975). Such a push should be followed by a clear shift towards a plan for permanent placement whenever restoration is determined to be impractical or damaging (Bush and Goldman 1982; Regional Research Institute for Human Services 1976; Stein, Gambrill, and Wiltse 1978). But Fein and colleagues' (1983) finding that children who had been returned home at least once were adjusting better than those who had not suggests that a single attempt at restoration, if based on a reasonable assessment of the situation rather than on agency inertia, is a risk well worth taking, although returning a child to his natural family should be prepared for and supported, just as would an exposure to any other change of placement (Rzepnicki 1987). In view of the inherent risk in permanently or repeatedly restoring children to families who are ambivalent or frankly reluctant to reclaim them (Tizard 1977; Fanshel and Shinn 1978), research is badly needed to develop guidelines to inform decision making for or against restoration (see chapter 5).

3 / HAS THE CHILD BEEN ASSESSED PRIOR TO ADMISSION TO CARE?

Littner (1970) has suggested that, wherever possible, a thorough diagnostic evaluation should occur before the child is removed from her family, and that temporary placements, whether emergency or diagnostic, should be avoided. As a consultant, the author is struck by the number of emergency placements that could – and should – have been anticipated, allowing the child to be brought into care on an elective basis. When placement becomes a *possibility* is the time to assess thoroughly the nature and depth of both the child's and the family's difficulties. Even when apprehension is unavoidable, one can often delay a placement long enough to perform an adequate prior assessment and to prepare those involved properly for placement. The more assessment and planning before a move, the fewer the unnecessary and potentially damaging replacements. To oppose assessment prior to placement on the grounds of excessive cost is a false argument. The cost, both in human and in economic terms, is small compared to the costs of not planning properly – increased breakdowns; loss of desperately needed experienced foster families; increasing damage to the personalities and development of children; and the greater long-term costs of residential treatment, chronic dependency, and repetition of inadequate and abusive parenting in the next generation.

There is a widely held notion that, until it takes a child into care and 'lives with him,' an agency cannot know what he is like or what to expect from him. This is often untrue, and acceptance of it invites unnecessary damage. One can often anticipate quite accurately from past behaviour, school reports, and an up-to-date psychological and/or psychiatric assessment the kinds of difficulties a child is likely to present following placement. This knowledge can then be used to select and prepare the type of setting that the child will need. But, all too often, such advance planning fails to occur for two main reasons.

First, there is often no time (Rowe et al 1984). In one agency, despite a stated policy favouring planned apprehensions wherever possible, 65 per cent of all placements occurred within forty-eight hours of the initial request (Catholic Children's Aid Society of Metropolitan Toronto 1975). A more recent report from another large agency showed that 75 per cent of cases were admitted within twenty-four hours of the request for admission (Report to Residential Family Resources Project Reference Group 1989). Non-urgent requests for consideration of possible placements were frequently ignored until resubmitted on an emergency basis some weeks later. One often can – if one is determined to do so – delay emergency admissions to allow an adequate prior assessment. Doing so will certainly favour a better understanding of the child's needs and allow the more appropriate matching and preparation of child and resource that are so often missing.

The parents of Chris (age eleven) were frequently drunk, emotionally abusive, and consistently rejecting. In response, Chris had developed a number of symptomatic behaviours (lying, manipulating, constant attention-seeking, frequent tantrums, disruptive behaviour in school) that the parents used to rationalize further rejection and abuse at home. An assessment of the family – which included a review of four previous unsuccessful attempts at preventive intervention – made it clear that Chris's family was unlikely to change, and that it was in his best interests to be removed from the home. But Chris was so skilled at provoking rejection, not only from parents but from neighbours, teachers, and caseworkers, that the agency considered the roots of his misbehaviour were already so internalized that he was thought to be unlikely to last in any available foster home. A psychological assessment was therefore obtained before moving him, even though this meant he remained in his inadequate family for three weeks longer.

An experienced and sensitive psychologist saw Chris three times, combining her clinical impression with the result of a battery of tests. At no point did she feel any relationship developing between Chris and herself. This, for her, was unusual; she usually made some meaningful contact with almost all the children she assessed. Chris, however, remained distant and, whenever he could get away with it, hostile and manipulative. At the end of each ninety-minute session, the psychologist felt unusually exhausted and drained.

Chris's test data suggested pervasive and barely controlled rage, which she interpreted as his response to intense feelings of helplessness and pervasive distrust of adults, even those who were kind and caring. She suggested that Chris's distrust was so intense that he dealt with all adults according to the principle of 'Get them before they can get you.' The projective tests repeatedly portrayed parental figures as rejecting, hurtful, and only pretending to care in order to lull children into a sense of false security. Careful questioning of Chris's teachers and parents revealed that Chris had never maintained a successful relationship with anyone, adult or child. His present teacher had tried particularly hard to befriend Chris. As long as she made no demands, Chris and she got along fine. But as soon as she expected Chris to settle down to work or stop talking, Chris became belligerent and complained of always being picked on.

The psychologist contrasted Chris with Ronny, a twelve-year-old she had assessed for the agency some months before. Although some of their behaviour was similar, on several occasions she felt she had gotten through to Ronny, and he had aroused a liking and caring in her – as did most children she assessed – that was quite different from the exhaustion, irritation, and hopelessness that Chris evoked. Ronny, too, had tried to manipulate, but unlike Chris, he cooperated once she gained his trust. Although his projectives showed distrust and anger at adults too, they also revealed a longing for a caring relationship with an adult who would love and protect him. He had had a number of successful friendships and cooperated well with teachers and adults whom he liked and who liked him, although he became disruptive and manipulative with adults when he sensed rejection.

The psychologist suggested that, while Ronny had the psychological strengths and relationship skills to adjust within a structured but caring foster family, Chris did not. She strongly advised against a foster-home placement, in which she felt he would likely provoke another rejection and disrupt the placement in short order. She advised placing him in a small staffed group home operated by the agency for children unable to cope with the demands of family living and unlikely to be tolerated by any foster family twenty-four hours a day, seven days a week.

For almost five years, Chris remained in the group home, to which the author consulted on a weekly basis. Again and again he demonstrated the wisdom of the psychologist's judgment. While eventually his behaviour improved and he provoked rejection less, he was one of the few children ever placed in the home who never developed a selective relationship with any of the staff or the other children. He learned to cooperate when it was worth his while to do so, but never to remain cooperative when frustrated or disappointed. Staff and teachers learned to work with him and to help him learn, but no one ever felt close to him. Having carefully considered – and rejected – the possibility that the psychologist's description had become a self-fulfilling prophecy, the author is convinced that no foster parents would have been able to live with Chris on a daily basis, so that the psychological assessment had avoided at least one – and probably many – unnecessary rejections.

Placements are often needlessly jeopardized by ignoring what has long been known about the effect of the foster parents' natural children on placement survival. If the foster family has a child less than five years old, the breakdown rate is roughly double that of placements in families without a pre-school child. If there is a natural child approximately the same age as the foster child, the breakdown rates rises from 25 to 40 per cent and, in planned, short-term foster homes, from 0 to 53 per cent (Berridge and Cleaver 1987, p. 180), although some clinical reports suggest that the same is not the case when an adolescent is being placed.

Workers are often reluctant to plan on the basis of someone else's assessment. There is often a major lack of trust and cooperation between child-welfare agencies and assessment and treatment resources, and often even between departments within the same agency. Too often communication breaks down between departments, or between Children's Aid societies and their consultants. As a result, agencies lose potentially valuable understanding, while consultants and clinical settings miss the corrective feedback they need to learn to make their recommendations realistic and practical. Good advance planning, based on the sorts of problems and behaviour patterns a child has shown and the type of resource he will need, will require an adequate history, a competent assessment, and trust and good communication between the agency and its consultants. In the lack of such collegial relationships either between departments or between agency and consultants, a renegotiation of the collaboration or consultation contract should be given high priority.

4 / ARE CHILD AND FOSTER PARENTS (OR OTHER RESOURCE) ADEQUATELY MATCHED AND PREPARED FOR PLACEMENT?

Wherever possible, admissions should allow time for adequate matching and preparation of both child and foster family for the coming placement (Kirgan 1983). Placement with a relative who can, and wants to, care for the child reduces the rate of breakdown of long-term placements significantly (Berridge and Cleaver 1987, p. 57). Children should understand as much as possible why they are coming into care. Proper preparation for placement takes time. It also requires pre-placement visits – not just a single token in-and-out visit but, especially for younger children, a predictable series of graduated contacts that will help them to get to know the family or setting to which they are going and to focus on and begin dealing with their feelings about their separation from their family (Westhues and Cohen 1987; C.R. Smith 1984). The effort taken to introduce a child to the foster family is a useful indicator of the placement's likely outcome (Berridge and Cleaver 1987, p. 177). Reactions to each stage of this introduction should be monitored by the worker and used to gauge the child's readiness for the next stage of the placement. Used this way, visits provide a sort of stress inoculation; they present the child with gradually increasing but tolerable amounts of separation anxiety, which allow him to begin preparing himself for the coming move. Keeping the process gradual helps protect the child from being overwhelmed at any one time by more anxiety than is tolerable. The more the child can, with help, recognize and deal with the feelings aroused by each stage of the process and the more familiar he is with his new family prior to placement, the greater the chance of that placement's succeeding, thus avoiding unnecessary, potentially damaging, and expensive replacements. In view of what is known about children's reactions to separation, it is shocking to learn how frequently children are placed with either no visit or only a single mechanical pre-placement visit with minimal attention to the feelings aroused by the coming move (Palmer 1974; Aldridge and Cautley 1975). Berridge and Cleaver (1987) found that 50 per cent of unprepared placements of children in long-term homes broke down, often within two weeks, compared to only 12.5 per cent of placements in which children had known their foster parents beforehand. The same authors found that placement-related problems caused about one-third of all breakdowns in either planned short-term or long-term admissions to care, and such problems also contributed, in combination with other factors, to additional breakdowns. They warned that agencies far too often ignore the importance of matching children and foster parents, the importance of proper preparation for placement, and the dangers of placing foster children in homes with younger natural children, all of which are associated with a high breakdown rate (Berridge and Cleaver 1987, pp. 74, 177, 178).

Foster parents, too, must be prepared in order to maximize placement success. Where the foster father, along with the foster mother, is involved in accepting a child, placements are more likely to succeed (Cautley and Aldridge 1973). Bush and Gordon (1982) and Katz and colleagues (1986) have stressed how participation of the child, the natural parents, and the foster parents in the decision-making process improves the quality of placements. Both children and foster parents seem more committed to the success of a placement they have helped choose. Berridge and Cleaver (1987) have confirmed the author's clinical impression that failure of foster parents to express prior reservations about a proposed placement, and failure of the placing agency to provide adequate, accurate information about the child to the foster parents, are both associated with a higher breakdown rate. Also undermining placements at this stage is the inadequate training and support of many foster parents and caseworkers (Berridge and Cleaver 1987, pp. 52–3, 183).

5 / WHAT CAN BE DONE AT THE POINT OF REMOVING
THE CHILD FROM HIS FAMILY?

How the child is removed from the original family may prove critical in the child's subsequent adjustment, and may do much to affect the stability of the placement.

a / *How is it possible to avoid taking total responsibility for the child from the parents?* Admission to care may reinforce family scapegoating, especially of a difficult child, thus decreasing the family's motivation to continue working to resolve the systemic problems that precipitated the child's coming into care. Once an agency accepts total responsibility for a child, it makes it easy for parents to feel excluded from the placement process or to believe that they no longer need remain involved (Weinstein 1960; Rowe et al 1984; Bampton 1982; Mech 1985; Schetky et al 1979). Many natural parents feel unwelcome and resented by foster parents and social workers when they visit; finding visits stressful, they make them irregularly or stay away altogether (Millham et al 1986; Thorpe

1980; Knitzer, Allen, and McGowan 1978). Particularly nowadays, when many parents deal with age-specific but normal conflict with adolescents by extruding the teenager and when children blame themselves for family breakdowns (Kufeldt, Armstrong, and Dorosh 1991), agencies risk exacerbating already serious family problems by excluding natural parents or by allowing them to foist total responsibility for their child onto the agency. Especially with older children and adolescents, whose admissions to care are usually temporary, prompt and energetic efforts should be made to protect the child's place in the family and to ensure that the parents see themselves as having a key role in solving the problem as long as any possibility of reunion exists (Palmer 1974; Allison and Kufeldt 1987; Watson 1982; Ryan et al 1981). Visiting patterns should be established early, since those arranged at the beginning of a placement tend to persist, and since withdrawal of natural parent interest and involved contact is highly associated with placement discontinuity, long-term drift, and failure of foster care to meet the child's needs (Millham et al 1986; Fanshel and Shinn 1978; Berridge and Cleaver 1987, pp. 64, 87–8, 177; Bush and Goldman 1982).

b / *How can the abuse of intermediate placements, either on a receiving or on an assessment basis, be avoided?* Ideally, a child's first placement will be her last. If an adequate plan based upon a prior assessment has determined in advance the likely duration and the type of home needed, that child should be admitted there directly.

Receiving homes are an intermediate resource that offer a convenient place of safety for the apprehending agency. It should be recognized, however, that the way they are commonly used can increase developmental risks, especially for toddlers and pre-schoolers, by encouraging them to replace their attachment to the natural parents by one to the receiving home parents, only to suffer a second – and this time avoidable – separation when moved to a permanent placement. This danger can be minimized if the receiving home is a staffed rather than a couple-operated setting, or if the couple ensures that the child is always aware of the transitional nature of the placement (Burke and Dawson 1987).

Is there risk in placing a child directly even on the basis of an adequate prior assessment? Certainly. But the risk is even greater of encouraging the young child to become attached to his receiving-home parents by leaving him there too long – in some agencies, such is almost routinely the case – only to uproot him again, this time unnecessarily. Frequently, the result is further sensitization to separation, compounding the effects of the earlier separation.

It is sometimes argued that it is safer to admit children to temporary receiving homes to determine their needs before deciding on a permanent placement. What is learned about a child in a receiving home, however, often has little bearing on the child's ultimate placement. When children leave or where they go usually has less to do with the child's needs than with where and when a bed is available (CCAS 1975; Berridge and Cleaver 1987, pp. 64, 87–8).

There are, however, three situations in which an intermediate placement is justified. First, when it is impossible to determine in advance the placement of choice, children should be placed in a receiving home but moved to a permanent placement as soon as possible. Otherwise, there should, ideally, be enough flexibility to extend what was originally planned to be an interim placement into a permanent one should the child be left there long enough to bond selectively to the receiving-home parents. If this is impossible, great care should be taken to keep the receiving home an interim placement, by regular and sufficient visits with natural parents for any children who may return to their natural families and by transferring those requiring long-term care to a permanent placement suited to their needs as soon as possible.

A second exception is the child who, through a prior evaluation, is suspected of being unable to form a selective relationship (see Chris's history cited earlier in this chapter). Children who can't or won't be part of a family should be spared the trauma and sense of failure that will almost inevitably result if they are placed in a family setting. Their least detrimental alternative is an institutional setting – a staffed rather than couple-operated group home, etc. – to avoid setting them up for predictable failure and avoidable rejection.

As to the third exception, Berridge and Cleaver found that, for children in long-term care, additional damage from failed placements compounded existing problems and undermined the stability of future placements (the breakdown rate was 56 compared to 32 per cent for children placed for the first time). Breakdowns did not serve for them as a learning experience that equipped them to cope better in their next placement. They noted that a relatively brief stay in a more territorially neutral children's home following an upsetting breakdown of a long-term placement cut the breakdown rate in their subsequent placement from 51 to 34 per cent (Berridge and Cleaver 1987, pp. 72–3; see also Fanshel, Finch, and Grundy 1990).

c / *Why is it important to intensity rather than decrease efforts to work with the family at the point where a child is brought into care?* A significant percentage, especially of those older children who are now the majority of children coming into care, are likely to return home on leaving care. The goal in such cases should be to return them to an improved family situation.

We have seen that taking a child into care risks even further disruption of an already disturbed family equilibrium. The more ambivalent the bonding, the more to be worked through if parents and child are ever to resolve the traumatic effects of their earlier experience of conflict and separation. The importance of this for the young child is obvious. But even the adolescent who is old enough to live alone will be emotionally scarred if the conflicts remaining from chronic discord and separation are not resolved.

Far too often, agencies unwittingly collude in blocking such a resolution once the child is in care (Bush and Gordon 1982; Rzepnicki 1987; Knitzer, Allen, and McGowan 1978; Steinhauer 1983b). At the very time when efforts to involve the family should be intensified, many family (or protection) workers reduce contact because the child is 'safely' in care, so that the social work task shifts from a family to a child-centred focus (Millham et al 1986). The child's worker, often a different person, meanwhile struggles to work with and plan for the child, often without understanding the family equilibrium of the problems that will continue following restoration. The worst thing for both child and family at this stage is total isolation in which to consolidate their alienation from and their scapegoating of each other (Kagan and Schlosberg 1989). Except in those relatively few cases where natural parents are either unavailable or so damaging that contact with them is contra-indicated, great care should be taken to avoid undercutting whatever bonding and sense of involvement parents and child have with each other.

Both children and families may strenuously resist further work on those problems that precipitated the family breakdown. Their resistances are often expressions of the same conflicts that required the admission to care. But parental rage may mask anxiety, grief, or guilt. A brief cooling-off period may lower tensions enough to allow tempers to settle and positions to be re-examined. Such is the optimal time to help both child and family begin resolving their conflict and preparing for a possible reunion. Otherwise, if the child returns, it will be to the same highly pathological system that had previously broken down (Ryan et al 1981; Allison and Kufeldt 1987; Watson 1982; Darnell 1988).

d / *The importance of worker continuity both to children and to foster families should not be underestimated.* Some agencies are so organized that the family service or protection worker who takes a child into care is replaced immediately by a new worker from the child care department. This change of workers is often considered merely an administrative routine of no significance to the child. However, the crisis caused by coming into care frequently encourages especially young children to form strong ties to the worker who protected them when they were most vulnerable. To lose this worker, suddenly and with little or no explanation that they can understand – just after they have lost their family and face the prospect of life with strangers – imposes an additional burden on children. The admitting worker is the natural person to help the child face and begin dealing with the feelings evoked by the family breakdown and separation. An abrupt change of workers can be avoided by having the family service worker, who brought the child into care, become the child care worker for as long as the child remains in foster care on a temporary basis, or by phasing workers in an out more gradually after the child has begun to settle and is starting to work through feelings about the separation. These strategies will minimize the child's sense of abandonment by the protection worker and will encourage the transfer of the positive feelings the child associates with her to the child-care worker.

e / *The more successfully the child works through feelings aroused by the initial entry into care, the easier if will be for that child to form a secure and effective attachment to parental surrogates.* The working through of the feelings of loss associated with the separation is important enough to be discussed separately (chapter 7).

Chapter Seven

Guidelines for the Clinical Management of the Sequelae of Separation

Prior to and at the point of separation of a child from his natural family, the first goal of effective management is to minimize stress and, thereby, the amount of anxiety confronting the child at any one time, since excessive anxiety encourages repression and the abortion of the normal mourning process. Anxiety is best minimized by taking the child into care on an elective basis wherever possible, thereby allowing sufficient time for the assessment of the child's needs, the selection of an appropriate placement, and the preparation of child and foster parents for each other. This preventive work is best done through the series of graduated pre-placement visits discussed in chapter 6, which simultaneously promote familiarity and stimulate a process of stress inoculation by evoking anxiety in graduated amounts, allowing the child to prepare a bit at a time (i.e., gradually to develop defences), assisted to this end by his worker.

In the 1960s, the author directed a ward of a children's psychiatric hospital providing long-term care for children with severe behaviour disorders. About 75 per cent of the patients were Children's Aid Society wards who had been hospitalized when their behaviour had precipitated the latest of their many foster-home breakdowns. The hospital would work with these children for up to three years. When it had done what it could, it would notify the responsible society, which would then provide a new foster home for the child. This process often dragged on while the child's behaviour, which had previously been improving, began to deteriorate, as the child sensed he was again in limbo. After a foster family was found, the child would then be discharged after several visits. Not surprisingly, many of these placements broke down, as, after a short honeymoon period, the new foster parents began to experience severe difficulties for which they were not prepared to cope. The author decided that the children and the foster parents were not ready for each other by the intended discharge date. In an attempt to correct this, he designed the following discharge protocol.

He insisted that the Children's Aid Society provide a foster family for each child three months before the expected discharge date, even if this meant paying a holding fee until the child was actually placed. Immediately, a program of visits was started. First, the new foster parents were given a clear picture of the child's history and what they could expect to have to deal with when he was in their home. Then, they visited the child at the hospital and were introduced to him as his new foster parents. Next, he began visits at their home, the first time accompanied by a familiar staff person, then on his own for two hours and a meal, next for a longer period, then overnight, and, as soon as all seemed able to tolerate it, weekly, from late every Friday afternoon to early Monday morning. After each contact, the child and the foster parents met separately with a social worker to discuss how the visit had gone, any difficulties – and there were few at the beginning, as both child and foster parents were trying to avoid them – and how each felt about the other and the visits. As soon as overnight visits had begun, foster parents and child were seen together, and the same process was conducted in each other's presence. As soon as the child was spending weekends at the home, a family therapy session was conducted soon after each return to hospital. By this stage, the child was having trouble remaining on 'company' behaviour and was beginning to test limits, while the foster parents were becoming more confident in dealing with his oppositionality and manipulation. The aim of the family therapy was to bring everything out in the open; thus, the boy's behaviour might be found comparable to ways he had acted in hospital, and the parents might be advised how they might handle him more effectively. The placement was not finalized until after the child had behaved as aggressively or disruptively in the foster home as he had in hospital, so that the foster parents had experienced him at his most difficult and had been able to cope successfully. The discharges were usually within, give or take, one month of the proposed discharge date. By this time, both child and foster parents knew each other enough that neither were dealing with an unknown quantity. The weekly family therapy sessions, of course, continued after the child's discharge. The post-discharge course following these graduated visits was more stable and much less stormy, even though some of the children had been through as many as fifteen foster homes in the past.

Immediately following placement, there is danger that the foster parents and/or social worker may fail to recognize or appreciate the significance of behavioural signs of the child's mourning. They may misinterpret the child's apathy, the cessation of protest, and his beginning to relate to them as signs that mourning has been completed, or they may collude in and help the diversion of the mourning process by distracting or cheering up the child. The child's defences against feelings of intense loss, superimposed upon conflicts and defences aroused by his earlier experience in the discordant natural family, often mask the mourning process. Insensitivity, excess sensitivity leading to denial, or an inability to tolerate the child's distress may lead to adult collusion.

No child can mourn successfully without adult assistance. The failure of key adults to assist the child's mourning may result from agency-related factors. These may include excessive caseloads, inadequate or insufficient worker training, too low a priority assigned to grief work, or a lack of support for workers through sufficient and adequate process-oriented supervision. Workers may be afraid to facilitate children's mourning for fear of antagonizing the foster parents. They, at times, resent having to deal with the child's upset and fear that contact with the natural parents will undermine the child's relationship with them. This is particularly likely if the foster mother has fantasies of being the child's *only* or *real* mother, which is likely to cause more than average difficulties and to predispose to breakdown (Berridge and Cleaver 1987, p. 182). Kufeldt, Armstrong, and Durosh (1991) had forty foster children, most between the ages of twelve and fourteen, rate the functioning of both their natural and their foster families, using the Family Assessment Measure (FAM), a standardized self-report survey of family functioning (Skinner, Steinhauer, and Santa-Barbara 1983). Of these children, 92.5 per cent viewed the overall functioning of their foster families as average or above. Those who reported problems in the foster families were as likely to be children who visited their natural parents rarely as ones who visited frequently, although weekly visits were associated with some decrease in feelings of closeness to the foster family.

Mourning is an uneven process. It follows the child's schedule, not that of the adults trying to assist it. No one, least of all a child, can tolerate unrelieved misery, so periods of active mourning alternate with long phases of renewed avoidance, denial, and repression, during which the child can appear quite untroubled. Children cannot be forced to mourn when they are not psychologically prepared to do so. Excessive, premature, or insensitive pressure towards mourning may, instead, encourage denial, intellectualization, acting-out, or other defences in the child.

The key to helping children mourn successfully lies in recognizing the behavioural indications that feelings originating from the loss are temporarily re-emerging into consciousness. A number of examples of this can be found in the case of Charlene (see chapter 3), especially in Charlene's repeatedly picking up and putting down and, eventually – only in the last session – playing with the police car. Again and again in Charlene's case, one sees themes of mourning accompanied by mounting evidence of sadness or upset, followed by periods of withdrawal by physical distancing or an abrupt change in the nature of the play. Such withdrawal protects the child from having to experience more upset than she can handle at the time. In real life, such withdrawals allow the temporary avoidance of mourning until some unexpected stimulus, such as another child in the home having a visit, a TV show that the child associates with her own home, being put to bed just as her mother used to put her to bed, reawakens it.

The foster parents, especially the foster mother, are often those best able to help the child mourn successfully. They spend more time with the child, do more for her, and are more likely to be there when the reactivated mourning breaks through the child's defences. S. Palmer (1974) has shown that, where an experienced worker is convinced of the importance of assisting the work of mourning, the child is more likely to mourn enough to be able to bond selectively to the foster mother, thus protecting later socialization. The child's primary guide through the work of mourning should be the foster mother, and social workers and/or consultants can best assist by helping foster parents recognize the signs of reactivated mourning and by increasing their sensitivity, understanding, and repertoire of techniques for facilitating it. Workers can also act as an additional adult from whom some children can gain assistance (e.g., practice) in the work of mourning. The workers' key role, however, should, wherever possible, lie in supporting the foster parents to assist the mourning, despite the pain and disturbance that usually accompany it.

Some agencies refer children newly admitted to care to play therapists, usually psychologists or psychiatrists. Kliman and Schaeffer (1984) have reported on two methods of using psychodynamic psychotherapy on 104 consecutively referred children entering foster care for the first time. Some received ten and others forty sessions of what the authors termed 'situational crisis psychotherapy.' In all cases, the natural and foster parents also received guidance in assisting the children's mourning. In a pilot study of 31 such children who received all the psychotherapy considered necessary up to and including several psychoanalyses, no foster home breakdowns and a decrease in children's compulsive need to repeat in their foster family old and dysfunctional patterns of behaviour and relationship were reported during the twelve months of the study. However, the groups receiving ten to forty psychotherapy sessions did not differ significantly from each other in most indices, or from a comparison group studied for rates of breakdown. There was only one exception: by applying Koppitz's scheme for rating indicators of emotional disturbance in Bender Gestalt test data, the extensively treated (forty sessions) children showed less evidence of emotional disturbance, while those receiving fewer treatment sessions showed no such improvement. This finding suggests that extensive psychotherapy for children entering foster care may provide some preventive advantage, though it is not clear whether the help was supplied by the psychotherapy itself, the guidance to the parents, or the fact that the feelings of the forty-session group were intensively worked with immediately after the placement. A highly desirable side-effect of this project was the stimulation experienced by members of those units of the child welfare agency involved with the study.

It is both unlikely and unrealistic to expect that, expect as part of research projects such as this one, there will ever be enough highly motivated psychodynamic therapists available for all children coming into care the first time (Offord et al 1989). Since no outside therapists are usually available, and since it is especially hard for many highly defended foster children to concentrate their mourning into the one or two hours each week that they meet their therapists – or social workers – the foster mother, given proper expectations, supervision, and support, is best able to provide the ongoing assistance most children need.

Possible Points of Entry into the Mourning Process

1 / *In relation to visits.* Children's visits with their parents, including ones that the parents cancel or fail to show up for, as well as those of other foster children in the same home often reactivate children's mourning. As important as the visit itself is the opportunity the visit gives the sensitive caseworker or foster mother to note and make a connection with how the child feels or behaves as the visit approaches, on the way to the visit, after returning from one, or when a visit is cancelled. This opportunity can facilitate the working through of repressed feelings stirred up by an actual or frustrated contact with the natural parents. Any changes in mood, activity level, expression, behaviour, fantasy, or play, or any marked withdrawal or increased aggression shortly before or just after visits or their cancellation should be considered and explored as possible reactions to feelings precipitated by the visits.

2 / *Concept of transference.* Many foster parents, and some social and child care workers, tend to interpret all difficulties between a child and the foster family on a transactional basis, as if the child's attitude and behaviour were a realistic response to the foster parents. But how foster children see and relate to their foster parents often has little to do with how the foster parents behave towards them. Many foster children's responses are based on the child's transferring onto the foster parents attitudes, motives, or feelings originating in the child's past experience and/or memories of his own parents. With help from their worker, many foster parents can learn to identify the marked over- or underreactions, displacements, or sudden changes of topic or mood that may suggest that a child's response is determined more by feelings transferred from the past than by current interaction. With help, many foster parents become adept at spotting the piggybacking onto present transactions of feelings transferred from key relationships of the past. The child may be mistrustful even when foster parents are consistently honest and caring. He may fear physical punishment even from a teacher who is fair and non-punitive. He may hate or feel picked on by a neighbour who has done him no harm. Such reactions, if recognized as out of proportion to the transaction in which they occur, can often be identified and traced to their source. Such displacements, distortions, and fantasy derivatives constitute the emotional re-experiencing in the present of unresolved feelings of deprivation and loss from the past. Feelings ex-

pressed in this way often derive from stereotypic expectations shaped by the internalized picture and feelings the child has of the lost parents.

'On the whole, things are going well,' a foster mother reported to her worker about six months after fourteen-year-old Lily had been placed with her, 'but there's just one thing that drives me up the wall; the way Lily acts whenever I try to discipline her or set any limit. No matter how reasonable I am, the response is always the same; she never accepts what I say, or argues or protests or gets angry, the way my own kids did. She just becomes very quiet, and withdraws. I see her standing there, but she's miles away. She just puts up a wall, and I can't get through to her. It doesn't matter how many times I tell her, "Look, Lily. If you don't think it's fair, tell me and we can talk about it. Don't worry, I won't be angry. You've been living here for six months already. Surely by now you can see that we can talk about things, and that we're not going to hold it against you if you disagree or tell us you think something is unfair. It would be much better if you would put what you think and feel out on the table as the rest of us do, instead of just putting up a wall."'

'Why do you think she's like that?' her worker asked.

'It's obvious. She doesn't trust us. She's afraid to do anything that might make us angry, and nothing we say do makes any difference, even after six months. It doesn't make sense.'

'Tell me,' her worker replied, 'suppose that you had grown up in a family where people were constantly attacking each other, where there was frequent and unpredictable violence, and where your father regularly exploded each time anyone questioned or disobeyed him. How would that have affected you?'

'Well, I guess I'd learn to keep my mouth shut when he was around. But it's not like that in our family. Why can't she see that? We're not like her family. Why does she keep on treating us as if we were? Why can't she trust us?'

'Suppose you had lived in that explosive family not just for six months, but for fourteen years. For fourteen whole years you'd been accustomed to parents who could go off the deep end at any moment, where any disagreement or expression of upset could lead to an explosion. After fourteen years of that, how easy would it be for you to trust others who *said* they were different, and to believe they really meant it?'

'I think I see what you mean. But how do we get it across to her that we *are* different? What can we say that will make her begin to trust us?'

'It's not a matter of saying. It's a matter of just being yourselves. Consistently. She'll come around in time, but not until she's ready. She needs more time to determine whether you're "for real." You *say* it's okay for her to speak her mind, but how can she know that you mean it and that you won't be just like her parents if she stands up to you? If you continue to be caring and open and predictable with her, in time she'll get up the nerve to test you, to see for herself if you really are different, or if, as she suspects, all parents are just the same. It takes a lot more than six months to undo fourteen years of conditioning.'

3 / *Recurrent themes occurring in the child's conversation, play, or behaviour.* The child's stories, play, drawings, dreams, and/or fantasies may, again and again, repeat common themes of children (or puppies, dolls, or baby birds) being abandoned, frightened, punished, deprived, or mistreated. Again, in such cases, the recurrent theme can be recognized as a derivative of a situation or feeling previously experienced and now being repeated in fantasy. This recognition can often be used to help the child expand on fantasies and feelings related to these generic themes.

4 / *The role of foster parents in assisting the work of mourning.* Many foster parents, with their workers' assistance, become very skilled at helping children recognize, identify, and gradually learn to connect up with their origin the feelings expressed in these derivatives of the unresolved mourning. Especially when the child has no conscious memory of the natural parents or can only intellectualize about them (with the associated feeling remaining isolated and unrecognized), it will be by noting and using those times when current expressions of repressed feelings of loss do break through the usual defences that mourning can be assisted.

The work of mourning is more than just a child and adult intellectualizing together about past events, or repeatedly talking about parents whom the child no longer remembers his feelings about. Intellectualization implies that the child's thoughts and feelings have become isolated from each other. Encouraging intellectualization merely strengthens the splitting of thought from feeling, thus reinforcing the child's inability to re-experience those feelings. But it is precisely the re-experiencing of the feeling, often stirred up by some current experience, that is required for mourning to proceed. It is only through reliving and thereby recognizing what he is feeling that the child can mourn. At first, feelings may not be about the parents at all; they may be transferred onto a teacher, a neighbour, one of the foster parents. Initially, it may be enough for the child to experience what he is feeling. Later, when he is more aware of his feelings, there will be time for him to think about why so many of his current reactions are exaggerated, understated, or displaced, and to help him trace the feelings to their original source. To force this process prematurely risks increasing the child's defences against his own feelings, and will prove counter-productive. Once the pattern is clear to the child, it can then sometimes be used to help him gradually become aware of how much of his feelings and behaviour are dominated by feelings left over from his experiences of the past. Only then can the child recognize how feelings originating from unmourned losses have become transferred and are contaminating his responses to the situations and relationships of today.

To facilitate this process, foster parents and worker must set a tone by the kind of people they are, consistently treating the child with care, sensitivity, and respect. These attitudes will do more than any specific thing they say or do to assist the child. Foster parents and workers must learn to sense and to utilize the right opportunities, and to respond to them in ways that encourage the child while avoiding criticism:

Example 1. 'I can't take it anymore! Every time you come back from a visit you're impossible. How can you expect us to put up with it?'

Example 2. 'You're not yourself when you come back from a visit. Something must be upsetting you. Lots of kids find their visits really tough: they look forward to them so much but, when they actually occur, they end up feeling disappointed. If you could just explain how your visits make you feel we could both understand better, and I'd be more able to help you. Also, you would probably feel better and find it easier for us to get along after visits.'

In the first of these examples, the foster parent is complaintive and critical, which is enough to make any child defensive. However, in the second example, through an accepting tone and the use of generalization to touch upon what the child may be feeling but cannot yet put into words, the reasoning is more likely to be accepted by the child. Some children are unable or unwilling to acknowledge their feelings, even when they are verbalized sympathetically, as in the second example. But that does not necessarily mean that the attempt to express what they might have been feeling has failed. Children unable to respond immediately will at least have had a clear example of their foster parents' capacity for empathy, even if they cannot use it yet, and every word may have sunk in despite the youngster's inability to acknowledge it at the time. Even for children who cannot recognize the connection between their current feelings and earlier separations thematically linked to them, the attempt to associate the two, as in the second example, may begin to help undermine the defences against long-buried feelings of loss. Even if they consciously reject the connection, the interpretation may linger in their mind, thus preparing the ground for a subsequent interpretation or spontaneous flash of recognition. Also, by respecting the youngster's right *not* to reveal what he is feeling, the foster parent or worker is establishing, at the very least, respect for the child's privacy – and, therefore, for the child himself.

Fourteen-year-old Donald was brought for treatment by his mother because he was sullen, oppositional, and defiant at home and badly underachieving at school. He was also stealing, although from what he revealed later, his mother had no idea how extensive this was.

Donald's father, with whom he had had a stormy relationship, died when Donald was nine. When he walked into his Grade 4 class the day after the funeral, the teacher, knowing that his father had cancer, had asked how his father was. 'Oh, he's dead,' replied Donald, sitting down and taking out a book with no outward sign of emotion. Throughout the entire mourning period, Donald distanced himself from his mother and sister. He claimed he just put his father out of his mind. He denied crying, or having recurrent or intrusive thoughts or dreams about his father, either then or subsequently. As far as Donald was concerned, his relationship and feelings for his father came to an end when the body was buried.

As Donald talked about his recent thefts, it gradually became clear that they occurred compulsively. For no understandable reason, he would suddenly be overcome with a feeling that he could identify only as intense and uncomfortable. Gradually, as his therapy proceeded, he became more aware of being overwhelmed at times by an overpowering feeling of emptiness or deprivation, that seemed to him to come out of nowhere. At one point, his therapist suggested that this feeling of emptiness might be a delayed reaction to his father's death, which he had never mourned. Donald burst out laughing, convinced that any attempt to link his current feelings of deprivation to the loss of his father was ridiculous.

From the therapist's vantage point, evidence that these intense bursts of deprivation were indeed related to Donald's never having mourned his father's death continued to grow, but Donald did not make the connection until one particular day, about four months later. He and his buddies had become friendly with a neighbour in his fifties, a mechanic who had set up an automotive workshop in his garage and who allowed the boys to work with him to learn the rudiments of auto mechanics. They spent more and more time working together, and became increasingly attached to him. One day after school, Donald rounded a corner of the house and, entering the driveway, suddenly looked up. He saw the mechanic standing there, his arm in a fatherly way around one of Donald's friend's shoulders. 'As soon as I saw it,' Donald recounted, 'tears began running down my cheeks and the bottom fell out of my stomach. At that moment, I realized what it was I had been missing for so long. It was seeing them stand there, so close to each other, that suddenly made me feel how much I had missed having a father. That one instant convinced me in a way that nothing you said ever could.'

Donald's spontaneous reaction, occurring as it did, finally broke through his defences, allowing him to recognize how his interpretation of what he saw between the mechanic and his friend was influenced by the previously repressed feelings remaining from the loss of his father. From that time, he gradually became more able to recognize and discuss his feelings of deprivation in his therapy. Simultaneously, the periodic bursts of intolerable emptiness became fewer and less intense, and with them the compulsive need to steal gradually weakened and, within months, disappeared.

During their past, most foster children's survival depended on their ability to protect themselves by concealing true feelings that, again and again, had been manipulated or attacked. Their fear that such will happen again often makes it hard for them to enter into therapeutic relationships, interfering with their ability to benefit from either regularly scheduled casework or psychotherapy, at least until they have had the experience of learning to trust some adult, usually their foster parent, enough to allow themselves to take the risk of forming an alliance, even though it means becoming vulnerable again (discussed in detail in chapter 15).

The question arises of when to challenge a child's defences and when to respect them by backing off. Excessive pressure, especially on the child with poor impulse control who cannot internalize tension, leads to the child's feeling invaded, controlled, and overwhelmed, and, in turn, intensifies the child's defences, causing withdrawal, acting-out, or any combination of the two. Any evidence that attempts like those in the example of Donald to verbalize what one thinks the child is feeling are proving counter-productive should lead to a temporary backing off, until the next appropriate opportunity arises.

One common and tenacious defence of many foster children is their unconscious need to repeat the past by provoking in the present the same kinds of situations and relationships that once proved so overwhelming (Littner 1960). Thus, it is not uncommon for children in foster case to fan marital conflict between foster parents, to set themselves up to be scapegoated, or even to seduce a foster father into sexually abusing them as they experienced intrafamilial sexual abuse prior to coming into care. (Of course, in such cases, the fact that the child was provocative in no way diminishes the foster parent's responsibility to resist the seduction.) These repeated behaviours can be understood in a number of ways. They may represent the behaviour of an anxiously or ambivalently attached child awkwardly seeking closeness and dependency in ways that alienate rather than attract. They may be evidence of a true repetition compulsion – a compelling need to repeat the past – in which the child is seeking to master anxiety by actively initiating experiences that, in the past, proved so overwhelming when they could be only passively endured. Such behaviours can also express what Hambridge (1962) has called 'secondary ego degradation' or Berne (1964) has referred has referred to as 'following a script.' According to both these formulations, the child has internalized his caretakers' opinion that, since he is unlovable and unworthy, he will ultimately be rejected. Therefore, he behaves in ways to make these self-fulfilling prophecies come true. At least that way he has some sense of being in control over what is going on. But, in all such situations, however the behaviour is formulated, the result is the same: as the cycle keeps repeating, the child, unaware of and therefore unable to change his own contribution to the vicious circle, repeatedly sets himself up for further rejection (Ney 1989; Pardeck 1984; also summarized diagramatically in figure 2.1). To interrupt such a cycle, someone, usually a foster parent, must succeed over time in gaining the child's trust. The resulting relationship can then be used to help the child, with or without recognition, to modify his contribution to the vicious circle.

Thus, the key to successful management of the foster child whose mourning has been aborted involves, first, demonstrating over and over again to a negatively conditioned child that adults can be trusted, and, then, using the resulting relationship to encourage the child to re-examine his own feelings and behaviour and to recognize how these are at times distorted by internalized feelings left over from past parental and other abuse, neglect, or abandonment. As the displacement is undone, and as the child becomes more aware of whom he is really angry at, his availability to work through his feelings about his natural parents and about being in care increases. The more aware he is of his feelings about the natural parents, the less need there is to transfer and act out these feelings via the foster parents and other current transference figures. The result is often a more realistic and less provocative and alienating response to them.

But what of the child who has so repressed the aborted mourning process that she genuinely can't recall or can only intellectualize about the original separation? Where such is the case, the child's thoughts have been so split off and isolated from her feelings subsequent to their original repression that the resulting isolation has proved impenetrable to attempts to reverse it. If the entry points suggested here do not succeed in re-establishing contact with the repressed feelings central to the mourning process, one may need to invoke some stronger stimulus to reactivate it. The routine, regular use of a 'Life Book' to provide some sense of historical continuity, a visit to a parent's grave, a drive past the house where the child first lived or where an adoptive placement broke down, a visit with the worker who originally brought the child into care – any of these may serve to reawaken repressed feelings and to rekindle a mourning process that has been aborted.

Debby, age ten, also lived in the staffed group home with Chris, whose entry into care was described in chapter 6. Debby had spent three years in the group home, and while her attention-seeking, aggressive, and disruptive behaviour had moderated somewhat, the staff remained worried about her limited progress. She had not formed any bond to any of the staff or other children. She did not care about how her behaviour affected others, and had no wish to modify it to get along with others. Staff had tried repeatedly to help Debby talk about her separation from her mother when she was four. All Debby could say was that she had gone to the bathroom and that, when she came out, her mother was gone.

As Debby had brought into care by the Children's Aid Society of a neighbouring county, staff did not know what to make of this, as they doubted that her mother would have left her under such circumstances. Debby easily and glibly talked about leaving her mother to come into care, but she never showed any evidence of being upset when she did so. For that reason, and because her behaviour showed no change in response to these superficial discussions, the staff considered them intellectualizations that were impeding rather than assisting the work of mourning.

In consultation with the author, it was suggested that we locate the worker who had originally taken Debby into care, and that we ask her to meet with Debby to discuss her coming into care. The resulting meeting was a dramatic one. The worker confirmed that, in the middle of a scheduled meeting, Debby had been excused to go to the washroom. Her natural mother had promised to wait for her return, but took advantage of her absence to bolt from the office without even saying goodbye. When Debby returned from the washroom, her mother had indeed gone. On hearing this, Debby began to cry and then got angry, first at the staff of the group home for not believing her, then at the worker who had taken her into care, for allowing her mother to leave before she returned from the washroom, and finally, only after all this, at her natural mother for abandoning her.

One of the group home staff, who had participated in this interview, was able following it to talk further with Debby about the feelings of betrayal and abandonment that surrounded her coming into care. Over the next few weeks, also, the staff noted that Debby frequently blew up in situations where she insisted that an adult (staff, teacher, neighbour) had broken a promise and let her down. Each time this happened, she was given a chance to ventilate her rage, and later her primary worker would link this to the original abandonment/betrayal by saying to her something like, 'Gee, Debby, I can certainly understand why that upsets you and makes you mad. After all, this isn't the first time that someone you counted on let you down, is it?' That was all it needed. Debby, in tears, would shout and swear at her current 'betrayer' and at all the adults who had let her down in the past, especially her mother.

Within a few weeks of the meeting with her original worker, Debby began showing signs of an early selective bonding to Joanne, who was becoming her favourite worker. Debby would ask others where Joanne was when she was on a day off, and when she would be back. She would seek her out when she was on shift, and was more likely to behave for her – or to be upset when reprimanded by her – than with other staff. A marked behavioural shift was observed, especially when it came to getting along with others and obeying rules.

Supporting children to work through the intense feelings mobilized by separation is one key to minimizing long-term damage to children in care. Members of the foster family, and especially the foster mother, are those most likely to be able to facilitate successful mourning, because of the child's dependence on them and their being the ones most likely to be present when mourning is reactivated. With proper training and appropriate back-up, many foster parents become very adept at guiding children through the mourning process. While occasionally it may be necessary for the child's worker or an outside therapist to catalyse the process of mourning, usually such professionals can help most by sensitizing and empowering the foster mother and family to fill this need.

Chapter Eight

Sharing a Child between
Natural and Foster Parents

Then came there two women, that were harlots, unto the king, and stood before him. And the one woman said, O, my Lord, I and this woman dwell in one house; and I was delivered of a child with her in the house. And it came to pass the third day after I was delivered, that this woman was delivered also: and we were together; there was no stranger with us in the house, save we two in the house. And this woman's child died in the night; because she overlaid it. And she arose at midnight, and took my son from beside me, while thine handmaid slept, and laid it in her bosom, and laid her dead child in my bosom. And when I rose in the morning to give my child suck, behold, it was dead: but when I had considered it in the morning, behold, it was not my son, which I did bear. And the other woman said, Nay; but the living is my son, and the dead is thy son. And this said, No, but the dead is thy son, and the living is my son. Thus they spoke before the king.

Then said the king: The one saith, This is my son that liveth, and thy son is dead; and the other saith, Nay; but thy son is the dead and my son is the living. And the king said: Bring me a sword. And they brought a sword before the king. And the king said, Divide the living child in two, and give half to the one, and half to the other.

Then spoke the woman whose the living child was unto the king, for her bowels yearned upon her son, and she said, O my lord, give her the living child, and in no wise slay it. But the other said, Let it be neither mine nor thine, but divide it. Then the king answered and said, Give her the living child and in no wise slay it; she is the mother thereof.

And all Israel heard of the judgment which the king had judged; and they feared the king; for they saw that the wisdom of God was in him, to do judgment. (1 Kings 3:16–28)

This quotation emphasizes the damage that can occur to children in care when the various adults in their lives – foster parents, natural parents, social workers – compete for exclusive possession or control of the child and try to keep others from playing their natural role in the child's life.

Experimental studies have shown that children who have ongoing contact with their natural families do best in long-term foster care (Wald, Carlsmith, and Leiderman 1988; Fanshel and Shinn 1978; Berridge and Cleaver 1987). This finding is supported by other evidence demonstrating how poorly foster children do without ongoing involvement with their natural families (Maluccio et al 1980; Gruber 1978; Wiltse 1976; Weinstein 1960). In view of this, one would expect that ongoing contact between foster children and their natural families would be encouraged in intermediate or long-term foster care. In fact, however, regular access to natural parents in long-term foster care is often resisted by both foster parents and social workers. Even when prescribed, it often finds little support within the foster care system (Berridge and Cleaver 1987); Ryan et al 1981; Fanshel and Shinn 1978). Why is there such resistance to natural families remaining involved?

Foster parents often vigorously oppose the continued involvement of natural parents, claiming that access to the natural family upsets the child and disrupts the foster family, which must live with the child's response to the visit. As evidence, they cite ways in which the child's behaviour deteriorates or shows signs of obvious upset prior to or after visits. They also argue that it is counter-productive to return a child, even for a visit, to a family that presents immoral, inconsistent, or antisocial behavioural models or provides inadequate care and supervision. Foster parents are frequently quite critical and judgmental of natural parents because of how they have treated the child in the past. They may try to protect children from further maltreatment by having all contact with the natural family terminated. There is an often black-and-white, good-and-bad quality to their position: the natural parents are bad because they have abused and neglected the child. In contrast, they, the foster parents, are good because they care for the child in spite of having to endure the difficulties resulting from earlier damage at the hands of the natural parents. At times, even if their criticisms of the natural family and their dislike of the child's visits are not made explicit, foster parents convey enough of their attitude subverbally that the child, in order to placate them, may shun contact with the natural parents in order to avoid upsetting or antagonizing them (Ryan et al 1981; Berridge and Cleaver 1987).

But with foster parents, as with all of us, motives given often rationalize and mask powerful but unconscious and less praiseworthy motivations that are consciously disowned. Foster parents' reasons for raising within their own families children who are so disturbed and disruptive are extremely variable. Many foster mothers, often the motivating force behind the decision to foster and those most involved in the day-to-day care of the child, acknowledge a need to be loved and appreciated by their foster children. It is not uncommon for even a seemingly stable placement to flounder when factors unrelated to fostering, such as the loss of a parent or of a natural child, marital problems, or illness, increase the foster mother's – or parents' – feelings of neediness. At such times, many foster parents either state directly that they are tired of constantly giving while getting nothing in return or demonstrate their neediness behaviourally through an increased frustration with the foster child's inability to respond. At the same time, foster children, despite their often exaggerated need for love, frequently show a diminished ability to tolerate or to return love. Their limited responsiveness frequently frustrates the needs of their foster parents (Ryan et al 1981; Berridge and Cleaver 1987).

A corollary of this need to be given to is found in many foster parents' rivalry with social workers, past foster parents, or natural parents, with whom they feel they are potentially in competition for their foster child's involvement. This rivalry can lead to their sabotaging, often without realizing it, the child's relationship with her social worker, thus decreasing her ability to benefit from ongoing casework. They may also attempt to undercut the child's continuing attachment to the natural parents through repeated criticism of them.

It is easy to see why foster parents, who, day after day, week after week, have to put up with frustrating and disruptive behaviour while doing their best for a difficult child, might resent that child's seeming to care more for the idealized natural parents than for them. Such may especially be the case when the natural parents' neglect or abuse was what brought the child into care and continues to upset her. This situation can lead to explicit comparisons, where the foster parents' criticisms of the natural parents are stubbornly resisted by the child. Foster parents frequently perceive this response as ingratitude by the child, whom they see as valuing the abusive and rejecting natural parents over those who have done so much for her. They fail to recognize that, because the child remains identified with her natural parents, she reacts to any criticism of them as an attack on herself. Such criticism, especially when repeated, not only undermines the child's relationship with the foster parents but, by intensifying her identification with the natural parents, further deflates her self-image by reinforcing her feeling of being bad, immoral, or otherwise unworthy, like her parents.

The foster parents' reaction is further understandable since it is their family who bears the brunt of the child's frustration after each new disappointment by the natural parents. They may recognize that much of her most distressing behaviours – the constant attention-seeking, the excessive demands, the distancing, the aggression and defiance – are displacements onto them of rage deflected from but never expressed to the natural parents. Also, when children are upset after a difficult visit or disappointed when parents fail to show up when expected, it is the foster parents who are left to deal with the child's disappointment and rage. To add insult to injury, their foster children may announce that, as soon as they reach the age of majority, they will return to the natural parents. Such statements are experienced by many foster parents as rejection. After visits, foster children often repeat their natural parents' criticisms to their foster parents. Such criticisms are common, since many natural parents resent others raising the child who has been taken from them, especially if the foster parents are doing a better job or if the child is beginning to become attached to them.

Natural parents, by contrast, typically feel inadequate, powerless, and stigmatized by society's taking away their child. Often, they defend against their guilt and their sense of failure by projecting the blame onto someone else, such as the child, the foster parents, the child-welfare agency, or the courts. The better the child does in care, the more they may see the foster parents as rivals who have succeeded where they, the natural family, had failed (Knitzer, Allen, and McGowan 1978). Often, their own self-esteem is so low and the need to deny and rationalize their overwhelming sense of failure so great that any realistic perception of the child's needs is impossible. As a result, their willingness to cooperate with the foster parents, who, unlike them, have succeeded with their child, can be undermined (Kieffer 1984; Hegar and Hunzeker 1988). Not uncommonly, such natural parents try to turn the child against the foster parents by criticizing them, by trying to buy her allegiance with inappropriately expensive gifts, or by directly encouraging the child to defy the authority of the foster parents. Their resentment and interference may negate the foster parents' readiness to share children with them, accounting for much of their opposition to ongoing access.

For all the above reasons, it is clear why foster parents might perceive a foster child's continuing involvement with her natural family as threatening her becoming a part of the foster family. But, if these are the positions of the foster parents and the natural parents, what about those of the social worker?

Social workers, like foster parents, tend to identify more with the child in care than with the natural parents, towards whom they may be critical and judgmental because of how they have damaged – and how they continue to let down – the children whom they are trying to protect. Because of the natural parents' guilt and feelings of inadequacy, and because the worker represents the agency that has emphasized their failure and helplessness by taking away their child, the natural parents are often extremely hostile, uncooperative, and defensive in ways that are likely to frustrate and antagonize workers. Some workers, especially those who see the natural parents as just as much the victim of their life circumstances as the child is of hers, can get beyond these defensive manoeuvres enough to empathize with the natural parents' underlying feelings of inadequacy and guilt. Many workers, however, are unable to do this. Having lost respect for the natural parents, they fail to recognize their continuing importance to the child in care.

Even if the child is receiving adequate care and is developing well, many workers are also ambivalent towards foster parents. Most workers appreciate and respect those foster parents who provide excellent care, but this is often tempered by their fear for the vulnerability of the placement. Some workers are reluctant to discuss potentially contentious issues with foster parents, lest they antagonize them. Since foster parents often oppose children's contacts with natural parents and are upset when they return to the foster home churned up from visits, some social workers find it hard to insist upon regular contact with natural families, except when the courts have made it mandatory. When feeling helpless in response to foster parents' opposition to such visits, they often fail to confront and work through the foster parents' resistance to them.

The social worker who lacks confidence in the foster parents faces an even more difficult situation. As dissatisfaction and concern mount, they are usually communicated, often subverbally. The foster parents, sensing the unspoken lack of confidence and other negative attitudes, become increasingly alienated from both worker and agency. At this stage, some social workers become competitive with the foster parents, convinced that they can do more for the child than can the foster parents, whom they no longer trust or respect. They may also begin to side with the child against the foster parents in conflicts arising between them. Particularly if the worker routinely sees child and foster parents separately, the casework risks becoming divisive. Such is especially the case if the worker, overidentified with the child, becomes increasingly critical and less empathic towards the foster parents. As foster parents respond to their workers' competitiveness, loss of confidence, and possessiveness, tension between worker and foster family can escalate, bringing disastrous results for the child and the placement (Stanton and Schwartz 1954; Darnell 1988).

In addition to competing with the foster parents in regard to who is more important, more capable of helping, or more loved by the child, social workers, at times, have other reasons for excluding natural families. Often they fear that, by undermining the child's relationship with the foster parents, such contacts will predispose to placement breakdown. The corollary is their hope that, by eliminating contact with the natural parents, the child will be spared being repeatedly upset and will eventually forget them, freeing her to form a secure attachment to the foster parents. But, as we saw in chapter 2, stopping all contact is likelier to favour idealization of the child's fantasy of the absent parents, thus interfering with the detachment needed for a selective reattachment to the foster parents. As long as social workers see visits as an obstacle rather than as a potential asset towards sustaining a placement, they are unlikely to promote regular contacts or to see them as being in the child's best interests.

Ample evidence suggests that a convinced social worker can often persuade foster parents of the importance of ongoing contact with natural parents to the adjustment and development of children in care. Such a worker can resolve their ambivalence enough to allow them not only to tolerate but to assist this through direct work with natural parents (Hazel 1981; Steinhauer 1988; Palmer 1974; Weinstein 1960; Allison and Kufeldt 1987; Ryan et al 1981). Foster parents' support of natural parents may even continue after the child has returned home (Steinhauer et al 1989). In such cases, natural parents, overcoming their initial antagonism and discomfort, can often learn to appreciate what the foster parents are doing for their child and to accept their help in becoming more effective parents, and, in some cases, can even acknowledge that an attempted restoration would undoubtedly have failed but for the continued availability and support of the foster parents (Steinhauer et al 1988). The key is having a social worker who sees clearly and without competition the unique but interrelated roles of social worker, foster parents, and biological parents in the interests of the development of the child (Galaway 1978; Eastman 1979; Howe 1983; Wald, Carlsmith, and Leiderman 1988; Steinhauer 1988). Any distortion in perception of the role that any of these participants in the foster-care system has to play risks undermining the effective functioning of the system as a whole, thus decreasing the likelihood of the child's receiving optimal care.

Shared Parenting: One Way to Protect Children's Best Interests

Thus far in this chapter, I have discussed factors that keep adults in the foster-care system from working together in the interests of the child. Moving from problems to solutions, I now address the question of how members of the system can best protect the child's best interests.

In spite of the extensive literature to the contrary (Fanshel and Shinn 1978; Weinstein 1960; Proch and Howard 1986; Berridge and Cleaver 1987), many professionals have overlooked the possible benefits to a child of growing up in a foster home while maintaining regular contact with natural parents. This oversight is often the result of either/or thinking. The concept of sharing a child between biological and foster parents runs against the widely held myth that children in long-term care should either be restored to their natural families or have all contact with them terminated to free the child for adoption. Behind this line of thinking lie a number of incorrect assumptions. These include: 1 / for the child in long-term care, the best way to ensure continuity of attachment to parental figures is through one or other of the two strategies outlined above; 2 / a child can be attached to only one set of parental figures at any given time; and 3 / any attempt to have a child maintain simultaneous attachments risks causing unnecessary confusion and conflict for the child, and, therefore, putting that child at risk of attachment failure.

These myths are so obviously contradicted by both clinical experience and current knowledge that it is surprising that they are still accepted by so many professionals in the child welfare and children's mental health fields. The first is discussed in some detail in chapter 2.

That the second and third myths continue to be believed as widely as they are indicates a failure to apply within the child welfare area what should have been learned from studies of multiple attachments in clinical observations of children raised in day care (Belsky and Steinberg 1979) and of those whose parents have separated and divorced (Wallerstein 1986; Wallerstein and Blakeslee 1989) to the situation of the child in foster care.

The rapid increase in rates of marriage breakdown and remarriage has exposed a growing number of children to simultaneous involvement – that is, concurrent attachment – to more than one set of parental figures. The result, of course, can be considerable role confusion.

The classical nuclear family of two parents and one or more children had closed boundaries. Either you belonged to it or you didn't. If you did, it was the only nuclear family of which you were a part. Thus everyone had a clearly defined place, either inside or outside the family's boundaries, and no one doubted where he stood in relation to them.

In contrast, the reconstituted family has open boundaries. As a result, its children may be considerably less sure as to which family (or is it families?) they belong. They know, of course, that they have a place in the reconstituted family in which they live most of the time, but that's not all, since they also have another parent who lives elsewhere and who, possibly having remarried, may have started a second reconstituted family. If the child belongs within the reconstituted family of the custodial parent, usually the mother, does he or she not also have a place in the new family of the non-custodial parent? Thus one consequence of membership in a reconstituted family with its open boundaries is an inevitable period of role confusion. This confusion will persist at least until the child has defined his relationships with both the original and the additional parental figures who, based on biology, history, or the act of recoupling, have some claim upon his allegiance, his respect, and his affection.

Now, obviously, the trouble that a given child will have resolving this confusion will vary, partly with his age, but even more so with how the adults involved handle the situation. How clear are they in their own roles and each other's? Is there continuing conflict or competition for loyalty of the child? Can each of them accept the importance of non-interference with the child's relationship with the others, thus minimizing the pressure the child feels while sorting out his own relationships with those adults who play key roles in his life? The more the adults involved can allow and encourage a spontaneous redefinition of roles and relationships – that is, the more open the boundaries – the better the child's chance of accommodating the conflicting demands of membership in more than one family.

But despite the potential confusion faced by children belonging to more than one family – many of whom become attached to more than one set of parental figures – most children survive family breakdown, parental remarriage, and dual family membership surprisingly well. After an upset lasting two to three years, many settle down and show no signs of lasting disturbance. Particularly interesting is Wallerstein and Blakeslee's (1989) more recent demonstration of disturbance appearing after three years in children who, one year following separation, denied and showed no obvious signs of distress. This process suggests one comparable to that described in foster children by Palmer (1974) in which active working through of immediate responses to separation from parental figures is associated with more immediate upset but improved long-term adjustment, whereas avoiding dealing with the child's early responses to separation – that is, collusion with the repression of the normal mourning process – results in less initial upset but increased long-term social, emotional, and educational deficits.

Consider deliberately encouraging a child to develop and maintain attachments to both a natural family and a foster family in any situation in which: 1 / the natural parents cannot and are unlikely to be able to meet in the forseeable future that child's developmental needs; 2 / the child is old enough to continue to remember and remain attached to the biological family; even if removed from it, he will consider it his real family.

Such children do poorly in adoption because they rarely become totally assimilated within the adoptive family, since they are unable to sever all attachments to past parental figures. Attempts to make them relinquish their psychological ties to the biological parents by permanently severing physical contact serve only to perpetuate their idealization and retention in fantasy of the natural parents; while acknowledging 'Sure, they have their problems, but they still love me,' they may persist with almost delusional force in defending their belief in the devotion of natural parents whom they have not seen in years (Kufeldt, Armstrong, and Dorosh 1991).

Whether or not the biological parents care about the child, even if they are consistently unable to meet the child's needs, does not affect the value of agencies encouraging children who are interested in maintaining contact to keep a simultaneous attachment to both natural and foster families. If the parents are caring but marginally adequate, having the child live in the parental home with the foster parents on deck to provide periodic short-term crisis relief in the foster home may provide the best possible placement for the child (Bush and Goldman 1982; Gabinet 1983; Derdeyn 1977, Steinhauer 1983b). Even if the parents are uncaring, rejecting, and/or inconsistent in following up planned contacts, an attempt to encourage the older foster child who remains attached to maintain contact with them is still indicated, although contact should not be forced against the wishes of the child. Such contact, and the cancellations and let-downs often associated with it, give the child a realistic picture of the parents' inherent limitations (Kufeldt, Armstrong, and Dorosh 1991). It can provide the catalyst around which the work of mourning takes place. Such disappointments will undermine the child's idealized fantasies of the parents, keeping before him the true reasons for his being in care. This awareness is frequently particularly important since highly ambivalent and guilty parents often tell their children that they want them home, blaming the agency for the family separation. As one ex-ward put it, 'Don't protect us so much. Especially at first, we won't believe what you tell us about what our parents are like. We have to find out for ourselves' (Fein et al 1983; Steinhauer 1983b). Unopposed distortion of reality in a child's fantasies encourages displacement of hostility from natural parents to agency and foster parents. The child is left both angry at and unable to bond successfully to the parental surrogates, thus undermining the stability of that and subsequent foster placement.

The following example is included to show how, given appropriate support by foster parents and worker, even a very young child can, at times, make the best of a bad situation if her parenting is shared between her natural and foster families:

I first met Sandy in April 1977, when she was four and a half years old. At that time, she had been living in a foster home since age three. She had arrived badly nourished, poorly cared for, withdrawn, frightened, and behind in her social, cognitive, and language development.

Sandy came into care when her mother, a chronic schizophrenic, who loved her but was unable to care for her, had been hospitalized. The mother was later discharged from hospital on medication. She never missed a chance to visit Sandy in her foster home, and told the agency that she wanted Sandy returned to her. The agency did not question her love for Sandy, but doubted her ability to meet her child's needs. Also in the mother's home was Sandy's eighteen-year-old sister and Sandy's father, a known alcoholic, who was constantly in and out. I was asked to help decide what plan was in Sandy's best interests. I did so by seeing Sandy in three situations. First, I saw her alone, then together with her foster parents, and finally in a third interview with her mother and teenage sister. I concluded by seeing Sandy alone twice more.

Sandy had clearly made excellent developmental progress in her foster home. Her physical health was good. She had given up a number of nervous mannerisms, and her speech, severely retarded when she came into care, was now age-appropriate. Her relationships with other children were increasingly normal. Most of the time she seemed much less sad and withdrawn, although she still withdrew when upset.

In her individual interviews, Sandy was one of the saddest and most pathetic little girls I had ever seen – inhibited, withdrawn, and unable to play. If she tried to, the result was joyless. She mechanically arranged doll furniture again and again. She barely talked and, when she did, could say only how much she missed her mother. As she did, she began to cry, and from that point there was just no consoling her. It was one of the few times in my then sixteen years of practice that I was totally unable to put a child at ease or comfort her.

When seen with her foster parents, however, Sandy showed active interest in what was being said about her. She related well to her foster mother, frequently initiating interaction with her and seeking her out for help or comfort. She played well and independently for most of the session. Sandy seemed surprised when her foster mother broke down while talking about the possibility of the court deciding to remove Sandy from her care. She asked her foster mother why she was in the foster home, and the foster mother replied that since her own mother was unable to care for her, they were doing the best they could. By the end of the first interview, I had concluded that Sandy was a very sad little girl who was badly missing her natural mother. Her mother still mattered a great deal, even though she had an excellent foster mother in whose care she was obviously thriving.

The next week, I saw Sandy both alone and with her natural mother and teenage sister. It was clear that however much her mother and Sandy wanted to be reunited, there was no way that this could work. The mother was apathetic and withdrawn. There was almost no meaningful contact between the two of them. Sandy perched uncomfortably on the edge of her mother's chair, remaining passive while her mother, inappropriately, stroked her. She never talked, looked, or responded to her mother. When asked about her plans for the future, the mother's judgment and planning ability were seriously defective. My conclusion at the end of that interview was that the mother's illness made it impossible for her to adequately care for Sandy, let alone meet her developmental and emotional needs. Sandy's eighteen-year-old sister, reluctantly and tearfully, agreed that any attempt to return Sandy home would be disastrous for both her mother and Sandy, especially since she was about to leave the home herself.

Thus, by this point, it was clear that Sandy's mother was important to Sandy and vice versa, but that the extent of the mother's illness and the unlikelihood of significant improvement made it extremely unlikely that Sandy could return home. When then? One possibility was to sever all contact between them, in the hope of forcing Sandy to detach herself from her mother to free her to form a substitute attachment to her adoptive parents. I decided against this tack as it was too risky. Sandy's age, the depth of obvious attachment to her mother, and the progress she had made in her foster home while enjoying ongoing contact with her mother made it inconceivable to deprive these two of each other.

Instead, it made more sense for Sandy to remain to maturity in the foster home, but to continue to visit her mother and sister on a regular basis. Our hope was that, over a period of time, Sandy would learn to turn to her foster parents to meet most of her needs while, at the same time, developing a realistic understanding of her mother's love for her, her mother's limitations, and why it was necessary that they live apart. Perhaps eventually more and more of the attachment needs would be shifted to the foster parents, so that the mother would increasingly become more like a member of the extended family (e.g., a caring aunt, grandmother) to be visited, but not to be lived with.

This course would ask a lot of Sandy's foster parents. We were asking them to care for a child whom they had come to love, bearing in mind that she would always have a mother of her own. They would never be her parents exclusively, and would always have to share her with her mother. The foster parents knew that this would be hard on them, but recognized that it would be best for Sandy. They agreed to try it. This situation, though by no means ideal, was, of the available alternatives, the one least likely to prove damaging as long as the following conditions could be met: if the foster parents could allow themselves to share Sandy, and to allow her, with their help and that of their social worker, to sort out, over time, her own relationship with her mother; if they could avoid competing with her mother for Sandy's affections and loyalty. If these were possible, Sandy would be free to maintain attachments to both her parents and her foster parents, taking from each what she could.

Time passed. For a number of reasons, related more to various participants' holidays, lawyers' commitments to other concurrent cases, crowded court dockets, etc., the court hearing was delayed by over six months. Therefore, I suggested to the supervising CAS worker that my six-month-old report might be out of date. I asked to reassess Sandy alone, with her foster parents, and together with her mother to see if the plan that had then seemed best remained valid. I want to describe one section of this reassessment in detail.

Sandy, who seemed much more secure, happy, and communicative than she had been when seen six months earlier, sat on her mother's lap, while her mother continued to stroke and caress her in a rather mechanical way. Sandy tolerated this without response. The mother asked Sandy if she liked living in the foster home. Sandy replied that she did, but that she would prefer to be at home with her mother. This pleased the mother, who smiled and repeated it to me. Sandy then, spontaneously, went on to state that, while she would prefer living with her mother, she was better off in her foster home. This confused her mother, who then asked if this meant that Sandy would prefer to live in the foster home. Sandy replied that she would prefer to live with her mother but that 'it is best' for her to remain with her foster mother because the foster parents took better care of her because her mother was sick. Her mother responded that she was better now. Sandy looked at her quizzically and replied, 'I don't think so. I think it's better for me to stay in the foster home.' Her mother, crying, put her arms around her, sobbing that she loved Sandy. Sandy replied, with great tenderness, that she loved her mother too, but that it was still best that she remain in her foster home because they could care for her best, although she would always continue to love and visit her mother.

What had occurred in the six months since the original assessment suggested that what we had hoped to achieve seemed possible. Sandy was flourishing in the care of her foster parents who were providing her with the security and stimulation she needed on a day-to-day basis. Changes in Sandy and in her ability to understand and tolerate the ambiguity of her situation had resulted from the work of the foster parents in interpreting the decision, and the reasons for it, and in helping her accept it. The visits with the mother, rather than interfering with Sandy's attachment to her foster mother, seemed to be helping Sandy develop a realistic picture of her mother's illness. She could see her mother as loving her but unable to care for her. This freed her to attach to the foster parents without guilt.

A follow-up conducted more than ten years later found Sandy a vital and well-adjusted adolescent. Well-integrated within her foster family, she was an honours student with a number of close friends and a variety of interests. While close to all members of her foster family, she also maintained a close relationship with her natural mother and sister, whom she saw at least weekly and talked to on the phone regularly. She was very appreciative of the agency's decision to take her into care, stating that it had worked out best for everyone, but especially her.

If a shared parenting arrangement is to be helpful rather than confusing, all the adults involved (foster parents, natural parents, and social worker) will need to be clear on and agreed as to what constitutes their respective roles in the life of the child, avoiding competion with each other for the child's allegiance. Any attempt by the natural parents of a child in planned permanent foster care to use visits to promise that the child will soon come home or to undermine her relationship with the foster parents will inevitably prove confusing and upsetting. Such parents should be warned that the shared parenting arrangement can succeed only if they are prepared to stop the tug-of-war for the child's affections and to respect and support the role of the foster parents as the child's primary caretakers. Some natural parents can do this; their children, as a result, end up getting the best out of both sets of parents (Ryan et al 1981; Bush and Gordon 1982; Gabinet 1983; Steinhauer 1983b; Kufeldt and Allison 1990). For those who cannot, terminating the visits at least temporarily may be necessary, should the resulting upset be more than child and foster family, even with support, can tolerate. Should the natural parents show that they can confine themselves to the role assigned them in the child's management plan, this decision can be reconsidered. At that point, visits might be cautiously reinitiated, if they appear to be in the child's best interests.

Chapter Nine

Visits of Foster Children
with Their Natural Families

The proper regulation of visits of foster children with their natural parents is an issue of great but often underestimated importance (M.S. White 1981). Far too often, decisions regarding visits are made either for or against with no rational basis whatsoever (Proch and Howard 1986). Yet a systematic policy regarding visits should be an integral part of every foster child's management plan. Whether or not a given child should have visits; the frequency and duration of such visits; where, when, and under whose supervision they should occur – all should be determined in advance. Courts, at times, order visits according to what they consider the natural parents' right of access. Wherever possible, Children's Aid societies should attempt to define and advocate the type of access best meeting the needs of a particular child. The following guidelines may prove useful in deciding upon and updating the visiting policy for a given child.

Visits can often be stressful for any or all of those involved, especially before a stable visiting routine has been established. Such is particularly true if any of those involved – foster child, natural parents, foster parents, or worker and agency – are opposed to visits that have been imposed upon them either by court order or by an agency's decision.

Visits are often accompanied by intense but mixed feelings. These may include excitement, happiness, sadness and loss, anger and loss of control, or fear of repeated abuse or of disruption of a placement in which a previously abused child feels safe. Visits may make a child feel guilty that she cannot meet the needs or expectations of either the foster or the natural parents. In his definitive discussion of this topic, Barnum

(1987) has pointed out that, at times, these feelings may be so intense that they may overwhelm, frighten, or upset any or all of those involved. Visits may precipitate signs of regression – whining, demanding, babyish behaviours – especially in younger children. Generalized tension as the visit approaches may present as hyperactivity and inattention, or as provocativeness and oppositionality in response to limits that can trigger verbal or physical aggressiveness or destructive behaviours. Older children may become depressed and/or withdrawn around visits, or may show other signs of anxiety, or such symptoms as headaches or abdominal pains, with or without frankly opposing the visit. Such feelings usually peak around times of transition from one family to the other, and although any of these behaviours may occur while the child is with the natural family, they are usually more common within the foster family.

The adults involved may also find visits difficult, adding to the difficulties of the child. Foster parents, as we have seen, are often competitive with and critical of natural parents. Some overtly sabotage visits imposed upon them by the sponsoring agency or the court. More often, however, their negative feelings about visiting are communicated unconsciously, increasing the child's uncertainties and guilt and arousing tension and anxiety at the time of the transition.

Natural parents may find visits difficult for a number of reasons. What may at first appear to be a lack of interest in visiting may be just that, but it may also be an avoidance of contact because of the feelings of inadequacy, depression, rage, helplessness, humiliation, and guilt that a time-limited and often stranger-supervised visit may evoke. The fact that the duration, timing, and location of the visit are controlled by others may increase feelings of loss of control. In response, natural parents may shy away from this whole complex of feelings, or, in a counterphobic manner, may be hostile or provocative to the supervising worker or foster parent. Alternatively, they may seek to consolidate their position with the child by lavish gifts or special activities, using these to assuage their guilt or to express feelings they cannot articulate. These actions may stem from an attempt to achieve a closeness they long for but cannot have, or may merely be their way of masking the conflicted feelings that both they and the child have about each other and about the awkward and unnatural situation in which they find themselves.

In view of such contradictory feelings, it is not surprising that there may be considerable resistance at times to visits on the part of any of those involved. Barnum (1987) has classified such resistances as arising from three sources: some stem from feelings and psychological conflicts of the child related to the visit; others originate primarily from the natural family; some originate within the foster family; usually, they arise from any combination of these. All too often, in practice, these resistances are viewed simplistically in either/or terms: the foster parents are seen as sabotaging the visits, or the child is accused of manipulating, or the child is considered to be upset by seeing the natural parents. But these are gross oversimplifications. A child can be upset because a visit stirs up feelings of sadness and loss, or because she is afraid that she will be abused on her visit as she used to be before coming into care. She might also feel guilty because she knows how upsetting the visits are to her natural mother or because she senses her foster mother's unspoken fear or opposition to them. She may be frightened because she is anxious about being dragged into a tug-of-war for her loyalties by a rejecting or abusive parent who uses the visits to secure the allegiance by trying to subvert her relationship with the foster family, whom she may fear losing. Obviously these are but a few of the many possibilities that may contribute to resistance to visits. Since all the principals may have their own difficulties around visiting, caseworkers and consultants may run into intense resistance when they attempt to explore exactly who doesn't want the visits, and why. The examples above are listed to illustrate the complexity and the multi-determined nature of resistance to visits, and to make the point that, until one clearly understands where the resistance is coming from in a given case, one cannot understand the problem or how to resolve it. Such clarity is often difficult to come by, since those opposing the visits may deny their opposition, externalizing and projecting it onto others in their attempt to achieve the desired disruption (Wald, Carlsmith, and Leiderman 1988; Berridge 1985).

Thus resistance to visiting is a sign of tension within the foster care system, but whether it reflects disturbance in the child, in the natural family, in the foster family, or in any combination of these will become clear only when one understands its basis.

In spite of these disincentives, most natural mothers, at least, do visit their children in care if the provision for their doing so on a regular basis is built into the agency's management plan for the child (Millham et al 1986). If regular visits are not scheduled by the agency, however, parents are much less likely to remain in contact (Proch and Howard 1986).

Regular visiting of children in care is highly associated with their returning home (Fanshel and Shinn 1978; Kadushin 1980; Zimmerman 1982; Mech 1985). Unfortunately, however, visiting plans often reflect more the general style of worker and agency than the needs of a particular child and family (Festinger 1983). Thus, even 30 per cent of children slated to return home had no visits planned for them (Proch and Howard 1986).

If, then, visits are so often resisted by all those involved, when is visiting in a child's best interests in spite of the tensions it may arouse?

1 / *Visits to avoid agency-created or court-created abandonment.* As long as a child may be returned to the natural parents, agencies must ensure that what was intended as a temporary or interim placement is not allowed, by neglect, to develop into a permanent one (Steinhauer 1977). This situation poses particular danger to infants and toddlers, who are especially vulnerable to remaining in limbo when separated for even a few days, from their major attachment figures. Despairing that they may never see them again, they rapidly begin to form a substitute attachment to the foster mother, who will, within days or weeks, eclipse the natural mother and become the child's psychological parent. Should the child then be returned home or moved to a long-term foster home, he would be subjected to a second, and this time unnecessary, separation, since the natural parents, whom the child has forgotten through the absence of visits, will have become psychological strangers (Goldstein, Freud and Solnit 1973). Having biological parents visit such children on a regular and sufficient basis helps protect the temporary nature of an interim placement by reminding the child – and by bolstering the attachment to – the natural parents. Such children, while remaining attached to the natural mother, will form a secondary attachment to the foster parent. To achieve this, daily visits for infants and children under age two, preferably with some active participation in the care of the child, and two- or three-times-weekly visits for children between the ages of two and four are recommended.

Such visits may be upsetting at the time, but so are visits of parents to a toddler in hospital. Being upset when the parent leaves is just the normal child's reaction to separation from a parent to whom she remains attached. It would be inconceivable to discourage parents from visiting children in hospital on the grounds that such visits are upsetting. It is no less necessary that infants and young children temporarily in care have their attachment to their primary caretakers protected, as long as any possibility of restoration to the natural family exists (Littner 1971).

There may, of course, be other reasons for the child's upset around visits, so the particular child's reaction should be explored, as described above.

For older children and adolescents coming into care, regular but less frequent visits may be no less useful, though here the developmental rationale for visiting differs. At this age, regular visiting is often intended to maintain, if possible, that child's place in the natural family that is in the process of extruding him, at least to protect for the child the possibility of improving family relationships as long as this remains an option, even if the child remains in care (Knitzer, Allen, and McGowan 1978; Wiltse 1978; Burke and Dawson 1987; Kufeldt, Armstrong, and Dorosh 1991). Most older foster children are likely to recontact or return to their families at some future point. For them, planned temporary admissions at points of crisis can, if properly managed, mobilize families' greater accessibility to intervention during crisis. Visits may make it possible to work towards improved communication, to increase members' ability to identify and begin to resolve their common problems, and to enhance their ability to cope more contructively with tensions that cannot be resolved.

Proposing visits may evoke resistance from children and/or from the natural parents, who, at the point of entry into care, may want nothing to do with each other. Agency collusion with such resistances risks exacerbating the existing scapegoating of the child. Also the interaction occurring on or around such visits can often be used to shift the natural family towards a more cohesive, less dysfunctional equilibrium. If this balance is achieved, then the child will not just be sent back to an equally or even more disturbed family system in which his behaviour is likely to regress significantly (Wolf, Brankmann, and Ramp 1987; Bank, Patterson, and Reid 1987; Rzepnicki 1987; Weinstein 1960). Even should the child remain in care, such efforts will not have been wasted, as they can do much to clarify the confusion leading to the original entry into care, thus providing the basis for an eventual understanding – and a coming to grips with – feelings and conflicts contributing to and remaining from the family breakdown.

2 / *Visits to catalyse the work of mourning.* As we saw in chapter 7, much of the work of mourning can be catalysed by alert and involved foster parents' and/or caseworkers' responses to feelings stirred up before, during, and after a child's visits. We have seen how tenaciously children seek to avoid the work of mourning, either by acting as if their

loss had not occurred or by dealing with it only in an intellectualized and mechanical way. We have also seen how the symptomatic derivatives of unsuccessful attempts to repress the overpowering rage, grief, anxiety, and mistrust evoked by the loss may result in displacement onto foster parents, teachers, social workers, or others, without the child realizing why he is so angry or whom he really resents. Initial attempts to suggest that much of this anger is a displacement are usually denied; even if the child intellectually recognizes a connection, it often fails to change his feelings or behaviour, which have lost contact with their source. Until feelings can be re-experienced, the child is not free to complete the work of mourning and will remain in limbo (Wilkes 1989). Without this re-experiencing, attempts to assist mourning by talking with the child about the separation or the parents he has lost are usually counter-productive. Visits provide one opportunity to re-establish this feeling of connection, thus reactivating and assisting the aborted mourning process.

Immediately following admission to care, often the last thing a child wants is contact with the family that has excluded him or from whom he has been removed. Nevertheless, the more abrupt and upsetting the separation and the less clearly and directly the reasons for it have been articulated, the more likely the child may be to blame himself for the family breakdown and the greater the potential value for child and family of facing each other in the presence of an experienced caseworker to confront and clarify their various perceptions of the issues and feelings around the breakdown (Weinstein 1960; Palmer 1974; Kufeldt, Armstrong, and Dorosh 1991). In order to mourn the loss successfully, the child must directly confront his feelings about it. This confrontation can sometimes be achieved only after the breakdown itself. Palmer (1974) has shown that children who *did* visit their families shortly after coming into care talked considerably more about their responses to the separation. While initially more visibly upset than those who had no further contact with their families, in the long run their adjustment was better than that of other children who had not been encouraged to mourn their loss.

For other children, the work of mourning may have been blocked. When there is no history of a child having mourned; when that child's relationships and behaviour are dominated by the signs of aborted mourning; when all attempts to modify the child's current attitudes and behaviour get nowhere while the inner core of depression, rage, and alienation remains untouched – then visits may be first discussed and then initiated in order to reactivate a dormant mourning process. The various ways in which visits can catalyse and assist a blocked mourning process are discussed in chapter 7. It is not just the visits themselves that are important; it is their use to mobilize memories and feelings that have been repressed. Thus, the dealing with the feelings and thoughts that accompany visiting, helping prepare the child, encouraging him to experience and verbalize his responses as visits approach or his reactions after visits are over can assist the work of mourning.

Many children whose mourning has been aborted may benefit from such visits. The child who complains of not having contact with his family but never asks that a visit be set up is a good example. Discussion of why he never asks for visits, the discrepancy between how he acts and what he says he wants, his feelings about a proposed visit, his reactions to the visit itself, and his altered behaviour following the visits may help the child re-experience feelings long repressed or avoided.

The child who either avoids mentioning or who idealizes what went on during each visit while consistently showing upset or withdrawn behaviour after them is providing behavioural clues suggesting persistent unresolved conflicts about his parents. Some children easily see the connection between their behaviour and the inner conflict stirred up by visits. Others may have to stop visits temporarily to gain enough control over the feelings they arouse to talk about them instead of acting them out. In either case, the visits, along with the reactions they evoke, may be the key to helping the child reactivate and proceed with the essential work of mourning. Again, while such behaviours may signify a resumption of mourning, there are also other possible reasons for them. The child's feeling about the visits and those of the natural parents and foster parents would have to be understood before the reason for the upset could be assumed.

Visits with key people from a child's past may help a child establish a sense of historical continuity and coherence. Children moved from family to family often lack such a sense, so that life, to them, seems not one continuous strand but a series of disconnected episodes, none of which seems very real. Visits with selected key figures, along with the discussion that precedes and follows them, may help make the past real, tying it together and connecting it with the child's present. (See example of Debby, page 155.)

3 / *The use of visits to undermine idealization of natural parents to whom a strong but negative bonding exists.* Some older children who have long

been without contact with parents whose inability to parent has been proved repeatedly and beyond a doubt may persistently demand such contact. Denying contact encourages them to idealize the love of the absent but, possibly, flawed parents in fantasy, thus alienating the child even farther from current caretakers. Their requests for visits may be symptomatic of their struggle with their feelings of unresolved loss. The child may need a chance to explore these feelings, and to compare them with what exists in his reality. It may be helpful to attempt to arrange one or more visits, with the fact that these are *just* visits – and not a step towards restoration – being made clear. Should the parents reject the requested contact, the feelings aroused can be discussed directly with the child. If the visits proceed, often the reality of what the child experiences will contrast so markedly with his idealized fantasies that he may be much more able to appreciate why he is in care (Fein et al 1983; Kadushin 1980). Again, it is not the visits themselves as much as how they are utilized to release the child's feelings and correct his fantasies about his natural family that can assist potential resolution.

4 / *The use of visits to encourage shared parenting between natural and foster parents.* Some older children and adolescents who are unable to return to their natural families remain attached to them even though well established in foster homes. Often their natural families, though unable to meet their needs, continue to care about them. For some such children, the least detrimental alternative involves their living away from home while maintaining regular access to the natural family (Gabinet 1983; see also the case of Sandy in chapter 8). Such an arrangement can work only when all involved – child, foster parents, foster family, and social worker – are clear on the reasons for and the limitations of the contacts. Initially, child and family may fantasize that the visits will eventually lead to the child's returning home. If so, the disappointment at having to live apart will come up around visits, demanding that the limitations and purpose of the contacts be spelled out and worked through, as they may need to be again and again.

5 / *Situations in which visits with natural parents should not be allowed.* Visits can, at times, be used by combative and/or litigious natural parents – or can be allowed by agencies that lack an effective and aggressive planning process – to block a child's being severed from even a severely and chronically neglectful and/or abusive family, thus blocking any possibility of such a child being placed on adoption. In some such cases,

visits may diametrically oppose the child's best interests. These, and not the wishes of the parents, should be the primary consideration in determining access for the child in care.

Visits without a purpose, or ones lacking a place in an overall plan of management, are rarely helpful. Visits without the discussion and working through that should accompany them may encourage wishful fantasy, thus helping the child and natural parents avoid rather than face reality. Some children, long after no realistic possibility of their returning to their families remains, continue to deny the finality of an unwanted separation. Such children may utilize ongoing visits, especially weekly ones often left over from a time when family reunion had not been decided against, to shore up their wishful fantasies. Such children are not free to form a meaningful attachment in their current placement, as long as they cling so desperately to the fantasy of family reunion in the face of what should be obvious reality (Gean, Gillmore, and Dowler 1985; Nickman 1986; Kufeldt, Armstrong, and Dorosh 1991). In such cases, spacing out or even discontinuing further visits, at least temporarily, may effectively force child and family to face the reality of the breakdown and the fact of separation. Again the reasons for doing so should be openly and clearly discussed, and acting out or withdrawal subsequent to the termination of visiting should be considered a response to the loss of family contacts. The basic principle remains: it is not the presence or absence of visits, but the degree to which the child faces and deals successfully with both the facts and the associated feelings and fantasies of his life history, that is the real issue.

Visits may, at times, be so upsetting, especially to an older child, that the child may request that they be discontinued. In such cases, the reasons for the upset and the request for termination should be carefully explored. Such exploration may allow the sensitive and alert foster parent or worker to help the child and/or families recognize and work through some of the pain related to the limitations of their relationships and/or their separations from each other. After doing as much as possible with this, the worker would normally leave the decision of whether or not to visit up to the older child, at least for the time being. If the child opted to stop the visits, the worker would then check back periodically to determine how the child was then feeling about the parents and about the earlier decision to terminate the contacts.

If the child, after discussion, as described above, remained so upset that his behaviour or distress related to visits could not be tolerated or contained, the worker would first explore the psychological and contextual factors contributing to the upset. If the role of the child's, the natural parents', and the foster parents' contributions and their effects on one another were understood, it should then be possible to identify and begin working through each participant's contribution to the problem. When this had been done, the worker would then try to achieve a consensus around whether or not to proceed with the visiting, in the same or a modified format, depending on the source of the difficulties identified. In doing so, she would make clear to the child and to the adults involved why the schedule had been altered and what emotional or behavioural changes would have to occur before the situation could be reconsidered.

Finally, one should, in investigating visits that have an aftermath of upset behaviour, attempt to pinpoint exactly who was most upset by the visits, the child or the foster parents. Foster parents hostile to or competitive with the child's natural parents can make a child feel disloyal to them if that child enjoys such visits. They may also exaggerate how upset the child was before or after visits in an attempt to stop them. The fact that it is the foster parents that are at the root of such an upset is usually obvious if one assesses the situation carefully. One would then attempt to work with the foster parents' resistance to the visiting process, hoping to help them allow the child to continue the visits without feeling disloyal to them. If, despite one's best efforts, the foster parents cannot overcome their opposition to the visits, one may have to review the child's plan of management and make a choice between continued parental access or risking the placement. In such cases, the choice would have to reflect the importance of each set of parental figures to the current adjustment and ongoing development of the child.

PART FOUR

System-Related Issues

Chapter Ten

The Foster Care Service System

An examination of the relationship between the child welfare agency, the foster parents, the biological parents, and the child in care will enable us to define how the caseworker can best enhance the quality and permanence of a placement. To begin, consider some differences between traditional and specialized foster care, summarized in table 10.1.

It is overly optimistic, at best, if not frankly naïve, to assume that the older and already damaged children currently coming into care will obtain the quality of care they need in most traditional foster families (Berridge and Cleaver 1987, pp. 182–3; Cooper 1978; Darnell 1987; Frank 1980; Hepworth 1980; Steinhauer 1970, 1983b). Such is especially the case when those families have been minimally prepared for fostering, while receiving only occasional and often irregular visits from an often inexperienced caseworker from the sponsoring agency. It is misleading, however, to suggest that in such cases a child needs 'specialized foster care,' since most children in 'ordinary' foster homes these days are just as disturbed – and equally disturbing to the day-to-day life of the foster family (Darnell 1988; Hochstadt et al 1987; Allison and Kufeldt 1987).

Experienced social workers and child welfare officials are already aware of this fact, but, in view of current funding and the organization of most foster care systems, they often have little option but to continue to repeat the wasteful and destructive process set in motion when a seriously disturbed child is placed in a foster family unable to tolerate and successfully deal with him (Steinhauer 1983b; Berridge and Cleaver 1987).

This change in the nature of the children coming into foster care has

TABLE 10.1
Comparison of traditional and specialized foster homes (Children's Servies Division 1979)

	Traditional foster home	Specialized foster home
Role of foster parents	Parent surrogates: provide basic care	Provide basic care and treatment program (i.e., parent-therapists, not parent surrogates)
Types of children	Chiefly infants and young children	Chiefly older and 'special needs' children with mental, physical, emotional, and behavioural problems requiring not just care but active treatment
Motivation	Primarily voluntary: not paid for time or service	Primarily a career choice; paid for time and services provided
Funding	Boarding and maintenance allowance	Boarding and maintenance allowance *plus* increment related to special services provided (treatment, etc.)
Goal	Normalization	Remediation
Training of foster parents	None required	Ongoing training and supervision would be expected; previous professional training might not be required, depending on program
Services offered	Contract to provide basic care and to cooperate in plan to return child home or prepare child for adoptive placement if possible or, otherwise, to foster to maturity	Contract to provide basic care and to cooperate with agency in implementation of management and treatment plan designed to meet the needs of the child. Might include work with biological parents towards a return home, preparation for adoption, providing a therapeutic milieu as prescribed, possibly recontracting to provide planned permanent foster or adoptive care
Disruption of family life-style	Usually minimal	Usually considerable

led to considerable role diffusion and confusion in the minds of many foster parents (Wolins 1963; Katz 1976; Berridge and Cleaver 1987, p. 183; Eastman 1979; Mietus and Fimmen 1987). Any change in a traditional role initiates a period of role confusion and heightened role conflict and anxiety. In itself, this situation can cause additional stress, both for the individual and for the system, of which each individual is just one part. Thus, change in the role of foster parents has necessitated a reciprocal adjustment in the role of social workers and in the working relationships with foster parents (Steinhauer et al 1988; Tinney 1985; Rosenblum 1977; Pasztor and Burgess 1982).

Many foster parents today are unclear as to whether they are *parent surrogates* (which they traditionally were, and which many would still like to consider themselves) or *surrogate therapists* (which, with the older age and higher levels of disturbance of children coming into care, they are increasingly forced to be). Many foster parents, without recognizing it, define themselves as the former but face all the pressures and frustrations, but few of the benefits, of the latter. While exceptions exist, by and large foster parents need to begin to see themselves – and to be treated by social workers and agencies – as surrogate therapists and colleagues instead of as parent surrogates and clients, since increasingly they are expected to provide not just accommodation but a therapeutic milieu within their home and family (Steinhauer et al 1988, 1989; Ryan et al 1981; Stapleton 1987). For this reason, traditional or 'ordinary' fostering is no longer sufficient to meet the needs of the average child in care (Allison and Kufeldt 1987; Steinhauer 1983b; Berridge and Cleaver 1987, p. 183). Standard care, to be adequate, must, in most cases, approach what in the past was once defined as specialized foster care (Burland 1980; Cooper 1978; Hepworth 1980; Lawson 1982; Darnell 1988; Appathurai et al 1986; Hochstadt et al 1987; Stapleton 1987).

The effects on a family of fostering a disturbed child are finally beginning to be discussed openly, although generally they remain insufficiently appreciated (Steinhauer 1970, 1983b; Gruber 1978; Derr 1983; Berridge and Cleaver 1987, pp. 165–7; Hepworth 1980; Wilkes 1979; Johnston 1989). There has been a curious reluctance to face and act upon what has been obvious all along. The chronic and, recently, increasingly acute shortage of adequate experienced foster homes in most jurisdictions has led, far too often, to many excellent foster homes being abused by being treated as if they had inexhaustible resources. Too little care is taken to avoid overloading them. They are given too little chance to express reservations about a proposed placement (Evertnam and Brazeau 1984; Lynes 1983). Foster families far too often receive inadequate training and insufficient supervision and back-up, and there is too little concern about the effects on them of fostering too many disturbed children at any one time (Wilkes 1979; Johnston 1989). This unintentional overtaxing of foster families results from the combined pressure of the general shortage of foster homes, excessive caseloads (Aldridge and Cautley 1975), an insufficient appreciation of the extent of the stress generated by the more disturbed children in care – funding sources have very practical (economic) reasons to deny any significant change in the nature of foster care – and agencies' desperate need to find placements for those children who have been rejected and extruded from everywhere else. The effects of such overloading on fostering families, and especially on their natural children and other foster children, who, prior to the overloading, were developing quite well, are often recognized only too late, after the family has lost the willingness to continue to foster. As long as foster parents continue to see themselves just as parent surrogates, they will place excessive and unrealistic expectations both on themselves and on the already disturbed children in their care. Until the change in their role is fully appreciated, both by agencies and by government departments of social services, foster parents will continue to go without the recognition, the remuneration, the training, the support, and/or the professional back-up they need. This situation has major implications for foster-parent recruitment, development, morale, and retention (Hazel 1981; Steinhauer 1983b; Smith and Guthiel 1988).

We know that there is an association between the experience level of social workers and their effectiveness in prevention (M.A. Jones 1985), in dealing with the sequelae of separation (S. Palmer 1974; Aldridge and Cautley 1975), and in preventing foster home breakdowns (Berridge and Cleaver 1987, pp. 154–5). There is every reason to suspect that experience is no less valuable in foster parents; that this is so is suggested by surveys that demonstrate greater effectiveness in foster parents over the age of forty (Berridge and Cleaver 1987, pp. 86, 124; Trasler 1960; George 1970). Therefore, the recent and accelerating loss of foster parents will affect the quality of fostering, as well as the quantity, choice, and potential for matching and preparation of services available. It will also contribute to foster-parent burn-out, ultimately leading many experienced foster parents to cease fostering, often after a more or less consciously recognized period of diminished commitment and sensitivity. It will, secondarily, contribute to increased alienation, as foster parents become distrustful, oppositional, contentious, and defensive in their dealings with the agency (Hepworth 1980; Steinhauer 1983b).

But exactly what does it mean to suggest that foster parents must be expected to function as surrogate or parent therapists? Part of taking and holding any therapeutic stance involves achieving and maintaining an appropriate distance from one's client, a difficult task under any circumstances, but especially so when the relationship continues without relief on a daily basis within a family setting. Nevertheless, some experienced foster parents recognize the protection provided for both them and the child when their role is primarily defined as therapeutic rather than parental (Barker 1978). Crucial to this redefinition is the acceptance of the foster parent as a team member rather than a client of the social agency (Freeman 1978; Reistroffer 1972). Thus foster parents must begin to see themselves – and, equally important, must be seen by workers – as the primary influence on the child, with the social worker's role centring less on direct casework than on supporting, supervising, and strengthening the foster family's ability to understand and help the child. Numerous reports suggest that foster parents who are treated as colleagues and are actively involved in decision making are more likely to obtain job satisfaction and less likely to burn out (Darnell 1988; Hazel 1981; Steinhauer et al 1988, 1989; Rubenstein et al 1978). There is no room for competition around who is more important to the child, foster parents or social worker; both are important, but in different ways.

The importance of worker continuity to both foster children and foster families is generally greatly underrated (Pardeck 1984; Steinhauer 1983b). Worker continuity becomes no less important if foster parents are acknowledged as the primary therapeutic influence on the child. The worker's role is analogous to that of the child psychiatrist or clinical psychologist treating a disturbed child within the natural family. Unless somehow that therapist or a collaborator can modify the family system so that it supports desirable functioning and attitudes in the child originally identified as the patient, any attempt to change the child via one-to-one therapy in one, two, or even three sessions a week is fighting an uphill battle. Furthermore, any experienced child therapist recognizes that, for any child caught in a struggle between therapist and parents, the therapeutic process stalls and the child deteriorates until the competition and/or conflict between them is successfully resolved. Competition between foster parents, especially experienced ones, and social

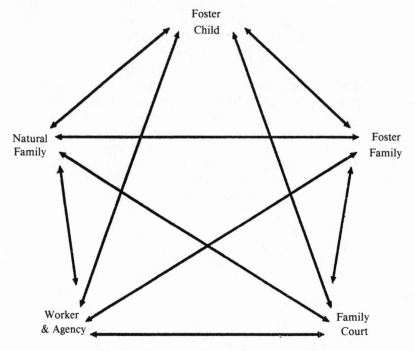

Figure 10.1   The foster-care service system

workers around who is more important or who can do more for a child, though often unrecognized, is much too frequent and always destructive (Harari, Hosey, and Sheedy 1979). Even the best social worker can no more take the place of the foster parents than a child psychiatrist can replace the child's parents. The sooner this is accepted, the more social workers will be freed to define their role vis-à-vis foster parents, and the more likely they are to begin to work with foster parents as colleagues rather than as clients. Thus, the emphasis will shift to defining how they, as social workers, can best ensure the effective working of the foster-care service system (Eastman 1797; Howe 1983; Wiltse 1978; Wald et al 1988), diagramatically represented in figure 10.1.

What matters in this redefinition is not whom the social worker sees. Workers may see the foster family together, or child and foster parents separately. Or they may vary their approach from week to week, depending on their personal styles and their understanding of the needs

of the case at any given time. It is far more important that their interventions take into account the tensions within the total foster-care service system rather than concentrate exclusively upon the needs of any
part (subsystem) of it.

One problem that commonly undermines effective collaboration between foster parents and social workers stems from an inability of each
to trust the other. Let us examine how this often appears from the
vantage point of each.

Foster parents are very much aware that the agency has the authority
to remove a foster child at any time, or even to close down the foster
home should it see fit to do so. They often feel trapped in a position
of forced dependency on the agency. The agency supplies their monthly
stipend, deals with any request for additional or out-of-pocket expenses,
provides regular or not-so-regular supervision or even occasional consultation, for which the foster parents may or may not see a need. At
times, decisions and demands of the agency, interpreted by their worker,
may have major and unpleasant repercussions on the foster family. And
yet, in many agencies, foster parents are rarely or minimally considered,
let alone consulted, around decisions that involve them as much as they
do the child – such as whether or not to place a foster child on adoption
or to recommend his return home (Darnell 1988).

Foster families often grieve when a child to whom they have become
attached is removed from them, either to be returned to parents in whom
they lack confidence or to be placed on adoption. They usually try to
support the agency, because they have been told that its decision is in
the child's best interests and because they want what is best for the
child. Still, in their hearts, they may question the agency's judgment.
Much of their questioning, however, is never raised directly, since many
foster parents fear that, should they object, they would open themselves
to criticism or retaliation, and might even decrease the chance of having
another child placed with them.

Often workers, even those who sensitively help foster children deal
with loss, are either unaware of the foster parents' grief at losing a child
they love or they feel that their job is to help the child, not the fostering
family, accept the separation (Berridge and Cleaver 1987, p. 166). Even
if the worker tries to help foster parents mourn the loss of a child, the
anger generated by their mourning may make them interpret the attempt
at helping as a further intrusion by a representative of the very agency
that caused their pain, so that they may be unable to accept it. Their
difficulty may be magnified by their belief that 'good' foster parents are

expected to facilitate children's moving on to adoption, and that they are not entitled to feel sad or angry since relinquishing the child is part of the job or since the child's best interests, not their own, are what matter. Some even feel that they have forfeited the right to have their own feelings considered by their unwillingness to adopt the child themselves. Other foster parents find it hard to share their grief with a worker whom they see as concerned only for the child, and not for them. Years later, such foster parents sometimes refer to how often in the past they grew, first, to trust and, then, to depend upon a worker, only to have her suddenly leave the agency or transfer to another department. Later, they were assigned a new worker with whom they felt ill at ease, and things were never quite the same again. Agencies, with all their talk about the importance of continuity to children, are constantly taking important people, children or workers, away from foster parents, often without seeming to realize with what consequences.

Not uncommonly, some months after such a change, the new social worker begins to notice a change. A foster family that was once described as open and cooperative becomes closed and defensive, or even oppositional and alienated. The worker becomes increasingly uncomfortable in their presence, and may even attempt to explore the reason for the change, but often to no avail. Soon the worker begins to fear that the quality of the fostering provided is deteriorating, but attempts to address this issue lead nowhere. Communication and relationship between worker and foster parents continue to deteriorate, until what was once rated a superior foster home is re-evaluated as marginal, or even substandard. Experiences in which foster parents met regularly in mutual support groups in both Toronto and Jerusalem suggest that some foster couples continue to nurse unexpressed bitterness for years, until, often in response to other group members expressing how they responded to similar losses, they finally air their unresolved bitterness and resentment. The presence and support of other foster parents allow them to recognize and to table these feelings in a way that sometimes even the most empathic social worker cannot. Such may be the case because many foster parents have the conviction that social workers, despite their formal training, cannot truly understand how they feel in the same way that someone who has been through a similar situation can (Steinhauer et al 1988; Steinhauer et al 1989; Arnowitz 1984).

But distrust and fears of being let down go two ways. Social workers must turn over to foster parents, even to those whose competence they sometimes question, responsibility for a child while retaining full accountability but no real control. Then, if they become concerned that the child's needs are not being met and begin to explore the situation, they often run into a blank wall of defensiveness or denial. They are in a bind. If they press to find out what they need to know to supervise the foster home appropriately, they risk antagonizing the foster parents, which could further complicate their relationship with them, possibly even enough to cause the placement to break down. But if they back off to appease the foster parents, they know they are not doing their job, and that the child may suffer from their ineffectiveness.

In some such situations, workers often react by moving to protect the child from the foster parents. Their doing so may serve to rationalize unrecognized feelings of resentment or competition, especially with the foster mother. Foster parents, in turn, respond to distrust, competitiveness, or high-handedness in the worker with their own anger and mistrust. Such a situation is ripe for mutual scapegoating: the social worker becomes increasingly critical of the foster parents' non-cooperation and their supposedly inadequate care of the child. The foster parents, meanwhile, grow more resentful and defensive towards the worker and the agency whose criticism and mistrust they resent, but with whom, because of their own internalized anger, they cannot broach the problems directly.

More than thirty years ago, Stanton and Schwartz (1954), discussing inpatient psychiatric care, noted that whenever two members of a therapeutic system were locked in unresolved conflict about a patient, that patient's care was jeopardized as long as the conflict persisted. Similarly, whenever foster parents and social worker, both key members of the foster-care service system, fail to recognize, face, and resolve their conflicts, both decision making and a child's adjustment, development, and placement will be undermined. Social workers, who represent the agency that has the authority to make ultimate decisions regarding the child and the foster home, must take the lead in establishing and, even more important, in maintaining open, two-way communication between foster parents and themselves. The relationship so established can be utilized to identify and resolve areas of potential disagreement or feelings of dissatisfaction as they arise. This is often difficult. Many foster parents and workers find it easier to avoid dealing directly with disagreement or potential conflict (Steinhauer 1983b; Berridge and Cleaver 1987, pp. 157–8). But, easy or not, unless open channels of communication are in place and carefully maintained *before* major disagreements occur – as, at some point, they surely will – the possibility of effective cooperation when most needed, at times of increased stress, is remote. The stronger the working alliance between foster parents and social workers – the more fully, openly, and directly each can express, hear, and negotiate areas of disagreement or tension with the other – the better the chance of the system working together to protect the foster child's chances of receiving maximal quality and continuity of care (see also Berridge and Cleaver 1987, pp. 157–8).

If maintaining an open relationship can help foster parents and workers work effectively as a team, how best can workers use this alliance to develop foster parents' capacity to provide better care? There are several ways, more than one of which can be operative at any given time. These include the following.

1 / *Helping foster parents feel understood.* If the foster parents, under stress, perceive their worker to be genuinely concerned, caring, and empathic, this perception will decrease their anxiety and avoid potential alienation, which might otherwise make it impossible for them to work together appropriately in the interest of the child.

2 / *Encouraging ventilation.* When foster parents' feelings of anxiety, discouragement, rage, guilt, or depression become intolerable, they are dominated by their own distress, which interferes with their ability to define clearly and respond appropriately to a child's needs. Foster parents may need to ventilate their own feelings before they can perceive those of the child without distortion, or accept the support or advice of others. The sensitive and available worker can often, first, facilitate ventilation and, then, help the foster parents make the crucial shift to constructive problem solving.

3 / *Assisting in cognitive restructuring.* After the foster parents have cleared the air through the ventilation of accumulated tensions, the worker can then help them recognize the nature of a problem, which, because of their previous upset and/or overinvolvement, they have not seen or understood clearly. Understanding the issue will then often make possible more appropriate attitudes and intervention.

4 / *Direct teaching.* In some cases, the worker's experience with other families, the objectivity available to her because of her greater distance from the case, or the appropriate application of her knowledge of child-development or other theoretical models can help foster parents reframe

an upsetting situation into one more manageable by the foster parents. By doing so, workers can often help foster parents develop more effective techniques of conceptualizing and responding to problems. Workers should always be careful, however, to avoid being pedantic, especially if they are unmarried and younger than the foster mother, in which case their age and lack of hands-on parenting experience frequently provoke defensiveness and resentment in older foster parents who easily feel patronized. Even the best advice is helpful only when it is wanted and when it is seen as useful by those to whom it is being offered.

5 / *Providing support.* Even those foster parents who resist direction often feel supported by their worker's serving as an empathic, non-judgmental, and non-critical sounding-board. This role can help them reorganize their own thinking and marshal their energies, as well as relieving them of the awesome feeling of total responsibility, which is so often the corollary of the looming fear of personal failure.

6 / *Increasing awareness and sensitivity towards foster children.* As foster parents and social worker work well together over time, many foster parents develop an increased skill at observing and interpreting children's behaviour accurately and sensitively. They learn to recognize that similar behaviours occur for very different reasons. Many learn to decipher for themselves the meaning of a particular behaviour at a given time, and to use their increased analytic skills to develop more useful interventions. Thus, over time, the social worker is, in effect, sensitizing and preparing foster parents to function as parent therapists, by teaching them to develop an attitude of observation and enquiry, how to utilize the child's daily behaviour to understand, to establish trust, to relieve distress, and to help the child identify and resolve conflict.

7 / *Increasing the motivation and commitment to fostering.* Almost always an open relationship between foster parents and social workers and inclusion in decision making regarding their foster child are experienced as supportive and helpful in restoring hope and morale at times of maximum stress. Foster parents often credit such factors with reviewing their motivation and their commitment to fostering (Steinhauer et al 1988, 1989; Hazel 1981; Rubenstein et al 1978; Galaway 1978; Stapleton 1987; Allison and Kufeldt 1987; Kieffer 1984; Wiltse 1978; see also chapter 15). However, alienation or competition between foster parents and social workers produces ongoing tension and mutual dis-

illusionment that sap the morale and undermine the commitment of both.

8 / *Developing the ability to differentiate between interactional and transference behaviours.* Foster parents often take a foster child's behaviour in an intensely personal way. They can be deeply hurt when personally attacked by children who are abusive or rejecting, especially when they have been caring and accepting, even when the child is difficult and they have done nothing to deserve the child's rejection or rage. Often, their worker can help them understand that apparently unprovoked hostile or distancing behaviour can be a child's way of transferring onto the foster parents – who are *there* – attitudes and motives originally experienced in that child's relationship with the natural parents – whom, since they are unavailable, the child cannot attack directly. Such children *unconsciously* displace their resentment of their natural parents – who did let them down – onto the foster parents, the only parental figures present and available. Most foster parents can learn to recognize this as a sign of the child's distorted perceptions and of his stereotyping of current parental figures because of the continuing internalized (psychological) influence of how he remembers his parents behaving in the past. Even though recognizing this may not change the child's behaviour, many foster parents can tolerate it better if they understand that the child is not aware of the displacement, and that he is attacking, not them personally, but (through them) his stereotype of those who were so punitive and rejecting in the past. That understood, many can better tolerate the attacks, while learning to understand and explore new ways of dealing with them and of helping the child learn to differentiate them from the stereotype. One illustration of this can be found in the example of Lily, in chapter 7. The following example illustrates how foster parents too can at times transfer their own unresolved feelings onto their foster children, thus inviting conflicts that they then misperceive as being primarily their own understandable response to the child's misbehaviour.

Ronit was a fifteen-year-old street girl, the daughter of immigrant parents one step ahead of the law, who had moved to Jerusalem from Morocco before she was born. After Ronit's third arrest for petty theft, she was placed in the foster home of a forty-five-year-old widow, also Moroccan-born, whose only natural daughter had died of leukaemia at the same age as Ronit several years before.

Mrs BenAmi was an extremely generous, warm-hearted woman.

She had not yet been able to mourn the daughter she had lost, although this was not fully recognized by the agency that had placed Ronit with her. Ronit, initially, thrived in her care. For the first time in her life, this deprived child, who so badly wanted love and security, suddenly had an excess of both. For a honeymoon period of almost eight weeks, she enjoyed being catered to, waited on, and adored so much that she did not challenge the curfew and other expectations that Mrs BenAmi set for her. Soon, however, the novelty wore off, and the predictability of her new life began to bore her. She began to long for her friends and for the excitement of her life on the streets. She started coming in at all hours and, in response to Mrs BenAmi's 'How could you do this to me? Aren't I good to you? Is there anything I wouldn't do for you? Haven't I treated you as if you were my own daughter?' she was bewildered.

First, Ronit tried to explain, but, when that did not stop Mrs BenAmi's attacks, she became defiant and abusive. When the foster mother's tears continued, Ronit rushed out of the house and did not come home. Her social worker, called on an emergency basis, found her and brought her back, negotiating a promise that she would live within the rules of the home. That led to a fragile truce, during which both parties nervously struggled to make it work. Ronit, genuinely touched by her foster mother's devotion and recognizing how much more cared for she was in this home than on the street, tried to keep her promise despite her growing boredom and malaise and a lifelong pattern of volatile emotionality and impulsivity. Mrs BenAmi, terrified of losing Ronit, tried so hard to keep her out of trouble that Ronit increasingly chafed at her constant control. Again she took off, to much mourning by the foster mother, only to find, much to her surprise, that the excitement of the streets was somewhat dulled by a sense of concern for the anguish she had caused the person who had been so good to her. Several more times she was brought back and the truce renegotiated, but the interim before the next run became shorter each time, until, one day, Mrs BenAmi threatened her with 'if you walk out this door, don't bother coming back. I don't ever want to set eyes on you again.' Ronit, of course, took off soon after, simultaneously relieved that the pressure was off but upset that the person whom she knew deeply loved her had told her never to return.

Mrs BenAmi, distraught by what she had done, broke down while telling this to the foster parents' group to which she belonged, ending with 'for the second time in two years, I have lost a daughter.' The group was warm and supportive and, after allowing her to ventilate for some time, its leader – who was also her social worker – pointed out that, while the loss of her daughter two years ago had indeed been tragic, her attempt to have Ronit take the daughter's place had been doomed from the start. Ronit had had fifteen years of street life and, even had she wanted to, she could never have fit the role that Mrs BenAmi had assigned to her.

This process was repeated within the group for several more meetings but, after the fourth such session, Mrs BenAmi made a decision: she and Ronit could not be mother and daughter – that she realized. She also knew that for them to live together again would be a disaster – they were far too different for that to work. 'But,' she went on, 'I didn't mean what I said about never wanting to see her face again. We can still be friends, even if not mother and daughter. If she wants to come and visit me, just for a chat and a cup of tea, I'd be glad to see her. There's nothing wrong with that, is there? After all, whom has she got?'

The group saw nothing wrong with that. Neither did the social worker. Nor did Ronit, who jumped at the chance to re-establish contact with the one person who had given her more than she had taken from her. At first, it was not easy; Mrs BenAmi still tended to come on strong; but, with the help of her social worker and the group, she learned in time to enjoy Ronit's visits and to stop trying to turn her into a substitute for her daughter. On those terms, Ronit could both give and take from her, and they continued to lead their own very different lives and to struggle with their own problems, though the life of each was lightened more than a bit by the friend-ship of the other.

9 / *Demand for placement termination.* Another way that social workers can help is through their dealing with verbal or behavioural demands, either by foster parents or by children, to terminate a placement. Many such demands are responses to transitional periods of severe frustration, disappointment, or feelings of inadequacy, rather than thought-through statements of what those involved really want. Workers who take such threats too literally will, by doing so, further escalate such crises, thus increasing the likelihood of placement breakdowns. (The case of Donny in chapter 6 serves as an example.) The worker who remains unflapp-able, however, can often absorb much of the accumulated tension and,

having done so, can negotiate to help all involved put the situation into perspective. In doing so, it often becomes clear that the threatened breakdown was merely a transient overreaction at a time of acute stress superimposed on chronic stress. In other cases, it becomes unavoidably clear that the relationship has, indeed, deteriorated beyond the point of no return, so that a replacement may serve a useful purpose. Distinguishing between these two situations, by providing the atmosphere and leadership by which they can be differentiated, and by actively taking the lead in negotiating towards the appropriate resolution will save many a viable placement while, at the same time, encouraging further growth in foster children and foster parents alike (Berridge and Cleaver 1987, pp. 154–5). Also, by responding calmly and rationally to such situations, workers demonstrate behaviourally a model for dealing with crises that, in future, may be picked up and successfully used by the family.

10 / Another key to minimizing damage to the child in care is the worker's *ensuring that there is at all times an up-to-date pro-active plan, both short-term and long-term, for each child*, as was described and illustrated in some detail in chapter 6. Above all, it is the worker's responsibility to prescribe, monitor, and balance the roles and responsibilities of all those who are part of the service system, of which the foster child is but one member. It is not for the worker, single-handedly, to design or execute the plan. The worker's responsibility is to ensure that a plan is in place and kept up to date and practical at all times. It is also her role to ensure that all members of the system (i.e., foster parents, natural parents, child, and worker) live up to their assigned commitments within it, that directives prescribed within the plan are indeed carried out and checked on a regular basis, and that the case is promptly brought to the attention of a supervisor if the focus is lost or if any objectives are not being met. Doing so is the best protection against allowing cases to drift aimlessly as a result of professional passivity or neglect (Wiltse 1978; Bush and Gordon 1982; Allison and Kufeldt 1987; Seaberg 1986; Katz et al 1986; Emlen et al 1978).

Berridge and Cleaver (1987, pp. 79–80, 143, 160–1) comment upon how frequently this commitment to active planning was not met by the agencies they studied (see also Finkelstein 1980; Gruber 1978; Maluccio et al 1980; Kadishin 1978). Many of their comments on the relative effectiveness of intermediate fostering are, in essence, an endorsement of active planning and active social-work involvement with both foster and natural parents, as opposed to the cursory reviews, minimal worker involvement, and poor coordination of services they found too often typified long-term care. The emphasis on permanency planning in North America is, essentially, a call for aggressive planning to keep children from drifting unintentionally into long-term care because of neglect on the part both of their natural parents and of the agencies whose job it is to protect them (Gruber 1978; Emlen 1977; Pike 1976; Maluccio et al 1980; Fein et al 1984; Lahti et al 1978).

Finally, consider briefly the negative consequences of natural parents frequently being discouraged and excluded from fully playing their part within the foster care system (Knitzer, Allen, and McGowan 1978; Gruber 1978). Both foster parents and social workers often encourage their exclusion, and each may blame the other for doing so. Active and regular visiting of foster children by natural parents, and an ongoing, cooperative and supportive relationship among natural parents, foster parents, and social workers, have been associated with a better experience for the child in care, fewer breakdowns, and a minimizing of the risk of drift into unplanned long-term foster care as a result of parental and agency neglect. Again, it is primarily the social worker's responsibility to try to keep the natural parents appropriately involved, except in that minority of cases where any such involvement is clearly contra-indicated.

It is social workers, as the representatives of the agency that holds the power, who must take the lead in establishing regular and as positive as possible relationships with natural parents, while doing what they can to catalyse a mutually supportive, understanding, and minimally competitive relationship between foster and natural parents whenever this serves the child in care's best interests (Berridge and Cleaver 1987, pp. 142–3, 158–9; Kadushin 1980; Kufeldt 1982; Cooper 1978; Kieffer 1984; Kufeldt and Allison 1990).

In summary, then, caseworker and agency, natural parents, foster child, and foster parents – along with the family-court system, whose influence will be discussed separately in chapter 11 – and their interactions with each other constitute the foster care system. It is incumbent on the social worker, as the professional responsible for the welfare of the child in care, to ensure that the contributions, effects, and relationships of all parts of the system are understood, and that the superordinate goal of the agency's involvement – ensuring that the system *as a unit* functions in the best interests of children in care – is indeed achieved.

Chapter Eleven

The Family Court System
and the Quality of Foster Care

It would be remiss to discuss the management of children in care without some mention of the key decision-making role played by the family court system. Although this chapter deals with issues as they occur within the family courts of the Province of Ontario, there is good reason to believe that the same issues are at least as problematic in child-welfare courts in most jurisdictions.

While it is the child welfare system that is responsible for the placement, supervision, and day-to-day management of children in care, except in that minority of cases in which a family voluntarily seeks the services of a child welfare association, that agency has become involved only after a family court has found the children sufficiently in need of promotion to allow the state to intervene and serve *in loco parentis.*

Society has traditionally held that a man's home is his castle, and that the state has the right to interfere in the affairs of the family only in exceptional circumstances. This belief is reflected in law, which has presumed that it is the role of parents, not that of the state, to protect the best interests of children. Usually they do, but parents' ability to perceive children's needs as separate and different from their own is frequently lost: 1 / by parents who are legally caught up in a marriage struggle in which both remain emotionally enmeshed; 2 / where either or both parents, because of past neglect or abuse at the hands of their own parents, mental illness, marital incompatibility, limited frustration tolerance, unbearable social and economic pressures, or chronic substance abuse, become neglectful and abusive; 3 / in cases where intrafamilial sexual abuse has occurred.

Courts have long recognized that where there is clear evidence of abuse, the child involved is in need of state protection. Thus, the family court system can legitimately be seen as a component of the foster care service system. But one can appreciate in this a potential dilemma. The family court must force intervention on a family only when absolutely necessary, that is, only when the parents of that family have been proved so grossly inadequate as to necessitate societal intervention. However, should the courts, in their wish to minimize their intrusion into family life, fail to intervene when necessary, the resulting neglect and continuing abuse may cause serious, even irreversible damage to children left at risk.

Thus, the court is responsible for determining when a family's situation has so deteriorated that the children's welfare and development are at risk to such a degree that state intervention is justifiable. In doing so, the court must take care to abrogate parental rights only when the combination of neglect and abuse is sufficiently damaging to merit such drastic action, and only when it is unreasonable to assume that the family's problems can receive adequate remediation without removing the children. Since vulnerability to even grossly unsatisfactory family functioning varies considerably from child to child, this can be a difficult decision to make in any given case (Anthony and Cohler 1987).

In North America, since the end of the Second World War, the balance has shifted in the direction of strengthening the civil rights of an individual when these conflict with that person's need for treatment of a psychiatric disorder that could, with consent, be treated. As a result of this swing of the pendulum, many matters that would once have been resolved in clinical settings between psychiatrists and psychologists, their patients, and the patients' families have, instead, become legal confrontations in which the civil rights even of individuals clearly lacking insight into even quite serious mental disorders are favoured above their need for treatment as seen by mental health professionals and other family members. Thus, the balance between mental health professionals and the courts has been profoundly altered, so that a great many of what, at one time, would have been considered clinical issues are now decided by law.

One of the effects of this increased legal decision making in what used to be considered the mental health field has been to legalize and legitimatize the struggle between patients who lack trust, who are hostile, who are oppositional, or who show an automatic need to reject or rebel against those in authority and those in the mental health – or child welfare – fields who are attempting to treat them. At times, the 'helper' seems to be seen as more of a problem than the underlying condition that he is attempting to treat. Another result of the rising legalization of the field is the enormous increase in time that must be spent by mental health and child care workers preparing for court, or repeatedly appearing before court or review boards to obtain the right to initiate or continue treatment. In the child welfare field, one effect of this trend has been a shift in the nature of supervision; an emphasis on recording procedures and accountability has replaced the traditional focus on the worker/client relationship and the casework process. Also, since this increased legalization of the child welfare field has not been accompanied by increased funding, workers who have to spend more of their time and energy in court-related activities now have less to share among their clients.

In cases of marital breakdown, our courts are much more likely to take into account children's needs in deciding upon custody and access than they were in the 1960s. At that time, there was little recognition of children's needs, and access was decided on the basis of parental rights or on the then-current belief that young children were always better off in the custody of their mother (except if the mother was of poor moral character, i.e., had had an extramarital affair, in which case they were likely to be awarded to the father). The appointment of a director of child representation in the Official Guardian's Office, and many other similar appointments in other jurisdictions, indicate how far the pendulum has swung towards a recognition that children's needs are not automatically perceived or served by their parents, and that their rights deserve articulation and protection in the legal process. In spite of this increased sensitivity and commitment to the rights and needs of children, there are still areas where children's best interests are frequently ill served by a court system designed with adults in mind. One such example is the process of cross-examination in the criminal courts, especially in cases of alleged intrafamilial sexual abuse, which will be discussed separately in chapter 16. Another area of difficulty is that, although some have recently been suggested, no clear-cut, replicable criteria have been experimentally validated for assessing parenting capacity. Thus, a great deal is left to the intuitive decisions of the individual judge who, in turn, is highly dependent on evidence supplied by clinicians. But clinicians, operating from widely differing data bases and with great variations in experience, skill, objectivity, and professional background, can at times overwhelm judges with masses of conflicting and confusing opinions from which it is hard to reach an appropriate judgment.

It is not uncommon, for example, for a judge to hear a case in which a child welfare worker urgently requests that children be brought into care to protect them from neglect and abuse at the hands of a single mother whose psychiatric problems, in the opinion of the agency, render her incapable of providing even the lowest standard of parenting necessary to protect the children's adjustment and secure their ongoing development. At the same time, the judge hears from the mother's psychiatrist that the parent regularly attends ongoing treatment and is continuing to improve. Assuming that the psychiatrist is better able to predict the parent's parenting capacity than the agency's social worker, the judge, often with some relief, accepts the psychiatric evidence and, accordingly, leaves the children in the care of the mother.

Facts that the judge fails to take into account include the following: 1 / The ability of psychiatrists to predict the future of a serious mental condition is much less precise than is generally recognized. 2 / One cannot directly equate *mental status,* of which psychiatrists can claim expert knowledge, with *parenting capacity,* about which most adult psychiatrists have considerably less knowledge than do most child welfare workers. Many general or adult psychiatrists are not even aware of the importance of the distinction between these, and cannot accurately assess the effects of parental emotional disorder on their patients' children's development. 3 / The psychiatrist who has a parent in ongoing treatment is under great pressure to support that patient's claim that he or she is, or soon will be, well enough to parent adequately. Failure to do so, or even a statement that the therapist is in no position to comment with authority, is likely to be seen as betrayal and/or rejection by the patient. The result may be to place the patient's relationship with the psychiatrist – and even the continuation of the therapy – in jeopardy, to say nothing of the threat of precipitating a depression or relapse should the psychiatrist so disappoint the patient. Thus even the conscientious and committed psychiatrist is likely, through often unrecognized subjective overinvolvement (i.e., counter-transference), to overestimate patients' ability to care adequately for their children.

But if judges cannot always rely on the accuracy and usefulness of psychiatric evidence, neither can they always depend upon the evidence of workers from a child welfare agency or Children's Aid Society. Such workers often lack full social work training and, because of the high burn-out rate, the experience they need to handle their far-too-heavy caseloads with insufficient or inadequate case supervision and back-up resources. All these factors can undermine workers' ability to perform effectively within the family court system. There is an increasing tendency to provide legal advocacy for children in care appearing in court for what once would have been considered matters requiring clinical (i.e., mental health and child welfare) decisions. The greater number of contested cases will increase the workload of the social worker, who has to spend much more time preparing for court. An unavoidable side-effect of this is a parallel decrease in the time available to workers for direct contact with children and families on their caseloads, which has been estimated at less than 30 per cent of workers' time on the job (Catholic Children's Aid Society of Metropolitan Toronto 1975; Report of Residential Family Resources Project Reference Group 1989). In addition, there are secondary effects: the net increase in pressure on the worker results in too little time, too much anxiety, too little job satisfaction, and too little chance to achieve the distance needed to keep the case in perspective. These effects may decrease the worker's ability to perceive clearly and present articulately to the court the needs of the child. Workers under extreme pressure frequently demonstrate decreased efficiency and are prone to excessive shortcutting and premature closure (leading to an inadequate data base) and/or to overidentification and power struggles (leading to a distorted data base).

Before leaving the topic of the completeness and reliability of the evidence presented by child welfare workers in court, one must consider the implications of the inherent ambiguity in the role of the Children's Aid Society worker. Such workers have, at times, two incompatible components to their jobs. Sometimes they function as mental health workers, assessing and trying to heal or stabilize families in which children are at risk. At others, they have the legal authority to take those same clients to court, using the data gathered during counselling as evidence of those clients' inability to parent effectively and, therefore, of the need to remove their child. Because child welfare workers' relationships with their clients are not privileged, as are those of lawyers, social workers can be forced to reveal in court what a client has told them in confidence. This double role of the child welfare worker (would-be helper but potential witness for the 'prosecution') is a source of confusion for workers and a potent and entirely understandable reason for distrust and non-cooperation on the part of many of their clients. The situation is often exacerbated by lawyers who, not inappropriately, not only warn clients that anything they tell their workers may be used against them, but go so far as to instruct them against cooperating in any way with any representative of any Children's Aid Society. While this advice may protect the client from potential abuse within the court system, it frequently has the undesirable side-effect of strengthening family mistrust and resistance. This effect undermines the potentially helpful role of the child welfare worker, not merely for those families where removal of a child is unavoidable, but also for others in which a therapeutic alliance with the worker would have been the best way to support the family and to prevent family breakdown. In view of this double mandate and the other factors listed above, it is understandable that there are often major gaps and distortions in workers' testimony. What is perhaps more surprising is that, in spite of their potential use of authority, child welfare workers are able, as often as they are, to gain clients' confidence and work effectively with families over whom they have considerable power.

Ultimately, it is the family court judge who must make the final decision about whether to take a child into care, to allow visiting between biological parents and their child in care, to terminate parental rights, or to resume contact with biological parents who have not seen their child for an extended period of time. In view of the number of possible sources of contamination, error, and disagreement among various clinicians involved in the case, it is perhaps fortunate that the judge is a neutral outsider whose job it is to make sense of the mass of conflicting evidence and to protect the rights of everyone involved. But most judges have had little or no training in child development and/ or child and family pathology. Nevertheless, they are expected to render judgments based on highly specialized data from clinicians who are supposedly expert – but who, in actual fact, will vary greatly in their competence, conscientiousness, and expertise – within their clinical fields. Judges, too, of course, show considerable variation in intelligence, sensitivity, commitment, experience, and understanding of these matters. They are placed in a problematic situation by being expected to render judgments in areas in which they themselves are not expert. How do they make sense of the mass of conflicting data from the bank of experts who may be – or may *appear* to be – contradicting each other? What is the danger of their favouring the evidence of an expert witness whose testimony is organized and glib, and sounds authoritative but is, in fact, based on a superficial, incomplete, or inadequate clinical assessment over that of a thorough and honest clinician whose presentation of the evidence is poorly organized and inarticulate? The danger is considerable; it happens all the time. In an attempt to make sense out of so confused a situation, judges tend to react in a number of ways.

Most judges do their best to resolve apparent contradictions or gaps in the evidence they have heard. The skill with which they do so generally varies directly with their understanding of children's developmental needs and those factors within a family and child welfare system that either facilitate or interfere with those needs being met.

Others, overwhelmed by the awesome responsibility divested in them and the frequent failure of mental health professionals to reach a consensus, react to the complexity and contradictions in the evidence by losing faith in all professionals and retreating to an exaggerated reliance on their own 'common sense.' As often as not, such 'common sense' is made up of their own personal but unrecognized biases and prejudices. Often they supplement or confirm these by insisting upon a direct encounter with children and/or parents in their chambers, using the information they derive from this single face-to-face chat as a check on that of the child welfare and mental health professionals who may have been involved in the case for years.

Still others react to the extreme responsibility placed on them by trying to avoid making *any* decision for as long as possible. The trouble with this alternative is that, by avoiding deciding, they are, in effect, making a decision of a different kind, that is, the decision to keep a child's living situation in limbo, instead of insisting that it be solved one way or another.

Thus the ultimate decision as to whether – or where – a child shall be placed is that of a judge, who usually has had little, if any, training in children's developmental needs, the assessment of parenting capacity, or the proper evaluation of clinical evidence. One experienced judge, speaking to this issue some years ago, pointed out that the judge has both the right and the duty to determine what clinicians, parents, agencies, and the child have to say when a child's future is in dispute. In the case of conflicting opinions or advice, these must be weighed against each other, against the rights of the child, against society's right to protect itself against the behaviour of the child, and against society's ability to provide the necessary resources, often at considerable expense to the taxpayers. He argues that, in arriving at his decision, the judge, who is a reasonable person, is aware that he is no clinician and is prepared to accept the advice of qualified clinicians, provided they can present and defend a credible plan of management in which no one's rights are abused (quoted in Steinhauer 1978a). Clinicians have no trouble with this concept, when the judge is, indeed, reasonable. But what about those who are not?

It is not good enough to state that an inappropriate judgment made by an arbitrary, arrogant, or idiosyncratic judge can always be appealed. While this may make sense in other areas of law, the appeal system, as currently constituted, has two major disadvantages within child welfare law. First, it takes time to prepare and hear an appeal, and during all those months the child, that child's foster parents, and possibly the natural parents remain in limbo while the already overextended resources of the Children's Aid Society are even further taxed. Frequently children's adjustment and development deteriorate dramatically whenever the plan for their future is up in the air. Secondly, the judges who hear cases on appeal typically have even less experience in family law and less knowledge of child development than do family court judges, and so are often in an even poorer position to evaluate the contradictory evidence with which they are confronted. For children to be well served, there must be a mechanism for immediate appeal heard by judges with experience in family and child welfare areas for all cases in which an appeal casts a youngster's disposition in doubt. There also needs to be an active and effective mechanism through which family court judges are held responsible for their decisions by their peers (Steinhauer 1978a; 1982).

In a later paper, the author has suggested ways in which our family courts frequently and unnecessarily, though unintentionally, undermine the adjustment, development, and interests of the children whom they are attempting to protect (Steinhauer 1984). Our judges, as a group, are no more or less competent or concerned for children's welfare than are child welfare or children's mental health professionals. Nevertheless, certain features built into the structure of the family court system predispose to unnecessary disruption and damage to the lives of children whose families have failed them and who, therefore, must have their future care and disposition decided in family court. These factors include the following.

1 / *Failure to appreciate the significance of neglect.* Recently, there is such a preoccupation with the prevention of physical or sexual abuse that our courts are in danger of abusing children by failing to appreciate the, at times, even greater damage done by continued exposure to severe and chronic neglect.

2 / *The developmental need for prompt decision making.* There needs to be far greater recognition by our judges of the importance to children of prompt decision making in order to spare children the destructive effects of drifting too long in limbo (A. Freud 1960; Steinhauer 1980b; Wilkes 1989). Tator and Wilde (1980), analysing 106 cases of child abuse brought before the Provincial Court (Family Division) in Metropolitan Toronto between January 1973 and December 1977, reported that the average case had 3.8 adjournments (lasting an average 92.8 days each) and required 454.3 days for final disposition. To minimize damage to children, the number of adjournments must somehow be decreased, especially those that represent delaying tactics by parents and/or lawyers more concerned with proving a point than with the welfare of children.

May, a four-month-old baby girl, was admitted to a major paediatric ward because of failure to thrive. Intensive medical investigation provided no explanation for her failure to gain weight. There were, however, significant concerns right from the day of admission that psychosocial factors were affecting her weight gain. Consequently the paediatric staff requested a psychosocial assessment from the hospital's Department of Psychiatry in order to understand and suggest how best to manage the problem. May gained weight steadily soon after being admitted to the hospital, and her psychosocial development, which had been significantly retarded on admission, showed considerable progress by the time of her discharge from hospital, three and a half weeks later.

While she was in hospital, the psychiatric investigating team was concerned by the fact that May's mother visited her only once during her almost month-long hospital stay, despite repeated requests by telephone and via her husband that it was important to May's attachment and well-being that she visit daily. She stated that she found coming to the hospital 'too upsetting' and that, besides, she was unconvinced that May was truly her child. She accused the hospital in which May was born of sending them home with someone else's baby instead of her own. This possibility was extensively investigated, and no evidence favouring it was found. On several occasions, the father demanded that blood tests be done to establish whether or not May was their baby, but when the hospital agreed to do this he withdrew his consent on the grounds that it no longer mattered; even if it was proved that this was their baby, he and his wife would not believe it, and if it turned out that May was someone else's baby, it would be too much trouble to switch at such a late date.

As part of the psychiatric investigation, arrangements were made to have May and her parents assessed by the hospital's Infant Psychiatry service. The parents failed to show for the assessment twice. After the second failure, they denied ever having agreed to participate in the assessment, which was patently untrue. In their dealings with the hospital staff, their family doctor, the public-health nurse, and their Children's Aid Society worker – who had originally been assigned prior to hospitalization when the mother had called the society to report that she had been given the wrong baby – the parents consistently took an adversarial stance. They were hostile and uncooperative, lying frequently and repeatedly omitting relevant data from their answers. They consistently denied that May had had any problems, or that they had had any difficulties with any of the professionals or agencies involved, although at other times they complained to each group of professionals about how badly each of the others had treated them. When, later, they began to concede that there was a problem, they totally absolved themselves of any responsibility and claimed that everything would have been fine if only the Children's Aid Society had never gotten involved.

Before May was six months old, representatives of all agencies involved met with paediatricians and child psychiatrists from the hospital and agreed that an attempt should be made to sever the bond between May and her family to free her for adoption. The court process was initiated at that time, but it was not until May was twenty-one months old that the case was finally heard and decided. There were numerous reasons for the delays, including the general overcrowding of the family court system; the parents changing their lawyer twice; strategic adjournments by the parents' lawyers; other lawyers, key professional witnesses, and the judge going on vacation at different times; the parents repeatedly failing to show for various scheduled appointments or assessments necessary for the preparation of the case. When the case was finally heard, some fifteen months after it was first submitted, the judge agreed to free May for adoption. By that time, she was securely bonded to a foster mother in whose care she had thrived but who, at age fifty-seven, was unprepared to adopt her. This meant that what could have been a relatively uncomplicated adoption had a decision been made within two or three months of the original submission had been greatly complicated by systemic factors into one in which May would have to go through the trauma of a separation from one set of psychological parents (the foster parents) in order to be adopted by another.

3 / *Problems related to appeals.* There must be greater recognition that the appeal mechanism as it now stands does little to protect children from inappropriate judicial decisions. Judges frequently remark that, if Children's Aid societies don't like their decisions, they can always appeal them. While this may make sense from the vantage point of the legal system, it makes none at all in terms of children's developmental needs. Appeals keep children in limbo longer. In an extended series of appeals and counter-appeals, either parents or a society may win, but whatever the ultimate disposition, the child is almost sure to lose.

4 / *Failure to recognize the importance of continuity of key relationships to the security and normal development of the child.* We have come a long way from the time when blood ties were routinely given a higher priority than psychological ties, thanks to the wider general appreciation of the developmental importance of attachment and bonding, and the introduction by Goldstein, Freud, and Solnit (1973) of the concept of the psychological parent. Many of our judges now understand the prime importance of the child's attachment to the psychological parent and do what they can to protect that attachment, be it to a natural, an adoptive, or a foster parent. Some of our judges, however, either don't understand this or idiosyncratically refuse to accept it. If they ignore it, an agency is left with two alternatives: to accept the clinically inappropriate disruption of the child's tie to the psychological parent or to launch an appeal, in which case the child's period in limbo is further prolonged.

5 / *Failure to appreciate the child's time sense.* Generally speaking, our courts still do not appreciate sufficiently the importance of a child's time sense. As a result, they contribute to unnecessary court-created abandonments or confusion. Precisely how long a given child can tolerate total absence from parents without a separation reaction being precipitated is unknown. We do know that, because of temperamental and other variables, some children are more vulnerable than others, even of the same age, but that, generally speaking, the younger the child

the shorter the period of total separation that can be tolerated before psychological abandonment occurs (Goldstein, Freud, and Solnit 1973). Thus, if a child is in care for any reason, including the result of a series of adjournment or even agency mismanagement, and is left in a temporary placement, that is meeting his developmental needs over a prolonged period during which he has no contact with the natural parents, he will protect himself from their loss by emotionally detaching himself from them, and replacing them by a reattachment to his substitute caretakers, who thereby become his psychological parents. It really takes only a very short time, and while the exact time is variable, for young children it is certainly far less than the average 454.3 days found by Tator and Wilde (1980). If, then, a few months later, the court orders the children returned to the care of the parents, they are forced through a second traumatic separation to be returned to biological parents who have been allowed to become psychological strangers.

6 / *Excessive reliance on what child/parents say in court or chambers.* The road to many a child's private hell is paved with the good intentions of judges who, responding to a parent's tearful testimony in court and caught up by a surge of compassion and the all-too-human wish to reunite parents and child, are sufficiently swayed by their own rescue fantasies to let their hearts, rather than their heads, deliver their judgment. When, in such a situation, a judge's feelings drift from empathy – that is, the capacity to understand what the parent is feeling – to sympathy – that is, the tendency to identify so completely with the parent that the distance needed for objectivity is lost – a child's future is very much at risk.

Along the same lines, I have considerable concern about the judge who, with the best intentions in the world, decides a child's custody on the basis of a private chat in chambers. How many young children, when they have seen their mother crying in court, will feel sufficiently free of guilt to tell the judge that they know they are better off in a foster home? How many, torn between two battling parents, both of whom they love, will change their minds many times a day about where they are more secure? How many children do not know what they want or, even more dangerous, want different things at different levels? How many sacrifice themselves to protect a parent, or are manipulated, bribed, blackmailed, or used as a weapon by, first, one parent and, then, the other?

Many family court judges feel it is important to establish personal contact with children and parents in chambers, in an attempt to de-mystify the proceedings and to establish them as humane and fair. Any-thing the judge can do to achieve such a rapport is in the best interests of all involved. This situation must be distinguished, however, from one in which a judge uses the time spent in chambers to obtain state-ments that, because the judge obtained them directly, are then used to dismiss out of hand even extensive and mutually consistent evidence from a variety of long-involved professionals. What a child says, at any single time, is not necessarily what that child thinks, wants, or needs. It is the tendency of some judges to overvalue the reliability of what the child says because she says it directly to them on that single occasion in a high-stress situation that constitutes the potential danger. The case of Carol, in chapter 5, is an example of how contradictory and complex the data provided by a confused child can be.

7 / *Excessive reliance on cross-sectional assessment and insufficient weighting of historical evidence.* Too often judges rely more upon a psychiatrist's or psychologist's one-time only (cross-sectional) assess-ment than on even a well-documented history of neglect or abuse pre-sented by a worker or agency (or a series of agencies) that has known and tried unsuccessfully to engage the family for years. Mental health professionals have contributed to this problem. Some psychiatrists and psychologists make dogmatic statements and predictions on the basis of far too little clinical evidence. Some social workers, either intimidated by being in court or unaware of what data are relevant or how best to organize them, fail to select and present their material effectively. As a result, the court may lack the relevant facts, or else the woods may be obscured by the trees. (Chapter 5 provides a guide for selecting and presenting historical data relevant to parenting ability, and discusses the hazards of overreliance on a one-shot assessment of a patient or client who may well manipulate the situation by withholding potentially damaging data or by obscuring the situation.)

The mother of two young girls, ages four and seven, was alleged by both daughters to have repeatedly involved them in multiple acts of sexual abuse, forcing them to drink urine and eat faeces, and using them in multiple Satanic rituals. The case itself was thor-oughly investigated, and at the end of a 150-day hearing, all contact between the mother and both children was permanently severed. With five lawyers (separately representing the father, the mother, the mother's then current boy friend, the local Children's Aid Society, and the girls, who themselves were represented by a lawyer from the Official Guardian's Office), the trial was sufficiently sensational to attract national attention and to inspire one carefully balanced book describing the legal proceedings (Marron 1988). All of the principals were examined by both psychologists and psychiatrists. Both children were in ongoing psychotherapy with a child psychiatrist; videotapes of her therapy interviews were used as evidence in court. A team of senior child psychiatrists examined 150 pages of process recordings kept by the children's very experienced foster mother to keep track of the children's gradual allegations over a six-month period. They looked at the quality and internal consistency of what the girls told the foster mother, and compared this with what the children had told a number of other responsible adults in a systematic attempt to establish the credibility of this indirect evidence.

One interesting aspect of the trial that was not reported in the book involved the two-day appearance in court of one of the two psychiatrists who examined the mother. This psychiatrist saw her on a single occasion for an extended two-and-a-half hour interview. On the basis of his examination, he concluded that the mother was not a significantly disturbed woman – 'she did not have a serious mental disorder, but only a mild personality disorder.' He concluded that she was more the victim of community hysteria than a victimizer of her daughters. Although this psychiatrist had available to him the results of all the other psychiatric and psychological examinations done of the mother, and had access to the record of the mother's involvement with two children's aid societies over several years, he chose not to contaminate the purity of his examination by reviewing this collateral information. He was content, he remarked at the conclusion of his testimony, to rest his opinion upon the mother's uncorroborated remarks.

The next day, under a withering cross-examination by the lawyer for the Children's Aid Society, he was confronted with undeniable fact after undeniable fact, carefully recorded over a period of almost seven years. In full retreat, he totally revised his assessment, concluding that the mother suffered a severe personality disorder and was likely, under severe stress, to become psychotic.

As an experienced forensic psychiatrist, this witness should have known better than to accept without corroboration the evidence of someone with a personality disorder. He should have known that one of the key characteristics of patients with personality disorders is their ability to dissemble and to present themselves as stable and well-functioning at any single point in time. It is only when one observes and records their functioning over a prolonged period that their instability and their inability to sustain successful relationships become apparent. This mother had withheld and distorted data in order to make herself look good. She was unable to maintain this façade with any who had followed her behaviour over months and years. To them, without exception, the high level of her disturbance was obvious. She could not conceal it from them, as she could from someone with whom she had to deal only once or twice.

This example illustrates how much more wrong the cross-sectional psychiatric or psychological examination of someone with a personality disorder is likely to be than is the longitudinal picture of that person's behaviour meticulously recorded over the years. Luckily, in this case, the effectiveness of the Children's Aid Society's lawyer, several conflicting psychological and psychiatric opinions, but, above all, the availability of the organized and well-presented history of the mother's past involvement with a variety of professionals and agencies belied the false conclusions of the expert witness who had met her just once. In other cases, which are more superficially investigated, where the case history is less well documented or corroborated, and where the individual is more able than this woman was to dissemble effectively in court, a judge who valued the polished but superficial one-time evidence of a psychiatrist or psychologist over the carefully documented historical record presented by the agency's social worker would clearly be deflected from a true understanding of the children's needs.

8 / *Issues related to legal advocacy for children.* Let us review some concerns around the widespread use of legal advocacy for children. On the whole, most mental health professionals welcome such advocacy as a sign of the growing acceptance of society's recognition of the need to identify and protect children's rights. Nevertheless, the prominence of the legal advocate for children in our family courts, while generally desirable, is not without potential drawbacks.

The first regards the question of which children are assigned a legal advocate, and how the decision is made. There are disadvantages in universal or automatic legal advocacy: greatly increased costs, and more backlog in the courts, leaving children whose disposition is in limbo waiting even longer for a decision to which they could begin to adjust. Another result of universal advocacy would be that Children's Aid Society workers, whose workloads are already far too large to allow them to be on top of all their cases, would spend even more of their time preparing for court, leaving them less available to serve the needs of the children and families in their caseloads. If the child's interests are indeed represented in court by parents or guardians, third-party advocacy is unnecessary and an intrusion on the integrity of the family or guardianship. When the child's interests are not being represented – i.e., when the child is caught between two adults, or groups of adults, who are so overinvolved that they have lost sight of the separate interest of the child – then legal advocacy is essential. Clinicians and lawyers need to be looking for ways of defining when parents and guardians (including children's aid societies) are capable of perceiving and representing children's interests and when they are not, in the hope of defining guidelines towards the more effective and selective use of legal advocacy.

Another concern with the role of the legal advocate is around how he decides upon his mandate. Does he merely represent what the child says he wants, as has been suggested by Justice for Children, one child advocacy group, and the Children's Services Division of the Ministry of Community and Social Services in Ontario? Or, does he seek consultation to determine what is in the best interests of the child and present that position, as suggested by the Office of the Official Guardian? This dilemma is summarized in the Minutes of Convocation of the Law Society of Upper Canada:

Is the child to be treated as any other client? Or, should the lawyer act as the child's guardian and advocate his opinion as to the best interests of the child which may or may not conflict with the child's wishes? Or, is some combination of these roles appropriate? Further, if the lawyer is to represent the child's wishes, does the solicitor/client privilege prevent him from disclosing facts he has learned from the child which do not support the child's position? Does it make a difference if these facts indicate the child may be in a position of peril, or if the child is of an age where he or she appears to be able to 'instruct' their lawyer? (Law Society of Upper Canada 1981)

The Sub-committee on the Legal Representation of Children, considering this issue, argued that, as the solicitor is not the judge of the best interests of the child, the lawyer should treat the child as he would any other client. There then follow a number of caveats, the most important of which are: that such treatment is dependent on the child's ability to instruct counsel; and that, should the child stubbornly, without reason, refuse to accept the advice of counsel, it may be that the child 'lacks the maturity to properly instruct counsel ... in which case counsel has no right to argue what in his opinion is in the best interests of the child ... in which case the lawyer is under a duty not to accept the instructions and to advise the court that the infant, in his opinion, is incapable of giving instructions ... in which case the Official Guardian should be notified.' It is at this point that the author's training and the ethic of his profession begin to cause trouble.

As a child psychiatrist, I am aware that the lawyer who is not supposed to be making subjective judgments is being called upon to make all sorts of them, for which his training does nothing to prepare him. What is judged as 'without reason' may be anything that appears unreasonable in the subjective view of the lawyer. Similarly, it is left to the individual lawyer to decide when the child lacks the maturity to instruct counsel. This situation is not without problems: some five-going-on-fifteen-year-olds are truly able to appreciate their situation and capable of giving instructions, while some fifteen-going-on-five-year-olds are not. To decide that a child is incapable of giving instructions would financially penalize the lawyer. I do not suggest that many lawyers would consciously exploit such a situation, but how many, when times are hard, might be subconsciously influenced to proceed inappropriately? Knowing the unconscious bias that psychiatrists and social workers can have if paid by one party in a marital conflict, I suggest that more than a few would. Finally, lawyers are steeped in the adversarial tradition. To what extent would they approach the child and interpret what he said from an adversarial set, thus producing new conflicts or intensifying existing ones? These dilemmas are well summarized in a discussion paper on child advocacy, entitled 'Implementing the Child's Right to Be Heard.'

We suggest that the definition of child advocacy as the child's right to be heard be broadened to include the child's right to be listened to and understood. This is important since it introduces the important distinction between the child's wishes and the child's needs and is in keeping with the ten principles enunciated by the General Assembly of the United Nations in their adoption of the Declaration of the Rights of the Child, specifically points five, six and ten.

Children express their needs both verbally and non-verbally. Their verbal and non-verbal communications may be either incongruous or even incompatible with each other. Often with your developmentally impaired and emotionally disturbed children, it is the non-verbal expression that is the more important. To understand how to make sense out of such discrepancies, and to avoid potentially dangerous simplifications, the listener should routinely have a thorough understanding of child development and children's mental functioning. Otherwise, since children's self-expression is so often contradictory, there is the real concern that the child's wishes, which are urgent, may obscure the non-verbal statement of more pressing underlying needs. (Harman, Lister, and Kligman 1981)

The Child Welfare Act in Ontario and similar legislation in many other jurisdictions contain a section that allows any interested party to demand a review of permanent wardship every six months without having to show substantial cause (Ontario 1978). As long as there can be no guarantees of permanence beyond six months ahead, children's placements remain vulnerable to being upset twice a year. Such a situation discourages both foster child and foster parents from committing themselves fully to each other, and both the quality and permanence of such placements are thereby systematically undermined. Furthermore, the reopening of permanent wardship, which results in the re-establishing of visits after psychological abandonment has already occurred, unnecessarily confuses and complicates the life and adjustment of many children. In view of the considerable potential for such a situation to destructive, the sole criterion for re-establishing contact after crown wardship (i.e., permanent wardship and separation) has occurred should be the interests of the child.

Two recent court cases in Ontario have emphasized the current dilemma of the child welfare worker: how can one avoid the drift that results from children remaining too long in care because no one has adequately planned for them, while, at the same time, avoiding giving up on parents too soon and thus undermining the chances of a successful reunion? These two cases – one in which the Children's Aid Society officials were charged with not being aggressive enough in removing a child from a mother who subsequently abused her and the other in which the society was held responsible for costs because the judge considered it too aggressive in seeking to remove a child to avoid abuse – indicate the perilous task of the worker caught between Scylla and Charybdis. Will it be any wonder if workers become increasingly defensive, more interested in protecting their own legal flanks than the needs of the children who are supposed to be their primary concern? The effects on workers' confidence and morale will increase with each such case that comes to trial, or where a conviction is handed down without trial on the front pages of sensationalistic newspapers.

Chapter Twelve

'Permanency Planning'

The program of the American Orthopsychiatric Association Annual Meeting (American Psychiatric Association 1980) stated: 'There is a consensus that children need and have a right to a stable permanent home, and that a child's own home and parents are best.'

A New York State committee on adoption, in a document entitled *Adoption: Service Needs and Goals*, discussed long-range planning for children, listing, in order of priority, three basic goals: 1 / to maintain the child in his own home; 2 / if 1 were not possible, to return the child to his natural family; 3 / if 1 and 2 were not possible, to free the child for adoption.

Af first glance, these goals seem both reasonable and humane. However, it becomes increasingly clear that to accept them uncritically would be simplistic. Yet this is precisely what is at times done in the name of 'permanency planning.'

But what is permanency planning and how can the above goals be faulted?

In some jurisdictions, there has been a major push over the last two decades to free all children in foster care, regardless of the length or quality of their placements, either for adoption or for restoration to their own families (Wiltse 1978). This policy is justified on the grounds that it gives these children their best chance to experience a 'stable permanent home.' Thus the rhetoric of many who call for 'permanency planning' at times equates permanency with adoption (Pike et al 1977). But this assumption avoids the major issue in permanency planning, the unavoidable tension around which children's best interests are served by restoring them to their natural family, which children are more likely to have their developmental needs met by a permanent placement excluding the natural family, and which children will do best with something between these two extremes, such as a planned permanent placement with continuing access to the natural parents (Derdeyn 1977; Madison and Schapiro 1970; Snowden 1989). It is important, however, to recognize that beneath the simplistic positions taken by some extreme advocates under the name of permanency planning can lie motives that are primarily economic and political, masked by a thin veneer of psychological-mindedness. One major reason that some authorities systematically urge indiscriminate disruption of long-standing and highly successful placements in the name of ensuring permanence is an economic one: the child in foster care is supported by the community, whereas a child who has been adopted or returned to the natural family is – temporarily, at least – no longer a financial burden on society. Here are just two examples of the climate that until recently pervaded the field.

Example 1. In Ontario, in the 1970s, Children's Aid Society workers were harassed by having to fill out a complex form *every three months* to defend their reasons for not having placed on adoption each child who remained a permanent ward, even if a plan to raise that child to maturity in her present foster home had been agreed upon years ago.

Example 2. At a meeting of Adoption Workers in Albany, New York, in 1976, workers told of a fourteen-year-old black, severely retarded, deaf girl who had lived in the same (white) foster home since birth. The agency was ordered by the courts to prepare her for adoption so that she might have the cultural benefits of adoption by a black family.

The above examples, and many more could have been included, violate several of the basic principles that should form the basis of rational and psychologically minded child welfare policies. Goldstein, Freud, and Solnit (1973) have advised that, when children are successfully bonded within families that meet their developmental and psychological needs, the state should make every effort to protect and support their placements wherever possible, be it in a natural, a foster, or an adoptive family. To disrupt a successful placement unnecessarily in the name of providing permanence – to remove children from families in which they are emotionally bonded and doing well in the hope of finding a not-yet-available-but-still-possibly-better alternative – means taking unnecessary chances with a child's adjustment and subsequent development. For child welfare or mental health professionals to collude with such a process without carefully determining whether the best interests of the particular child are being well served is frankly irresponsible.

Several authors (Maluccio et al 1980; Fein et al 1979, 1983; Maluccio and Fein 1983; Sachdev 1984) have drawn attention to the difference between what is *legally* a permanent placement and one that is *experienced as permanent* by the child and parents involved. Lahti and colleagues (1978) add that the child's sense of permanence, not the legal status of the placement, seems most closely related to the child's sense of well-being. Bush and Gordon (1982) have found that foster children can judge effectively which settings are supportive and what characteristics make them supportive. It is one thing to legally define a placement as permanent, but doing so in no way guarantees either that placement's quality or its permanence. Thus neither placing a child on adoption nor restoring that child to her biological parents offers any guarantee of permanence or stability. Furthermore, removing a child from a foster home that is experienced as permanent by both the child and the foster parents in order to return her home or place her on adoption elsewhere may do violence to that child's best chance for permanence in a misguided attempt to secure it. Pike and colleagues (1977) and Maluccio and Fein (1983) suggest that the term 'permanency planning,' rather than being used as a synonym for 'adoption planning,' should refer to aggressively clarifying and deciding upon the purpose of a given placement and, during temporary care, actively seeking and implementing a plan for permanence, as has been urged in chapter 6.

There is a common belief that adoption reliably provides a higher quality of commitment and caring than does fostering. This is a myth. A number of methodological problems have made it impossible to draw firm conclusions from even those few studies of long-term foster care that do exist. Most of these are prospective but uncontrolled, while a minority are retrospective studies relying on often incomplete and not necessarily accurate charts, or on interviews of past events with social workers or, in one case, ex-wards. Both such designs have questionable validity, as most variables are reported or recalled only subjectively, and the experimenters lack the power to control for or dismiss other possible explanations.

Only one study, that of Stein, Gambrill, and Wiltse (1978), had an adequate experimental design containing both pre- and post-placement measures and random subject assignment. The later outcome studies, despite more complex methodology, remain inconclusive since their outcome measures vary from study to study; they include criminal behaviour (Kraus 1981), intelligence testing (Bohman and Sigvardsson 1981), decrease in problem behaviours (S.E. Palmer 1979), and a sense of wellbeing or variations in adult functioning, often very narrowly defined (Meier 1966; Festinger 1983; Rest and Watson 1984). The time lag between the exit from foster care and the measure of the outcomes also varies, and the longer the interval the greater the possibility that additional intervening variables are contaminating the effects of the foster care in either direction. Finally, the sample sizes and the percentage of the sample lost to follow-up varied considerably, from a population of 13 (Rest and Watson 1984) to one of 491 (Kraus 1981). Rest and Watson were able to study only 18.6 of their original sample, while Festinger obtained the cooperation of 72.6 per cent of hers. As a result, there is little reason to alter Prosser's (1978) conclusion that little is known with certainty about the differential effects of various types of long-term placements. Certainly, some reports support the opinions of experienced workers in the field that long-term foster care need not be as destructive as is generally assumed, and that some ex–foster children seem to manage their lives well (Fanshel and Shinn 1978; Festinger 1983; Zimmerman 1982; Fein et al 1983; Rest and Watson 1984; Fanshel, Finch, and Grundy 1990). Some studies show that ex-wards do not have particularly low self-esteem (Seligman 1979) or high rates of delinquency (Runyan 1985) or behaviour problems (Palmer 1979; Leitenberg et al 1981). One that followed 585 highly traumatized children over eighteen years showed that an encouraging 60 per cent went on, after foster care, to lead well-adjusted lives (Fanshel, Finch, and Grundy 1990). Some foster children clearly prefer remaining in care to returning to their natural parents' homes (Lemmon 1975; Bush 1980), and studies have demonstrated that foster children lose many of the benefits achieved while in care if returned home (Block 1981; Rzepnicki 1987; Wald, Carlsmith, and Leiderman 1988; Wolf, Braukmann, and Ramp 1987).

The fact is that there is considerable overlap between foster and adoptive placements in terms of both quality and permanence. Several authors, in fact, have noted that the relationship of fostering and adoptive care to each other is changing. With a decreasing number of healthy infants available for adoption; an increase in the number of older, disturbed, and/or multiple handicapped children requiring long-term placement; and the emergence of such intermediate alternatives as subsidized or open adoption, planned permanent foster care, and foster care with tenure, there appears to be a major convergence between the two extremes once represented by traditional foster and adoptive care (Bowyer 1980; Cooper 1978; Hepworth 1980; Kadushin 1980; Steinhauer 1983b).

Many children who would once have been considered unadoptable are now placed on adoption under a variety of different arrangements, ranging from traditional adoption up to and including forms of adoption that permit ongoing access to key attachment figures from the child's past. Foster parents, who, until twenty years ago, were routinely considered 'overinvolved' if they sought to adopt one of their wards, are now seen as, preferred to be, and even, at times, pressured into becoming the adoptive parents of choice. Their choosing not to adopt a difficult child is often interpreted as proof that they lack commitment to the child. Some agencies then move rapidly to remove that child for placement with a family that is prepared to adopt him. But, many foster parents who are prepared to foster a child to maturity balk at adoption, not because of a lukewarm commitment, but because they are realistic enough to anticipate major difficulties for the child and their family during the child's adolescence. For this reason, they do not want to cut themselves off from continued access to support services available freely to foster children but not to adoptees.

The family accepting an older and 'unadoptable' child or sibling group on adoption probation may sincerely intend to offer a permanent home, but good intentions are no guarantee that such a placement will succeed. It is misleading, therefore, when planning for an older or multiple-handicapped child, to fail to consider the merits of both planned permanent foster care and adoption, since each may have its advantages, limitations, and risks for a particular child. Theoretical arguments for one alternative or the other that are applied rigidly and dogmatically – ignoring the possible superiority of the other for a given child – are more likely to be damaging than a more flexible approach that considers all possible available alternatives (Bush and Goldman 1982). In the United States, federal legislation stressing only adoption or restoration to natural families fails to recognize the need of that substantial segment of foster children whom the foster care system can rescue from anti-social careers, dependency, and other life failures (Fanshel, Finch, and Grundy 1990).

For some children, foster care can be every bit as good – and, as Derdeyn has pointed out, for selected children may even be much better – than moving them to adoption (Derdeyn 1977; Steinhauer 1983b; Rest and Watson 1984). Other placements, either foster or adoptive, clearly offer an inferior quality of care. The psychological and developmental needs of children living in inadequate and/or rejecting homes, be they foster or adoptive, will not be met.

There is a second, frequently held belief that adoption can be counted upon to guarantee greater continuity than can foster care. Research on foster care is weighted in the direction of investigating failures. With a few exceptions (Zimmerman 1982; Festinger 1983; Fanshel, Finch, and Grundy 1990), there is little in the literature regarding unbroken, permanent, or planned long-term placements. Madison and Schapiro (1970) stress the importance of distinguishing planned permanent foster care from the at best indifferent long-term fostering resulting from lack of planning, from drift, from inadequate service, or from agency neglect (see also Bush and Goldman 1982). In a similar vein, Wiltse (1979) and Wald and colleagues (1988), reviewing the work of Fanshel and Shinn (1978) and other studies, concur that there is no proof that continued foster care is 'demonstrably deleterious,' but that permanency in living arrangements and continuity of key relationships (rather than whether a home is foster or adoptive) emerge as the critical variables. This issue raises a number of related ones concerning research design, which will be returned to later in this chapter, and also brings us to a discussion of 'drift.'

Most child welfare workers use the term 'drift' to refer to the situation of the child brought into care who, more through agency neglect, passivity, or inefficiency than from design or active planning, unintentionally ends up in long-term foster care, abandoned both by his natural parents and by the agency that is supposedly protecting his welfare (Miller et al 1984). But for some of the more extreme advocates of planned permanency, all long-term foster care is considered harmful, as is illustrated by a 1979 report of the National Commission of Children in Need of Parents, entitled 'Who Knows? Who Cares? Forgotten Children in Foster Care.' According to that report, 'foster care provides little love and virtually guarantees insecurity and instability for many children in its embrace' (see also Gruber 1978). In taking this extreme position, the authors fail to distinguish the indifferent long-term foster care derived from drift and inefficiency from the planned permanent foster care designed to preserve permanently a foster-care placement of high quality that is perceived as permanent by both the child and the foster parents involved (Rest and Watson 1984; Bush and Goldman 1982).

But is there only one form of drift? The drift of the child already in care is already well recognized. But there are other forms of drift that, though less commonly referred to as such, are similar in their origin and no less destructive in their effects.

The first of these consists of allowing a child to drift towards increasing psychosocial deterioration in a natural family that has given ample evidence to its inability to meet that child's developmental needs. Thus failure to take a child into care, when a careful assessment of parenting capacity would have indicated that to do so is in the child's best interests, is one form of drift (Wald, Carlsmith, and Leiderman 1988; Lamb et al 1985; Schneider-Rosen and Cicchetti 1984; Egeland, Sroufe, and Erickson 1983).

Another form occurs when an agency ineffectually allows a child to drift – 'bounce' might be a better word – in and out of care by repeatedly restoring that child to ambivalent and/or frankly rejecting natural parents who could reasonably have been identified much sooner as incapable of meeting that child's minimal developmental needs. Rzepnicki (1987) warns that the return home from foster care should always be considered as a new placement, with agencies providing all the accompanying preparing and assistance both in advance and subsequently that would be afforded any other well-handled placement. Wald and colleagues (1988) suggest that, since most of the benefits of foster care appear to be lost when children return home, and since efforts at family reunification are favoured by judges and social workers in the absence of physical danger, policy makers and social planners need to develop and advocate more effective forms of intervention on behalf of abused and neglected children. The same authors hypothesize that the relationship between natural mother and child appears to be a critical factor. Those children who do worst come from families with long histories of rejection and lack of structure, whereas the provision of predictability, structure, freedom from abuse, and the opportunity to learn more effective social skills seems to be the main factor preventing further deterioration and assisting the children in their development.

The drift in and out of inadequate families (Bank, Patterson, and Reid 1987; Wolf et al 1987; Block 1981; Rest and Watson 1984; Tizard and Rees 1974; Turner, 1984) may result from a failure of the court system rather than agency inertia, when judges, in spite of convincing evidence of parental incapacity, elect, nevertheless, to return children to inadequate families (Wolf, Braukmann, and Ramp 1987). This form of drift, drift within the legal system, was discussed in chapter 11.

One reason for the reluctance of many agencies and courts to support planned permanent foster care is the frequency with which foster homes break down when children reach adolescence. Many do, of course, but then many natural and even infant adoptive families also show signs of severe strain and/or disruption as their much-less-damaged children reach adolescence. One wonders, also, how many of those foster placements that *do* break down in adolescence deteriorate because of inadequate case planning and management prior to adolescence (Rowe and Lambert 1975; Rowe et al 1984). I am referring here to the widespread prevalence of inadequate assessment and placement techniques and insufficiently aggressive or systemic casework and planning reported by Palmer (1974) in Ontario; by Aldridge and Cautley (1975) in the United States; and by Berridge and Cleaver (1987), Rowe et al (1984), and Vernon and Fruin (1986) in Great Britain (see also Bowyer 1980; Snowden 1989; Bush and Goldman 1982).

It would be irresponsible, however, to blame welfare agencies for society's failure to provide the conditions – the smaller caseloads, the necessary professional back-up, and the range and quality of casework and back-up services – that will maximize the chance of children growing to maturity within their own families. The complexity of the children coming into care is increasing while the revenues available for caring for them are shrinking. Further exacerbating the problem are increases in the amount of paperwork to be attended to, the time spent preparing for and appearing in court, the hours required to investigate thoroughly the increasingly frequent sexual abuse allegations, and so on. The inevitable result of all these factors is that workers' caseloads increase, forcing them to shift their focus away from planned or preventive interventions in order to meet even the minimal service needs of one crisis after another (Vernon and Fruin 1986). Too often, overloaded workers who spend less than 30 per cent of their time actually seeing clients (Metro 1989) are dragged from crisis to crisis, ineffectually attempting to lock the barn door after the horse is already out rather than having the opportunity to stand back, plan, and implement adequate preventive and early intervention services or a well-formulated management plan on an ongoing basis. Surely such ongoing systemic neglect, however unintended, is a major factor in placement breakdowns and worker burn-out, both of which eventually add to the cost, human and economic, of inadequate resources and insufficient services (Berridge and Cleaver 1987; Snowden 1989; Metro 1989; Lawton and Magarelli 1980).

Generally speaking, children, adoptive parents, social workers, and society at large expect more of adoption than they do of foster care. Adoption usually implies the hope and intention of the adoptive family to integrate the child as a part of the family. But the child or sibling group who come with set personalities and well-established problems of their own, those with strong memories of and a continuing attachment to their natural parents, those who have been severely damaged prior to coming into care, or whose capacity to relate and to respond to the affection of others has been blunted by multiple rejections and breakdowns prior to adoption placement – for all these, the potential for forming the quality of attachment implied by adoption may just not exist. One worker presented for adoption a twelve-year-old girl who had been passed through fourteen foster homes in slightly more than three years, all placements ending in disaster. This child had been suggested to an inter-agency conference as a good candidate for adoption. All her placement breakdowns were rationalized as having nothing to do with her; it was just her bad luck to have been placed in fourteen consecutive inappropriate foster families. There was no recognition whatsoever that the child might have psychological problems that had contributed significantly to any of the breakdowns. Without realizing it, the worker presented evidence strongly suggesting that the girl's capacities for trust and relating were severely limited; that she had serious problems in peer relationships, impulse control, and the ability to focus her attention enough to permit school success. Without ever having been assessed by a psychologist or psychiatrist, she was being placed for adoption as a normal child. This case is by no means an isolated example. To present such 'normal' children, naïvely or dishonestly, as good candidates for adoption is unfair both to the children themselves and to potential adoptive families.

In summary, then, adoption may offer more than planned permanent foster care:

– if the child is young enough (i.e., under the age of three or four) and legally and psychologically free to form the kind of total attachment that almost all adoptive parents need and expect; or
– if adoptive parents are able to accept and to commit themselves to

a child age four or over both knowing (intellectually) and appreciating (emotionally) that whether or not the child may ever be truly integrated within their family may not be known for years; *and*
- if both child and adoptive family, with the assistance of whatever supports are and will continue to be made available, are considered able to survive the period of testing, acting out, and emotional withdrawal that may go on for months, for years, or forever.

However, planned permanent foster care, with or without access to the natural parents, depending on the needs of the children involved, may offer more than adoption:

- for the older child who has lived as much of his life as he can remember securely attached in a foster family, which he perceives as a permanent placement, as long as his developmental needs are being met, his development and adjustment are either good or improving, and foster parents are willing to commit themselves to raising the child until maturity;
- for the older and more disturbed foster child, where the risk of removing her from a foster family that can accept her in spite of her disturbance, and in whose care she is at least holding her own, is greater than that of preserving the present placement;
- for the child over the age of four who remains obviously attached to an ineffectual but loving parent who, while incapable of providing the care he needs, is prepared to visit the child regularly and can do so without undermining the child's identification of the foster parents as his primary caretakers;
- for the older child who remains intensely but anxiously attached to natural parents who are neglecting or abusive; unless that child can be helped to accept the loss of those parents as final and to complete the mourning process, which is frequently impossible, that child is unlikely to join and integrate within an adoptive family to the extent that most adoptive parents expect and demand.

In their model study, Stein, Gambrill, and Wiltse (1978) have demonstrated that having experienced caseworkers with smaller caseloads – presumably acting through more intensive work with all members of the foster care system – was correlated with successful permanency planning. Other associated factors have included environmental ones, such as a lack of housing and financial problems; parent-related ones, such as frequent visiting, especially during the child's first six months in care; and, in a single study (Fein et al 1983), a child having a temporary trial at returning to his own home as part of an active planning process. However, both Sherman, Newman, and Shyne (1973) and Block and Libowitz (1983) found that at least 25 per cent of restorations break down and the children are returned to care at least once. While Lahti and colleagues (1978) found a somewhat smaller recidivism rate, one cannot be sure to what extent this is a reflection of high-quality, goal-directed casework or just a function of a shorter follow-up time. Child-related factors associated with success include the age of the child at which the permanent placement is made and a decrease in behaviour problems after coming into care. Levitt (1981) has talked of the advantages of a contractual approach, but one cannot be sure whether those advantages are attributable to the contracts themselves or to the fact that they are one example of the goal-directed case planning that Lahti and colleagues (1978) associated with affording permanence. There is no reason to doubt that the early intervention and active casework and tracking found effective by Stein, Gambrill, and Wiltse (1978), Levitt (1981) and Fanshel, Finch and Grundy (1990), often in association with others of the factors listed above, would also tend to protect permanency. However, an increase in the total number of placements and being a teenager at entry into care have been associated with a lack of successful permanency planning (Claburn and Magura 1977; Block and Libowitz 1983).

These principles are intended to serve as guidelines for the selective use of long-term placements. Neither set of guidelines is complete, and one could envision additional circumstances that might modify their application to a given case. They should not be followed unthinkingly, but, until research provides more clear-cut guidelines than are currently available, they can serve as a basis for deciding the cases for which each of the major forms of long-term placement seems most appropriate. Usually, if one has the facts and formulates them carefully, one can evaluate the advantages and disadvantages of each type of placement for a particular child. The worker or consultant who routinely considers both alternatives and then settles on the least detrimental one is less likely to do unnecessary harm than the one dogmatically committed to either alternative. There is also a need, largely unmet, to involve regularly all recipients of service, including natural parents and the children involved, in systematic decision making and program evaluation (Bush and Gordon 1982; Bush and Goldman 1982; Cooper 1978; Rowe et al 1984; C.R. Smith 1984).

Much of what has been suggested in this chapter is opinion – that of the author, based on more than twenty-seven years of continuing involvement with several local children's aid societies. It also reflects the opinions of many respected colleagues, both social workers and child psychiatrists, from whose thinking and experience he has learned a great deal. It is consistent with his reading of the professional literature that he has found useful and helpful. This whole area is one in which there is little solidly proved fact, while much that is glibly presented as fact is, rather, mere opinion.

This brings us to the final point, the need for more carefully controlled research into the outcome of various forms of child placement. In order to clarify rather than merely perpetuate and appear to legitimize continuing confusion, research must sufficiently take into account such issues as:

– the psychological status of the child prior to removal from the natural family;
– the age at separation from the natural family;
– the number of breaks in continuity (i.e., placements, returns, and replacements);
– placement techniques and casework or other services utilized, including a description of the number of pre-placement visits; the degree to which feelings stirred up by separation were dealt with in casework; the nature and extent of casework services provided;
– the presence or absence of contact with the natural family while in care; and
– the amount and quality of casework support given the placement throughout the period in care.

The above list is by no means exhaustive, but it at least draws attention to the extreme difficulty of developing research procedures that allow a valid comparison between the success rates of planned permanent foster care and adoption. Every attempt should be made to design studies that are sufficiently rigorous to provide firmer guidelines for the selective use of adoption and planned permanent foster care, in order to better serve older children needing families. In the meantime, we should be aware of the lack of adequately validated comparisons between planned permanent foster care and adoption. In their absence, we should be prepared to base our interventions not on dogma or simplistic rhetoric but on systemic planning and the careful application of principles of child development and attachment theory and their clinical applications.

Chapter Thirteen

Potential Contributions of
Mental Health Consultants
within the Child Welfare System

This chapter discusses different ways that child psychiatrists and psychologists are utilized as consultants by child welfare agencies and explores the benefits and some limitations of each.

The Client-Centred Case Consultant

Psychologists and psychiatrists are most often utilized by child welfare agencies to provide client-centred case consultations, that is, clinical assessments of children or families that are then used to guide case planning, usually at a point of crisis, or to support the agency's position in court. There is no doubt that effective client-centred consultation can be helpful, especially if it is appropriately timed and followed up by adequate two-way discussion of the practicality of the consultant's conclusions and recommendations with those directly responsible for caring and planning for the child. There are, however, limitations to the value of this form of consultation, especially when it is the only way that an agency utilizes its consultants. These include the following.

1 / *Lack of expertise of the worker.* The value of client-centred case consultations varies directly with the clinical skill and experience of the worker and/or supervisor requesting them. Unfortunately, those who utilize client-centred consultations most are usually those who need them least. Less sensitive and inexperienced workers are less likely to recognize the need for consultation, or may initiate it only after the case has so deteriorated that little can be done to alter its course significantly.

Experienced, skilled workers are also better equipped to focus the consultation around the questions they need answers to, and to understand and utilize the suggestions of the consultant, than are less sophisticated workers.

2 / *Cost-effectiveness of client-centred case consultations.* The client-centred case consultation is a relatively inefficient use of a consultant's time. It requires a relatively large investment in a single case, often with little carry-over to the worker's functioning with other clients. Attempts to economize by shortening the time available for the consultant to assess child and family or by substituting a written report for a face-to-face discussion of conclusions and recommendations significantly increase the risk of skewing the consultation. Under such conditions, consultants risk generalizing from an insufficient understanding of the case, are often unclear as to what exactly the agency wants from them, and are unsure as to whether or not their recommendations are seen as practical, relevant, and workable.

3 / *The triangulated consultant.* In the client-centred case consultation, consultants risk being inadvertently caught up in internal agency conflicts or power struggles that they fail to recognize or to understand. For example, a request for consultation may be a worker's attempt to go over the head of a supervisor or a supervisor's attempt to pressure a worker into conformity. While, at times, consultation can be used appropriately to resolve disagreements around clinical issues, its success will depend on the consultant's ability to avoid getting caught up in political in-fighting and to maintain the focus on the needs of the case. When the request for consultation is, in effect, an attempt to select and manipulate a consultant so as to increase one professional's power over another (e.g., worker over supervisor; supervisor over worker; child-care worker over protection worker), the consultation is in danger of being, at best, unhelpful and, very possibly, counter-productive. Most seasoned workers and supervisors have previously worked with a number of consultants and are skilled at selecting one whose decisions, from past experience, are likely to support their point of view. This tendency adds to the danger of such a consultation providing a vehicle for acting out instead of problem solving. The more a request for consultation *substitutes for* rather than *supplements* a full, open, direct, and rational discussion of the needs of the case, the more likely it is to prove unhelpful, or even destructive.

Earlier, reference was made to the attitude of the mental health consultant to the consultee. Caplan (1963, 1970) has pointed out that respecting the consultee's areas of competence is essential for effective consultation. But many mental health professionals tend to be unsympathetic or patronizing towards front-line child welfare workers. With their primary interest in intrapsychic pathology and in psychotherapy, many child psychiatrists and clinical psychologists fail to recognize how much of that which is possible in their private office or clinic is meaningless or unrealistic in the less-protected world of the child welfare agency. Unlike them, the child welfare agency does not have the luxury of refusing to work with 'impossible' cases. It must continue to struggle with multi-problem families who are rarely motivated to seek treatment and who, even were they to initiate it, would soon be considered unmotivated, resistant, and/or unsuitable for psychotherapy. To rate workers' attempts to deal with such families by the same criteria used to evaluate a psychiatric resident's or a psychological intern's treatment of a middle-class, reasonably motivated child or family is unfair and potentially degrading. An overemphasis on intrapsychic conflict, if it ignores familial and social aspects of a foster child's family and social context, may be irrelevant and unhelpful, even if the dynamic formulation of the case is accurate. A psychodynamic or systemic emphasis can be invaluable, however, if it accurately links intrapsychic or interpersonal conflict with their behavioural expression in a way that leads front-line staff to improved understanding and better management. The consultant who, failing to recognize the limited potential of a case or the limitations imposed on the consultee by too large a caseload, too little training, and/or inadequate or insufficient supervision, places unrealistic expectations on a worker who is thereby left feeling unduly responsible, overwhelmed, and demoralized will do more harm than good (Malucchio et al 1980).

However, a number of factors can maximize the usefulness of client-centred consultation. These include the following.

1 / *Timing.* Elective consultations (i.e., those sought when a case is not yet in crisis) are more likely to be helpful than are emergency consultations (i.e., those initiated only after the case is in crisis or a major management change such as a foster-home breakdown has already occurred). Elective consultation allows time to achieve an adequate assessment of the psychological and systemic issues involved and to

compare management alternatives, thus minimizing the pressure on all those involved. Consultants, too, can be immobilized by excessive pressure and/or expectations, which can detract from the usefulness of their impressions and recommendations.

Finally, while consultants can, at times, propose concrete solutions to practical problems, they are often unable to provide the clear-cut direction workers would like, especially if called in only after a case has deteriorated to the point of no return. Thus requests for emergency consultation are often equally frustrating to consultant and consultee; the consultants feel that they have been set up to fail and, possibly, to be scapegoated for their inability to keep the case from deteriorating farther. Meanwhile, the consultees, still lacking the answers they wanted but not realizing the impossibility of their questions, dismiss the process as an exercise in futility. Thus, their belief that consultation is a waste of time is reinforced, setting them up to repeat the self-defeating cycle in the future.

2 / *Preparation for the consultation.* The more effectively the workers have pulled together their understanding of the case and focused their questions, the greater the consultant's chance of proving helpful. At times, the process of standing back and preparing for consultation may in itself prove almost as helpful as the consultant's input.

3 / *Two-way communication between consultant and consultee following the assessment.* Most consultations are only as valuable as the extent and quality of the communication between consultant and consultee(s) in response to the consultant's initial recommendations. These should be placed on the table not as a final statement, but as the starting-point for negotiations between consultant and agency. All too often, however, such a dialogue fails to occur for a number of reasons including the following.

a / *Too little time.* Lack of time is often used to explain the failure of consultant and consultee to meet together to discuss the recommendations. Often, however, this factor is a rationalization for too little interest on the part of the worker, the consultant, or both.

b / *Consultant defensiveness.* Some consultants have an inflated opinion of their own importance and cannot tolerate anyone questioning or disagreeing with their initial impressions and recommendations. The more consultants become defensive, rigid, or angry in the face of attempts to point out realistic obstacles to the carrying out of their recommendations, the less likely they are to receive the corrective feedback they need to learn what is realistic and possible in the real world of the child welfare agency. Thus they lose a chance to fine-tune their understanding and recommendations to the point where they become practical, relevant, and, therefore, useful.

At the root of such defensiveness is the issue of the basic nature of the relationship between consultant and consultee. Those consultants who picture themselves as having all the answers because of the superior knowledge and insight stemming from their professional status are much less likely to prove helpful than are those who appropriately value their consultees' greater knowledge and expertise regarding problems common to the child welfare field. Thus, while the consultant may know more about intrapsychic conflict, family relations, or hyperactivity, the case worker knows much more about the social context of child welfare families; how realistic it is to expect to modify a pattern of neglect or abuse that has gone on for years; and the realistic limitations arising from having to carry too large a caseload in an underfunded, understaffed, and undersupervised agency. Consultants' ability to recognize and acknowledge the limitations of what they know and to respect and learn from their consultees' areas of greater experience and expertise may be more important than the correctness of their formulation or recommendations in determining their effectiveness.

c / *Consultee resistance.* The consultee may fail to express directly any questions or disagreement with the consultant's conclusions or recommendations. Reasons for this behaviour may include lack of respect for the consultant; frustration or anger at the recommendations; an inability to understand what the consultant is saying, which may be the result of the consultant's hiding behind professional jargon and communicating poorly rather than of any inability of the consultee to understand; intimidation by the personal or professional qualifications or manner of the consultant; difficulty in challenging the consultant, who is seen as a competitor or as an authority figure; or interprofessional rivalry. Instead, the consultees may read the consultant's report or sit passively through a scheduled attempt to discuss recommendations without raising even important questions, doubts, or objections. Then, after the consultant has left, consultees may ventilate to each other the criticisms and/or hostility that should have been expressed directly. This approach deprives the consultant not only of a chance to modify or augment unclear, impractical, or inappropriate recommendations, but also of the opportunity to learn from the corrective potential of the workers' experience.

Whenever a consultant's advice seems wrong or impractical, workers should courteously but directly point out where she seems to be off base. The responsibility of the consultant in such a situation is twofold: she, as the more powerful participant in the consultation, should actively and routinely elicit sufficient feedback from the consultees to focus, and adapt if necessary, the original recommendations, being careful to consider any feedback without defensiveness or retaliation.

The Consultee-Centred Case Consultation

In a consultee-centred consultation, a case example is used primarily to expand the knowledge or clinical skills of the consultee(s). In this way, the impact and efficiency of the consultation can be increased. Consultee-centred consultations are often seen by agencies as useful only after an initial period of client-centred case consultations, during which the consultant has proved herself as potentially helpful and able to contribute to case management without being too critical or threatening. Because there is more emphasis on the professional functioning of the consultee, this form of consultation can be more anxiety-provoking, even though the explicit focus remains case-centred.

The consultant should always bear in mind the limits of the consultation mandate: her job is to improve the consultee's professional performance. Where possible, this improvement will be achieved by their examining together the needs of the case or by respectful questioning of the process of case management. The validity of unwarranted assumptions or of general principles or problems illustrated by the specific case may be pointed out. As the consultant recognizes a recurrent pattern of omission or commission, she may draw attention to a repeating sequence of events or stereotyped responses that seems to interfere with the conduct of the case. The definitive discussion of the effective management of such situations, termed 'theme interference,' remains that of Caplan (1970), which has yet to be improved upon. The process is illustrated late in this chapter in the section on working relationships between consultants and consultees.

Consultants should be particularly wary of administrators who invite them to discuss or treat what they describe as the 'problems' or 'psychopathology' of their staff. Therapy for agency staff, if indicated, should be sought outside the agency, and not masked under the guise of supervision or consultation. To accept any such invitation goes far beyond the mandate of the ethical consultant, and usually ends up undermining the trust on which a successful consultation relationship depends. Neither administrator nor consultant has the mandate to focus upon the personal conflicts of the consultee as if he were a patient. Although these conflicts may be recognized and their derivatives may be dealt with by the consultant in displacement – that is, by helping the worker understand or manage the case more effectively – their direct resolution is the job of the consultee and, if necessary, of his personal therapist; it has no place within the power structure of the agency in which he works. If a referral for consultation comes to be seen as an invitation for unwanted analysis or focus upon the personality of the worker, consultation will be seen as an unwarranted intrusion, and the relationship between consultant and agency will inevitably be undermined.

A consultee-centred case consultation can take different forms. The first example illustrates how what was originally presented as a client-centred case consultation was modified to deal with theme interference on the part of the consultee. A second example of a consultee-centred case consultation is found in the description of the 'Balint-type' seminar, which will be described below.

An experienced worker sought consultation because of an inability to shift a repeated pattern occurring in a family where both parents were stubbornly oppositional and the wife was, in addition, excessively dependent. Any time the worker tried to focus on how husband and wife undermined each other, they would mysteriously manage to derail her intervention and disrupt her therapeutic focus.

The consultant asked the worker to play two or three segments of a videotaped interview in which the unrecognized manoeuvre had occurred. Replaying one section, she then asked the worker what the wife had achieved by getting upset and claiming to be misunderstood just after the worker had confronted her with undermining her husband. In answering the question, the worker realized that the mother's attack had diverted her from the examination of the mother's undermining behaviour. When the consultant asked if this sequence was a repeated one, the worker replied that whenever she asked the wife to examine her behaviour, she would either get upset or aggressively demand that the worker explain to her exactly what she wanted her to do. In this way, she would again and again catch the worker off balance, putting her on the defensive and diverting the demand for self-scrutiny.

The consultant then asked about the husband's role. Was he always as cooperative as he seemed on tape, or did he, too, have ways of preventing a focus upon his contribution to the pathological interaction? The worker stated that, until she had been asked the question, she had not realized that he, too, blocked progress, but in different ways. For the most part, by sitting silent, he put steady pressure on his wife to reveal herself, and therefore her contribution to the family problem, to the worker. Then, when he did talk, he presented a picture of sweet reason personified, although the children repeatedly snickered and remarked that there was a big difference between how he behaved in the sessions and how he acted at home. Once these repeated patterns had been recognized, the consultee had much less trouble dealing with them in future sessions.

The consultant suspected that this worker, usually quite perceptive, failed to recognize so obvious a repeating pattern because of a selective inattention or 'blind spot' related to some personal (i.e., counter-transference) meaning of the sequence. The consultant made no attempt, however, to explore the psychological reasons for the blind spot. Instead, she chose to help the worker overcome it in displacement by helping her see the aspects of the case that she was failing to appreciate.

THE 'BALINT-TYPE' SEMINAR

Michael Balint, the British psychoanalyst, met with groups of physicians to advise them around the management of psychosocial issues occurring in their practices. The participating doctors would discuss in the group their patients' difficulties and how they had attempted to deal with them. The groups, under the leadership of Dr Balint, would sensitize the participating physicians to psychological nuances that helped them understand and respond more effectively to their patients' psychosocial needs.

Some agencies utilize consultee-centred consultation extremely effectively by having a group of workers meet regularly with a consultant to discuss work-related problems as they arise. The consultant uses the case material to increase the understanding, skills, and confidence of the participating professionals in their job performance. Such seminars differ from group supervision in several important respects. First, the consultant remains outside the power structure of the agency. For such a seminar to work, the participants must feel free to discuss even – or especially – those aspects of their work in which they feel least confident or secure, knowing that such disclosures will not in any way be used against them. For the consultant within such a contract to relay to a supervisor or agency administrator a negative evaluation of a worker's contributions would represent a breech of trust and constitute un-professional behaviour. The consultant's position as an outsider will allow her an objectivity and distance that those within the agency, over-whelmed by the responsibility for decision making, may have lost.

Also, the consultant's position outside the power structure of the agency will, ideally, leave her untouched by tensions and politics that, within the agency, may contaminate clinical decision making. This same dis-tance may allow the consultant to be supportive in a way that someone caught up in the inevitable power struggles that occur in agencies cannot be. It goes without saying that a prerequisite for the consultant to func-tion effectively in this role is the ability to remain outside agency pol-itics. Consultants who support one agency faction against another sooner or later lose the credibility needed to provide this particular form of consultation. Partisanship might but need not constitute a barrier to an administrative consultation in which the consultant's mandate is to advise the agency administrators as to how to improve agency efficiency and functioning.

Program-Centred Case Consultations

A still more cost-effective use of mental-health consultation occurs when the child psychologist or psychiatrist consults to a department or pro-gram within the agency. Here the goal of the consultation is to augment the knowledge and skills of a group of staff involved, for example, through in-service training designed to help staff master a particular technique or better understand a particular problem of practice.

The author was asked to consult on a situation involving Annie, an eighteen-month-old girl who was being considered for adoption. The complicating factor was that Annie had an eleven-year-old sister, Holly, who visited Annie faithfully each month, looked for-ward to the visits, constantly talked about Annie, and was extremely affectionate whenever she saw her. She had just missed one visit, because of chicken pox when Annie was ten months old. On the next and subsequent visits, Annie's behaviour towards Holly had changed. Whereas previously she had gone to her readily and played easily with her, subsequent to the missed visit, she hung back, looked away, and cried when Holly approached her; only after ten to fifteen minutes did she warm up and play with Holly, as she had in the past. Holly's child-care worker was convinced that, while Holly visited her mother as often as the mother's inconsistency would allow, it was Annie who mattered to her more than anyone else in the world. She argued that, if Annie were placed on adoption, one of the conditions should be a willingness of the adoptive family to allow Holly to continue her visits. Annie's worker, however, felt that ongoing contact with Holly would complicate Annie's adoption, so she wanted the contact between the sisters terminated.

The author suggested a meeting with all workers in the child-care and adoption departments of the agency branch involved. After a brief description of the major forms of attachment (see chapter 2), he questioned Annie's foster mother and the workers who had known the two children and supervised their visits with each other about how they behaved towards each other during their visits. He used the information received to demonstrate that Annie was attached to her foster mother and foster siblings, but not to her natural mother or to Holly. In doing this, he was careful to point out the evidence on which he based his conclusions, so that the workers would know what information to gather in other cases to assess the quality of a one-year-old's attachment to various family and foster-family members. He then explored Holly's relationships with her mother and Annie, pointing out the evidence needed to confirm the worker's statement that Holly seemed more attached to Annie, suggesting how one could distinguish whether this was normal but overly exuberant play (which it was) or a sign of a potentially serious sibling rivalry (which it was not).

The author then tackled the significance of the change in Annie's responses to Holly after the missed meeting. He talked about how not seeing Holly for two months at Annie's age would alter Annie's perception of Holly (by converting her from someone known into a stranger), and how it was only at or after eight months of age that infants begin to 'make strange' with those they do not know well. Thus Annie's modified responses were an age-appropriate response to someone who, by absence, had become a stranger, in contrast with her close relationship to her foster siblings, to whom she was securely attached. We also examined Annie's responses to separation (e.g., when the foster parents left her with a sitter) for some clues as to how she would likely respond to moving from the foster home to an adoptive family, and discussed ways in which the reaction to the separation could be minimized.

Finally, we turned to the question that had prompted the consultation. The author confirmed that this was a question with no satisfactory answer: what would be in Annie's best interests (i.e., adoption with access to the foster family at first but not to Holly) would be against Holly's best interests, and vice versa. The fact that the consultant was just as unable as they were to find an easy, painless way around the conflicting alternatives was reassuring to the assembled workers, whose interest, high level of involvement, and expressions of thanks suggested that they would find the approach useful in deciding similar questions in other cases.

The specific areas in which a given consultant will be able to assist an agency will depend both on the consultant's personal interests and expertise and on the needs of the department, program, or agency. A specific contract acceptable to both consultant and agency should be drawn up and agreed upon, and should be reviewed and, if necessary, renegotiated at least every six months, or even more often in agencies with rapid staff turnover, in order to ensure that the consultation remains relevant and acceptable, both to the consumers and to the consultant. While the following list is by no means complete, there are a number of areas in which mental health consultants often can contribute to staff development of a child welfare agency through in-service training or other forms of program consultation.

1 / *By increasing workers' knowledge of child development and assessment.* A significant number of those who plan for children in care lack even the most basic knowledge of children's developmental norms. Since an understanding of the range of normal is essential in order to identify accurately what is abnormal, the consultant who can help staff learn to assess accurately developmental norms – and developmental needs – will thereby increase their capacity for accurate assessment and planning. This is essential to effective case management.

Two social workers in a Children's Aid Society commented with surprise and pleasure on the ease with which a two-year-old, who was being assessed for adoption, would go to complete strangers without any evidence of anxiety whatsoever. Questioning made it clear that this child had no special relationship with anyone: he was just as likely to go off with or seek comfort from a stranger as he was from his foster parents of six months. Thus what the workers had mistakenly viewed as evidence of security, social confidence, and readiness for adoption was, in fact, a manifestation of failure of attachment resulting from long-term and extreme parental inadequacy, inconsistency, and, subsequently, multiple moves. The correct understanding of this behaviour obviously had major implications in choosing an appropriate placement for the child and in predicting his future.

2 / *By increasing workers' skills at formulation and treatment planning.* Accurate formulation is the key to effective intervention. Formulation is the process, following an adequate assessment, of interpreting the results of that assessment, using an adequate knowledge of developmental principles. The goal of formulation is to achieve an understanding of those biological, familial, social, and psychological factors that, singly and in interaction with one another, predisposed to, precipitated, and are perpetuating symptomatic behaviour and emotional problems. A good formulation also pinpoints those protective factors that can be utilized to help child, family, and foster family avoid or master recurrent crises.

Many front-line workers intervene without first having achieved an adequate understanding of child and family. The more clearly the child's situation in the context of his family is understood – that is, the clearer the worker's formulation of the case – the less likely that worker is to intervene inappropriately. Most workers can learn in a relatively short time to improve their formulation and treatment planning skills greatly. Providing them with models for formulation and workshops in applying these to case planning can be an excellent use of a well-chosen consultant.

3 / *By expanding the consultee's awareness of factors contributing to the problem.* Earlier it was suggested that the child psychologist or psychiatrist who is aware *only* of intrapsychic (i.e., psychological) or familial conflicts or tensions may be of limited use as a consultant to Children's Aid societies. However, the consultant familiar with intrapsychic dynamics and with the ability to correlate these with familial and social factors perpetuating ongoing conflicts can prove extremely helpful, es-

pecially to workers who think almost exclusively in terms of social and interpersonal behaviour, regularly missing the extent to which these are related to – and perpetuated by – intrapsychic pathology.

For example, a worker who understands repeated conflict between a child and his foster parents just in ongoing interactional terms (i.e., their response to the child's misbehaviour; the child's reactions to their attempts to limit his misbehaviour) will miss the boat if a major contributor to the child's behaviour is residual anger transferred from his natural parents, whom he sees as having abandoned him. Should this be the case, helping the child recognize and deal more directly with his continuing sense of abandonment will do more to undermine the displacement by the child and circular acting out between child and foster parents than a purely interactional or behavioural focus.

4 / *By serving as a resource person and a source of specific skills, e.g., techniques of understanding and communicating with young children through play, or of family or group assessment and counselling.* Some workers and agencies may have considerable skill in the techniques of assessment and formulation, but may wish to increase their ability to intervene effectively to help children change. In other agencies, supervisory and administrative staff, while acknowledging the potential usefulness of a particular skill, may lack either the expertise or the teaching skills needed to introduce the technique successfully to the staff. In such cases, a consultant with expertise in the particular technique can train staff in the new intervention with benefit to the agency as a whole.

5 / *By providing cognitive structures (models) and special areas of knowledge in key areas* such as attachment and separation theory; assistance in the work of mourning; assessment of parenting capacity; effective organization of case material for presentation in court; assessment and management of cases where sexual abuse is alleged. These can help workers understand and organize their clinical experience.

Many front-line workers, while dealing day to day with some of the most difficult children and families in the community, lack the theoretical models needed to understand – and, therefore, to plan and deal appropriately with – children's and families' behaviour. The reasons may be related to a variety of educational backgrounds not always relevant or sufficient to the work of a child welfare agency, or to rapid staff turnover, which frequently forces agencies to break in new workers inexperienced in the child welfare field. Almost from their first day on the job, workers must, often on the basis of limited understanding, make decisions on which children's futures depend. Such is the case even if formal decision making is vested in the supervisor, since the data supplied to supervisors are filtered through the primary worker.

There is a body of knowledge, however, that can be used to make sense out of much of the behaviour that the new worker is expected to understand and deal with. Thus, the worker who correctly sees that a child's behaviour represents that child's response to separation and the work of mourning will understand that child differently than will the worker who, failing to see the reasons for the behaviour, responds just to its nuisance value. Thus an understanding of the course and manifestations of normal reactions to separation in children of different ages, ways in which children mourn at all levels of development, and the criteria that can be used to assess and predict parenting capacity can greatly increase workers' accuracy and confidence in making necessary day-to-day decisions. Particularly at a time when many child welfare agencies have responded to financial constraints by de-emphasizing supervision of assessment, clinical understanding, and casework skills and process in favour of a supervision stressing mainly recording procedures and accountability, consultants can often provide a real service by supplying the necessary theoretical base, and by showing workers how to organize their ongoing work around it. (Of course, not only mental health consultants can provide this service, and not all psychologists and psychiatrists are able to do it successfully. Nor can the best consultant be effective in an agency that places little value on helping its workers develop the sound knowledge base essential to effective casework.) But, in agencies where this need is recognized, consultants, in collaboration with the agency's director of in-service training, may be of great help in filling this gap.

In other agencies, a consultant, noting such a gap and the agency's failure to appreciate its existence and/or significance, may first need to demonstrate to the agency's administrators how, repeatedly, the quality of the service offered is being compromised by the lack of an adequate knowledge base. In view of the rapid staff turnover common to many child welfare agencies, any such program should be under continuous review, as even an adequate introduction to the models considered most useful may need to be repeated at least yearly if new staff are to receive the necessary theoretical grounding.

6 / *By providing guidance as to when to support and when to confront defences.* One result of recent work on responses to stress (Caplan 1981) and on some children's remarkable ability to survive successfully even the most adverse environmental situations (Rutter 1979b; Anthony and Cohler 1987) has been the recognition that the same psychological defence mechanisms at times used pathologically may, even in the same child, be used at other times to protect coping ability, stability, and adjustment. This raises two questions: when are defences stabilizing, and therefore deserving of support, and when should they be confronted? Also, in the latter case, how can individual or family defences be confronted so as to ensure that the confrontation proves therapeutic, rather than counter-productive? This issue is important, since the inappropriate timing or wording of even an appropriate confrontation may increase anxiety, defensiveness, and symptomatic behaviour, instead of freeing the individual or family to deal with the underlying issues more directly and successfully, as intended.

Especially in an era when the process of casework is often de-emphasized in supervision, the mistaken belief that calling a spade a spade will always prove helpful has often been used to rationalize a great deal of destructive and irresponsible behaviour by mental health and child welfare professionals who should know better. Whether it arises from professional naïvety or is an acting-out of the 'helper's' frustrations is, at this point, immaterial. The point remains that effective casework depends on the worker understanding defences, and having the professional judgment to know when these should and should not be disturbed, along with the knowledge and ability to confront defences appropriately and constructively. While mental-health consultants are not the only ones able to help workers learn to deal with defences appropriately, in some agencies (particularly those that de-emphasize the casework process in ongoing supervision), consultants may help workers learn to evaluate and confront defences more selectively and effectively. At times, one of the principal functions of an agency's consultant may be that of emphasizing the continued importance of ongoing process in an agency where, because of workload, recording demands, accountability procedures, and the burden of preparing for court, it is insufficiently stressed.

7 / *By emphasizing realistic goal setting.* One common reason for requests for case-centred consultation is workers' feelings of desperation,

frustration, and/or guilt at their inability to effect change as completely or as quickly as they, often mistakenly, feel they should. While at times such expectations can be reasonable, at others they reflect unrealistic goals that come more from the rescue fantasies of the worker than from the realistic potential of the case. When workers set themselves impossible goals and feel pressured to achieve them, their inability to do so can evoke self-criticism and discouragement, which undermines both morale and efficiency. At times the most useful aspect of such consultations is the consultant's ability to reframe the problem to demonstrate that there are limits to what anyone can do. This reframing may be followed by a demonstration of the importance of setting realistic goals and the demoralizing effect of excessive expectations and by empathizing with workers frustrated by the strains of trying to effect change in chronically overwhelming and multi-problem situations. Often the recognition that the consultant (i.e., the expert) appreciates that their failure to achieve more is not proof that their work is inadequate and that they really are doing all that can reasonably be expected with an extremely difficult case is enough to release workers from the repeating cycle of excessive expectation and self-recrimination that so often contributes to otherwise avoidable burn-out (Berridge and Cleaver 1987; Snowden 1989; Metro 1989) or to inappropriate referrals for residential treatment that cost much more, that may not be able to achieve the unrealistic expectations made of them, and that may further fracture the child's sense of historical continuity and trust.

8 / *Help the worker separate myths from facts.* Decisions in child welfare are often based on myths that are widely accepted as facts. Some such myths (e.g., any child does best with the biological parents; any foster child is better off being adopted; the least-intrusive alternative is always best; if a child and the foster parents are in conflict, the best solution is to remove the child; the only way to anticipate how a child will behave in care is to observe that child in a receiving or assessment home) are potentially destructive, especially when regarded as having universal validity and used dogmatically as a basis for case planning. Helping workers unfamiliar with the gaps and contradictions in the professional literature separate in their own minds what is known (i.e., proved) from what is mistaken for fact while remaining unproved (i.e., myth or opinion) may help release workers from the errors induced by simplistic stereotypes.

9 / *Modelling of a 'research attitude.'* In busy and understaffed service agencies, the pressure for service often discourages workers from standing back and critically reviewing their own performance in the way that is essential for further honing of their sensitivities and casework skills. The encouragement of what might be termed a 'research attitude,' i.e., the readiness to stand back, examine, and re-evaluate and, therefore, to learn from ongoing clinical experience, will beneficially affect both ongoing service and staff's continuing professional development. Effective mental-health consultants, by their example and by the nature of their questioning, can do much to stimulate the growth of such an attitude in front-line personnel; even more than can formal clinical research in which agency workers and consultants may collaborate, such consultation can help in the rigorous clinical evaluation of – and therefore the learning from – the experience of direct service.

10 / *By supporting the agency from within the community.* Because of the increased difficulties presented by children and families with whom they must deal, the financial constraints that arise from chronic recession and inadequate spending on social services, larger-than-optimal caseloads, and the unrealistic expectations of the media and the community, who expect the impossible and then condemn any error, real or imagined, child welfare agencies often badly need community understanding and support. At the same time, such agencies feel very much alone and vulnerable to 'trial by headline' or ill-considered criticism by colleagues in higher-status – and much less stressful – agencies, clinics, or university and governmental departments. Attempts by social workers or administrators to reply to public or professional criticism are often written off as defensive or self-serving. Often the agency's consultant, as someone aware of the difficulties under which the agency operates while possessing an independent professional identity and a base outside the agency, can speak up publicly for the child welfare agency in a way that its own staff cannot. By doing so, consultants do more than simply provide support for beleaguered colleagues within the agency. In addition, they are actively contributing to the modification of community attitudes. Until these are shifted, child welfare agencies will continue to have low priority in the allocation of limited public funds, and will remain vulnerable to being scapegoated for their inability to resolve the social problems of which the community would rather not be reminded, such as child neglect and abuse (Schorr 1988).

Administrative Consultation

Some agencies use consultants primarily as advisers to the director or top administrative staff. Such a consultant may help the administration look critically at the nature and quality of programs in operation, help rank priorities, and identify gaps within existing service patterns and suggest ways of eliminating them. She may use her knowledge of systems to help the administration spot and modify unnecessary areas of tension and/or poor collaboration between different departments or programs within the agency. Finally, the administrative consultant may use her ongoing relationship and influence with the administration to lobby for clearer conceptualization and more effective intervention, as long as this is done in a manner that is respectful of the autonomy of the agency and the consultant's position as an invited guest. In so doing, the consultant may, at times, temporarily be in a position of supporting one faction within the agency against another. If so, it is essential that the consultant's motives be beyond reproach, and that she not abuse her position of trust in the pursuit of personal power or influence. In such cases, it is recommended that the consultant openly declare her agenda, and use negotiation, demonstration, research, and persuasion rather than manipulation to bring about change. If change cannot be achieved in this way, it is essential that the consultant respect the agency's right to chart its own course, even if this includes rejecting that aspect of her input.

Advantages/Disadvantages of Mental Health Consultants as Providers of Long-term Psychotherapy for the Child in Foster Care

Let us consider the usefulness of long-term psychotherapy for the child in care. If, as recent reports indicate, most children coming into care are, by and large, already seriously disturbed, should they not be receiving the benefit of intensive (i.e., insight-oriented) psychotherapy or play therapy with well-trained and experienced psychotherapists, rather than more superficial counselling and management with workers who are often less trained and experienced? The answer to this question is an unequivocal no. Chapter 14 describes in some detail the prerequisites for successful involvement in psychotherapy. These are rarely met by children in care. Those foster children who can utilize psychotherapy over a period of time are more often the exception than the rule.

What, then, are the roles of the child's social worker and the agency's consultants in the management of disturbed and disturbing foster children? These will vary, depending on the sensitivity, willingness, and commitment of the foster parents in any given case. Ideally, the omnipresent foster parents will become the primary influence on the child. Social workers will structure their interventions to help child and foster family deal with tensions affecting the foster-family unit by providing regular back-up and encouragement to the foster parents via direct support and by making available opportunities for ventilation, for cognitive restructuring, for refocusing and goal setting, for temporary relief, and for direct guidance to child and/or foster parents, when needed. When, as may occur, the foster parents are unwilling or unable to serve as surrogate therapists, many of these functions will, instead, be assumed by the social worker. While often necessary, this recourse is less than ideal. Social workers serving in this capacity are subject to most of the same limitations that apply to child psychologists or psychiatrists, although their greater access to the home and more extensive experience in dealing with social problems and psychosocial crises, given adequate time and back-up, often give experienced child welfare workers an advantage over psychiatrists or psychologists at times of crisis.

The agency's mental health consultants' greatest contribution to such a process may be through timely and flexible case-centred consultation with worker and/or foster parents. In the course of such consultations, issues and goals can be clarified, problems anticipated, and guidelines for future management outlined. The occasional (i.e., once or twice yearly) consultation in support of the therapeutic milieu of the foster home can do much to clarify and resolve difficulties. In particularly difficult cases, the consultant's continuing flexibility and availability by phone to adapt her approach to better meet the needs of the foster parent/social-worker team at periods of confusion or crisis may be crucial in sustaining a therapeutic family milieu and process.

Some psychologists and psychiatrists will undoubtedly object to the statements above on the grounds that only a mental health professional is qualified to provide 'treatment.' It is well known that there will never be enough trained psychotherapists to serve this group of children, and even those foster children who request therapy are usually unable to sustain it long enough to give treatment a fair chance. One recent superlative province-wide epidemiological survey (the Ontario Child Health Study) has shown that only one in six of those children needing treatment for behavioural, emotional, psycho-physiological disorders is likely to receive it (Offord et al 1989; Rae-Grant et al 1989). But, if children can avoid treatment, the one unit that they, like it or not, cannot avoid is the foster family, and it is within that family that most disturbed and conflicted behaviour occurs. Since the foster family must in some way respond to the child – there is no way that one can avoid responding to behaviour one has experienced – the question boils down to whether the consultant chooses to place her knowledge and experience in the hands of those who have the best chance of influencing the child or, instead, to retire behind a protectionist position, withholding her knowledge of children and the therapeutic process from those most in a position to help. Despite a full awareness of the risks involved in the former position, the author suggests that it is far preferable to the latter alternative.

Characteristics of the Working Relationship between Consultant and Consultees

Common difficulties that arise between social agencies and their mental health consultants are well analysed elsewhere (Caplan 1970). At this point, a few major, recurrent themes will be touched upon. Both consultees and consultants are strongly urged to read and digest Caplan's definitive discussion of the mental health consultation process, to make their collaboration more stimulating and productive for themselves and more fruitful for their clients.

1 / *The essential ambivalence of the contract between consultant and consultee.* Many requests for consultation are more or less ambivalent. At the same time that the consultee seeks help from the consultant, she fears that, if the consultant comes up with a solution – one that the worker basically feels she should have been able to produce unassisted – it will merely confirm what the worker has feared all along: that she is inadequate. Several important repercussions ensue. Without realizing it, consultee(s) may withhold or distort data to make it harder for the consultant to succeed. The alert consultant, aware of this possibility, must be as sensitive to what *has not* been revealed as to what *has*.

2 / *How to offer criticism in a supportive and constructive way.* The effective consultant, sensitive to the consultation's potential for confirming the worker's feelings of inadequacy, however unrealistic, will constantly and consciously strive to say what must be said so as to avoid any real or perceived assault on the self-esteem of the consultee. This

does not mean that the relevant issues must be avoided, but rather that they must be discussed in a way that is always respectful. Probably even more important than the actual words is the basic attitude of consultant towards consultee. If it is – and is perceived as – empathic and collegial, the consultation is likely to be successful; if not, there is real danger of its proving to be counter-productive.

3 / *Effective consultations in an atmosphere of mutual respect.* For effective consultation, the consultant must have respect for the expertise of the consultee within his own areas of professional functioning, a genuine appreciation of the difficulties of the consultee's professional role, and an awareness of the limits of her own area of expertise. Consultants who lack respect for workers who are less sophisticated in those professional skills in which the consultant considers herself expert have no place consulting to a social agency. It goes without saying that consultants who, feeling critical or condescending towards a given worker, attempt to mask their superior attitude by avoiding dealing with important areas of difficulty will come through not as supportive but as patronizing or withholding and, therefore, unhelpful. Also, consultants who are unaware of the difficulties that they would soon experience if suddenly expected to take over the job of the front-line worker – including an inability to reject all but 'suitable' cases; excessive caseloads; uncooperative and hostile clients; a host of social and psychological factors constantly interfering with the establishment of a therapeutic alliance; and the lack of an orderly casework process – have a high potential for being destructive. Thus an appreciation of the difficulties of the consultee's role and an awareness of the difference in the participants' distinct areas of professional expertise is a prerequisite for effective consultation.

4 / *The need for a consultant to have a concurrent involvement in direct clinical service.* The clinician who provides only consultation to agencies – who lacks the sometimes humbling ongoing experience of directly struggling with resistant patients or clients – risks becoming glib or oversold on pat solutions, and losing sight of how much easier it is to recognize someone else's blind spots than it is to overcome one's own. Some consultants use consultation to enhance their own self-esteem by having available for every situation an example of a similar one that, in the past, they handled brilliantly. Those who do so are in danger of intensifying their consultees' sense of failure and inadequacy. Many

effective consultants find it useful, at some point, to refer routinely to examples in which they had similar difficulties, directly making the point that every mental health professional, consultants as well as consultees, will have difficulty from time to time. Their doing so gives consultees permission to examine their own difficulties with less sense of personal inadequacy since the consultant, the outside expert, is human; she, too, sometimes makes mistakes.

5 / *Dealing with difficulties arising from the consultee's counter-transference.* Particular care must be taken in dealing with difficulties related to the consultee's counter-transference, that is those blind spots or inappropriate interventions in which workers' response to a client is driven by the unrecognized intrusion of feelings remaining from their own unresolved conflicts and sensitivities. This happens to all mental health professionals from time to time, consultants as well consultees. The more important the contribution of this unconscious distortion, the more difficulty the worker is likely to have in spotting its effects, and the more defensiveness the insensitive consultant is in danger of arousing by attempting to label or confront the counter-transference directly.

In general, the author endorses Caplan's technique of handling what he terms 'theme interference' (Caplan 1970). Caplan recommends avoiding any direct confrontation and, in such situations, dealing with the issue indirectly, being careful not to challenge the displacement. For example, with a worker who repeatedly backed away from mothers who became aggressive and attacked whenever challenged, one would focus not on the worker's personal feelings about aggressive mothers but on the mother. One would explore in detail the nature of her difficulties, how best to understand and utilize her areas of potential strength, and ways of approaching her other than those that were proving unsuccessful. In so doing, one would help the worker move past his inability to deal effectively with this type of mother without ever explicitly labelling this as his problem. Caplan suggests that, if the consultant's perception of the difficulty is accurate and the suggested response appropriately focused, it will successfully mobilize the worker to deal more effectively not just with the case at hand, but with other similar cases as well. At times, the process may have to be repeated with two or more cases illustrating a similar problem.

6 / *Avoidance of any therapeutic involvement with staff of an agency to which one is consulting.* Under no circumstances should consultants

become involved in the treatment of, or in the exploration of personal conflicts of, workers with whom they are involved in a consultant–consultee relationship. Such is true even if the attempt to move from a consultation to a therapeutic relationship is initiated by the consultee. Once one has become involved in a therapeutic way, an entirely new dimension is added to the consultant–consultee relationship, a dimension that is liable to interfere with the primary (i.e., working) relationship.

Consultants are wise to handle the occasional attempts by workers to involve them in their own personal problems by a gentle but firm statement that, since they are professional colleagues, the consultant is not the best person to help with such difficulties, as doing so would risk complicating what has been a successful working relationship. Should the worker persist in trying to use the consultant in a therapeutic way, the consultant would be wise to suggest referral to an appropriate therapist not involved with the agency, with whom the worker could pursue the personal issues further, if desired.

7 / *Establishing a balance between the ideal and the practical.* One issue that every consultant to a child welfare agency must face repeatedly is that of establishing the right balance between the ideal and the practical. Consultants who expect too little of consultees are likely to collude with their periodic avoidance, denial, defensive rigidity, and inertia. However, those whose expectations are excessive and unrealistic, given the conditions in which the worker is functioning, are in danger of producing more frustration and demoralization than assistance (Malucchio et al 1980).

8 / *The consultant as a role model.* Often more important than what the consultant *says* is the way that the consultant *is* in her dealings with the agency. The consultant's attitudes; her respect or lack of respect for clients, workers, and other agencies; her innate sincerity; her organized approach to understanding clinical situations; and her commitment to a high standard of practice will often be among the most useful things that the consultant has to offer, at least to those workers who use that consultant not just as a source of ideas but as a role model. This does not mean that the consultants should 'assume' a role or pretend to be different from what they are. Those who do so are soon recognized and, because of the artificiality of the poses they assume, are frequently discredited. Nor does it mean that consultants should actively try to turn

consultees into carbon copies of themselves, instead of recognizing and helping each consultee develop his or her own personal style. Rather, it means that, in seeking a consultant, the agency is wise to select one whose personal and professional qualities, approaches, and attitudes are those that the agency values in its staff.

9 / *The importance of flexibility and continued availability.* Nothing gives consultants more credibility than their willingness to remain available to meet the needs of the agency on a continuing basis. Most agencies have had multiple experiences with consultants who came, did their thing, and moved on, leaving all sort of instructions as to how the agency should function in the future but not remaining available to help it implement their suggestions or to answer questions and resolve difficulties occurring as consultees try to put them into practice. There is an increasing tendency these days for agencies to invite charismatic professionals to give one- or two-day workshops on topics or skills in which they are expert. These are offered not only because the consultants' names give them box-office appeal, but with the expectation that workers, having been brushed by the expert, will come away ready to apply the particular skill. Such workshops are often of limited value, and may even prove destructive unless followed by an adequate ongoing opportunity for supervised practice in the techniques involved. Lacking such an opportunity, one of three unfortunate results all too commonly occurs. In some cases, workers are intimidated by how much they are expected to assimilate and by the skill and ease of the expert, so that they are afraid even to try to apply what they have seen. Others, to their client's detriment, plunge in where angels fear to tread, and, soon beyond their depth, get into trouble, with results that are often destructive both for their clients and for their own confidence. Finally, there are those who, seeing a charismatic expert demonstrating an impressive technique, seize upon that technique as a gimmick, missing entirely the sensitivity of the expert's assessment of the client, the careful selection and application of the technique, and the ongoing context of the relationship that existed between the expert and the client. Failing to recognize the importance of these, the worker becomes a 'groupie' of the 'guru,' blithely and repeatedly applying the technical manoeuvres with little or no awareness of the sterility of the technique when applied outside the context of a genuine relationship. To avoid such abuses, agencies are advised routinely to follow such workshop demonstrations by an adequate period of supervision in the technique thus introduced.

It would also help if recognized experts in a given skill or area would demand as a prerequisite for providing such a workshop a plan of how the agency was intending to follow through, to ensure an opportunity for supervised practice in the technique being promoted.

Conclusions

Effective mental health consultation can be a stimulating and beneficial experience for both the consultant and the consulting agency. Under the conditions outlined above, it is also an extremely economical use of the 'multiplier effect,' a way of placing the skills of the mental-health professional at the service of those front-line workers who deal with the most disturbed youngsters and families in the community, many of them among the five out of six who are unlikely ever to have received treatment (Offord et al 1989). The union between a child welfare agency and its ongoing consultants, like any marriage, needs continual scrutiny and adjustment in order to remain an open and mutually beneficial one. Such a relationship rarely benefits one party unless it is beneficial for both. Should this be the case, both consultant and consultee – to say nothing of their clients – end up professionally, and often personally, enriched by the ongoing collaboration.

One of the rocks upon which many potentially successful consultations founder is the failure by the agency to take sufficient responsibility for shaping the nature of a consultation by promptly and directly airing sources of dissatisfaction. Such a situation makes it harder for consultants to adjust their input to better meet the agency's perceived needs. Meanwhile, agency dissatisfaction, if not directly tabled, continues to mount, further interfering with the frankness and openness necessary for successful communication. The partnership eventually breaks down as the agency finally decides that the present consultant is not meeting its needs and begins the search for a new one. Many agencies could avoid such breakdowns and get much greater value from their consultants if they actively exercised their right as consumers to shape the nature of the consultation and to make explicit their expectations and areas of need and dissatisfaction. Frankness and directness on both sides are essential to the establishing and maintenance of a consultation that is – and that remains – vital, responsive to the needs of both agency and consultant, and rewarding to both.

Chapter Fourteen

The Role of Psychotherapy
and Residential Treatment
within the Child Welfare System

By now, it should be clear that a conflicted and rejecting family life prior to coming into care exacerbated by the effects of separation from the natural family is likely to cause disturbance in the foster child which will affect his ongoing adjustment in foster care. The frequency and severity of this disturbance will probably increase with each successive repeat of the cycle of rejection and loss. Most foster children show signs of psychological and/or social disturbance and, frequently, of serious learning problems. These, in themselves, often play a major and increasing part in repeating the cycle of rejection by foster parents, peers, teachers, and the community, which progressively undermines their self-concept and self-esteem (Littner 1960; Steinhauer 1983b; Fanshel, Finch, and Grundy 1989). Particularly important is the often unrecognized role that emotional and behavioural symptoms stemming from the child's psychological disturbance play in undermining successive placements and threatening the permanence and continuity of relationships needed for normal development (figure 2.1).

But, if many foster children are psychologically disturbed, why, then, was the statement made in chapter 13 that foster children who can benefit from ongoing psychotherapy are more often the exception than the rule? Often staff of child welfare agencies, frustrated by their inability to achieve the results they aspire to with the severely damaged children in their care, hold unrealistic expectations of psychotherapy. The frequently refer such children for treatment in the belief that mental-health professionals or clinics can help the child more than they can (Wilkes 1989). If, as most child psychiatrists and psychologists would agree, many foster children – especially those who have experienced multiple separations – are among the most vulnerable and disturbed children in the community, what do psychotherapy and residential treatment have to offer them?

The truth, unfortunately, is often very little. Exceptions do exist: there are scattered reports of individual therapists who have successfully engaged and maintained a particular foster child in prolonged out-patient psychotherapy (Miller 1980). But such successes are uncommon. By and large, foster children are poor candidates for psychotherapy. They rarely see a need for it. Even if they do, they can only occasionally sustain their motivation long enough to commit themselves to therapy to the extent needed for a significant result. Most foster children are understandably preoccupied by the instability of their daily lives. They are so often overwhelmed by environmental factors beyond their control that they can rarely focus enough to work successfully on psychological (i.e., internalized) conflicts or on their contributions to the chaos in their lives. Unless the criteria defined below are met, a referral for out-patient psychotherapy is likely to produce just one more failure and to be perceived by the child as yet another rejection. Such a perception will confirm once again his conviction that those who claim to help and care are unlikely to live up to their promises. Such failures merely consolidate the youngster's narcissistic determination to avoid future involvements, since they may rekindle a glimmer of hope that all too soon fades into yet another disappointment.

Some might argue that the above holds true only for psychodynamic or insight-oriented psychotherapy, and that long-term supportive psychotherapy differs, and might, in fact, provide the meaningful relationship over time that foster children so badly need. While at times such is the case – Frank, described later in this chapter, is an example – the average foster child is much more likely to find such a relationship within the child welfare system – from foster parents, social workers, or group-home staff – than within the mental health system. Also, with only one child in every six who need it ever receiving treatment (Offord 1989), there will never be enough therapists for the majority of the children in the child welfare system, and the inadequate supply of trained psychotherapists can be used to far greater advantage with children satisfying the criteria listed below than if squandered on youngsters largely impervious to their particular skills.

Mental health practitioners are under great pressure to keep up with the demand for their services. As a result, they tend to select for treatment cases that come closer to the criteria discussed below. They generally resist taking into psychotherapy clients with many and massive social problems, including gross environmental (e.g., placement) instability and (foster) parents who refuse to participate actively in the treatment. Child welfare professionals at times consider mental health professionals' reasons for refusing to treat such cases a self-serving rationalization used to avoid involvement with multi-problem clients and families. However, such cases rarely benefit from those skills in which child psychiatrists and psychologists are best trained – those used to help the child deal with verbal or play expressions of intrapsychic conflict reproduced within a scheduled treatment hour. In view of the unmet demand for the services that experienced psychotherapists are better qualified to provide, they can better assist child welfare professionals in a back-up or consultative capacity, leaving those more experienced in the day-to-day management of complex social and multi-problem situations – e.g., those in the child welfare field – to provide the ongoing relationships and support (Steinhauer et al 1988, 1989; Fanshel, Finch, and Grundy 1989, 1990).

What, then, are realistic criteria for referring a foster child for long-term psychotherapy?

1 / *The child has demonstrated an ability to form and sustain at least one meaningful relationship.* Otherwise, she will be unable to forge the sort of alliance with a therapist essential for successful psychotherapy.

2 / *The child has shown some ability to internalize (contain) psychological tension within herself, rather than having to discharge it immediately via poorly controlled and outwardly directed behavioural explosions, technically referred to as 'acting out.'* If this criterion is ignored, the tension and frustration generated by the psychotherapy will be acted out. Should such behaviour occur, not only will it undermine the therapy but, even more important, it may threaten the stability of the child's placement, thus straining even farther that child's already limited support system.

3 / *The child must not only have serious psychological problems, but must recognize at least some of these as problems within herself, rather than attributing them all to an unsympathetic family or environmental situation.* She must be motivated to change some aspects of herself. The child who sees herself purely as victimized by neglect or mistreatment

by others (parents, foster parents, agency, teacher, peers, fate, etc.) is not a candidate for psychotherapy. Even if her perceptions are accurate as far as they go, to benefit from psychotherapy she must identify and be willing to change her own self-defeating behaviour. This behaviour, while resulting originally from the internalization of conflicts and from the defences originally generated by familial stress or distorted parental expectations, has itself become internalized, and so repeats itself independent of the environmental situation.

Steve entered care at age four, having spent his early years with a deprived mother who had been neglectful, punitive, and rejecting. He presented as an affection-starved and hyperactive youngster with significant cognitive, emotional, and social-developmental delays. His insatiable demands, his inability to be satisfied, and his repeated tantrums when even minimally frustrated had led to the rapid breakdown of three foster-home placements in less than eight months. Each breakdown further exacerbated Steve's distress, causing even greater demands, less satisfaction, more tantrums, and less ability to tolerate frustration.

Because of the recognition, albeit too late, that Steve was too disturbed and disturbing to be helped in a foster home, he was admitted to a small, professionally staffed therapeutic group home run by the agency. There, trained and well-backed-up child-care staff were able to combine acceptance and warmth for Steve with firm but reasonable limitations of unacceptable behaviour. It took two years before Steve reached the point of tolerating any attempt to limit or frustrate his impulses as anything but a further deprivation. Until then, he consistently misinterpreted staff's behaviour and motives, because of his expectation that all adults (like his natural mother and his three sets of foster parents) would end up rejecting him. During this entire period, he developed no special relationship with any member of the group-home staff. He related to all adults (staff and strangers) according to the same basic rule: as long as you do what I want, you're my friend; as soon as you frustrate me or make any demands, you're the enemy.

During these two years, Steve was not an appropriate candidate for individual psychotherapy. Despite many problems that would have been helped had he been able to engage successfully with a therapist, he could neither relate well enough to form a therapeutic alliance nor acknowledge and begin to work on his part in perpetuating and distorting the adult responses that so devastated him. As far as Steve was concerned, he had no problems; it was just that nobody ever did enough for him, while, at the same time, everybody frustrated and bossed him around.

4 / *As a corollary to the above, a reasonable candidate for psychotherapy should be able to reflect upon the part he plays in perpetuating his unsatisfactory relationships.* However, he also needs the ability to make note of, to recall, and to express via play or discuss at a set time, hours or days later, situations that have bothered him. It also helps greatly if he has some ability to recognize and reflect on his personal contribution and reactions to problem situations.

> In his third year in the group home, Steve's behaviour gradually began to change. He selected one of the staff, Joanne, as his special friend. He spent as much time as he could with her, asked for her when she was not on shift, and began to seek and to express affection for her. Even more important, he would accept limits and some frustration from Joanne, at times even showing evidence of wanting to please her.
>
> At about the same time, other aspects of Steve's behaviour also changed. He threw fewer tantrums. The school, for the first time, stopped complaining about his aggressivity. As well, Steve began to show signs of significant depression. He seemed sad and withdrawn much of the time, lost interest in activities that had previously fascinated him (e.g., scavenging and bringing home discarded clocks, radios, and other mechanical equipment to dismantle and rebuild). Often, especially with Joanne, he would cry and insist that he was no good, that nobody could love a boy like him, that all he ever did was cause trouble, and that his situation was hopeless because, even though he knew it, he couldn't help being this way.

At this point, Steve clearly satisfied the criteria for psychotherapy listed so far.

5 / *The final and least negotiable criterion to be met before referring a foster child for psychotherapy concerns the stability of that child's environment.* The child who has experienced extreme and repeated deprivations and/or abuse may require years of psychotherapy for it to prove helpful. Even children who have some ability to internalize tensions go

through periods during their therapy in which depression and/or acting out precipitated by the treatment will cause difficulties for the foster parents who have to live with them on a daily basis. It is unwise to involve such a child in psychotherapy unless three conditions are met.

a / The foster parents have sufficient commitment to the child *and to the therapy* to maintain the placement, accepting and supporting the child throughout the regression and upset that are likely to be stirred up by the treatment. At the same time, the agency, on its part, should be prepared not to initiate a voluntary change of placement or status for a child involved in psychotherapy – including a shift from foster care to adoption probation – without the therapist being informed at least several months in advance and having input in the decision-making process. Of course, the strength of the foster parents' commitment and what they will be able to tolerate cannot be predicted with certainty. However, they should be informed directly about what is involved, and the depth of their commitment should be explored before beginning therapy. Should the placement break down as a result of the therapy or should be child have to be withdrawn from treatment prematurely to protect the placement, one risks having done more harm than good, as the child will interpret it as one more proof of either failure or unacceptability, with all that that implies.

b / Severely deprived children are highly ambivalent and mistrustful about treatment. Much of the initial stage of therapy – which may take several years – requires the therapist to form an alliance with the child by forging and sustaining a connection with the positive component of that ambivalence. When the child begins to act out the negative component by failing to attend, as most foster children do at some point in their therapy, agencies, their resources often severely overextended, often take the child's resistance as proof that the therapy is not working and unilaterally decide to terminate. Missed sessions are especially difficult for child welfare agencies to accept, since psychotherapists in private practice, paid by the hour, usually demand that they be paid for failures to show or late cancellations until either the resistance is successfully worked through or it becomes clear that the therapy is not viable. In the long run, one can force a child to see a therapist, but cannot impel that child to form an alliance or to use treatment. As a result, any child really determined to sabotage therapy can eventually do so. Should the agency demand termination during a stage of temporary resistance, the whole process will have been undermined at a point where a sudden disruption may be particularly destructive to that child. An example would be when the child's acting out represents his attempt to deal with feelings of vulnerability by testing to see how committed and caring the therapist really is, prior to succumbing and becoming involved in a therapeutic alliance.

Child welfare agencies are constantly short of funds, and can always find other legitimate financial demands to rationalize withdrawing and diverting funds needed to sustain a highly resistant child's therapy. To use this excuse to justify a premature termination is to risk betraying a commitment by precipitating a significant loss in a child already sensitized to loss. Agency support must be both financial, that is, involve a willingness to assume the cost of the therapy unless a different arrangement has been negotiated in advance, and parental, that is, involve a commitment to cooperate with the therapist to do all within reason to protect the continuity of the therapy during the inevitable phases of increased resistance, which can be especially difficult when it takes the form of failed appointments.

Ron was an extremely bright and personable fifteen-year-old who had been in care since the age of three. An honour student, he had considerable leadership ability, and was an excellent artist and athlete. Superficially, Ron was very popular with his peers, but he was unable to sustain a deep or trusting relationship with anyone. He had periods of extreme depression, usually triggered by a crisis in a friendship. Over a six-month period, Ron had been becoming increasingly despairing about his inability to sustain fulfilling relationships. He strongly pressed the agency for psychiatric help, and was seen by the author at a stage in his professional career when he was somewhat more sanguine about what psychotherapy could accomplish for boys like Ron.

Ron related extremely well to the author at first. He mentioned his inability to sustain a relationship, though he had no idea that he might be in any way contributing to the difficulty. He talked very openly about his unhappiness, so much so that at times I felt the need to slow him down to keep him from being overwhelmed by the amount of sadness dredged up in each session. Always, though, he drew a complete blank after describing what had gone wrong each week and how terrible he felt. Any attempt to explore what he might be contributing to his repeated interpersonal crises led nowhere, and was usually interpreted as criticism or an attack, no matter how supportively I tried to phrase it. Or, if I merely accepted what he told me and tried to empathize with what he was feeling, he would become furious, accuse me of not really caring, and insist that I was wasting his time. No matter what I tried, all it did was frustrate him. Since he saw the problem as lying entirely outside himself, he felt that all he had to do was tell me about it and that I, in some magical way, would do the rest. I understood what he was doing as a transferring onto me of all the feelings of deprivation and rage that he had been harbouring for years against his parents and all other adults whom he felt had let him down. There was no way that I could meet his expectations by providing the rapid relief he came into therapy seeking. By my failure to do so I became just the last in a chain of adults who had disappointed and frustrated him.

About this time, Ron began to act out the rage that he could not express or resolve by talking. He began to miss sessions. After he missed the first, I called him at home. I suspect that it was more my concern for him and the fact that I cared enough to call rather than anything I said that registered, but he then came in for two sessions. Then this pattern repeated itself several times. After each missed session he would be more talkative at the next, but would soon close up again. During this stage of his therapy, he was so fearful of getting emotionally involved and so angry at my inability to produce rapid relief that he would stay away again after each one or two sessions to discharge some of the helpless rage he could not handle any other way.

After his third missed appointment, I received a letter from the society that had referred Ron for treatment. It stated that the agency understood that since I was holding an hour for Ron I was entitled to be paid for that hour, but that since it was a public agency, it would no longer be able to pay if Ron missed any more appointments. I met with the supervisor involved, and stated that this put Ron's therapy in jeopardy. To establish my trustworthiness to Ron would take time, and during that time, Ron's acting out and missed sessions were very likely to continue periodically. I could not go on with the process of trying to establish my credibility and caring without some guarantee from the agency that the next missed session would not be Ron's last. The supervisor claimed that he could see my point, but that he could not alter the agency's position. He even refused to give me time to bring Ron's therapy to a gradual close so as to minimize his sense of abandonment.

The next session, as objectively as I could, I explained the situation as it had been presented to me, pointing out that only if Ron could handle his frustrations other than by missing sessions could his therapy proceed. I made it clear that I hoped it would be possible for us to continue, but he flew into a rage. He insisted that his therapy had been the one thing in his life that gave him any hope, but that he had been a fool to let himself think that it might be helpful. Once again, the adult world had let him down. As he stomped out, he yelled that this just proved that the agency didn't give a shit about him and that all I cared about was money. He never came back, despite several phone calls and letters.

Following that day, Ron's behaviour deteriorated significantly. He became more antagonistic and belligerent. He moved from being an occasional marijuana user to smoking hash on a daily basis. His energy, school performance, and athletic activities deteriorated. Any attempt by his foster parents or social worker to reach him was met by either 'Fuck Off!' or 'What the hell do you care?' Clearly his introduction to therapy had aroused in him a sense of hope, which, when the therapy broke down, intensified his bitterness and alienation. I, too, found the termination traumatic, since I was convinced that may attempt to help him had merely ended up reinforcing his global mistrust and adding to his difficulties.

Whether Ron and I would have been able to achieve anything had I found a way of keeping him in therapy, we will never know. However, my clinical impression is that Ron would have been better off had we never attempted to engage with each other in the first place.

Agencies should not undertake therapy unless they are prepared to support it on a continuing basis in spite of other legitimate claims on their already overextended resources. A change of workers or supervisors, early and short-lived behavioural change occurring long before the resolution of the intrapsychic conflicts from which it originates, or a series of missed sessions is often enough to prompt many agencies to withdraw foster children from treatment prematurely, against the advice of the therapist. Such agencies often interpret as overinvolvement or overprotection the therapist's objections that the agency is betraying the contract made with both child and therapist. Many therapists refuse to accept referrals from child welfare agencies because of having been burned by such an experience. Prior to beginning therapy with such cases, one should with a written contract describe what the agency can expect from the psychotherapist and vice versa, and confirm the agency's willingness to accept the recommendation of an independent consultant with expertise in both psychotherapy and child welfare should agency and therapist be unable to resolve a disagreement about when to terminate.

c / The therapist taking on a seriously deprived child in therapy should meet certain special qualifications. First, such therapists must appreciate before beginning that treating these youngsters involves committing themselves, possibly for years, to remaining involved with a patient who will be extremely resistant and whose therapy is likely to be painfully slow. Second, such therapists should have some understanding of the usual course of treatment with chronically deprived and abused children. They should know the kinds of frustrations they are likely to face and, even more important, must be prepared to wait them out before expecting the child to make a similar commitment. Third, they will need to be secure enough in themselves and in their abilities as therapists that they don't lose confidence in themselves or in their work, even during prolonged periods of resistance and despite repeated pressures from agency, foster parents, and/or the child to give up on a case to which they are committed. Fourth, such therapists should have enough gratification in other areas of their lives that they are not so dependent on succeeding with each child that they pressure themselves and the child by demanding more than the child can deliver. Such excessive expectations will surely prove counter-productive. Finally, therapists must not be so self-centred that, in stages of resistance, they use the always available argument that they can better use their time with more motivated children, even if at the moment that is so, to rationalize welching on the commitment undertaken by beginning treatment with such a child. Once having accepted such a case, the ethical psychotherapist must be prepared to see it through, however frustrating and unprofitable it may seem for long stretches of time, even though ultimate success is by no means guaranteed.

In spite of the factors noted above, a therapist is sometimes able, through a heroic effort, to engage and maintain even a severely deprived child in therapy. The following example of a boy treated by the author will give some indication of how demanding and difficult treatment can be when undertaken in cases that fail to meet the criteria for long-term psychotherapy listed above.

Ken was thirteen when first seen, the oldest of five siblings, all of whom had frequently been in and out of care. His parents had separated when he was five, and his father had remarried a woman who resented and competed with any attempted contact between him and his children from the previous marriage. Ken's mother was, at times, overpermissive and seductive. At others, she claimed that she was just too nervous to care for so many children, at which point she would neglect them until neighbours' complaints would end in their being taken into care, only to be returned home a few months later to repeat the cycle once again. Ken later recalled what to him was one good, caring family among the five foster homes in which he had lived. This placement, unfortunately, broke down after the death of the foster father. He describes having been the recipient of repeated and cruel beatings in two of the foster homes, and of being homosexually seduced by the foster father when drunk in another. Though he claims he reported the latter, he insists that nobody believed him or, to his knowledge, seriously investigated the allegations.

Ken was referred for consultation at age thirteen when, while sleeping nude in the mother's bed, as he normally did, he was sufficiently aroused to propose intercourse. His mother, feeling she had lost control of the situation but unaware of her part in provoking it, panicked. She called the Children's Aid Society because her 'nerves could no longer take it.' Ken was again placed, and a psychiatric assessment of Ken and the family was requested. It was suggested that Ken remain in care, as there was no evidence from her past behaviour that his mother had the capacity to assume an appropriate parental role or to modify her seductiveness. She would agree verbally with every suggestion, but her behaviour and attitudes never changed.

When first seen at the clinic, Ken was antagonistic, negative, and uncooperative. He saw no reason to be in care or to see a psychiatrist, since he was not crazy. I agreed, and tried to define in general terms why the referral had been made. Ken stopped talking, and refused to say a word to me for over a year. During treatment sessions, he would hide under the desk, or occasionally would sit, head hanging, in a chair, looking sullen, provocative, and, I thought, sad. At such times, I would try to verbalize what I thought he was feeling, but he never gave me clear indication, verbal or behavioural, of whether or not I was correct. He resisted any attempts to engage him in drawing, play, or discussion. Needless to say, he aroused a whole maelstrom of counter-transference reactions – frustration, rage, dislike, anxiety, feelings of personal inadequacy, guilt for not being more effective, etc. There were only two reasons that I continued to see him. I had noticed that Ken usually arrived early for each appointment. I interpreted this as evidence of some positive component of an ambivalence, the negative half of which I was experiencing much more directly in the office. I was also afraid that, if this hypothesis was correct, Ken would interpret my terminating his therapy as another rejection, one that he could ill afford. And so I continued, not knowing where this would lead and feeling at least as much a captive as he.

By his second year in therapy, I felt committed to Ken, though by no means optimistic or even wanting to remain trapped in a process I felt was going nowhere. I agreed to see Ken as a non-paying private patient, since I no longer worked at the clinic. At that point, although his social worker reported that his behaviour at school and in the foster home had improved significantly, the foster parents broke up their marriage, and Ken, along with four other children, was displaced again. This time Ken was placed in a group home, as there had been no indication of any meaningful relationship in any of his last four foster placements. Six months later, he began to talk enough in his therapy to complain about how the others in the group home were picking on him. He blamed his therapy for this, since it gave the others something to feel superior to and to tease him about. He insisted he didn't need to be in therapy, even though nothing in his life was working out for him. Although it sounds as if by this stage Ken was talking freely in therapy, this was not true. He would never cooperate with any attempt to have him amplify, develop, or tell his feelings about any of his complaints. For most of each session, he would just sit there, sullen, angry, depressed, and non-cooperative. Finally, after two and a half years, and just at a point where I was beginning to wonder if I was seeing a minimal increase in his willingness to work with me, he suddenly announced that therapy was making him crazy. He had said the same thing several times before, but I remember at that session thinking, 'That makes two of us.'

After that day, Ken flatly refused to return. I wrote him a letter, suggesting that, even if he was determined to stop, he should come back at least once to discuss his decision and bring his treatment to a close. I later heard from his social worker that he'd torn up the letter after reading it. I remember at the time feeling relieved to be released from a therapy that I found as unsatisfactory and unpleasant as Ken did, but I also felt resentful and saddened by what I then considered my naïve persistence in a gamble that seemed not to have paid off. I felt I'd been a fool to waste so much time in arriving at what seemed a foregone conclusion, and could not help but wonder how much it was my inexperience rather than his psychopathology that had kept Ken's treatment from succeeding. No one at that time could have convinced me that my work with Ken had been anything but a failure.

Almost seven years later, out of the blue, I received a phone call from Ken. He had dropped out of school and had been unemployed for almost three years, because he was too anxious and felt too inadequate to apply for a job. He had joined a supportive group-therapy program in an outlying hospital. He soon complained that he was getting nothing out of the group, and told the leader that the only involvement by which he had ever felt helped was the one with me seven years earlier. The group leader suggested that he see if I would be willing to work with him again. Surprised, humbled, yet very aware how much the encounter in which I felt so little had happened must have meant to him, I agreed to see him on two conditions. First, I expected him to pay two dollars in addition to his health insurance for each session. Second, in order to obtain the money, he would obviously have to get a job. Ken said he would think about it and call me back.

Two weeks later, Ken announced that he had found a job and asked for his first appointment. I gave him one within the week, and there then began a therapeutic involvement that, with several extended intermissions, lasted over a period of fourteen years. For much of the first three years, Ken was still sullen, angry, and un-willing to speak. Gradually there were more and more times in which he was willing to talk and to listen to me. Bit by bit, I learned of the rage that he feared could be potentially homicidal if it es-caped; of his hatred of both parents, whom he felt had abandoned him; of his difficulties at work because he felt so self-conscious, inferior, and anxious that he just had to get away and find another job; of his rage at all his bosses and at anyone in authority who told him what to do; of his feeling that I, along with everyone else, just pretended to be interested in him, but that sooner or later, I too would show my true colours and take advantage of him; of his rage at his father for letting his new wife become more important to him than his own children; of his wondering whether his mother was aware of the many ways that she stimulated him sexually; of feelings that, whenever he went anywhere, people looked at him as if they knew he was inferior, which made him wonder if they thought he was homosexual. At times, Ken thought I looked at him as if he were homosexual, and he suspected that one day I would make a pass at him, even though, by that time, we had worked together for three years (in addition to the earlier two) without anything remotely physical between us.

This stage in his therapy coincided with a period in which Ken was homosexually promiscuous; desperately seeking a surrogate father, he let older men use him sexually as long as they first went through a period of kindness and fatherliness. In this way he acted out his fantasies of them desiring him because they obviously found him attractive and wanted him as their son. There followed a period of male prostitution and, soon after, he began socializing with an exclusively homosexual crowd. He consistently denied any real sexual interest in homosexuals, claiming that he circulated with them only because they were kind to him, because they gave him presents, and because, instead of his having to go through the anxiety involved in approaching an attractive girl, he could sit back and let gay men court him. They upset and angered him when they insisted he was homosexual. He was sure he was not, since his sexual desires and fantasies were predominantly, though not exclusively, heterosexual, and since his interest was not in the sexual aspects of his encounters; rather, he endured these to obtain the admiration and the chance to feel fathered that came with the sex. For several years, he lived with one of his previous sexual partners, refusing any sexual involvement for most of this period but claiming that he liked having his friend care for him. After months of preoccupation with whether he was heterosexual or homosexual, he decided in favour of the former, and gradually began to confront his anxiety about approaching girls. At the same time, he was trying to overcome anxieties about going back to complete high school, which he had dropped out of at Grade 10, and around trying to find a job that he knew he wanted and for which he qualified but was afraid to ask. In every area of his life, he seemed stagnated, knowing what he wanted in each case but claiming it was too hard to make the necessary move.

Several times, earlier in his therapy, Ken had suddenly, and without warning or explanation, disappeared for months or over a year at a time, only just as suddenly to drop back in some months later. He would not explain these absences, although they usually seemed to occur when he was angry; I suspected he left therapy to avoid having to deal with the negative component of his ambivalence to me. On this occasion, however, for the first time, I took responsibility for stopping Ken's therapy. I pointed out that, in all major areas of his life, he knew what he wanted but was unprepared to confront the anxiety that must be overcome in order to succeed, and that he had been stuck at this level for over a year. Talking about his problems in therapy seemed to have become a substitute for his doing something about them, rather than a way of preparing himself to pursue his goals. I therefore suggested he take a recess from therapy, coming back when he had committed himself to a course of action. I made it clear I would accept whatever he chose, but that he had to make some decisions and act upon them for his therapy to be meaningful.

Ken was furious, but returned eighteen months later, clearly much more involved and having faced some of the challenges he had been avoiding. Despite great anxiety, he had registered at a community college for an upgrading program. By hard work, and despite a low normal intelligence, he managed to achieve a high-school graduate level. He then attempted a vocational retraining program at the same college, but found this beyond him and could not cope with it. He used his therapy to deal with the disappointment, and decided to return to work, soon finding a job despite a high level of unemployment.

By this time, Ken was living with an Asian woman ten years older and obviously brighter than he. He was ambivalent about this relationship. Although he was highly self-conscious about her colour and age, he hoped that here, at least, was someone who would meet all his needs unconditionally. Initially, she indeed seemed prepared to give him the unlimited gratification he craved, but soon she, too, began to make demands of him. At that point, the totally satisfying relationship of his fantasies rapidly deteriorated into one in which she became increasingly demanding, accusing, attacking,

and degrading. Endlessly she berated him for his multiple inade-
quacies and failure to meet her needs. At first he battled against
these accusations, but increasingly slipped into a passive withdrawal, becoming depressed and self-critical. At a time when the
relationship was becoming increasingly sado-masochistic, I left the
country for a year's sabbatical. While away, I received a brief letter
from Ken, wishing me well, thanking me for being 'more like a
father' to him, and asking to see me again on my return. I replied
that he could, and gave him the name of a colleague whom he could
consult if necessary in the interim.

Ken called for an appointment within a few days of my return.
He had seen the colleague, but, though he was 'very nice,' it 'just
hadn't been the same.' Ken was deeply locked in a destructive
relationship with the Asian woman, who had become increasingly
derogatory and emasculating over the year I'd been gone. Ken felt
stripped of whatever self-confidence he had by her attacks, and had
been left feeling useless, weak, and thoroughly inadequate. Although
acknowledging that the relationship was destructive, Ken found the
prospect of leaving her 'too frightening.' He seemed totally vulnerable to her abuse, and wholly incapable of protecting himself in
the face of her taunts. He knew that the relationship was destructive,
but could not end it. At about this time, his partner took matters
into her own hands and threw him out.

Ken was crushed, and rapidly became seriously depressed and
agitated. He was not sleeping, was losing weight, and had no energy
for anything. In his therapy, he talked of the lost relationship in
idealized terms; he would repeat again and again how much he
loved her, how she had destroyed him and how devastated he was
feeling. He could not see the transference significance of her abandonment, and seemed utterly unable to examine any of his positions, so much so that communication between us broke down
almost totally. Again, he became suspicious and withholding, and
his agitated depression continued unrelieved. He blamed himself
entirely and uncritically for the breakdown of the relationship. He
had lost his ability to critically examine what she said about him,
and accepted as true – and castigated himself for – all the ways she
claimed he had let her down, which he used as proof of his innate
worthlessness.

At this point, concerned by the depth of his depression and my
inability to make meaningful contact with him despite an attempt

to use cognitive behaviour therapy to modify his repeated self-castigation, I began Ken on anti-depressant medication. This rapidly decreased his agitation, and once again he became accessible to psychotherapy. He was then able to stand back a bit to re-examine both positive and negative aspects of the relationship, to consider its effect on his self-esteem, and to see how his extreme passivity and internalization of anger had sustained so destructive an equilibrium for almost five years. As he recognized this, he became aware of intense rage at the girlfriend, an anger that he had dared not express lest he kill her. By this stage, Ken no longer showed signs of clinical depression and, just as I began to reduce his anti-depressants, he again disappeared, discontinuing the therapy without warning.

Ken next showed up a year and a half later. He had been living for six months with a divorcée with whom he was on the verge of beginning a serious involvement. He was hesitating, however, because his last relationship had proved so destructive that he was fearful of getting deeply involved. He was no longer depressed. He had interests, friends, and, at times, could enjoy himself. He no longer worried about the extent of his rage. He realized that he was well accepted everywhere, and that people seemed to like him at work and also in his neighbourhood. Although many of the adolescents in the neighbourhood clearly admired him, he decided that he would never have children, 'at least until I'm a lot better than I am now ... when I can be sure that I won't screw them up the way my parents did me.'

Ken is now reconciled with both parents and visits each of them occasionally. He is ready for a meaningful relationship with his father, who parries his attempts at closeness, because they make him (the father) too anxious. Ken sees his therapist as his best friend and confesses to thinking at times of how different his life would have been if the therapist had been his father. The extent of his idealization at times makes me uncomfortable, and I remind him that it's easier to be objective and understanding with one's patients than with one's own family. Sometimes he wishes we could see each other outside office hours, always adding that he knows it cannot be, but that he can't help wishing it. This causes me some guilt, but apart from his being my patient, there are differences in age, intelligence, interests, social class, etc., that make this impossible. I suppose we are both learning to live with the fact – which we have discussed – that I will never be able to be for him all that he would like me to be. I am reassured to note that he is now able to get annoyed at me when I am slow to understand something that he thinks I should be picking up faster.

There are other isolated reports of successes in ongoing psychotherapy with seriously deprived youngsters who do not meet the criteria for involvement in psychotherapy listed above (Miller 1980). Clearly, in the exceptional case, it can be helpful. Ken's case is described in detail to demonstrate what a therapist must be prepared to wait through to work successfully with such a youngster. Many more such arrangements fail than succeed, and such failures can be devastating to the foster children involved. It is because of unsuccessful attempts to work with other severely deprived children that the author suggests the guidelines listed above for readiness for psychotherapy. Each of them represents numerous lessons learned the hard way. They are intended to save time and to avoid inadvertent damage to inexperienced therapists and deprived youngsters who are more likely to be harmed than helped by premature and naïve involvements, most of which are destined to fail.

If, then, many of the most seriously deprived youngsters are almost impossible to involve successfully in out-patient psychotherapy, what can they gain from residential treatment?

Recent controlled studies of residential treatment for children with severe undersocialized conduct disorders are seriously lacking, so the answer here must be a qualified one. Given appropriate residential treatment, a number of these youngsters can be helped significantly. But the residential treatment needed by youngsters who fail to meet the criteria for psychotherapy described above usually takes at least three and, more often, four or five years. There are few centres that provide both the necessary quality of treatment and the long-term commitment that are required for successful results. The author knows only four such settings, two in Britain, one in Israel, and one formerly in Canada; the latter no longer meets these criteria. Other settings that will take on and stick with such youngsters no doubt exist, but they are few and far between. The successful ones share certain characteristics.

1 / They recognize that, to treat severely deprived children (including what Winnicott [1960] would call 'false-self' children and what DSM-III (American Psychiatric Association 1980) would label 'children with unsocialized conduct disorders') adequately in residential treatment will

require an average of three to five years, with at least part of that time being spent in a setting from which they cannot escape (Vaillant 1975).

2 / Most of the first two years will be needed to allow a relationship to form with a child who has learned through past experience to fear any involvement as a prelude to abandonment. One cannot manipulate a child into relating until he is ready to do so. One can, however, expose the child to a milieu that is sensitive and caring yet, when necessary, strong and firm, with a staff able to set and consistently enforce limits when necessary, but not needing to exercise their authority out of their own insecurity, frustration or need for control.

3 / Such settings recognize the need for consistency within the milieu, and the importance of providing the security, structure, and continuity that even the most suspicious child will eventually learn to trust, when he realizes that the basic therapeutic stance and attitude of the staff can be counted upon to remain the same. At least at first the setting must be one from which the child cannot escape, since only if a child is forced to remain in the milieu long enough to become convinced that adults can be relied upon – by experience, that the staff can be trusted to perceive sensitively and respond accurately to each child's individual needs, an experience he missed earlier because of his own parents' inability to provide 'good enough parenting' as defined in chapter 2 – will he eventually allow himself to enter into an experience that contradicts, and thus forces him to re-evaluate, his former stereotype of all adults as neglectful, punitive, abandoning, and rejecting. Until a child realizes this on his own, all adults will continue to be mistrusted, and the youngster will rely on attempting to establish and maintain an omnipotent control through manipulation or intimidation, since only by remaining in control can he ward off the feeling of helplessness that he associates with having been abandoned and betrayed by those on whom he depended in the past. Until that time, any appearance of caring or warmth on the part of staff may be exploited or even enjoyed, but the child's apparent responsiveness and cooperation will evaporate at the first sign of unwanted expectations or limits. Then the child's apparent cooperation will be replaced by aggressive, manipulating, or intimidating behaviour that serves both to ward off feelings of helplessness and to force the staff to reveal what the child is convinced are their true (that is, abandoning and punitive) colours.

4 / In order to pass the test in spite of the child's provocation, such settings devote considerable time to selection, support, and ongoing training of staff. There is a strong commitment to regular supervision, in which the emphasis is not just on correctly understanding the needs of the children but on the exploring workers', as well as the child's, role in their mutual transactions. In some such settings, staff are encouraged to enter personal therapy; in others, personal issues may be dealt with in the course of supervision. In either case, however, there is an explicit understanding that anyone who works in depth with such demanding and disturbing children for any length of time will, by doing so, be forced to deal with areas of personal difficulty or unresolved conflicts that, if not recognized, are bound to block and distort the sensitivity, clarity, and appropriateness of his or her professional responses.

Such centres maintain a consistent emphasis on individualizing the milieu's response to each child's needs. This demands regular communication and frequent meetings among staff at all levels working with a given child. Each attempts to integrate the perceptions of the others, so that staff as a whole will understand and respond to the child in a consistent way. One result of this emphasis on staff development and support is that the average length of time a child-care worker remains in such a setting is in the vicinity of four to five years, as opposed to a much more rapid turnover (less than half that) in settings where staff support is not given such a high priority. Thus, some benefits of the commitment to various forms of staff supervision, development, and support include high staff morale and smaller staff turnover, despite the extreme pressures inherent in the work, which make possible greater consistency both in staff continuity and in the conceptualization and delivery of the treatment program.

5 / Individual psychotherapy is usually not provided for most children until they have been in the setting long enough to have demonstrated the ability to trust and to relate that is central to forming a therapeutic alliance. Signs of their readiness for psychotherapy are similar to those indications for out-patient therapy mentioned earlier in this chapter (i.e., demonstration of the ability to form and sustain a relationship, to internalize tension, to recognize and acknowledge problems that the child is motivated to do something about, and the willingness and ability to discuss these after the fact). For most of these children, it takes at least the better part of two years to develop enough trust to form their first relationship.

For the above reasons, it is not until the third year that most such children are reasonable candidates for successful psychotherapy. If they are routinely discharged in two years or less – a policy common in North America, where a two-year stay is considered long-term treatment – it is not surprising that the results obtained are disappointing. What else would one expect if, having worked for the better part of two years to overcome lifelong distrust and just having reached the stage where one is tentatively letting an adult, often for the first time, become important, one is then discharged on the grounds of 'institutional policy'? Such a discharge often occurs at the very point where that crucial first trusting relationship is just beginning to form. The real tragedy in this is the self-fulfilling prophecy involved: by redefining what are really inter-mediate institutions as long-term, and by routinely discharging young-sters from them at the height of their dependency, one succeeds only in proving again and again the initial false premise that such children have little to gain from residential treatment or from letting themselves care about others.

Unfortunately, a lack of controlled follow-up studies by those few settings that are prepared to offer truly long-term care (i.e., three to five years or more) has resulted in a lack of experimental proof of the efficacy of the minimal criteria listed above (Barker 1978; Stone 1979). In eval-uating those studies that do exist, there are problems in the definition of how to measure success in residential treatment. Much of the research emphasizes narrow but objective criteria, such as recidivism rates or criminal convictions. Others (for example, Balbernie 1966, 1974) are crit-ical of these measures, which they claim may be indications more of behavioural conformity or of more effective antisocial functioning than of true psychosocial improvement: 'A child who avoids a brush with the law but who never succeeds in forming a relationship with anyone is considered a success, while one who gets into trouble once after dis-charge but then goes on to form successful relationships and to function well in every way is considered a failure. There are too many variables involved for meaningful research' (Personal communication).

Balbernie and his colleagues at the Cotswold Community in England gauge success in terms of character change, productivity, and the ability to form and sustain successful relationships. (These sets of criteria may often be complementary rather than mutually exclusive.) In spite of the difficulties and disagreements encountered in arriving at a definition of 'success' that is objective, clinically relevant, capable of accurate measurement, and acceptable to those working in the field, until generally agreed-upon measures of success in residential treatment are adopted, it will not be possible either to prove or to disprove the major point being made here. As a result, the criteria discussed in this chapter summarize the consensus of a number of experienced clinicians who understand and utilize the implications of attachment theory for both the development and the treatment of severe character pathology in chronically deprived and unsocialized children. (A more comprehensive review of other models of residential treatment is provided by Quay [1986].) Only studies that systematically satisfy the criteria listed above can establish experimentally the effectiveness of truly long-term residential treatment of children with undersocialized conduct disorders. There is a desperate need for controlled follow-up studies to clarify this issue one way or the other.

In North America, foster children are overrepresented in the populations of the so-called long-term – usually intermediate – residential treatment centres (Barker, Buffe, and Zaretsky 1978). This finding is not surprising, in view of the extent of their pathology and since the major criteria for admission to residential care are negative – i.e., an inability of the family or community to tolerate the child's behaviour – rather than positive and specific (Winsberg et al 1980; Kashani and Cantwell 1983; Ney, Mulvihill, and Hanna 1984; Rae-Grant 1978). Foster families are less likely to tolerate severe and prolonged disruptive behaviour from someone else's child than would most natural families from their own. Foster children, as we have seen, are usually limited in their ability to form and use relationships to modify unacceptable behaviour and to mediate tension. It is not surprising, therefore, that foster families and the community are less tolerant of the disturbed foster child's behaviour, so that many such children are admitted to residential settings, both to protect foster families and the community from their behaviour and to shield them from the community's reaction to it. These may be very appropriate reasons for short-term admission, since there is a limit to how much extreme, repeated, and uncontrolled antisocial and aggressive behaviour families and communities can tolerate. Also, it should be recognized that many of these youngsters cannot be successfully treated while remaining in the community as long as their behaviour remains consistently uncontrolled. The ability to contain the antisocial and aggressive acting out of such youngsters is a prerequisite for successful involvement in treatment. Unless such containment is achieved – by the youngster's own assertion of controls, by the influences of those in the child's living environment, or through the input of a therapist – that child will not be meaningfully engaged in out-patient treatment.

It may be appropriate, on a temporary basis, to admit such children to short-term residential settings for the protection of the community, of the child, or of the placement. But how therapeutic are such admissions? For the vast majority of children as severely disturbed as those under discussion, these admissions are therapeutic only to the extent that they provide a brief cooling-off period that allows a disengagement between the child and those caring for him who, at the moment, can no longer tolerate the child's behaviour. If such a break allows enough draining off of tensions to save a placement that was in jeopardy, or to let a child who has temporarily lost even what little impulse control he normally has to regain it, then it will have served a useful purpose. Also, such short-term admissions can provide a focus and opportunity for crisis intervention, during which the temporary overwhelming of the child's, the family's, or the setting's usual defensive operations may leave all more accessible to limited behavioural interventions. However, two features of such short-term admissions bear mention.

Often the request for residential treatment comes from a worker who is under great pressure from a foster family, the community, her workload, that worker's supervisor or his or her anxiety to 'do something quick' to cool off a situation in crisis. At times, this sense of urgency, especially when superimposed on an insufficient understanding of the dynamics of child and family, the day-to-day environment, and how these affect each other, can lead the worker to seek admission to residential care as the safest, and therefore the best, alternative for all involved. Such admissions, unless based on an accurate assessment of the strengths and weaknesses of the service system of the foster child, not only may unnecessarily disrupt the life and continuity of the child but may undermine the system's confidence in its own ability to do its job. Wherever it is possible to restore control to the system without emergency admission, through consultation or through appropriately timed back-up by experienced mental health professionals, such is always advisable, even if an elective admission is indicated later in the best interests of the child.

Unnecessary short-term admissions of such children just confirm for members of the system – and for children – their inability to resolve crises using their own resources. Admission, at such times, may relieve the immediate situation at the cost of undermining the confidence of all involved in the system's inherent usefulness. Thus, after one such admission, the confidence of all involved in their ability to cope successfully with the next similar crisis is compromised. Also, the more that adults in such a situation rely on short-term admission, the more they convey the message: 'You can't be expected to control yourself and we are unable to help you do so. Therefore, we will admit you to a setting that can supply externally the controls that you and we lack.'

This places the emphasis on external controls rather than on mobilizing inner controls that, if within the child's and the system's capacity, are always preferable. There is also the danger that the deprived child will find so much dependency gratification in the residential setting that he may stop trying to cope and may precipitate crisis after crisis to force others to take him in and take care of him again and again.

Thus, an accurate assessment of the coping potential of child, the family, and the system of which they are a part is crucial in response to a demand for emergency admission. Many unnecessary and potentially compromising admissions can be avoided if thorough assessment and appropriate back-up at the point of crisis are available to help the system identify and mobilize strengths that, in crisis, it had lost sight of. If, however, not enough capacity for coping is available within the system, an emergency admission may be the only realistic alternative.

A key factor in any such crisis assessment is a thorough understanding of the role of the crisis worker or team. How well does the worker understand child and family? How actively and effectively has the family been dealt with during the crisis? Is the worker's anxiety, whatever its source (e.g., realistic evaluation of the nature of the crisis; pressure from community or agency; reaction to family distress; lack of understanding and/or skills; counter-transference/theme interference), inflating the anxiety and thereby immobilizing the potential controls of child and family? Should any of these be true, can the worker be helped to regain control of the situation again, and can that worker, given appropriate back-up and/or consultation, help the family resolve – or at least contain – its crisis?

We mislead ourselves if we consider it therapeutic to admit children who require long-term care to residential settings that are not prepared to continue working with them for sufficient periods of time. Such admissions are an exercise in self-delusion (Wilkes 1989). There is currently a trend in North America against truly long-term residential treatment of any form. It is expensive, at a time when most agencies are underfunded. Because those operating the truly long-term settings able to treat successfully asocialized children are clinicians rather than researchers, and because of the difficulty in agreeing on how to define and measure what constitutes a successful result, available data merely confirm what we have long suspected: that up to two years of residential treatment of such children does not work (Lewis et al 1980; Schain, Gardella, and Pon 1982; Shamsie 1981; Romig 1978; Quay 1986).

At the same time, there is as yet no experimental proof that even the more extensive residential treatment described above can indeed help, not just to contain but to resolve the underlying character pathology of such youngsters, freeing them to live more useful and productive lives and, even more important, releasing them from the need to repeat the cycle in the next generation. Until such evidence is available, economic and political pressures against sufficiently long-term residential treatments adequate both in quality and in duration will continue. In the absence of such treatment facilities, short-term cooling-off admissions (at points of crisis; between foster-home breakdown and replacement in a newly selected and adequately prepared foster or group home; and as a back-up to programs providing a therapeutic milieu within highly motivated, well-trained and adequately supported foster families [see chapter 15; Chamberlain and Weinrott 1990] staffed group homes, or other reasonable community alternatives) may be both more honest and less damaging than continuing to admit youngsters to intermediate institutions for periods that we know risk damaging the children involved. If we continue to ignore this, our credibility as mental-health professionals, our pretence of being able to offer to treat what are all too often these days referred to as 'impossible' children, as well as the children themselves, will be the losers (Webb 1988; Hawkins et al 1985; Friedman 1987). Unless we, as a society, are prepared to fund truly long-term treatment institutions, enriched foster care as the basis resource, supplemented in times of crisis by short-term admissions, offers probably the most effective and least potentially detrimental placement there is for seriously disturbed foster children (Chamberlain 1990; Chamberlain and Weinrott 1990; Martin and Pilon 1986).

Chapter Fifteen

Four Innovative Models
of Foster Care

The value of foster care as a service for children requiring placement has recently been challenged by a number of prominent mental health professionals and government officials who question whether long-term foster care is so innately unstable that children unable to be raised in their own families would be better served by a return to institutional placements. A number of factors have contributed to their taking this position: difficulties in both recruiting and retaining foster parents; the frequency with which placements break down; the high numbers of foster children requiring institutional placements; the number of failures of the foster care system who leave care showing severe and persistent disorders of personality, socialization, behaviour, and emotional regulation; the frequency with which these patterns recur in the next generation, repeating the cycle of neglect, abuse, and multiple separations that the parents, as children, experienced. In some jurisdictions the result has been a serious call for a return to institutionalization as an alternative possibly less detrimental than foster care.

Some authors, however, while well aware of the potentially harmful effects of indifferent fostering, attribute many of the shortcomings of the foster care system to the widespread failure to recognize and respond appropriately to the changing nature of the children coming into care (Bush and Goldman 1982; Steinhauer 1983b; Wald et al 1988; Wiltse 1979; Fanshel and Shinn 1978; Fanshel, Finch, and Grundy 1990). A number of alternative models of foster care have been designed and evaluated under experimental conditions. These are adapted to the needs of the foster children of today. Four such innovative models of foster care will be described and compared, after which some of their common features will be discussed.

The Parent-Therapist Program

The Parent-Therapist Program (Rubenstein et al 1978) was developed by the Chedoke–McMaster Centre in Hamilton, Ontario, as an alternative to residential treatment for emotionally disturbed children and early adolescents. It attempted to combine the positive aspects of both institutional and foster-family care while minimizing the risks and disadvantages of each. It was a gold-medal American Psychiatric Association Achievement Award winner in 1977.

The Parent-Therapist Program attempted to develop a therapeutic system consisting of an 'extended family' network of foster families that could: 1 / provide the security and stability of a residential treatment centre; 2 / eliminate the effects of institutionalization on emotional/ social maturation of children; 3 / minimize the rejection and extrusion of difficult children from foster homes. Unlike other programs, which placed disturbed children in specialized foster homes and provided psychotherapy for them and long-term casework for the specialized foster parents, this program trained the parent-therapists to serve both as foster parents and as surrogate therapists. The families, not mental health professionals, were the primary treatment resource. The supportive elements in the treatment program were provided by other parent-therapist families, with mental health professionals serving only as consultants and supervisors. An extensive evaluation component was built into the program, so that the effectiveness of parent-therapist homes and residential treatment centres in dealing with disturbed children could be compared.

Recruitment for the Parent-Therapist Program was through an extensive advertising campaign via radio, the newspapers, and pamphlets left in public places. Interest in the program exceeded expectations, producing 300 enquiries, from which 75 families were extensively interviewed. Each potential parent was assessed as an individual; so was each marital dyad, and each family as a unit, with particular reference to problem-solving skills, communication, satisfaction with role assignments, sensitivity, and flexibility when faced with deviant behaviour. Thirteen parent-therapist families were selected, varying considerably in age and social and educational backgrounds, as well as in motivation. Four of these withdrew during the project, but were easily replaced. All applicants were seeking an interest to supplement their occupational and/or leisure activities, but whereas some had pre-school children and were dissatisfied with being full-time mothers and housewives, others had grown children who had or would soon be leaving the family. Still others seemed drawn by the opportunity for further academic knowledge and practical skills in the areas of child and family behaviour.

The parent-therapists were organized into three stable extended-family groups, each consisting of five couples who, together, formed a single interactive system. All members shared common goals for all children managed within that group system, although individual couples bore specific responsibility for those children living in their homes. Thus each child had not just foster parents, but a network of foster aunts, uncles, and cousins as well.

Educational and supervisory processes were delivered to each parent-therapist couple via the groups. First came a four-week period of orientation. Then, following placement, each group met weekly for a three-hour session in which members were encouraged to use the groups to improve their communication and problem-solving skills; to work through difficulties that any child, couple, or family were experiencing; and to provide and obtain emotional support. The groups shared their experiences, analysing together behavioural transactions and noting ways in which the child elicited negative parental reactions and responses that facilitated or inhibited more appropriate behaviour. Over time, the focus of group discussion shifted from the management of specific behaviours, such as truancy and theft, towards increasing couples' understanding of psychodynamic issues and specific therapeutic responses.

Parent-therapists audiotaped the sessions for future reference, and, when indicated, videotapes, films, seminars, and selected readings were used to augment the training. The parent-therapists were introduced to basic concepts of normal growth and development, to the understanding of disturbed behaviour in children, and to the significance of the family system in developing and perpetuating both normal and abnormal behaviour in children. Thus, through the groups, the couples were trained to go beyond traditional fostering to become surrogate therapists who were better equipped to manage disturbed behaviour effectively and to apply specific management techniques.

The groups allowed the foster children to be contained within an extended-family system, whereas, without them, the only alternative when a placement broke down would have been a referral for institutional placement. For example, when an unexpected pregnancy led one couple to leave the project, their foster son was placed with minimal disruption in the home of another couple from the same group who already knew him. Weekend visits of foster children with their foster aunts and uncles were encouraged, both to give the children contact with alternate parental figures and to afford parent-therapists some relief from caring for such difficult children on a daily basis.

Before reporting the results of the study, it should be noted that only 25 per cent of the children involved were wards at the beginning of the study, while 75 per cent were placed with the parent-therapists directly from their own homes. All of the thirty-six children placed were between six and eleven years (later six to fifteen years) old, and, in addition to their behaviour problems and/or emotional difficulties, functioned academically well below their estimated potential.

The average child remained in the parent-therapist home for eighteen and a half months (range nine to twenty-six months) and received no casework or psychotherapeutic services while in the program. Fifty per cent could not be maintained in regular classes, and required special educational placements or individualized remediation. The only other service available to children in the program was a weekly activity group led by a child care worker.

Relationships between natural parents and parent-therapists were rather complex, in part because initially the program had unintentionally discouraged contact between them. Later on, the program shifted its goal, encouraging carefully monitored contact. As the parent-therapists became more experienced and confident, they increasingly began to handle contacts with natural parents on their own, at times providing considerable emotional support and advice on child-rearing. In only a minority of families, especially those in which the natural parents had made a decision not to take a child back home and were emotionally separating from that child, was there conflict between natural parents and parent-therapists that could not be resolved by the latter, alone or with the help of the available professional consultants. In every case where the natural parents wanted to maintain contact regular visits were arranged.

Only four of the thirty-six children in the study were unable to be maintained in a parent-therapist home and required replacement within an institutional setting. In general, children in the program made substantial gains in developing social and interpersonal skills, in academic achievement, and in decreased symptomatic and maladaptive behaviours. The parent-therapists became increasingly psychologically sophisticated in their appropriate use of theoretical constructs in managing children, and in the manner in which they used the resources of the groups and their supervisory staff.

As to the evaluative component of the study, parent-therapist satisfaction was suggested by the fact that eleven families remained active in the project for four years, two families for three years, and two more for two years. Estimates of cost-effectiveness suggested that children in parent-therapist homes did about as well as those in residential treatment centres, but at approximately half the cost.

The Alberta Parent Counsellors Program

The Alberta Parent Counsellors Program (Larson, Allison, and Johnston 1978), operated by the Child Welfare Branch of the Alberta government, was an attempt to provide therapeutic services within community homes for children and adolescents with such severe emotional and behavioural problems that most foster homes would not be prepared to cope with them. An alternative to institutional care, the project involved the integrated development of fifty parent-counsellor homes and four assigned social workers over the period from June 1974 to March 1977.

It was recognized from the start that the intensive demands placed on parent-counsellors would require careful selection of participants from a large pool of potentially interested families. Since social workers were not considered either particularly interested in or skilled at recruitment activities, the project utilized and studied three distinct routes for generating recruit families. Of these, systematic use of public media proved the most effective and, in the long run, the most cost-effective recruitment strategy. Despite fears that the media approach would cost too much, this project demonstrated that systematic media recruitment cost less per contracted family. Potential families were located by the media, leaving the social workers more time to spend on family selection and preparation.

The media campaign featured an explicit, realistic, and descriptive picture of what was expected of potential parent-counsellors. It stressed that recruits would have to commit themselves to working in their own homes with children with serious behaviour and emotional problems. They would receive training and supervision in providing parent counselling that would serve as an alternative to hospitalization. Potential candidates were encouraged to see parent counselling as a career, and as a second income for the family. The campaign attracted responses largely from married couples under the age of forty with one or more children under the age of twelve, the husbands typically skilled tradesmen or labourers and the wives generally unemployed at the beginning of the project.

In addition to careful recruitment and selection procedures, the Alberta Parent Counsellors Program featured extensive parent-counsellor training prior to each placement; the careful and purposeful matching and placement of children with parent-counsellors chosen to provide maximum benefits to child and natural family; and planned involvement of child, natural parents, parent-counsellors, and social workers in developing, implementing, regularly reviewing, and, when necessary, revising an ongoing plan for case management and subsequent discharge. The program design featured weekly meetings of the parent-counsellors in groups comprising approximately six couples for advice, mutual support, and a continual and ongoing review of case management. An evaluation component was included as part of the program design.

The educational component of the program recognized the impossibility of training the parents to become experts in child management prior to placement. However, it decreased their anxiety and improved their performance by helping them develop a repertoire of practised responses to problems that could be anticipated prior to placement. The parent-counsellors' role was defined clearly vis-à-vis the child, the natural family, the social worker, and the agency. The training program, beginning prior to the initial placement and continued subsequently by the parent-counsellor groups, was designed to increase the parent-counsellors' ability to relate to children and to solve management-related problems, while enhancing their confidence in their work with the children and their awareness of the dynamics of the foster care system and of the results of placing children in care. The groups of parent-counsellors were expected to function as an extended family, providing mutual support and assistance in problem solving and formulating a specific plan for each child.

The evaluation component revealed significant changes in the children's self-esteem and other personality dimensions, more so for those children remaining in parent-counsellor homes at the time of the recording than for those already discharged. The children (almost 100 per cent), the parent-counsellors (about 90 per cent), and the social workers (about 70 per cent) noted some improvements in overall functioning over the course of the parent-counsellor placements, especially in self-esteem and school performance. Improvement in the relationship with natural families was one problem area reported least improved. In interpreting the latter finding, note that in only 29 per cent of cases were the natural families rated by social workers as co-operative participants in the program.

The Kent Special Family Placement Project

The Kent Special Family Placement Project (Hazel 1981) was originally developed to challenge two key assumptions in English child care thinking that had important implications for child-placement practice: that a large number of children and adolescents were 'unsuitable' for family placement, and that there was a shortage of residential placements for children and young people.

Basing their recruitment efforts in part on the findings of the Alberta Parent Counsellors Program, the Kent Special Family Placement Project sought its recruits via an intensive and systematic saturation of all local media. This campaign produced sixty applicants, only one of whom was obviously unsuitable. Group selection supplemented by individual interviews was then undertaken. Nearly all families applying were accustomed to having two incomes, although in some the wife/mother had for some years given hers up while her own children were young. The average applicants were described as clear and confident in their own relationships. They were attracted by the challenge of the project as described accurately in the media blitz, which they saw as adding meaning to their lives and stretching their capabilities in an area of considerable importance.

The Kent team sought to determine whether, if society were prepared to spend as much on developing family placements in the community as it costs to care for a child in a residential treatment centre, it would be possible to provide more effective help for those adolescents with severe problems who could not be managed within their own families. It further sought to determine whether ordinary people in their own homes could effectively help teenagers with severe behavioural and emotional problems and, if so, which of them could respond to family-based forms of 'treatment.' Treatment was described by the Kent team as 'any defined program of care and/or help directed towards producing changes likely to improve the child or young person's ability to live successfully within society.' For these fourteen- to seventeen-year-olds, a time-limited placement in a treatment home was intended to provide a bridge to adult life.

In line with the basic premise that it is legitimate to spend as much on a specialized family placement as on one in a residential treatment centre, the program paid a professional fee, usually, at the families' request, to the wife in the participating families. By doing so, the project sought to recruit a new population of foster parents with the knowledge, experience, and personal qualifications needed to confront difficult teenagers. It was considered crucial that the fee be high enough to compete with alternative and competitive sources of a second income for such families (see Campbell and Downs 1987). The Kent Special Family Project took a systemic view of the foster-care system. The foster parents were seen as the child's focal therapist, and social workers were warned not to weaken this relationship or to consider the foster parents as working for them. In many cases, the foster parents took responsibility for work with the natural families of their foster children as part of their role as fee-earning, free-lance professionals who undertook to achieve certain objectives within a specified time. All placements, which were intended to be problem-solving, were based on three written contracts, each of which tried to specify the tasks to be undertaken by the project family, the natural family, and the adolescent. Unlike the situation in the Alberta Parent Counsellors Program, the natural families involved in the Kent Project, with a few notable exceptions, supported the foster placements as preferable to those institutional placements in which their children had been prior to the beginning of the project. Natural parents were keen to meet the prospective foster parents and eager to visit their homes. Global objectives were usually easily defined and agreed upon. As in the Alberta Parent Counsellors Program, teenagers and families were carefully matched in an attempt to provide a family able to meet the needs and deal with the problems of each adolescent involved. While the initial twenty-one adolescents placed in the project remained for variable periods ranging from less than one year to more than two years, it is noteworthy that some of the teenagers chose to remain permanently in their foster homes after reaching age eighteen. The Kent team found that time-limited therapeutic placements for adolescents differ from foster placements of younger children in that having natural children of the same age in the foster family is more an advantage than a threat to the placement. The foster children seem to accept without significant jealously and rivalry the role and status of the natural adolescents, while the latter are sufficiently rooted in the local community to help the newcomer find a toehold in the local peer group. Many of the adolescents involved did well at work and school, and seemed to lose interest in delinquent activities (Hazel, Cox, and Ashley-Mudie 1977). It is noteworthy that, in the first two years of the project, 'except for a few brief sorties, no one had run away.' Foster families generally reported great satisfaction from their involvement in the project, and over the first two years only one family dropped out.

For a brief description of the Kent Special Family Project, including an outsider's assessment of one of the participants and her foster parents, see Barker (1978). The definition description of this project is to be found in Hazel (1981).

The Foster Care Research Project

The Foster Care Research Project (Steinhauer et al 1988, 1989), jointly developed by a collaboration of the Children's Aid Society of Metropolitan Toronto and members of the Division of Child Psychiatry at the University of Toronto, was originally designed as a controlled study comparing two models of foster care. Families agreeing to participate in the study were randomly assigned either to a control group or to an experimental group. Those in the control group received all routine services and educational opportunities available within the Children's Aid Society of Metropolitan Toronto. Couples assigned to the experimental group were assigned to one of four foster-parent support groups, each of which was jointly led by an experienced foster parent couple (the FPCLs) and a social worker (the SWCLs). The FPCLs provided relief for group members in times of crisis, and shared leadership of the support groups with the SWCLs. The groups themselves were to provide support for participating foster parents, to play a major role in foster-parent development and ongoing case planning, and to perform many of the functions ordinarily supplied through individual casework. Families in the group model had access to emergency psychiatric consultation, although routine psychiatric assessments were provided by the agency's usual consultants. Once each month, the leaders of the four support groups and their supervisors spent two hours with a senior child psychiatrist (the author) who directed the project. The time was used to coordinate the service and the research components of the project and to provide a case-centred program consultation.

The Foster Care Research Project (FCRP) differed from the other 'extended family' models of foster care described in this chapter in several important respects. First, the others were all designed as alternatives to residential treatment for disturbed children, but the Foster Care Research Project was intended to provide an enriched service for currently fostering families. Second, in the three other programs, the participating foster parents were specially recruited, specially trained, specially matched, and paid a salary. The FCRP, however, selected and randomly assigned to groups regular foster parents who received only the agency's routine per diem. Third, only the FCRP had groups jointly led by senior foster parents and a social worker acting as co-leaders. Fourth, only the FCRP built in an ongoing program consultation with a child psychiatrist, and occurred within the services of an existing child welfare agency, the Children's Aid Society of Metropolitan Toronto.

Various aspects of the Foster Care Research Project have been summarized (Steinhauer et al 1988, 1989) and described in more detail in a number of companion papers (Barker and Kane 1985; Santa-Barbara and Kane 1982a, 1982b; Hornick 1983; Steinhauer 1985; Johnston 1989). In its first objective, that of increasing foster-parent satisfaction, the group model parents were consistently more pleased with the support they received from the social work co-leader, the society, and other foster parents than were those receiving individual service. Those receiving group service unanimously agreed that the support groups had increased their skills as foster parents. Significantly more foster parents receiving individual service planned to discontinue fostering. Members receiving group service also indicated greater satisfaction in their feelings of being listened to by the agency and in being helped by the agency to accept difficult decisions and to deal with their feelings. Group model parents were significantly more likely to feel that the children in their care had profited from the service that they (the foster parents) had received. 'In addition, Group Model participants were more satisfied with their relationship with their social workers than were participants in the Individual Model on the average. The types of complaints made by foster parents in the Individual model were typical of those identified in other studies (Aldridge and Cautley 1975; Hampson and Tavormina 1980; Jacobs 1980; Jones et al 1976; Reistroffer 1972; Wiltse 1976). Only one Group foster parent identified poor worker service as a dislike' (Santa-Barbara and Kane 1982a, p. 20). A comparison of the group (experimental) and individual (control) groups suggested a trend towards fewer breakdowns among those families receiving group service, but the difference was not statistically significant. The number of home closures in both service models was low, and their infrequency allowed no conclusions to be drawn. Most of those few foster parents in the group model who left fostering indicated that they had enjoyed and felt supported by group service, whereas all foster parents in the individual-service model who withdrew from fostering were dissatisfied with the service they had received.

One objective of the Foster Care Research Project had been to compare the efficacy of the two models of foster care in reducing the incidence and severity of emotional disturbance in foster children. As there is no single, simple index of emotional disturbance for children over a wide age range, a number of different measures were used (Barker and Kane 1985; Santa-Barbara and Kane 1982a). Results at follow-up – six months after the child left the FCRP home or six months after the end of the research phase of the project, whichever came first – showed few differences between the children from the two models of care. The few statistically significant differences found were small in magnitude and did not favour either model of care. Many of the measures used suggest that the group model children were functioning better, though in most cases not to a statistically significant degree, than those receiving individual service.

Nonetheless, the Group Model Children indicate a consistent pattern: slightly fewer placement breakdowns for those who remained in care (16.6 vs 22.2 per cent), a slightly higher proportion who attained or exceeded their individualized goals (79 per cent vs 72 per cent); greater goal performance with respect to Behavioural Control issues (54 per cent vs 21 per cent). In addition, the younger children (under 5 years of age) from the Group Model for whom data was available, were functioning (developmentally) at their age appropriate levels.

An important finding from the present study is that children from both models of service tend to show important gains while in care and at follow-up. There is a consistent (if not always strong) pattern of gains for children from one or both models of service on social competence, school behaviour, individualized goals areas, and recidivism – both in terms of returning to care and with respect to needing mental health service. These children were also rated at follow-up as generally doing 'well' or 'fairly well' on many measures of family and peer activities, as well as in the area of self-esteem. The picture of these children at follow-up is considerably different from that indicated at their entry point into the Foster Care Research Project. (Santa-Barbara and Kane 1982b, p. 21)

The improved relations between the foster parents in the group model and the agency and its staff were viewed as central to the delivery of effective foster care, especially since the changes in foster-care delivery found in the group model were ones that foster parents themselves have been advocating (Aldridge and Cautley 1975; Cautley and Aldridge 1973; Hepworth 1980; Darnell 1987; Hampson and Tavormina 1980; Jones et al 1976; Steinhauer et al 1988; Santa-Barbara and Kane 1982a; Hegar and Hunzeker 1988). A major reason for the high morale and the positive attitudes of the group-model parents was their satisfaction with the support groups to which they were assigned.

The FPCLs and SWCLs of each support group shared a common supervisor. All co-leaders and their supervisors met for two hours monthly with a child psychiatrist who, as acting director of the project, provided a case-centred program consultation. Steinhauer and colleagues (1988, 1989) have described in detail nine processes occurring within the support groups that seemed central to their effectiveness.

- *A feeling of being understood.* This decreased feelings of loneliness, isolation, excessive responsibility, and alienation.
- *Cognitive restructuring.* Issues that, at the time, had seemed overwhelming to the foster parents were focused upon, analysed, partialized, and reframed, leaving foster parents understanding them and, therefore, feeling less helpless and out of control.
- *Teaching.* This occurred when group co-leaders or other group members suggested new ways of viewing a situation or of dealing with it.
- *Ventilation.* Members not infrequently came to meetings so anxious, enraged, discouraged, frustrated, or depressed that they were at first paralysed by the intensity of their own feelings. At such times, they needed an opportunity to ventilate in the safety of the group before they could utilize cognitive restructuring or teaching to plan an approach to the previously overwhelming situation. At the appropriate time, the co-leaders would then shift the group to move from ventilation to active problem solving.
- *Support.* Group members received support from each other both during and between the meetings, from FPCLs and SWCLs and, indirectly, through the leaders from high-profile members of the operational team.
- *Relief.* Requests for relief were less frequent than had been antici-

pated, and were often met informally by other group members, who knew each other's children.

– *Increased sensitivity to the needs and feelings of the foster children.* The greater sensitivity and awareness that members developed over time helped them perceive, understand, and respond more effectively to their foster children's needs.

– *Increased motivation, commitment to fostering.* Resulting from many of the factors listed above, this contributed to the high morale and sense of accomplishment that resulted in almost twice as many group-model foster parents indicating that they planned to continue fostering (74 vs 40 per cent: Santa-Barbara and Kane 1982b).

– *Sense of shared responsibility.* Group members and co-leaders often reported intense relief at being able to share the stress of coping with a difficult child with the group, rather than having to shoulder it alone.

The members of the operational team, all of whom had had previous experience working within an individual-service model, felt that the quality of the foster care provided within the group-service model had produced greater improvements in emotional and behavioural functioning of the children than had been demonstrated at a statistically significant level by the research design. Two papers, one by the author (Steinhauer et al 1989) and the other by an independent senior researcher unassociated with the project (Hornick 1983), have analysed the experimental design and suggested that the gains seen clinically but not proved statistically were underestimated as a result of problems in the research design. For summaries of the project and a critique of the research design, see Steinhauer and colleagues (1988, 1989).

Long-term Follow-up

The one of these innovative models for which long-term follow-up data are available is the Parent-Therapist Program. Its effectiveness was examined in a longitudinal study of all the emotionally and behaviourally disturbed latency-aged children of Hamilton, Ontario, who received residential treatment between February 1972 and May 1975. These children had been treated either in one of two institutional settings, one all-male, the other co-ed, or in the Parent-Therapist (PT) program. By comparing the three groups, a 1986 study by Martin and Pilon makes some interesting observations about the PT program and suggests reasons for its possible success.

A trained interviewer administered an in-depth, semi-structured interview to each subject that focused on the child's life history from the time of discharge from residential treatment until the follow-up study (approximately six years). Information was obtained about the youth's changes of residence, school performance, employment, emotional problems, antisocial behaviour, health, and social-service use. Also, the interviewer assessed the child's academic achievement (reading, spelling, arithmetic) using the Wide Range Achievement Test (WRAT) to compare levels achieved at follow-up with those obtained at the beginning of the program.

Social functioning was compared by noting the proportion of children in each group who experienced police contact or incarceration during the six years between discharge and follow-up, and information was validated with school, police, and child-welfare-agency records. Finally, a gross measure of relative emotional health was estimated by comparing the proportion of children from each of the three groups that had attempted suicide or had undergone psychiatric treatment during the same period.

While the three groups did not suffer in academic progress or social outcome, there was a significantly higher rate of suicide and mental-health-service use among the members of the PT group. These suicide attempts were positively related to placement with biological parents upon discharge from residential treatment.

Based on these results, the authors suggest (Martin and Pilon 1986; Pilon 1988) that the main cause of failure in the PT program is the removal of the child from a structured and healthy living arrangement to return to the chaotic home environment after discharge from treatment. Martin and Pilon suggest that this movement 'may counteract any progress accomplished while in the residential treatment' (1986, p. 9). Pilon suggests that were the child able to remain in the program, gains could likely be sustained. Since foster families are often in a position to make long-term commitments to children, permanent planning can, and should, be a part of the ongoing treatment process. Because 'long-term stability is probably the single most important factor in determining a positive placement outcome' (Pilon 1988, p. 23), an enriched foster care program where a child could remain in the setting where he had made his major gains until reaching the age of majority should minimize the chance of losing hard-won gains by returning the child yet again to a highly pathogenic family situation. Pilon suggests that such a program would prove economically as well as therapeutically advantageous: 'where the need to remove children from their homes cannot be obviated, the foster care system needs to develop mechanisms that would ensure stable placements. The long-term impact of enabling families to adequately parent their own children and of upgrading foster care services would undoubtedly be to reduce the need for very costly residential programs, (p. 6). Based on the results of the study, Martin and Pilon recommend that the Parent-Therapist Program be discontinued as a separate program, but that its positive aspects be incorporated into other foster-care services. Were this done, it would result in a program very similar to the Foster Care Research Project, as described above.

Summary and Conclusions

What can we learn from what these four models have in common that can serve as a guide to improving the efficacy of foster care?

1 *Change in role.* All four of these models have foster parents serving in a parent–therapist or surrogate–therapist role, rather than just as parent surrogates.

2 *Change of payment pattern.* Three of these models pay a salary either to one member of the foster-parent couple or split between the two. The fourth (the FCRP) would not have had its effectiveness interfered with had the parents been paid; indeed, the staff of that project felt that payment along the lines of the other projects would have been fairer to the foster parents and could only have augmented the success of the program.

3 *Change of contract.* As a consequence of foster parents' changed role definitions and their receipt of a salary over and above the usual boarding and maintenance allowance, the directors of the first three projects were able to contract for – and insist upon – a prearranged level of cooperation in implementing an individually formulated management plan along the lines of those examples described in chapter 6. The salaries also made it possible for them to insist upon attendance at all group and training activities. The one project that did not pay a salary (the FCRP) had to depend entirely upon the motiva-

tion and good will of the foster parents. It could have profited from the additional leverage available through payment of salaries in increasing foster fathers' active involvement.

4 *Change in recruitment.* Utilizing the change in role and payment patterns discussed above, the first three programs relied heavily for recruitment upon advertising campaigns heavily utilizing the public media. All found this an effective method of obtaining an adequate supply of satisfactory recruits. The fourth program, which was dependent upon the parent agency's usually methods of recruitment by social workers, had more trouble finding an adequate number of potential candidates.

5 *Change of model.* All four models relied heavily upon foster-parent groups to which all participating foster parents were assigned as the major source of support, training, and supervision supplied in traditional foster care by social workers. All four models cast the foster family as the major therapeutic influence on the child, and saw social workers and other mental-health professionals as having primarily a supervisory or consultant role.

6 *Provision of relief.* All four models built into their programs the provision of relief during crisis for overstressed foster parents in order to decrease the risk of foster-parent burn-out.

7 *Systemic view of the foster-care system.* All four models developed their programs around a systemic model of the foster-care system which took into account the interactive effects of foster parents, natural parents, foster child, and sponsoring agency on each other.

These four, in many ways similar, models of enriched foster care basically replicate each other, which suggests that foster care can substantially overcome many of the barriers to effective service delivery while avoiding the dangers inherent in institutionalization if based on a model similar to those described above. While not all foster parents or social workers will be comfortable within an essentially group-based model of foster-parent supervision and support, these projects have demonstrated that many of the problems that have contributed to pessimism about the efficacy of long-term foster care can be overcome by appropriate adaptations in service delivery. It is suggested that the major obstacles to a widespread utilization of the knowledge obtained from the experimental evaluation of these models has been the lack of general awareness of these experimental programs and an unwillingness by government social-service departments to pay foster parents a salary because of the fear of the cost to the child welfare system of doing so. If one takes into account the long-term costs of *not* providing such a model, such economy is likely in the long run to prove false indeed.

PART FIVE

Issues Related to Sexual Abuse within the Foster Care System

Chapter Sixteen

Developmental, Clinical, and Legal Implications of Children's Testimony

Why a Chapter on the Assessment of Children's Allegations of Sexual Abuse?

There are two main reasons for including a chapter on the evaluation of allegations of sexual abuse in a book dealing with the more generic aspects of foster care. The first is that many children who have been abused will end up in foster care, and that the sequelae of their having been abused may lead to difficulties within their placements. Often, the first evidence of their abuse may come to light only after they are safely in care. An understanding of how children are affected by abuse and some guidelines for the assessment and recording of allegations of abuse and for preparation for court testimony regarding them should be helpful for foster parents and for case workers dealing with such children. Second, foster children are making allegations of sexual abuse against members of foster families in increasing numbers. Such allegations may be extremely difficult to evaluate. Even if false, their investigation, while necessary, can be traumatic to the foster families and may lead to damaging and unnecessary placement breakdowns and loss of foster homes. Alternatively, inadequate investigation of such allegations may lead to unnecessary prolongation of the abuse or of exposing more children to foster parents who should have been recognized as abusive.

There is no doubt that some children and adolescents who have previously been sexually abused within their own families tend to set themselves up for repeating the abuse at the hands of members of the foster family (Littner 1960; Avery 1984). Usually adult and older adolescent members of foster families are quite aware of this possibility and are careful to avoid being compromised. In other cases, however, the lack of an incest taboo, whether or not the foster child plays an actively seductive role, may make it easier for weak and/or unscrupulous foster parents or foster siblings to take advantage of the situation and to repeat the abuse.

False allegations of having been sexually abused have, at times, been used by older or adolescent foster children to break up an unwanted placement, either as a deliberate manipulation or because a child or teenager who had previously been sexually abused within her own family fears a repetition of the same situation. The resulting allegations against members of the foster family may, especially if the child is genuinely convinced or fearful that they are true, be extremely difficult to verify. Because of the importance of protecting the child who has been abused and of understanding the issues related to sexual abuse and providing a framework for evaluating such allegations with the foster family, this chapter has been included in spite of its presenting a somewhat different aspect of foster care than others in this book.

Historical Introduction

For at least a century, North American society did not recognize childhood sexual abuse (Sgroi, Sarneck-Porter, and Caufield-Blick 1982; Freedman, Kaplan, and Sadock 1976). For decades before and after Freud, allegation of abuse were assumed to be either fantasies or lies. On those rare occasions when sexual activity was acknowledged, the child was usually blamed for seducing the adult (Berliner and Conti 1981).

The Woman's Liberation Movement challenged this situation, stimulating clinical and research interest. Solid epidemiological studies determined that one in four females and one in nine males were in some way sexually molested by their eighteenth birthday, although it should be noted that the broader the definition of abuse, the higher the statistics (Finkelhor 1979, 1984; Russell 1984; Badgley Report 1984). Many professionals become concerned about the extent of the problem and were dismayed with a social system that had failed to protect young victims. This concern was channelled into child advocacy with the motto 'children must be believed,' (Sgroi 1982). This attitude led to uncritical evaluations of some sexual-abuse allegations, which not only damaged some alleged offenders who were falsely accused, but also undermined the credibility of true victims.

Increased awareness, particularly through the media, resulted in a great increase in reported cases. It also focused increased attention on false allegations and false denials. Summit (1983) described the common experience of children taking back or falsely denying true allegations because of threats from the offender or their family. Meanwhile, false allegations received increasing publicity, despite the much lower rate at which they were reported, and were used to discredit true allegations of sexual abuse by encouraging the myth that it was impossible to believe what children were saying.

The Assessment of Abuse Allegations

A knowledge of important clinical and developmental factors is needed to clearly and systematically decide upon the validity of abuse allegations. Three stages are involved.

1 / *Determine whether or not the child is competent to recall and describe an abuse experience.* To understand this, one must have an appreciation of that child's developmental capacity for:
– reliability
– memory
– reality testing
– language/cognitive development
– conceptual level, as a function of the child's age
since all of these will affect the child's presentation of the abuse allegations.

2 / *Assess the quality of the child's description,* by applying a set of established criteria to determine whether or not – and how strongly – these support or undermine the validity of the allegations.

3 / *Examine the child's social context* to obtain additional relevant data, including:
– secondary (indirect and/or hearsay) data
– evidence of the child's being influenced by the opinions of others:
   a / to keep things secret, as in the 'Accommodation Syndrome' described later in this chapter, and b / to tell a story that is not true (i.e., false allegation).
Let us review these three stages of an adequate abuse assessment in turn.

TESTING THE COMPETENCE OF THE CHILD'S RECALL

First, how does one determine whether a child is able to recall and describe an abuse experience? What can be learned from what is known about the developmental capacity of children at different ages to remember and report with accuracy what has occurred during an episode of abuse?

The current professional literature provides both experiential and experimental evidence of each of the following statements.

Reliability. Children are at least as reliable as adults when it comes to telling the truth (Loftus and Davis 1984; Marin et al 1979; Melton 1981; King and Yuille 1987). Young children are generally more direct/frank in giving information. They lack the sophistication to lie deliberately. However, they may stress different aspects of an experience than those recalled by an adult, and their different use of concepts may invite misinterpretations. To a small child, for example, a short adult may still be a big man.

Direct and leading questions can distort memory both in children and in adults (Loftus and Davis 1984; Dawson 1981; Cohen and Harnick 1980). Children are vulnerable to suggestion in some circumstances, but resistant in others (Hoving, Hamm, and Galvin 1969; Fodor 1971). They appear particularly susceptible to suggestion when they are pressured to comply with an adult's expectations (Loftus et al 1984; Nurcombe 1986). There is no clear evidence that this finding is significantly related to age once they reach the age of six years, although three-year-olds were found by Goodman and Reed (1986) to be significantly more suggestible than were five-year-olds. However, although the children, especially the three-year-olds, were less able to resist false information offered in suggestive questions, the suggested information was unlikely to appear in their own free reports or to be elaborated beyond a tentative 'yes' or 'no' (Goodman et al, in press). Under extreme stress, some children exhibit perceptual and cognitive mistakes (Terr 1985b) and fantasy elaborations (Terr 1985a; Terr and Watson 1988). Other factors, such as interest value, delay interval, language development, and the kind of test used, may be just as important as age in determining a person's vulnerability to suggestion (King and Yuille 1987; Jones and Krugman 1986).

To test reliability:
1 / Ask the child the difference between telling the truth and telling lies.
2 / Ask the very young child who is unable to answer abstract questions to give examples of telling the truth and of telling lies.
3 / Give the child examples, some of which are obvious truths and others obviously untrue. Ask the child which are true and which are lies.

To test suggestibility:
1 / Having asked the child to tell about a familiar event (e.g., a birthday party or what was done on Hallowe'en), repeat the story back, altering some details and adding others. If the child does not spontaneously reject the alterations, ask if the story was repeated correctly or if any mistakes were made.
2 / Tell the child a short story of about a paragraph in length. Then, after having gone on to and completed another part of the examination, return to the story and ask a number of leading questions, the answers to which were not contained in the original story (e.g., 'What colour was the car?' 'On which side was the black eye when the injury was not located in the original story. The child's responses should be scored by a clinician who is aware of suggestibility norms for adults and for children of that child's age.

Memory. Children are able to recall past events more accurately than is generally believed (Nelson 1984; Jones and Krugman 1986). Though recall memory is not very sophisticated in young children, it improves with age, while recognition memory is well developed by age two (Perlmutter and Myers 1979; Perlmutter and Ricks 1979). Although, generally, children's recall is less than that of adults, what they do recall is largely correct (Marin et al 1979) and they are better at picking up apparently irrelevant details that may establish authenticity (Neisser 1979). Since their capacity for recognition exceeds their capacity for recall, children may require specific clues or questions to make an association. Disclosures that are volunteered spontaneously in the child's ongoing life or in free play or during an assessment are more reliable than those given in response to leading questions. This finding also raises the important clinical issue of how to cue the child sufficiently to stimulate recognition without leading or distorting the child's testimony (Donaldson 1978;

Price and Goodman 1985; Wehrspann, Steinhauer, and Klajner-Diamond 1987).

Two sorts of memory distortions occur in young children: first, children under age two can misinterpret an event, or can fuse two distinct
events by condensing them into a single happening that they believe
occurred. This tendency lessens with age (Nelson 1984).

Novel events, or ones that evoke strong emotions, are remembered
more clearly than routine and/or repeated events (Gislason and Call
1982; Fivush 1984; Hudson and Nelson 1983; Linton 1982; King and Yuille
1987).

In summary, most children by about age three can reliably register,
retrieve, and describe an episode of abuse in response to questioning
that appropriately stimulates recognition rather than just relying on
recall. Under age three, confusion and fusion make recollections less
reliable. In children younger than three, ongoing behaviour is often a
more reliable indicator of what they have experienced than what they
say they have experienced.

Distortions in children's evidence may be caused by fear of retribu-
tion, guilt experienced because of the child's relationship with another
person, or the influence of an overinvolved parent or professional. Such
distortions are unlikely to represent a deliberate attempt (at least by the
young child) to alter the course of justice or to victimize an innocent
party.

To test long-term memory:
1 / Ask the child to describe a major event, such as his birthday
party or what she got for Christmas.
2 / To estimate internal consistency, ask the child to describe the
same event on a subsequent meeting, or later in the same meeting.
3 / To estimate external consistency, check the child's description
against that of the parents and/or siblings.
4 / For further evaluation, tell the child a paragraph-long action
story, and repeat steps 2 and 3
5 / The child's responses should be scored by a clinician who is
aware of long-term memory norms for adults and for children of
the child's age.

Reality testing. There is a common belief that children are unable to
separate fact from fantasy. In fact, school-age children's abilities to sep-

arate fantasies from memories of real events are almost as good as those of adults (Johnson and Foley 1984). Between the ages of two and seven, children are in the pre-operational stage of cognitive development. In this stage, they are developmentally unable to invent fantasy without some prior experience on which to base it, so their imagination is dependent on what they have experienced (deYoung, 1986). Therefore, without some basis in experience, the young child cannot concoct elaborate lies or fantasies, although the fantasies of young children remain susceptible to the influence of the important adults in their lives.

To test reality testing:
1 / Ask the child the difference between 'real' and 'make-believe.'
2 / If the very young child cannot answer (i.e., if the question is too abstract), ask the child to give an example of something that is real and something that is make-believe; a situation that is real and one that is make-believe; a person/man/lady who is real and one who is make-believe.
3 / If a further estimate is desired, have the child sort out age-appropriate examples from each of these categories provided by the examiner.

In this pre-operational stage, the child's characteristic concreteness, egocentricism, and centring of thought may make what she says confusing, although, in some cases, the nature of the detail provided and the child-centred thinking may increase the impression of validity. For example, a child perceives and defines an object in terms of the function that child knows; this is called 'centring' the object. Thus, ejaculation is called 'peeing' by the young child, which may add confusion to the story. If, however, details of the 'peeing' are consistent with the ejaculation of semen, then the child's centred thinking supports the validity of the allegation (see Wehrspann, Steinhauer, and Klajner-Diamond 1987).

Conceptual level as a function of the child's age. Children's emotional development and their dependence on parents and others whom they cannot afford to alienate leave them especially vulnerable to appearing in court to confront directly those who have abused them.

Young children have a basically egocentric view of the world, which predisposes them to assume inappropriately that they are responsible, often stirring up intense guilt. This dynamic makes children prone to enormous emotional stress during court procedures, so that, if they are to be treated fairly, they should be well prepared, and the court should take into account their vulnerability.

Their egocentric view leaves children easily intimidated by adults, especially by those on whom they depend for survival. The judicial principle of allowing the accused to confront the accuser carries enormous threat to young children who have been and/or are being intimidated by the accused, especially if that person is a family member.

Children who have been mistreated by a parental figure still remain attached and anxious to please, though ambivalent, towards that person. Thus it is hard for them to give evidence if they fear that it will betray or hurt their abuser. Their fear and guilt will be increased if they have been told that, if they tell what happened, they will be responsible for breaking up the family, for sending their father to jail, and so on.

Children are especially vulnerable to the emotional stress of long waiting periods before threatening events, such as court hearings. Since these may provoke and perpetuate enough disturbance to seriously undermine intellectual, emotional, and social development, the waiting periods prior to court appearance should be kept to the absolute minimum.

Language/cognitive development. Children can accurately communicate their information and their opinions, as long as a method of cognitive processing appropriate to their developmental level is used. The child's developmental level must be taken into account both in posing questions and in interpreting the child's answers. Clinicians can assist courts in determining how developmental issues affect and/or distort children's testimony. It is important that clinicians assessing abuse allegations also look for evidence of adult influence affecting the child's testimony.

Age may limit the reliability of direct verbal allegations of children younger than two, and those of some children between two and three years of age. By age three, vocabulary limitations usually do not affect the reliability of children's allegations, and by age four children's grasp of languages differs from that of adults more in terms of style than of number of errors.

The younger the child, the greater the difficulty that child will have with abstract factors, such as time relationships. To expect young children to locate an event precisely in time is expecting the impossible. In recalling traumatic events, children are likely to get the sequence wrong (Terr 1985a). Even up to age seven or eight, children are still unable to locate past events within a given hour, day of the week, day of the month. They can, however, place the event in some context (e.g., day or night; near Christmas or their birthday; summer or winter).

To test language/cognitive development:
1 / Compare the child's expressive language to norms for children of that age.
2 / Do not expect the young child to give dates or times, but the child should know:
- whether it was light (day) or dark (night)
- whether it was hot (summer) or cold (winter)
- whether it was a school (or day-care) day or a stay-home day (weekend)
- who else was home when it happened
- in what room the events occurred

EVALUATING THE VALIDITY OF A CHILD'S TESTIMONY

Consideration of how the information was obtained is required for the evaluation of a child's testimony. The larger the data base, the more opportunity one has to assess the credibility of what the child has said.

To obtain an adequate data base, examine what the child has said:

1 by obtaining a videotaped/audiotaped interview, especially as early as possible after the child has begun making allegations. The advantages of a taped interview over a dictated statement are twofold: first, it captures directly the words of the child and, even more important, the feeling-tone that accompanies the allegations. These may play an important role in assessing their validity. Second, it allows the viewer to observe the role played in the interview by the adult conducting it. To what extent did the examiner lead, suggest, or reinforce the child's allegations? To what extent did the examiner stimulate recognition without undue leading or suggesting?
2 Via dictated statements, especially those made soon after the alleged event. Note that the first telling is often the most accurate account of what occurred.
3 By a sworn witness reporting what the child said verbatim. The judge has two checks on the accuracy and validity of the witness: the witness is under oath and the judge can estimate the reliability of the witness. The same semi-objective criteria that can be applied to assess the

validity of what the child says directly are equally applicable to in-direct evidence (i.e., statements made by the child to others).

4 By the child in person presenting evidence in court: via videotape or closed-circuit TV, or in the courtroom. In assessing a child's direct or indirect testimony, always look for evidence of pressure to keep things secret or to tell a story that is not true.

What criteria, then, can help to determine the validity of a child's allegations as to whether or not sexual abuse has indeed occurred? The occurrence of abuse can usually, but not always, be determined by care-fully applying the following criteria to what the child directly tells the examiner, along with what the child has said to other credible adults. While any one of these criteria may be absent from a given case, it is the overall picture that usually establishes the credibility, although sometimes one will never be sure whether or not abuse has occurred.

1 / *Medical findings.* Venereal disease in a pre-pubertal child, semen deposits near vagina, anus, mouth, and/or severe trauma to genitals or anus are highly suggestive. However, because of the elasticity of normal vaginal tissues, the large variety of sexual behaviours that can occur, and the lack of normative statistics, an absence of such signs, especially after a week or more has elapsed, cannot be taken as proof that abuse has *not* occurred (Wooding 1985).

2 / *Criteria arising from the child's presentation (direct or indirect)* (Wehrspann, Steinhauer, and Klajner-Diamond, 1987)

a / *Spontaneity.* It is important to evaluate whether what the child said or is reported to have said was offered spontaneously or in response to the questions or comments of the informant or an examiner. If a videotaped recording of each such conversation is not available, the adult should, as soon and accurately as possible after the event, record the relevant discussion verbatim in the form of a dialogue to allow others reviewing the record to determine for themselves whether the adult's contribution to the dialogue was leading and, if so, if the child merely took that lead or went far beyond it, spontaneously volunteering much more than was asked for.

Her foster mother reported that, one night, Margaret was alone in her room, making up a song while going to bed: She sang,

I'm getting ready for bed.
Nobody can hurt me here
Mommy loves us, but she sticks her fingers in us
And we're going home some day.
But Mommy can't hurt us now.
I'm getting ready for bed
Mommy can't hurt us now ...
They stuck it in you, too, Cathy.
And now I have to go pee
And I want a drink
'Cause I'm going to bed.

b / *Repetitions over time: internal consistency and external consistency.* Repeated statements that complement and are consistent with each other support the credibility of allegations. These may take several forms:

- Repeating basically the same story to more than one person.
- Repeating the same story to the same person(s) with variable but consistent detail over time.
- Repeating the same basic theme through more than one medium. For example, the child's drawings, puppet play, doll play, responses to the 'three wishes' and the 'animal' questions (Broder and Hood, 1983) may all confirm the allegations.
- Several involved children repeating a consistent story:

  The details of many conversations over a period of eight months in which Joanne and Christine described abuse by their father differed from time to time, but all were consistent with each other. They were also congruent with what both girls had, on other occasions, told their social worker, the worker who had conducted the original abuse investigation, and their therapist.

There can also be consistency in false allegations, for example, from a younger child under adult influence or an adolescent using false allegations to attack or intimidate parents or surrogates. An example would be the foster child who, having been abused in an earlier home, falsely alleges abuse to disrupt an unwanted placement (Terr 1986). Young children, especially, will often answer if asked who told them to say what they have just said. One should at least suspect adult influence if a child somewhat mechanically repeats progressively more elaborate versions of what supposedly occurred, especially in the absence of any accompanying evidence of repression (as in the 'Accommodation Syndrome,' described later in this chapter), with a lack of age-appropriate detail, and with affective responses inappropriate to the allegations. A comparison of stories told by mother and child can provide other signs of adult influence (Benedek and Schetky 1985; A.H. Green 1986).

c / *Embedded responses.* An embedded response occurs when a child's recognition is suddenly and unexpectedly triggered by a chance occurrence that is cognitively or affectively linked to memories of past events that, because of repression and/or developmental limitations, are unavailable to spontaneous recall. The stimulus, a not-unusual event embedded within the ongoing flow of everyday life, has no special meaning to the average person, but provides for the sensitized child a connection to the repressed experience, thus evoking an idiosyncratic reaction (Weick 1971; Nelson and Ross 1980).

> While eating lunch one day, Christine suddenly vomited all over and burst into tears. She immediately apologized: 'I'm sorry, Aunt Mildred, but the salad dressing looks like the stuff that people rub on pee-things.'
>
> (*Christine* (relaxed; eating Jell-O for dessert at lunch): 'My mom has jelly in her pee-hole.'
> *Foster mother:* 'I see.'
> *Christine* (angrily): No, you don't see. I see. With my own little flashlight. I get to look right up my mommy's pee-hole.'

Embedded responses are more commonly found in data gathered through the careful ongoing observations of the child by a parent or foster parent, or in what is revealed to a therapist or social worker over a period of time. The presence of embedded responses supports credibility.

d / *Amount/quality of details.* Sometimes children tell a story so rich in age-appropriate details that we are convinced that only by experiencing the events could the child have produced the same quality and amount of detail (DeJong 1985). Such detail is clearly beyond what a child of that age could know, fantasy, dream, or have seen (e.g., pornographic videotape; direct observation of sexual behaviour in adults or older children), although fusion and confusion of real memories with what the child may have seen or been told by others should be considered (Nelson 1984). Where the abuse occurred, what participants were wearing or what they took off, where other family members were at the time, timing the events using a child's chronology (related to birthdays, school-day vs weekend, or what the child had seen on television), or other idiosyncratic details related to the assault further favour credibility.

Joanne and Christine, on three separate occasions, talked about the differences in the taste of warm vs iced pooh. They described how, unlike cold pooh, warm pooh sticks on the teeth and on the bathtub. They told how Donald would sometimes argue with their mother or try to help them hide when she was going to make them eat pooh, and how if you brought up when you were eating it, their mother hit them and made them eat it again.

The more novel, traumatizing, and singular the episode of abuse, the more details a child can be expected to produce. The more frequent the repetitions, the less specific details the child can give of any single episode (Hudson and Nelson 1983; Fivush 1984).

e / *Story told from the child's viewpoint.* Sometimes the way children tell their story strongly suggests that it is being told from a child's viewpoint. Faller (1984) has argued that children present what has occurred in a highly personal way, identifying 'who' did 'what,' 'when,' 'where,' and 'how,' along with other discriminating information consistent with the developmental and experiential limitations of the child. Their choice and combination of words, and especially their naïve attempts to describe events they do not understand, may give their story the stamp of authenticity.

Once both girls insisted that they knew it was their mother's urine and not Donald's that they had been forced to drink. When asked how they could be so sure, they unhesitatingly replied that it tasted different from what it was like when they were gagged by the towel into which Donald had peed (i.e., ejaculated) after rubbing his pee-thing.

f / *Evidence of child's emotional state consistent with disclosure.* Such evidence includes both the child's state of mind at the time of the abuse as related by the child or others, and also the child's emotional state when telling what occurred. Common reactions include embarrassment, disgust, anger, anxiety and fear, and such psychophysiological reactions as trembling, flushing, loss of bladder or bowel control, topic-related hyperactivity, or a marked dissociative response. Avoidance, hesitation, or refusal to talk may be an indication of the overwhelmed child's attempt to avoid having to re-experience the feelings associated with the event and should not be dismissed simply as an indicator that the alleged events never occurred.

Sometimes Suzy would shiver and shudder uncontrollably when she talked about something her dad had done to her. Her brother, Teddy, would become frantically overactive in an attempt to distract her, either wetting or soiling if he could not do so. Once when Suzy told about the time she was forced to perform fellatio, she became pale and said she had a pain in her stomach, as if she were about to throw up.

A flat, withdrawn response is compatible with either a defence against overwhelming feelings associated with the abuse (i.e., a dissociation), or with a mechanical account of a false allegation (Summit 1983; Green 1986). These must be distinguished between on clinical grounds (see pages 311–19 of this chapter).

g / *Consistency in the face of challenge.* If the child responds to a direct challenge by confirming the original allegation, the child's credibility is thereby strengthened:

	Verbatim report	Interpretation
Joanne:	'Those things we said this morning were just a dream.'	Note use of 'we said,' not 'Chris said,' i.e., I, too, said it.
	'I thought it was true but I had a dream, I was dreaming.'	The frank admission is followed by attempt to take it back, claiming it was all a dream.
Chris:	'Oh yeah, Joanne! Really Joanne! A dream, eh? It's true, Joanne. I don't tell lies. It's crazy but we do everything.'	Chris reaffirms her original statements and, by insisting that it is true and she doesn't tell lies, questions, by implication, the truth of Joanne's denial.

Joanne: 'Yeah, but I shouldn't say   Joanne herself concedes that
            that stuff. Mother will give   it really did happen.
            me a licking. You always get
            me into trouble.'

h / *Sexually Specific Behaviours.* The repetition of sexually specific behaviours by a pre-pubertal child highly discriminates sexually abused children from others who are psychiatrically disturbed without having been abused (Friedrich et al 1984). What the child says may reveal a level of sexual knowledge, experience, or preoccupation inconsistent with the age, as can the child's fantasies, free play, art, or excessively sexualized behaviour. These may be self-directed (e.g., insertion of foreign objects into the anus or vagina; excessive, compulsive, and prolonged masturbation from which the child cannot be dissuaded, carried on without an age-appropriate sense of privacy). Even stronger is evidence of the child repeatedly initiating sexual behaviour involving younger children or adults. Occasional masturbatory and exploratory behaviours are both common and normal (DeJong 1985), but their intensity and recurrence can imply sexual overstimulation and/or trauma. They suggest sexual abuse, except in rare cases where normal sexual behaviours used for self-stimulation or for relaxation by severely deprived children are exaggerated by an extreme overreaction based on distorted parental sexual attitudes. These are usually obvious when looked for (Kempe and Kempe 1984; Yates 1982).

i / *Evidence of the 'Accommodation Syndrome' (i.e., of suppression due to intimidation).* (Summit, 1983) Evidence of delayed, conflicted, or unconvincing disclosure with or without subsequent retraction should always suggest the possibility of the child 'accommodating' to external threats or pressures. Rather than being taken as proof that the child's testimony in unreliable, evidence of fear or intimidation, as represented in the withholding, modification, or retraction of allegations, should support, not undermine, the child's allegations.

Mother will be mad at us for telling. I'll get a licking. You shouldn't say we do it. Mom did all those bad things to us even before we knew Donald. Why did she hurt us so much? ... We'll be in trouble when we go home, that's the subject. Mother will say we're lying, but it's the truth. Why does Mother tell us it's not true? Mom knows it's true. She's the one not telling the truth. She's lying, Joanne. She knows it's true, so why does she say it never happened?

It is commonly assumed that children quickly report abuse to a trusted adult. But the behaviour of sexually abused children usually challenges our expectations. The child typically keeps the abuse a secret (Finkelhor 1984), does not protest, tells only part of what happened (often unconvincingly), and may then retract the allegations. These responses have often been misinterpreted as proof that the child enjoyed the contact, imagined it, or lied about it (Herman and Hirschman 1981; Finkelhor 1979; Russell 1983).

In 1983, Summit described the 'Accommodation Syndrome' to explain children's responses to their parents' or others' attempts to intimidate them into suppressing details of abuse or retracting what they had already said. Direct evidence of bribery or threats by the alleged perpetrator against a child who feels helpless in the face of them, associated with the child's substantially changing or withdrawing the allegations, is highly suggestive.

There are five essential components to the Accommodation Syndrome as described by Summit. They include:

- *Secrecy.* The adult misuses his authority to establish the activity as secret, using bribery, intimidation, or direct threats to reinforce this point. Unbelieving or frightened mothers may collude with these threats.
- *Helplessness.* The child – especially the young child – is helpless: she cannot stop the abuse, nor can she escape from the situation, because of her extreme dependency on her abuser.
- *Entrapment.* By remaining silent and by passively submitting to repeated abuse, children may avoid the threatened consequences, but they remain conflict-ridden and confused. Their ongoing inner conflict may cause a variety of emotional and behavioural symptoms.
- *Delayed/conflicted unconvincing disclosures.* Given the child's conflict, the threats to which she has been exposed, and her feelings of helplessness and domination, it is understandable that disclosures are often partial or confused and may alternate with retractions.
- *Retractions.* The fact that the child takes back or alters significantly the initial allegation does not necessarily mean that the child is an unreliable witness. While she may be correcting a mistake in earlier testimony, the recanting may also be an indication of the Accommodation Syndrome in action. Distinguishing between these two is usually possible by a clinician with adequate awareness of typical responses of children at all developmental stages to the stress of sexual

abuse (De Francis 1969; Terr and Watson 1988; Wald 1975; Sgroi, Porter, and Blick 1985; see also pp. 306–11 of this chapter).

The 'non-offending' spouse may collude with the perpetrator in persuading a child to keep the secret or to recant. Even non-perpetrating parents who know that abuse has occurred often fear the effects of the truth coming out on their marriage or on the family (Berry 1975; Henderson 1972). There can be either direct or indirect evidence of parental influence. Direct evidence would include the child stating that she had been told what to say or threatened about what would happen if she repeated the allegations, or direct observation of the parent trying to change the child's story. Indirect evidence of influence, suggested by intimidation in the presence of either parent or marked ambivalence in the child's reaction to the parent(s), or evidence of the accommodation syndrome, always merits careful exploration.

j / *Confirmatory evidence obtained from other sources/informants.* Courts, traditionally, are reluctant to accept indirect (i.e., hearsay) evidence. However, the sworn testimony of others (the mother, a foster parent, the caseworker, a therapist) may give a better picture of the young child's experience than the one that even an expert examiner, who is a stranger, can obtain directly from the child, especially in a pressured interview situation. Thus the systematic evaluation of indirect evidence can allow a qualified expert to comment under oath on its contribution to the total determination of credibility and reliability of allegations. Such is the case only if the methodology of collecting and reporting avoid excessive pressure and leading and if the data satisfy the criteria developed earlier in this chapter.

VALIDITY OF THE ABOVE CRITERIA

The above criteria can be applied to either direct or indirect (i.e., hearsay) evidence when used in conjunction with an appropriate assessment methodology.

Research validity has not been established for any such criteria except by Undeutsch (1982), who reported his results with 1500 cases, of which his criteria suggested that 90 per cent were truthful. In 95 per cent of those whose statements Undeutsch found truthful, the perpetrator was convicted. None of those was ever proved innocent by the subsequent discovery of conflicting information. In several questionable cases in which Undeutsch's criteria suggested credibility but were in conflict with such evidence as an alibi or a medical report claiming impotence of the alleged perpetrator, further investigation often confirmed the accuracy of the psychologic examination. Undeutsch denies that additional evidence contradicting a psychologic determination via his criteria was ever obtained in over thirty years of practice.

Research validity has also been established for sexually specific symptoms. Friedrich, Beilke, and Urquiza (1984) compared three groups of young children: a sexually abused group, a psychiatrically disturbed group, and a normal group. Both the sexually abused and psychiatrically disturbed groups were equally disturbed, and significantly more so than the normal group. Sexually specific symptoms significantly discriminated the sexually abused from the psychiatrically disturbed group. In another study, Faller (1984) evaluated the criteria of 'presentation' and 'quality' against the independent measure of admissions of abuse by the perpetrator. In 76 per cent of those cases where there was some sort of admission (full, partial, or indirect), the criteria for presentation and quality were met.

The suggested criteria also have consensus validity, as they are widely used by professionals across Canada, the United States, and Germany. The criteria listed above (except for 'embedded responses'), despite minor variations in terminology, are those utilized by Faller (1984), Green (1986), Sgroi (1982), D.P.H. McGraw Jones (1986), Nurcombe (1986), Undeutsch (1982), and Steller, Raskin, and Yuille (1987), all of whom have contributed significantly. With these, Wehrspann, Steinhauer, and Klajner-Diamond (1987) have suggested the inclusion of two additional structural criteria: embedded responses and consistency in the face of challenge. These, along with sexually specific behaviours and the systematic collection and examination of confirmatory evidence obtained under oath from additional sources, can enlarge the data base to which these criteria can be applied.

It is crucial that workers in the child welfare and abuse fields develop and practise techniques of stimulating young children's recall while minimally contaminating their replies (Wehrspann, Steinhauer, and Klajner-Diamond 1987). To overcome the widespread assumption that children's allegations of sexual abuse cannot be trustworthy, it is not enough to expect the courts to accept clinician's opinions on a child's credibility on faith. Rather, clinicians must marshal their evidence so that judges can see the raw data, understand the methodology and criteria applied to them, and follow the logic the clinicians used to reach their conclusions, while ruling out the credibility of other competing explanations via the same data and methodology. The better this is done, the more effectively children who have been abused will be protected; at the same time, the naïve and damaging acceptance of false and/or parentally influenced allegations that threaten to entrap the innocent and draw professional credibility into question can be avoided.

Situations Commonly Associated with False Allegations

Young children rarely initiate false allegations without the influence of an adult intending (consciously or unconsciously) to prove the allegations true.

Four situations are commonly seen in which a child, under adult influence, is likely to make false allegations.

1 / *Post-traumatic stress disorder.* Women or girls who were sexually abused in the past may repress the intense feelings and memories associated with the abuse and go on to develop a chronic post-traumatic stress disorder (American Psychiatric Association 1980). This disorder may evoke in them periods in which intrusive and recurrent thoughts, feelings, or behaviours burst through their usual denial, often in response to an environmental stimulus. At these times, they may feel and act as if the abuse that they experienced earlier is recurring. Some even go so far as to recapitulate aspects of their own abuse in their relationship with their own children (Gelinas 1983).

Adolescent girls suffering from post-traumatic stress disorder may convincingly describe an abuse that they say occurred recently. Their confusion of present and past events may lend their reports an intensity that suggests credibility, making it difficult to determine the truth of current allegations.

Mothers suffering from post-traumatic stress disorder as a result of past sexual victimization may overidentify with their child, particularly when she reaches the age at which their own abuse occurred. They may then become convinced that the child has been sexually abused. While such a response can be triggered by actual abuse, it can also be precipitated by any situation that, while in itself non-abusive, contains elements or elicits feelings reminiscent of the mother's past abuse. In either case, the mother's extreme overinvolvement with the child's alleged abuse, along with her tendency to fuse and confuse present and past events, may add to the difficulty of assessing credibility, especially when the mother's disturbance is superimposed on allegations of an abuse that did indeed occur. Such a mother's overinvolvement in false allegations of abuse to her child is usually easier to identify if the examiner considers the possibility.

> Mrs H's viewing of a street-proofing film with her three-year-old daughter prompted her to report that her daughter had been sexually abused by her estranged husband. Mrs H saw her daughter squirm during the film. Therefore, she questioned the child and 'discovered' she had been fondled. Mrs H audiotaped her talk with her daughter. This revealed that the questioning process was coercive, leading, and highly suggestive. In assessment, the mother related a long-standing incestuous relationship with her own father that was seriously affecting all areas of her life. In interview, she confused and blurred present and past concerns of her own and her child's sexual abuse. The child's assessment did not confirm the mother's concern.

2 / *Serious psychiatric disorder.* Another potential source of false allegations lies in the combination of a serious psychiatric disorder in the mother (especially schizophrenia, a borderline personality disorder, or Munchausen-by-Proxy) combined with a symbiotic mother/child relationship (D.P.H. Jones and McGraw 1986; Goodmin, Sahad, and Rada 1978). In such a situation, psychiatric examination reveals a mother who has delusions that her child has been abused, along with an enmeshed mother/child relationship with clear evidence of a self-other boundary disturbance (Steinhauer and Tisdall 1984) such as the child being incessantly interrogated and pressured by the mother to repeat false allegations. It is the mother who usually initiates such disclosures. These she may increasingly embellish over time, often supporting her allegations with copious notes. If the child makes a statement, it is usually remarkably similar to the mother's, lacking in detail and told in the absence of an appropriate emotional response.

> Mrs W. said that her young boys, ages five and two, had been molested by their maternal aunt. Mother recounted that the older boy, shaking with fear, had told her how his aunt had 'touched his dink.' In subsequent interviews, the mother made increasingly fantastic allegations. In individual sessions, the older boy disclosed, almost verbatim, the same allegations, but without any upset. The mother became increasingly agitated and admitted that she had

been spending much time talking with the child about the abuse, and that she found it more difficult to discriminate fact from fantasy. The situation culminated with the mother's hospitalization for a paranoid disorder, at which time the boys' disclosures stopped.

3 / *Custody/access disputes.* Perhaps the most common cause of false allegations of sexual abuse is their precipitation by an ongoing custody/access dispute. It is usually the child's mother, shortly after the marital separation, who alleges abuse by her ex-husband, though on occasion the father may accuse the mother's new partner. It is revenge, driven unconsciously by the accuser's inability to handle the loss of the spouse, that motivates the accusing parent to exaggerate acceptable physical contact that occurred while the child was on a visit into an allegation of abuse. The child's dependency, along with the fear of parental disapproval or loss of love, persuades the child to go along with the parent's false allegations.

Mrs B., after losing a court bid to restrict access of her ex-husband to their four- and one-year-old daughters, said that her oldest daughter had told her she had been abused by her father. In interview with mother and daughter, the child asked her mother to talk about the abuse because she thought her mother could tell it better. In individual interviews, the daughter talked of her father bathing her and rubbing her genitals (pee-pee) with a washcloth. She said her mother thought it had hurt, but it had not. When the older daughter's court case turned for the worse, mother said that the youngest daughter had rubbed her pee-pee and said, 'Daddy hurt pee-pee.' This allegation was not corroborated by the child's day-care or by investigative interviews.

4 / *Professional bias.* False allegations may occur as a result of professionals who, overly identified with a young child, prematurely commit themselves to believing an allegation through overvaluing, misinterpreting, and/or distorting some data while failing to heed others. Such a bias may skew their evaluation, with the effect of seriously damaging the lives of those falsely accused, which, in turn, can be used to call into question true allegations.

The fact that clinicians' errors can contribute to false allegations must be recognized, but this should not be taken as a suggestion that it is more of a problem than professionals' denial of true allegations. A balanced stance by the clinician, combined with an awareness that both false positives and false negatives can occur, is a prerequisite for the responsible assessment of such difficult cases.

A young girl had disclosed to her aunt that, on weekends over the preceding year, her father had fondled her many times. However, the child's psychotherapist was so convinced the abuse had occurred that she was unable to see any mother–daughter pathology or anything positive in the relationship between the daughter and her father. She went on a single-minded campaign to get her client's father convicted, eventually organizing a demonstration outside the provincial premier's office. The judge dismissed the case on the grounds that the therapist's behaviour so influenced the child as to make a determination impossible.

Summary

In assessing children's evidence, three questions need to be answered: 1 / Has the child the developmental capacity to remember and describe the abuse? Determination involves an understanding of the child's memory, reality testing, language, conceptual level. 2 / Is the quality of the child's description suggestive of credibility (i.e., of the validity) of the allegations? 3 / Does the child's social context reveal relevant data, including secondary (indirect) evidence, evidence of influence, evidence of accommodation?

Failure to assess, to interpret adequately, or to consider appropriately the evidence relevant to all three of these stages will result in avoidable discrimination against children within the justice system. The information obtained by the three-stage clinical assessment described above should be presented and interpreted (translated) to the court by one or more professionals with appropriate clinical knowledge of children and their developmental competences. Such experts should be expected to substantiate their opinions in a number of ways, including:

- describing their data base, and how it was obtained (videotape/process recording)
- describing the methodology they applied to gather and interpret that data
- systematically applying at least one set of semi-objective criteria to

the evidence supplied directly (from the child) or to that supplied indirectly (from others to whom the child has spoken)
- providing evidence of supportive statements from the established professional literature
- indicating why the evidence does not fit alternative explanations.

The routine utilization of these five principles avoids the risk of expert statements that depend for their validity simply on who made them. Furthermore, these positions would be available to responsible criticism by comparable experts representing the other side.

Court-Related Issues

The criminal court, intimidating even to experienced adults, was not designed with children in mind. Due process, designed as it was for adults, becomes grossly inappropriate when society attempts to fit children into it without the modifications needed to ensure that they are given the same rights, taking into account their developmental status and needs, that adults already enjoy. As long as children continue to be treated by our governments and courts like little adults, they will rarely see justice done in our criminal courts.

Recent legislation has, in some jurisdictions, offered a few crumbs to children, but these are largely of a cosmetic nature. After much controversy and concern about the potential for falsifying videotape evidence, some jurisdictions have decided to allow videotaped interviews as evidence. A clock running on camera is a good safeguard against cutting/editing of videotapes. Many lawyers are concerned that clinical interviews can be distorted by the interviewer leading the child, thus slanting the child's evidence, which can, indeed, be a problem at times. The videotaping of interviews can be particularly helpful in revealing the contribution of the clinician to the interview. Instead of a psychiatrist or psychologist presenting abstract conclusions to the judge and expecting to have them taken on faith, the evidence from which the clinician draws his conclusions can be reviewed by the judge, who is free to reach his own decision as to whether or not the clinician was leading the child excessively or interpreting correctly.

A major inequity is that the young children who are alleged to have been abused are still required to appear in court to face examination and a prolonged and often hostile cross-examination in the presence of the alleged abuser. We recognize that the rights of the child to be spared additional trauma in the course of court proceedings must be balanced against the rights of the alleged abuser to a fair trial. But there are ways other than through the intimidation of children by which this end can be achieved.

1 / First, in order of preference, is allowing the child to testify via videotaped interviews, and by having other adults, including clinicians to whom the child has talked, present under oath videotaped or verbatim accounts of what the child has told them (Jones and Krugman 1986; Skoler 1984; Notes 1985; Ordway 1981). Then a clinician with special expertise in the sexual-abuse area would be expected, under oath, to interpret what the child is saying, to explain how he arrives at his conclusions on the basis of the data available to the court, and to state what criteria he used in arriving at those conclusions and in rejecting others.

This raises the question of the acceptability of hearsay evidence in court in such cases. In his 'Reasons for Judgement' in the recent case of the Children's Aid Society of Hamilton-Wentworth (Ontario) against D.C. et al., Judge Thomas A. Beckett wrote: 'It is evident to me that if society is to protect young children from sexual abuse, some traditional rules of evidence do not and cannot apply. The best evidence we are likely to get from young children may be in the form of statements that they make to others in the investigative or assessment process.' Judge Beckett also quotes Lord Devlin, in *Official Solicitor to the Supreme Court, V.K. and Another* (1965) A.C. 201 (H.L.): 'There are also rules of less importance designed to aid in the administration of justice and to regulate procedure. They are rules of convenience rather than of principle; and the rule against hearsay, which I shall later have to consider, is among them. No one would suggest that it is contrary to natural justice to act upon hearsay' (p. 238). Judge Beckett also quotes Lord Devlin (pp. 242–3) as saying, 'an inflexible rule against hearsay is quite unsuited to the exercise of a paternal and administrative jurisdiction.'

Judge Beckett also quotes the judgment of the Court of Appeal, delivered by Mitchell, J.A., on appeal of the decision on *W.M. and D.M.V. Director of Child Welfare for Prince Edward Island* (1986) 3 R.F.L. (3) 181 (P.E.I. S.C.) [App. Div.]:

the general rule excluding hearsay has never been regarded as absolute by the courts. Over the years the common law has recognized numerous exceptions when it became necessary to do so in order to reach a just determination of an issue and the out-of-court statement in question was made in circumstances under which its trustworthiness could be relied on by the court.

The list of exceptions has never been closed. Just because certain hearsay evidence is not admissible according to any of the traditional exceptions to the exclusionary rule does not mean that a court would not be justified in admitting it if circumstances warranted the making of a new exception.

Oftentimes in cases of alleged sexual abuse of a young child the only evidence available is contained in a statement made by the child to some third party. Usually such statements are not made in circumstances that would meet the criteria for admission under the traditional exceptions to the hearsay rule. *If the child can not or for some valid reason does not testify about the fact asserted in the out-of-court statement and hearsay is excluded the court will be deprived of hearing what could be the most relevant of evidence.* Faced with that situation, the court may admit the third party's evidence as proof of the facts contained in the child's statement, even though that evidence be hearsay, provided that, as groundwork for its admission, sufficient evidence is first led to establish the reliability of the out-of-court statement, and of the circumstances which establish the need to introduce the contents of the child's statement through hearsay. In such cases, the court must always proceed with great caution both with regard to satisfying itself on the question of the reliability of the child's statements, as well as with respect to those circumstances which justify the need for the admissibility of the out-of-court statements.

The problem with the hearsay evidence in the case at bar is that the trial judge received it without first hearing any evidence to justify receiving it on the basis of its necessity or reliability. (p. 185; emphasis in original)

2 / To avoid intimidation to which young children are especially vulnerable, the child should not be expected to give evidence in the presence of the accused and/or family or other supporters of the accused. (This avoidance of intimidation could be managed by the mechanism listed in 3, below, or, if the child were testifying in court, by allowing the accused and/or supporters to watch and hear the testimony from outside the court on closed-circuit television.)

3 / The child could be interviewed in another room, by an expert in the psychiatric/psychological interviewing of children. The interviewer, preferably one who is known to the child and non-threatening, would have special expertise in interviewing children of the particular age and knowledge of how developmental factors affect the giving of evidence in alleged-abuse situations. The goal of the clinician would be to put the child at ease and to get the child to tell his or her story. The interview process could be monitored in court by closed-circuit TV, and the in-

terviewer could present to the child questions submitted by the attorneys, the judge, and the accused in a non-threatening way.

4 / Another possible solution, suggested by Terr (1986), would be to try cases of intrafamilial physical or sexual abuse or neglect (other than homicide or attempted homicide) within the juvenile- or family-court systems, instead of within the criminal courts.

5 / Having the child appear and be cross-examined in the presence of the alleged abuser is the least fair alternative from the child's point of view (Avery 1984). The abuse story is complicated and complex, and the child needs a sympathetic interviewer and a relaxed situation to convey the story/tone correctly. Children, especially young children, can easily be discredited by cross-examination, but that does not necessarily mean that their original allegations were untrue. Rather, it means that children are developmentally lacking in the skills necessary to defend against a determined and hostile cross-examination. Their insufficient grasp of abstract reasoning, around which most cross-examination is based, and vulnerability to intimidation by adults leave them likely to lose at an intellectual game for which they are developmentally poorly equipped (Parker 1982). A known and trusted person should be present at the child's side during cross-examination. Children should always receive adequate preparation before appearing in court, and sufficient debriefing following testifying (Pynos and Eth 1984; Terr 1986).

6 / Time delays should be avoided or, at least, minimized, since children are especially vulnerable to the emotional stress of long waiting periods before threatening events.

PART SIX

Adoption as an Alternative to Long-term Foster Care

Chapter Seventeen

Factors Related to
Success or Failure
in Adoption*

It is generally agreed that success or failure in adoption depends primarily on the relationship between the adoptive parents and the adopted child. This relationship, is determined by the interaction of three sets of factors: characteristics of the adoptive parents; characteristics of the adopted child; the fit or integration between them, stemming from the ability of each to meet the other's needs and to accept the other's limitations.

Characteristics of Adoptive Parents

Qualities generally sought in prospective adoptive parents are summarized in table 17.1. While this and the subsequent tables reflect what has appeared in the adoption literature and are consistent with the clinical experience of the authors, they have not been empirically validated.

Other crucial qualities of adoptive parents that have been considered related to success in the adoption of older and multiply disadvantaged children are summarized in table 17.2.

Given the range of these qualities and attitudes, especially since many applicants lack some of them at either conscious or unconscious levels, a thorough psychological and psychiatric assessment of potential adoptive parents should ideally precede any adoptive placement. The older

---

* Margaret Snowden, co-author.

TABLE 17.1
Qualities generally sought in prospective adoptive parents*

---

1. Good physical health
2. Solid emotional, social adjustment
3. Emotional maturity
4. A stable marital relationship
5. Positive feelings regarding children
6. Absence of continuing distress regarding their own sexuality and/or sexual vulnerability, including, where relevant, those stemming from their inability to conceive a child of their own
7. Appropriate motivation for adoption
8. Genuine recognition and acceptance that no predictions can be made as to whether or how a child will change
9. Ability to accept a child as is, even if the *child does not improve*
10. Ability to remain committed to a child who does not seem to be benefiting from their care
11. Ability to seek and accept outside help when the need arises
12. Honest recognition of the fact that, but for the grace of God, they might be in the shoes of either the birth parents or the adoptee

---

* Humphrey (1969), Klibanoff and Klibanoff (1973), Jewett (1978), and Snowden (1989)

the child – and thus the more complicated the situation – the more rigorous this pre-adoption assessment should be. Realistically, however, agencies are increasingly willing to accept adoptive applicants who are only marginally qualified because of their age, state of physical and psychological health, or marital relationship, in order to obtain adoption homes for children who would once have been considered 'unadoptable.' These are older, difficult, and often multi-handicapped children, and/or ones who retain strong emotional ties to members of their natural or previous foster families.

Generally speaking, adoptive parents are older and, despite qualifying medical examinations, less healthy than biological parents (Bohman 1970; Grey and Blunden 1971; Maas 1960). Humphrey (1969) has demonstrated that adoptive parents whose relationships with their own parents were strained, whose self-esteem is low, and who have not separated successfully from their own families of origin are particularly likely to run into difficulties raising another's child. Adoptive parents who have resolved their feelings about their own infertility sufficiently to have transcended the need to deny that there are differences between their own and a biological family are more likely to be able to communicate

TABLE 17.2
Qualities crucial to the successful adoption of older and handicapped children

1. Ability to honour their parenting commitment to their natural children in the face of ongoing stress, precipitated or exacerbated by the adoption
2. Truly non-judgmental acceptance of the rights of the birth family – or a foster family with whom the child continues to have a significant relationship – and the child to maintain or re-establish contact with each other
3. Honest recognition of the need to communicate openly with the spouse, with both natural and adopted children, and with helping resources
4. Ability to live comfortably with the prospect of being called upon at any time to deal with the unexpected or the unknown
5. The stubbornness or determination required to 'hang in,' even in the face of chronic and at times agonizing adversity, and to see the adoption as something that they believed in and take responsibility for; as something that they will, therefore, see through

freely and relate successfully to each other (Kirk 1964; Sorosky, Baran, and Pannor 1977).

Adoptive parents with significant needs of their own left unfulfilled can experience enormous strain trying to meet the needs of problematic older adoptees. For adoption to be an older child's least detrimental alternative, the couple in question must have enough other gratifications in their own lives and relationship that they are not dependent upon the child's ability to meet their emotional needs at the time of the adoption – or, possibly, ever.

Characteristics of Adoptive Children

Apart from the work of Witmer (1963), Bohman (1972), and Hoopes (1982), there has been little controlled systematic research comparing non-clinical populations of adopted and non-adopted children. Even the Hoopes study may not be entirely representative, since it consists largely of volunteer white, middle-class, high-school seniors of at least average intelligence who had been placed in their adoptive families before two years of age by an agency that followed ideal placement procedures (Stein and Hoopes 1985). Nevertheless, despite considerable controversy on methodological grounds, it is reasonable to conclude that adopted children are moderately overrepresented in mental health clinical populations. Critically reviewing the British, Canadian, American, and Swedish literature, Hersov (1985) suggests that adopted boys are more likely to be disturbed than are girls, and that conduct and character disorders are more overrepresented in adoptees than are emotional and anxiety disorders. Steinhauer's (1983b) review of possible reasons for this increased vulnerability to stress in adopted children is summarized in table 17.3.

A number of clearly identified characteristics negatively correlated with success in adoption have been identified. These are summarized in table 17.4.

Little controversy remains about at least some of the psychological conflicts specific to adoptive status that are almost universally experienced by adopted children. Adopted children need to face and resolve complex problems in establishing a clear sense of their own identity, as this process is complicated by their having at least two sets of parents in their lives (Frisk 1964; Blum 1976; Schwam and Tuskan 1979; McWhinnie 1969; Schechter et al 1964; Sorosky, Baran, and Pannor 1975). Identity confusion during adolescence is exaggerated for many adoptees (American Academy of Paediatrics, 1971; Sorosky, Baran, and Pannor 1975, 1977; Stein and Hoopes 1985; Schoenberg 1974), partly because of the complications of attachment that undermine the origins of the child's sense of identity and partly because of the continued presence in fantasy or in real life of a second set of parents, the birth parents. This presence tends to favour excessive reliance on the use of splitting (i.e., idealizing one set of parents and denigrating the others) as a psychological defence. Splitting, in turn, hinders the child's ability to fuse good and bad images into a single introject, thus undermining the child's achievement and stabilization of a clear, constant sense of his own identity (Schechter 1960; Schechter et al 1964; Sorosky, Baran, and Pannor 1975). These issues of the complications of identity formation in the adopted child are discussed in more detail in chapter 4.

Beyond these issues, however, adopting parents are vulnerable to potential stresses unique to their special (i.e., adoptive) status. These include the competition, real or imagined, from the ghosts remaining from biological and/or much loved foster parents; the prior history and biological inheritance of the adoptee (McWhinnie 1969); unresolved feelings of sexual vulnerability related to their own infertility (Kirk 1964; Sorosky, Baran, and Pannor 1977; Frisk 1964; Rickarby and Egan 1980; Blum 1976; Schwam and Tuskan 1979); oversensitivity to adolescent strivings for independence (Frisk 1964; Sorosky, Baran, and Pannor 1977); the results of adopting a child across racial lines (Fanshel 1972; Chimezie 1975; Kim 1980; Ladner 1977).

TABLE 17.3
Possible reasons for the increased incidence of disturbance in adopted children

Factor	References supporting this factor as a major contributor to the increased incidence of disturbance in adopted children
1. Biological inheritance	Cadoret (1978) Clarke (1981) Cunningham et al (1975)
2. Poor parental/perinatal care of unmarried teenage mothers	Crellin et al (1971) Hausknecht (1972) Osofsky and Osofsky (1970) Vaitenas (1981)
3. Neglect, abuse, lack of continuity of placements and/or attachment figures prior to adoption	Clarke (1981) Jewett (1978) Rutter (1972) Tizard (1977)
4. Problems of adoptees' consolidating of their psychological identity related to the continuing presence (in reality or fantasy) of at least two sets of parents	Schechter et al (1964) Sorosky, Baran, and Pannor (1975) Triseliotis (1970) Schoenberg (1974) Frisk (1964) Sants (1964) Wieder (1978) Blum (1976) Rickarby and Egan (1980)
5. Experiences in the adoptive family	Jewett (1978) Klibanoff and Klibanoff (1973) Steinhauer (1983b) Toussieng (1962) Ward (1978) Easson (1973) Sokoloff (1977) Sorosky, Baran, and Pannor (1977) Schechter (1964) Wieder (1977a) Lawton and Gross (1964) McWhinnie (1969)

TABLE 17.4

Factors negatively correlated with adoption success in adoption

Factor	References supporting this factor as one negatively correlated with adoption success
1. Previous severe deprivation, especially within first two years of life	Kadushin (1970) Rutter (1979a)
2. Multiple placements	Kadushin (1970) Rutter (1979b) Steinhauer (1980a)
3. Diagnosable conduct disorder prior to placement	Kadushin (1970)
4. Sudden removal from successful long-term placement (e.g., foster family) in which child has bonded and is developing well	Steinhauer (1980b) Goldstein, Freud, and Solnit (1973)
5. Adoptions involving severing a strong emotional bond to a birth parent, foster parent, or natural sibling (unless access is granted and supported)	Goldstein, Freud, and Solnit (1973) Kadushin (1970) Steinhauer (1983b)
6. Adoptions in which the child, as a result of prior experience, has developed an established personality, set ways of behaving, and/or exaggerated needs likely to decrease acceptability to adoptive parents	Eldred et al (1976)

Adoptive boys are significantly more vulnerable to disturbance than are girls (Bohman 1970; Tizard 1977), and adoptive children are more hostile, insecure, and attention-seeking than those who are not adopted, though less so than those illegitimate children raised by their own mothers or restored to natural families after a period in care (Tizard 1977; Tizard and Rees 1974). Although there is controversy about whether and how much the age at placement affects adoption success, difficulties that occur following adoption are more likely to result from social, behavioural, and emotional problems than from overt resistance to reattachment or integration within the adoptive family (Eldred et al 1976; Jaffee and Fanshel 1970; Kadushin and Seidl 1971; Tizard 1977). Adopted status, then, involves increased vulnerability and risk, and can be expected to interact with and potentiate other risk factors.

Factors Affecting the 'Fit' between Adoptee/Adoptive Family

ASSESSENT: MATCHING AND PLACEMENT

How can one use a knowledge of these issues to match children and adoptive parents successfully? One begins by ensuring that it has carefully been determined that adoption by this family is the best plan available for a particular child in the opinion of placement personnel, the adoptive parents, and the child herself, as much as is consistent with her age and potential for understanding. One must carefully explore how much each member of the prospective adoptive family is likely to be able to meet the needs and honestly accept the limitations of the others. This exploration should begin with a thorough and realistic mental health assessment involving all those who know the child best and including a self-assessment by the child herself, to the extent that she can participate wherever possible, in order to determine specifically the child's complex needs. Prospective adoptive families should be selected for their ability to meet the identified needs of the child, giving due consideration to the abilities of all family members, including all children, natural and adopted, to give and take. Movement towards placement should be deliberately slow and thoughtful, since it is during the placement process that the foundation for a successful adoption is either established or not. At this stage the process of integration of the adoptee into the adoptive family really begins. Given natural anxieties, this period is necessarily a difficult one. No stone should be left unturned to identify and resolve any danger signals, since the placement process is liable to ignite unresolved unconscious conflicts, producing behavioural and emotional symptoms that can often not be avoided or ignored. Children, adoptive families, and placement personnel may be tempted to hurry this process along: siblings may begin to complain; adoptive parents may become apprehensive about behaviour that contradicts their family's values; normal family routines may break down, causing unexpected anxiety; one parent may be hurt by the other's excessive preoccupation with the adoptee.

It is crucial to discuss and fully work through all such difficulties at the time, since the communication and problem-solving processes set up at this stage are likely to be needed again and again over the years. Such is especially the case since issues avoided at one stage become even harder to face and resolve successfully the next time round. Placement should not be completed until everyone is satisfied that an adequate familial problem-solving mechanism is in place. The older the child or children involved, the more complex the placement process can be (Rowe et al 1984), but if the adoptive parents are comfortable with a child's heritage and if the child (age permitting) honestly desires adoption, the subsequent handling of the child's status within the family should not constitute a major problem.

AGE OF ADOPTION

The definition of 'older child' for adoption purposes is very vague and, indeed, involves a number of personality and emotional factors that must be evaluated carefully in every case. Some agencies call any child over age one an older child for adoption purposes, since that child's basic personality will already have been established and she will have to experience a separation from her caregivers prior to adoption. Any child below the age of six is almost totally at the mercy of adults who decide for or against an adoptive placement. Most legislation considers children able to speak for themselves as of age twelve, although we have all met children (e.g., Sandy, in chapter 8) who could do so effectively at a much younger age, and others who cannot even when they are much older. The principle of total involvement of each child in her own life decisions is whole-heartedly supported. However, it must be recognized that these are very complex and delicate issues, involving different levels of awareness, understanding, and insight. To be clear as to whether a given child is ready and able to make a meaningful commitment to adoption, if indeed that is possible, requires the wisdom of Solomon and the patience of Job. Despite repeated exploratory and supportive discussions of what the contemplated change is likely to mean, even after a careful assessment of how the child, if beyond infancy, has progressed through the work of mourning her natural and/or previous foster parents, and even given the most realistic possible estimate of how able the intended adoptive parents will be to accept any social, emotional, behavioural, and academic problems and limitations of the child, everyone involved – that is, the child, adoptive parents, placement personnel, foster parents, and even natural family (if they are still in the picture) – must ultimately be prepared to take a leap of faith. A prerequisite for success, whatever that may mean, is that the child truly wants the adoption to succeed and is prepared to cooperate with all involved to make it work. This point is stressed because frequently children request adoption but with little realistic awareness of what it involves, and, often, with even less awareness of their own (often largely unconscious) feelings and motivations than do many prospective adoptive parents. This topic will be discussed later in this chapter.

INTERACTION BETWEEN CHILD AND PARENTS RELATED TO
ADOPTED STATUS

Several authors note a general reluctance of adoptive parents to discuss their child's biological parentage and pre-adoption history candidly and comfortably (Jaffee and Fanshel 1970; Sorosky, Baran, and Pannor 1977; Triseliotis 1970). Although there are exceptions, primarily derived from abstractions from clinical data (Schechter 1960; Goodman and Magno-Nora 1975; Wieder 1977a, 1977b, 1978), most authorities suggest that the child's adoptive status be open for discussion from day one, with the child receiving freely and comfortably sensible amounts of information at appropriate times along the way. The greater the empathy of the adoptive family for the birth family and the less threatened they are by their own special (i.e., adoptive) status, the more easily and naturally will this openness occur (Kirk 1964; Sorosky, Baran, and Pannor 1976). The more secure the adoptive parents, as individuals and as marital partners, the better prepared they will be to handle difficult and poten-tially threatening questions. All this appears obvious and straightfor-ward on paper. In practice, however, we are dealing with complex people, whose at times conflicting personal needs affect the situation. Often unrecognized needs of adoptive parents – such as their drive to assert their adequacy in the face of infertility or their fear that their adopted child will never be theirs – or of children traumatized by separation – who bring repeated rejections upon themselves – are, at the time, more obvious to others than to the participants themselves. It can be even harder to recognize the unconscious needs demanding some sort of fulfilment that are inevitably present in both parents and child. It is crucial that, as these surface, they be communicated honestly and ad-dressed. If, instead, they are suppressed and repressed, they will fester and undermine the integration and, in some cases, the solidarity of the new adoptive family. Adoption, especially of the older child, is *not* a natural process, and it is one experienced differently by each individual involved. This fact must be openly acknowledged whenever issues emerge, in order for the process to succeed.

WAYS IN WHICH SPECIAL STATUS IS HANDLED IN ADOPTIVE FAMILIES

Both adoptees and their adoptive parents know that the adopted child's biological inheritance differs from that of other family members. This fact establishes the child as 'special,' and any child with special status is particularly vulnerable to scapegoating and/or rejection in response to sustained high levels of individual, marital, or family pathology or stress, especially if this special status is combined with a shortage of effective mechanisms for family problem solving (Steinhauer 1984). Inherited temperamental factors and/or the long-term sequelae of deprivation and discontinuity make many special needs older adoptees hard to accept, let alone love. If natural children are conceived only after the completion of an adoption undertaken because of supposed infertility, many adoptive parents – angry, discouraged, yet guilty for feeling so rejecting – may ascribe any difficulties occurring with a more limited and less satisfying adopted child solely to genetics and/or prior experience. In so doing, they may distance the child while, at the same time, absolving themselves of any need to modify current attitudes and interactions that are contributing to the problem (Tooley 1978; McWhinnie 1967; Hoopes 1982).

Two particular problems related to the special status of the adopted child bear consideration. The first involves the issue of how the child's special status as an adoptee is dealt with between parents and child. As this is closely related to the development of the adopted child's identity, it is explored at greater length in chapter 4.

Reference has already been made to the reluctance of some adoptive parents to discuss openly their adopted child's biological parentage and/ or pre-adoption experiences with their child, and to the controversy as to the best age at which to begin discussing their adoption with adopted children. Failure to discuss adoption and the child's origins openly can be related to a general lack of openness in parent–child communication, to marked overprotection, or to the parents' need to deny that anything is special about their adoptive status (Jaffee and Fanshel 1970; Sorosky, Baran, and Pannor 1975; Triseliotis 1973).

There are two major reasons for the authors' encouraging adoptive parents to be as frank as possible with adopted children consistently from day one. At some point, all such children will learn of their adopted (i.e., different) status. Attempts by parents to hide this fact from them are usually symptomatic of the adoptive parents' attempt to deny that adoption is, in any way, different from the process of having and raising a natural child. Such attempts at distorting reality usually reflect significant discomfort with their status as adoptive parents. Unless this issue is effectively resolved, it places the parent–child relationship and the child's subsequent development at increased risk.

Second, since at some point all adopted children are likely to learn about their special status, it is better that they first do so gradually over time, in a matter-of-fact and comfortable way from trusted parents, than that they have the facts withheld from them. The vulnerable child who first learns the truth of her origins from an outsider who confronts her in an unexpected or hostile manner risks being shocked not just by the truth, but by the fact that the parents have, uncharacteristically, concealed it from her (Triseliotis 1973; Lawton and Gross 1964; Glatzer 1955; Sorosky, Baran, and Pannor 1976, 1977; Stein and Hoopes 1985).

Parental shame related to infertility may be less of an issue these days than it was a generation or two ago, since the Women's Liberation Movement and changing social attitudes have made childlessness more acceptable to some, while providing women with ways other than the production of children to establish their worth. The tone and attitude in which such discussions take place may be even more important than the actual information exchanged. The greater the adoptive parents' comfort with their special status, the more easily and naturally such discussions are likely to go, and the less anxiety and sense of stigma they are likely to arouse.

What and when the child is told about the adoption is an important issue. While there is no single right way – all parents must say and do what is natural for them – a number of guidelines are suggested.

Parents should begin with a simple and concrete statement as soon as children begin showing an interest in where babies come from. By this time, toddlers should at least have been introduced to the word *adoption*, even though they will not yet understand it. Beyond that, children should generally be told what they want to know, no more and no less. If they sense that the topic is an open and acceptable one, they will request more information as they are ready for it. Their questions and the fantasies on which they are based will vary with age.

Ambivalent or anxious but conscientious parents, determined to do what is right for their child even if they find it unsettling, may excessively and unnaturally stress adoption from an early age to the point of ramming it down their child's throat. When this occurs, their subverbal communication will convey their conflicts about the child's special status, rather than providing the open and supportive atmosphere they are intending. In summary, the context in which disclosure takes place matters more than the content of disclosure itself in sustaining successful family relationships (Lawton and Gross 1964; Sorosky, Baran, and Pannor 1977; Stein and Hoopes 1985).

DIFFICULTIES DEALING WITH THE HOSTILE COMPONENT OF NORMAL PARENT–CHILD AMBIVALENCE

The second major problem common to adoptive families is the increased difficulty that both adoptees and adoptive parents frequently have handling the angry or hostile component of their natural ambivalence towards each other. Children can, at times, use anything at their disposal to manipulate their parents, depending, of course, on their own stability and security. Some adoptees soon realize that confronting their parents with their adoptive status gives them an ideal weapon that natural children do not have at their disposal. Secure adoptive parents are not conned by this tactic, and so deal appropriately with the child's attempted manipulation. Some adoptive parents, however, fear that the child is not securely bonded; the more anxious they are made by the child's use of his biological parentage to intimidate them, the more complex the parent–child problems that may result. Depending on other emotional stresses and supports available to the parents at this time, a real crisis can develop in the parent–child relationship (Sokoloff 1977; Sorosky, Baran, and Pannor 1977; Stein and Hoopes 1982).

Some adoptive children handle much of the hostile component of their ambivalence to their parents by exploiting the parental anxiety that they are not securely attached by using claims that they feel unloved or by hints of longing for reunion with their birth parents in order to manipulate or make excessive demands on the adoptive parents. The parents, if too vulnerable to say no, can be blackmailed into condoning outrageous behaviour and demands. In response, already insecure parents become increasingly anxious, then resentful, and finally guilty. In some psychologically susceptible parents, the extreme guilt evoked by mounting anger and rejection that cannot be expressed for fear of alienating the child forever and acknowledging that the adoption is in trouble is defended against by *reaction formation*. Here the hostile component of the parents' ambivalence is turned into its opposite and masked by extreme overindulgence, overinvolvement, and excessive permissiveness. These, in turn, block the parents' ability to limit or discipline the child, whose infantile tendencies to resist socialization are thereby reinforced, predictably producing, in time, a behavioural Frankenstein. Other adoptees experience different difficulties handling the hostile component of their ambivalence. Some, especially those who have been repeatedly told that their adoptive family chose them, thus saving them from a life of poverty and degradation, may feel so obligated that they cannot allow themselves the right to express or even feel anger towards the parents that have done so much for them. Others report feeling that just as they were once 'chosen,' so may they be 'unchosen,' should they become too unappreciative or rock the family boat too much. Either of these defensive patterns can distort the open expression and normal resolution of anger so necessary to the ongoing maturation of child, family, and the parent–child relationship.

By the time their adoptive children reach adolescence, the adoptive family may be stretched to its limit, with all members at low emotional ebb. Mother may be struggling with the menopause; father burned out by career pressures and by the demand to raise many thousands of dollars to finance the children's education. The children may be at a variety of stages, each with its own developmental tasks and hazards to be dealt with in more or less constructive ways. The family may be stressed by the growing demands of elderly, ill, or dying grandparents. These are just a few of the simultaneous stresses commonly affecting families at this stage in their life cycle, a stage when many families – not just those facing the additional pressures resulting from adoption – are in need of outside support: informal, professional, or both. These combined pressures connect with the earlier discussion on assessment for adoption, where the importance of the desire to communicate, the building-in of techniques for problem solving, and the need to put into place support systems at the beginning of the adoptive process were stressed.

Support is more likely to be considered acceptable if it comes from others who have been in a similar situation, hence the potential usefulness of post-adoption groups. The need for these may not be appreciated at the time of adoption, so that the initial assignment to such a group might have to be mandated as an expected component of the normal adoption process (British 1988). The ability to recognize the need and to seek help when necessary (Jewett 1978) will depend upon the personalities and psychological defences of the adoptive parents as well as on their experience and appreciation of support systems, mandatory or voluntary, with which they have had contact in the past. The frequent tendency of adoptive parents to deny or minimize even what others report as major problems until after rejection of an adopted child is already well advanced has often been noted (Bohman 1970; Cohen and Westhues 1987; Jaffee and Fanshel 1970; Schechter 1960; Tizard 1977). All adoptive families should, therefore, be strongly encouraged to have such supports in place and to know how to activate them, since a time of need will almost inevitably come (Hartman 1984; Snowden 1989; Stein and Hoopes 1985).

ISSUES RELATED TO THE ADOPTED CHILD'S HAVING
TWO SETS OF PARENTS: THE MOVEMENT TOWARDS
MORE OPEN ADOPTION

There are two sets of parents involved in any adoption. One may exist only psychologically or may be actively involved in an ongoing way with the child, but in either case the birth parents are very much present in the child through their contribution to the child's biological inheritance and temperament. However constructive the adoptive environment, it may be called upon to balance inherited tendencies, which, generally speaking, have an above-average tendency to produce a psychosocially vulnerable child (Cadoret 1978; Cunningham et al 1975). Clarke (1981) has demonstrated that children adopted early resemble their biological parents more than they do their adoptive relatives, and the authors have observed the phenomenon reported by Sants (1964) and Wieder (1978) in which obvious differences between adoptee and other adoptive family members have served to create difficulties in the normal identification process, thus interfering with personality integration. Vaitenas (1981) stresses the importance of perinatal risk factors resulting from low birth weight, prematurity, foetal alcohol syndrome – all of which can increase the risk for the child who will be placed, and reacted to, within the adoptive home.

Children have no control over the various sets of parental figures that have contributed to making them what they are, but most of them, at some point or other – and, almost all, during adolescence – will fantasize about their birth parents, often building on memories, dreams, and pure fantasy to compare them to their adoptive parents and press them into the service of unmet emotional needs. This issue should be one that adoptive parents expect and prepare themselves to accept with equanimity. One hopes that adoptive parents will feel securely enough bonded to their adopted child to support the child in his search for roots and identity with a genuine belief in the birth parents' good intentions, and without experiencing the child's interest as an intolerable threat to their own self-esteem or their mutual connectedness. At some point, the child will be ready to consolidate his own sense of identity. What matters then is the comfort, commitment, and sincerity of the adoptive parents in supporting this attempt. Efforts to block the child's coming to grips with her origins or to interfere with the consolidation of her identity through deceit, by withholding known information, by hostile criticism of the birth parents, by implications of disloyalty, or by becoming upset and angry may, temporarily, derail the search, but only at the cost of even further increasing internalized tensions. These will then intensify and complicate the child's subsequent attempts to resolve the issue of her own identity.

In contrast, an issue that is recognized as universal – one that adoptive parents are prepared for and interpret either as natural or as minimally threatening – can be dealt with gradually, that is, at a pace that both child and adoptive parents can tolerate without unbearable distress.

Adoption is not the natural way to have a family. Successful adoption depends on the ability of adoptive families, including the children, both natural and adopted, to continue to strive honestly to do what they can to balance the rights and needs of the adoptee against those of all members of the adoptive family. Adoption does not guarantee the fulfilment of the usual needs aroused in parents by the process of child-raising.

OPEN ADOPTION: AVAILABILITY OF RECORDS AND REUNION
WITH BIRTH PARENTS

Much has been written since 1975 on the concept of open adoption, about the disclosure of information, the unsealing of adoption records, and reunions with birth parents. It is not surprising that, in the present social climate, where individual rights and the concept of knowing one's 'roots' are highly valued, adoptees are beginning to insist upon having the right to satisfy these long-buried demands. As with so many other facets of the adoption process, open adoption is far from straightforward, primarily because of the somewhat conflicting needs of the various parties involved.

The literature reflects this controversy. There is much support for the opening of sealed adoption records (Baran, Pannor, and Sorosky 1976, 1977; Dukette 1984; Pannor and Baran 1984; Semancik 1979). Those supporting this position submit that, while adoption of older children has been open for many years, all adoptions should be similarly open, in order to minimize those psychological problems of adoptees and their biological and adoptive parents currently perpetuated by the secrecy, anonymity, and mystique of closed adoption. Dukette (1984) suggest that the maintenance of biological ties for older adoptees, often seen as a disruptive threat to current ties, may, instead, facilitate the establishment and maintenance of enduring relationships within the adoptive family. We must recognize, however, that although Sorosky, Baran, and Pannor (1975) reported that 80 per cent of adult adoptees studied claimed to have found reunion with their birth parents satisfying, 10 per cent of birth parents and considerably more adoptive parents reacted negatively. How does one satisfactorily address the needs of adoptive children, without inflicting undue damage upon any of the other parties in this complex triangular relationship (Weidell 1980)?

Aumend and Barrett (1984) found that those adoptees who did not seek out their birth parents had more positive self-concepts and more constructive attitudes towards and relationships with their adoptive parents, whom they perceived as emotionally more involved with them. Triseliotis (1973) also distinguished between adoptees demanding reunion with their biological parents and those seeking only non-identifying information about them. The reunion-seekers showed long-standing dissatisfaction with family relationships; low self-esteem; chronic problematic adjustment in many aspects of life; non-disclosure or uncomfortable disclosure, only of information disparaging to the birth parents by the adoptive parents.

In an unpublished 1978 pilot study of seventy-nine adoptees over the age of majority seeking non-identifying information and/or reunion with their birth parents, D'Iorio and Steinhauer basically replicated Triseliotis's results, with one additional finding. They found that those seeking reunion rather than just non-identifying information divided naturally into two groups. The first was a group of chronically maladjusted and dissatisfied *urgent seekers* who demanded immediate access to their biological parents as a matter of right, regardless of how either the biological or the adoptive parents felt about it. The second was a group of apparently normally adjusted *non-urgent seekers* who, while sympathetic to both their biological and adoptive parents' feelings about their search, had an interest in at least meeting their birth mothers. These non-urgent seekers saw reunion more as a way of helping clarify their own identities than as the magic answer to what they perceived of as 'a life of misery,' which they attributed almost entirely to their having grown up in adoption (see also Kowal and Schilling 1985). D'Iorio and Steinhauer's non-urgent seekers seemed, at least outwardly, to be emotionally and socially well adjusted, although their urgent seekers, like those of Triseliotis, were severely, chronically, and pervasively disturbed. The urgent seekers' response to reunion was often mixed, and such reunions at times had severely disruptive effects on the lives and marriages of the searchers, including a not-infrequent involvement in incestuous relationships, which, while rationalized at the time, seemed, at least in part, to be desperate attempts to facilitate and/or force bonding. However, even when the reunion itself involved bitter disappointment, and/or ongoing disruption up to and including marital breakdown, the urgent seekers claimed to have found the contacts helpful in coming to grips with their identity, whether or not this was accompanied by evidence of objective behavioural change.

The disappointment experienced by some urgent seekers following reunion is not, in any way, an argument against reunion; rather, it emphasizes that reunion can precipitate a psychological crisis that can be a necessary, though possibly painful, stage in that adoptee's finally coming to terms with his personal reality.

These data, along with those of Jaffee and Fanshel (1970) who also found an association between long-standing dissatisfaction, problematic adjustment, and complaints of insufficient and/or hostile disclosures about the birth parents, suggest the importance of adoption agencies routinely supplying background information to all adoptive parents, along with the strong suggestion that this information be shared as freely and naturally as possible well before the children enter adolescence.

These data also suggest that requests for either non-identifying information or reunion be viewed not as isolated events, but as important stages in an ongoing process of adoptees clarifying and/or consolidating their sense of identity. Sensitive casework from a worker familiar with the convolutions of identity formation in adoptees can be extremely helpful at this point to the adoptees themselves, to their adoptive families, and, at times, to the birth parents. Obviously, workers who are seen as part of an ongoing support network (i.e., the adoptive agency), rather than someone newly introduced in response to the request for information and/or reunion, will have a substantial advantage in being helpful (Kowal and Schilling 1985).

In 1977, Minnesota passed legislation allowing the release of a sealed birth certificate to adult adoptees upon the consent of their birth parents (Weidell 1980). Stephenson (1975) discussed the controversy surrounding the Canadian (Manitoba, New Brunswick, Ontario, Saskatchewan) adoption reunion registry, enabling reunion after the age of the adoptee's majority given three-party consent. More recently (July 1987), amendments to the Child and Family Service Act (Bill 77) have brought into law some very progressive changes in Ontario, although the question of integration of the birth-family experience in adoption is somewhat more advanced in Great Britain (Snowden 1989). As a result, the government will conduct an active search for parents, grandparents, or adult siblings on the request of an adult adoptee without the consent of adoptive parents.

In evaluating these changes in legislation, we would first argue that a solution that will be completely satisfactory to all parties in all situations is probably unattainable. However, if one considers children as being 'on loan' to parents, whose job it is to nurture them in the direction of independence, how can one justify parents denying children the comfort that comes with consolidation of their personal identity? We know that some adoptees require more information and contact, and others less. The situation is further confused since earlier adoptions took place under guarantees of anonymity to both biological and adoptive parents, which, in many jurisdictions, no longer apply. Meanwhile, contemporary adoptees and their prospective families are being prepared for a variety of possibilities that may address identity-related issues in the future.

The author agrees with Baran, Pannor, and Sorosky (1976), Dukette (1984), Semancik (1979), and Pannor and Baran (1984) that any adoptee at the age of majority should have the right to contact birth parents, if the latter are in agreement. We strongly question the right of adoptive parents to try to veto such reunions by withholding their consent. For them to do so seems analogous to the attempts of some natural parents to control their child's career, marriage choices, etc., by going far beyond adding their input within the dynamics of a mutually respectful and constructive relationship.

There is no question that this position is somewhat unfair, especially to earlier adoptive parents who were promised an anonymity that is no longer available. We can only suggest, however, that change is a part of our lives, and that we are living in a time in which societal attitudes have so shifted that the rights of some are given priority over those of others. We argue that this attitudinal shift, when the adoptee that we are dealing with is an adult, merits giving the choice to the adoptee, even in the face of adoptive parents' disapproval. Until the adoptee reaches the age of majority, however, we would argue that adoptive parents' agreement should generally be a necessary condition for reunion, unless the adoptive family has so broken down that the adoptive bond exists only at a legal level.

We recognize that these proposals are not without some risk during what we are labelling a crisis point in the life of adoptee and adoptive family, one during which the availability of external support for any or all of those involved is highly indicated. We would submit that mandatory professional counselling to all parties involved in an actual or proposed reunion, wherever possible occurring within an already established relationship, is strongly indicated in order to ensure empathic and objective help towards avoiding potential disruption and resolving issues reactivated for all involved by the search process.

Factors Correlated with Lack of Success in Adoption

1 / *Children with a history of severe deprivation and multiple placements,* especially within the first two years of life (Kadushin 1970; Rutter 1979a, 1979c), are at higher risk of adoption breakdown. Such children are likely to have more frequent problems in school and in their behaviour outside the home, and continuing difficulty in their social relationships. Taken together, these difficulties will inevitably place additional strain on their relationships with their adoptive parents, however accepting the latter may be.

2 / *Children with a diagnosable conduct disorder* prior to adoptive placement are at higher risk of adoption breakdown (Kadushin 1970).

3 / *Children who are removed from a successful long-term placement* with foster parents who have become their psychological parents also face an increased risk of adoption breakdown. Currently, in North America, there is strong pressure towards adopting or restoring to their birth families all children in long-term foster care on the grounds of ensuring permanence. Many of the sources of this pressure seem political, racial, and even economic – they aim to eliminate the cost of maintaining children in foster care or to return children to a particular racial or religious group – rather than attempts to address realistically the children's psychological needs. The arguments that foster homes are inherently unstable, that the permanence of even planned permanent foster placements cannot be guaranteed not to suffer breakdown during

the child's adolescence, and that foster parents seeking tenure must be only minimally committed or they would proceed towards adoption – all at times true – have been used dogmatically to demand permanent (i.e., adoptive) placement. But one cannot, by legal means, ensure the permanence of a given placement, however good the intentions (Emlen et al 1978). A number of authors have suggested that foster placements in which children have formed a stable attachment and are developing satisfactorily deserve to be supported and stabilized, not to be undermined and disrupted by agencies and governments operating in the name of the child's 'stability' (Cooper 1978; Derdeyn 1977; Goldstein, Freud, and Solnit 1973, 1979; Rae-Grant 1978; Steinhauer 1980b, 1983b; Wiltse 1976; Allison and Kufeldt 1987; Bush and Gordon 1982; Lahti et al 1978; Bush and Goldman 1982).

To accommodate such situations, a variety of intermediate alternatives, such as 'planned permanent' foster care, foster care with tenure, and 'subsidized adoption,' are being utilized increasingly for children developing well in stable foster placements within families disinclined towards adoption in the normal sense (Derdeyn 1977; Steinhauer 1983b; Allison and Kufeldt 1987; Watson 1982; Ryan et al 1981; Rowe et al 1984). In the absence of reliable experimental evidence as to the least detrimental alternative for this group of children, we recommend careful planning on an individualized case basis, utilizing the full participation of all those involved in a given child's life in order to find the currently available solution most likely to provide maximal continuity for that child (Wiltse 1978; Cooper 1978; Bush and Gordon 1982; Katz et al 1986).

4 / *Adoptions involving a child who continues to retain a strong emotional tie* to members of the birth family or to a foster family are vulnerable to adoption breakdown unless the existing attachment is not merely tolerated but actively protected, with continuing access guaranteed, even in jurisdictions where adoption with access is not possible under the law but must be privately negotiated and left to the good will and co-operation of all those adults involved. In such cases, forced separation is likely to favour retention and idealization in fantasy of the lost attachment figure, thus interfering with the child's ability to attach successfully to competing adoptive parents (Goldstein, Freud, and Solnit, 1973; Kadushin 1970; Steinhauer 1980b, 1983b). Access, of course, has its own practical, as well as emotional, cost in terms of the greater or lesser degrees of disruption it can cause, and therefore frequency and duration

of access have to be suited to the individual case in order to minimize such disruption.

5 / *Adoptions in which one or both adoptive parents have excessive expectations of the adopted child* are at high risk. In some such cases, the child is so badly needed to meet the exaggerated expectations of the adoptive couple (for example, to replace a dead child; to be the ideal companion for an only child; to fill an empty nest; to give the adoptive parents' lives meaning) that the parents have difficulty accepting the child as he or she is (Schechter 1960).

6 / *Adoption in which the child, as a result of previous experience, has developed a well-established personality,* set ways of behaving, and/or exaggerated needs that interfere with acceptability and integration within the adoptive family is at higher risk of breakdown (Eldred et al 1976).

7 / *Age at adoption has influence on its success.* Controversy remains about how much the age of adoption affects the likelihood of adoption success (Eldred et al 1976; Jaffee and Fanshel 1970; Kadushin and Seidl 1971; Rae-Grant 1978; Tizard 1977). Humphrey and Ounsted (1963) found a higher rate of disturbance, especially in boys placed prior to six months, but both Offord, Aponte, and Cross (1969) and Kadushin and Seidl (1971) found that frequency and severity of antisocial behaviour varied directly with the age at adoption. However, other studies (Eldred et al 1976; Menlove 1965) suggested that the age at adoption did not significantly affect adoptive outcome. So did that of Jaffee and Fanshel (1970), while Kadushin (1970), in a follow-up of children placed on adoption between the ages of five and twelve, found that only 14 per cent of adoptive parents expressed dissatisfaction. This figure has been widely used to support the claim that older-child adoptions are as likely to be successful as infant adoptions, and, in fact, most adoption studies report a parent satisfaction rate of 78 to 85 per cent regardless of the age at adoption (Tizard 1977). However, since these studies rate adoptive success according to parent satisfaction only, and since adoptive parents typically deny even what others report as fairly major problems until after rejection of the involved child has occurred (Bohman 1970; Cohen and Westhues 1987; Jaffee and Fanshel 1970; Schechter 1960; Tizard 1977), these findings may be unduly optimistic, especially since some studies include only adoptions that have successfully survived the probation period (Jaffee and Fanshel 1970), while others (Eldred et al 1976) are

harder to evaluate since the precise criteria by which success was defined are not clearly stated. Nevertheless, although available data certainly suggest that the risk in adoption of older children is considerably less than was previously believed, it is generally accepted that, to minimize the risks, adoption should occur at the earliest possible age, wherever feasible.

Chapter Eighteen

Placing the Older Child on Adoption*

Since, as has been indicated, the adoption of 'special needs' children currently represents two-thirds of extra-familial adoptions (Hepworth 1980; Rowe and Lambert 1973), let us examine specifically the older-child (and often sibling group) adoptions that represent so large a part of this population. Some agencies consider a child to be 'older' (for purposes of adoption) following the first birthday. Most agencies consider potential adoptees older children by age four years.

1 / *Adoption of the older child normally initiates a family crisis.* It has been suggested that some sort of family crisis almost inevitably follows the adoption of an older child and/or sibling combination. Ward (1978) describes this in terms of the influx and pressures of merging, while Katz (1977) points to the multiple stresses acting on all members of the family system. Snowden (1987) likens the process to a marriage, but one lacking the romance yet possessing as many potential spouses as there are family members, all of whom, including those who wanted nothing to do with the process in the first place, must somehow integrate into a united whole. The imminent danger, perhaps for years, is that the amount of love, energy, and wisdom required of the new parents will be overextended and eventually depleted by excessive demands.

2 / *Adoption as one alternative.* Beginning with the planning stage, adoption of the older child should be carefully considered as one alternative

* Margaret Snowden, co-author.

TABLE 18.1
Factors useful in comprehensive planning for placement of the older child

1. Early deprivation (especially within first two years) and multiple placements
2. Pre-existing behavioural tendencies
   - Diagnosable conduct disorder
   - Pre-existing personality with characteristic behavioural traits
   - Known academic, psychological, and social problems
3. Demonstrable evidence of the child's level of ability to reinvest in relationships
4. Significant connections with key attachment figures from the past, including: natural parent(s) or siblings or foster parent(s) or siblings
5. Child's understanding of what is involved in adoption, and level of child's motivation to make the adoption succeed
6. Ability of the particular potential adoptive family to satisfy the qualities crucial to the successful adoption of older children summarized in table 17.2, with respect to the particular child/sibling group being considered for adoption

on a continuum of well-thought-out permanency-planning options for a child, taking into account all of that child's complex and interlocking needs. It should never be assumed that adoption is bound to be the best plan. Economic arguments or a rigid philosophical stance that simplistically equates legal permanence with actual permanence and children's best interests should always be avoided.

3 / *Key factors useful in comprehensive planning*, already cited in earlier chapters, are summarized in table 18.1.

Under no circumstances should an older child who retains significant connections to key attachment figures when considered for adoption have an important existing bond undercut in the interests of hoped-for but unpredictable legal permanence. While there is much still unresearched in the areas both of older-child adoption and of planned permanent foster care, it is strongly suggested that, as a working rule, emotional connections to natural or foster parents established by children old enough to continue to remember and value them should be very carefully considered before they are in any way undermined. Bonding is critical to any child's adjustment. If a child legally freed for adoption remains emotionally bonded to natural parents, the accessibility to the birth family, which is more common in foster care than in adoption, might result in less pressure on the dynamics of a foster family than of an adoptive one. In some such cases, planned permanent foster care with tenure might involve less risk for both child and parents than might adoption, even if access could be guaranteed, in jurisdictions where this is permitted (Bush and Gordon 1982; Lahti et al 1978; Bush and Goldman 1982; Steinhauer 1983b).

4 / *Assessment, preparation, and mandatory support services.* When adoption is the least detrimental alternative for a particular child, the gradual approach to assessment, preparation, and mandatory intensive support services for adoptive parents recommended in chapter 17 should be put into place. Potential adoptive parents should be told clearly and directly that, while many couples who adopt older children report satisfaction, they themselves should expect and be prepared for a long period of excessive demands, disruptive behaviour, indifferent school performance, and/or distancing and rejection by the child. They should consider in advance the potential effects of disruptive and manipulative behaviour on the existing family. They should also, if possible, be aware in advance that they may have to put up with anger and distrust transferred onto them, the feeling of being unfavourably compared to birth parents and of being attacked or even hated for what they consider responsible and reasonable parental behaviour. They may find it even more difficult to tolerate indications that, by proceeding with the adoption, they are upsetting and/or hurting their own natural children, or may be upset by the recognition of a growing dislike for the child or children they have committed themselves to integrate at such great cost. Some will be hurt by finding themselves shut out of previously fairly predictable family relationships. For others, the greatest difficulty may be tolerating criticism from neighbours, extended family, and friends should the adoptee's behaviour even temporarily exceed the limits of acceptability. The more of these reactions that are experienced, recognized, and discussed openly before the final placement, the fewer surprises there will be afterwards (Ward 1981). Unless open discussion, active problem solving, and the ability to utilize external – including professional – supports are in place prior to the placement being completed, the chance of the family being able to seek and utilize the help they are likely to need later is diminished. Until the adoptive parents have experienced most of these feelings, they are probably insufficiently prepared for placement completion.

Claudia Jewett (1978) has spoken of the effects of very refined abilities to manipulate; sibling rivalry among adopted siblings; the rush and strain of constant problem solving with the adoptees, leaving the natural children to take care of themselves; the effects of incomplete mourning, withdrawal, and emotional isolation; impulsive, aggressive, and poorly controlled behaviours; repeated tantrums; the impact of transition from one social class to another; the splitting by the child of two sets of parents; parental confusion and guilt in response to their own over-reactions, especially when fatigued. Just telling potential adoptive parents what to expect is not enough. Parents who have developed a crush relationship with a child whose appealing picture they have seen in the newspaper or on television have an amazing capacity to deny that the child could ever present them with the same problems that have been described by others. Too often it is only in retrospect that such parents can say:

I heard what you told me. But I just could not believe that he would be that way once he was a part of our family. I was sure that once he experienced being a part of a loving family, he would change – he would have to change. The behaviour you told me about I dismissed as his reaction to how he'd been hurt in the past. I never dreamed that he would be like that with us, or that he might one day provoke us to the point of violence or despair. If only I'd really heard what you said ...

Such a tough approach can be criticized in that it may scare off some potential adoptive parents, and so it will. It remains, however, critically important that prospective adoptive parents see things as they are, and that they undertake the challenges involved in the adoption of an older child with optimal understanding of their own motivation, vulnerabilities, and tolerances, because the buck stops with them. They may be the ones whose extended-family members will say, 'I told you so'; the ones with police cars in their driveways; the ones whose neighbours refuse to allow contact with their children; the ones whose own children will at times show signs of pain and dislocation. Also, they will be the ones left to struggle with various levels of guilt resulting from the pain precipitated by the adoption, for which they feel responsible. Jewett (1978) mentions the 'sense of enormous personal growth' that can be a by-product of a successful older-child adoption. The destructive fall-out in the process, however, while preventable in some cases, can be tremendous, especially when the child fails to show the hoped-for personal growth. The promise that 'adoption is forever,' however well meant, does not always turn out as hoped for. Furthermore, there are many situations where families are left in limbo because of unresolved – and sometimes unresolvable – issues that may remain with them for the rest of their lives. For these reasons, we suggest that prospective adoptive parents and adoptees alike are done a major service by a thoroughly frank and even hard-line, but compassionate, approach to this undertaking.

5 / *Anticipating future needs for support.* Families adopting an older child or sibling group are likely to need, at first, continuing and, later, periodic external support, even after the adoption is made final. They should be helped to anticipate that, in some cases, the period of adoption probation may be like a honeymoon, the calm before the storm, with some of the more disturbing forms of behaviour being suppressed until after the adoption is finalized. It is important that they establish open communication and problem-solving mechanisms within the family prior to the actual placement, and that there be an alliance with the placement agency that can survive both the stresses prior to placement and those of the adoption probation periods (Steinhauer 1990).

Adoptive parents should be alerted at the point of adoption to the possibility that, during adolescence, their adoptee(s) may seek information about their biological parents and/or express a wish to meet them. They should be told in advance that an adolescent adoptee's showing interest in the birth parents during adolescence is not unusual or necessarily abnormal, since it may represent an attempt by the teenager to consolidate his or her identity rather than a negation or rejection of the bond to the adoptive parents. They should be aware in advance that adolescence is a time of increased stress for many adoptive families. They should be encouraged to reactivate their contact with the placing agency for help or for an appropriate referral in order to ensure that this developmental crisis in their new family's life cycle is negotiated with as little stress and fall-out as possible. It goes without saying that agencies placing older children on adoption should have both the philosophical stance and the resources to allow them to respond and assist at such points of crisis in the life of the adoptive family.

6 / *Ongoing contact with attachment figures to whom the older adoptee remains connected.* Prospective adoptive parents should be helped to see how the support, and not just mere tolerance, of ongoing contact via letters and/or visits with parents, foster parents, and siblings with whom the older adoptee retains important connections at the point of placement is in the best interests both of the adoptee and of the adoptive-

family unit. The question of which existing relationships should be maintained for the child's sake and the reasons for each such decision should be made clear to potential adoptive parents prior to the agreement to place the child. Situations and relationships may change over time; some relationships that may at one stage have been important to a child may become much less so over the years; in other cases, the reverse can occur. What is crucial is that it is possible to reconstitute, whenever necessary, a conference to consider input from all those currently involved in a child's life, ideally chaired by an objective professional, preferably one from or recommended by the placement agency and acceptable to the adoptive parents. The goal of such a conference would be to determine just what arrangement constituted the adoptee's best interests at that given time – in the hopes of helping those adults involved to recognize, understand, and support the child's developmental needs, not undermine them.

In summary, adoptions of older children are not without their risks, and attempting to overlook or minimize those risks only exacerbates them. Despite these risks, however, the successful adoption of older children who would once have been considered unadoptable occurs more frequently than we would, at one time, have thought possible (Triseliotis and Russell 1984). It is by careful consideration and application of the principles outlined in this chapter that these risks can be minimized, and the hopes of such adoptions succeeding can best be realized.

PART SEVEN

Summary and Review

Chapter Nineteen

Summary and Review: The Preventive Use of Foster Care

There is a widespread belief that long-term foster care is inherently unstable and generally damaging (Filkelstein 1980; Gruber 1978; Maluccio et al 1980). Cooper (1978) suggests that, while short-term fostering in preparation for adoption has a clear purpose, intermediate and long-term fostering lack a clear definition of task and are so inherently unstable that they promote insecurity for all involved. Numerous authors (Maluccio et al 1980; Gruber 1978; Steinhauer 1980a; Fanshel and Shinn 1978; Prosser 1978; Wiltse 1976) have expressed concern about the number of foster children who, more from inadequate planning than from any conscious decision, end up drifting into permanent foster care, abandoned by parents who no longer visit and neglected by the agencies supposedly caring for them. But it is important to differentiate the effects of the indifferent foster care resulting from indecision or drift from those of planned permanent foster care. A number of authors (Frank 1980; Steinhauer 1980b, 1983b; Goldstein, Freud, and Solnit 1973; Fanshel and Shinn 1978; Wiltse 1976, 1979; Madison and Schapiro 1970; Anglim 1980; Derdeyn 1977; Fanshel, Finch, and Grundy 1989), while well aware of the dangers of indifferent long-term placements, hold that, for selected children, especially those whose relationship capacity and behaviour are severely disturbed, high-quality planned permanent foster care resulting from an appropriate placement and receiving adequate agency support may provide the least detrimental alternative available (Chamberlain 1990; Chamberlain and Weinrott 1990; Wilkes 1989).

Adequate Foster Care – A Definition

To be adequate – that is, maximally protective of a child's current adjustment and ongoing development – foster care should meet the following requirements:

1 It should provide for the physical and emotional needs basic to all children, including those for caring, structure and consistency, reasonable expectations, and intellectual stimulation.
2 It should meet those emotional needs that are special to foster children, including:
   - those resulting from disturbing experiences and relationships, neglect, and/or abuse experienced in families of origin prior to coming into care;
   - those resulting from the separation from the natural family, and not infrequently exacerbated by a subsequent series of separations;
   - those resulting from persistent problems of feeling, behaviour, and relationships that continue to disturb the child's adjustment and relationships in the foster family and in the surrounding community;
   - those resulting from continuing uncertainty about the future, and feelings of helplessness and lack of control over it;
   - those resulting from the special status (stigma) of being a foster child, and the stresses of having to reconcile oneself to having more than one set of adults – i.e., foster parents and social workers and/ or natural parents – performing some aspects of what, for other children, would be provided by the parents.
3 It should be guided by an active, informed, and proactive planning process, rather than by one that merely lets things drift while responding to crises.
4 Foster children should be kept informed about and allowed to participate in the planning process, to the extent that is possible, considering their developmental capacity.
5 The plan should protect, as much as possible, the child's major attachment relationships, such as those with natural parents, siblings, other relatives, except when these are specifically contra-indicated. Wherever possible, a child coming into care will remain within his or her ethnic or racial community.
6 The plan should, as much as possible, protect the child's sense of historical continuity by:

- protecting relationships with key attachment figures, as above;
- considering the promotion of multiple attachments wherever indicated;
- minimizing the number of moves to which any child is exposed;
- minimizing the changes of worker to which any child/foster home is exposed;
- keeping the child aware, through ongoing discussion, the use of lifebooks, etc., of his or her life story.

7 Every possible effort should be made to ensure that the components of the foster-care system – child, natural parents, social worker, and agency – are aware of and work together in the best interests of the child.

Biological, Psychological, and Social Factors Contributing to Failures of Long-Term Fostering: Potential Pitfalls to Be Avoided

Many of the failures of long-term fostering can be attributed to the interacting effects of a number of pathogenic variables, as illustrated diagramatically in figure 19.1 (Steinhauer 1980a, 1983b; Oates, Peacock, and Forrest 1984; Hersov 1985). These include the following.

1 / *Biological (including temperamental) vulnerabilities of the child.* The precise operation of these is not yet fully defined, but genetically determined temperamental factors undoubtedly make some children easier and others more difficult, at least as perceived by their primary caretakers (Thomas 1981; Bates 1980, 1983; Dunn and Kendrick 1982). Temperamental factors have been implicated in at least some cases of anxious attachment (Crockenberg 1981; Campos et al 1983), and a difficult temperament has been identified as one additional stress on already overstressed mothers that increases the risk of undermining further the quality of their child care (Wolkind and DeSalis 1982). Rutter (1978a) has shown that those children of parents with marital problems who have adverse temperaments are most likely to be scapegoated during periods of family difficulty. Both Rutter (1972) and Garmezy (1984) describe patterns of temperament that can protect children from the impact of familial and other psycho-social stresses, while Kagan and colleagues (1987, 1988) suggest others that predispose to excessive anxiety and inhibition. In general, one might conclude that temperamentally difficult children are most vulnerable to high levels of family stress, and are most likely to become permanently scapegoated by exacerbating and

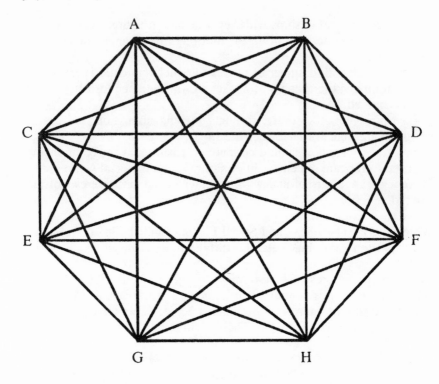

Figure 19.1   Potentially pathogenic factors that interact with each other in
the course of long-term foster care, where:

A = biological (incl. temperamental) vulnerabilities of child; B = continuing
(internalized) effects of exposure to natural family prior to entry into care; C = effects
of removal and separation from attachment figures; D = inadequate matching and/or
preparation for placement; E = insufficient assistance in work of mourning; F =
ongoing interactional difficulties in new setting; G = too little, inadequate, insufficient
systematic casework; H = social factors, including socio-economic vulnerabilities,
stigma.

Source: 'The preventive utilization of foster care,' *Can. J. Psychiat.* 33
(August 1988): 460

focusing familial distress on themselves, especially in already disorganized families. Their development is, in turn, likely to increase the
negative (i.e., attacking, shaming, and rejecting) reactions of their fam-

ilies (Lerner 1982). At least in some cases, therefore, biological and temperamental factors undoubtedly contribute to a child's increased vulnerability to family breakdown, to children coming into care, and to difficulties adjusting following placement. (The effects of temperament on attachment and adjustment are discussed in more detail in chapter 2.)

2 / *The continuing internalized effects of parental conflict and violence, rejection, neglect, and abuse experienced in their family prior to coming into care* (Herrenkohl and Herrenkohl 1981; McCord 1983; Egeland and Sroufe 1981; Hetherington and Martin 1979; Hinde 1980; Fanshel, Finch, and Grundy 1989). As a result of their prior experiences of neglect and/ or abuse, foster children are more likely to have formed an anxious attachment and to be less compliant, more easily frustrated, more aggressive, and more prone to behavioural and antisocial disorders than are children whose family background was less conflicted. Also, the more hostile and oppositional the child at entry into care, the more conflicted his adaptation to foster care, and the poorer his adjustment was likely to be on exiting from foster care and in adult life (Fanshel, Finch, and Grundy 1989).

3 / *The effects of removal and separation from major attachment figures.* A variety of factors influence the severity of each individual child's response to separation. Any separation can prove traumatic (Bowlby 1973), and the role of multiple separations in predisposing to permanent detachment and to a variety of emotional and behaviour problems has been well documented (Maas and Engler 1959; Eisenberg 1962; Steinhauer 1983b; Yarrow and Klein 1980; Hensey, Williams, and Rosenbloom 1983). Egeland and Sroufe (1981) have demonstrated the disturbing effects of patterns of attachment in foster children, while Kunkel (1983) has described a number of stages of alienation children go through when placed out of their families. Presumably related to their inability to trust others and a result of their disturbed pattern of attachment, this alienation will prejudice their ongoing adjustment in and beyond the foster family. Also, through the reactions it invites from others, it may undermine their place in, and even the stability of, the foster family.

4 / *Inadequate matching of child and foster family, and inadequate preparation of both for placement.* Poor matching or preparation of children and foster parents prior to placement is common (Berridge and Cleaver

1987) and invites renewed instability and breakdown (Littner 1970; Steinhauer 1984), thus undermining the child's chance of obtaining the stable and tolerant family relationships that have proved beneficial to so many children in care (Triseliotis 1980, Hersov 1985).

5 / *Insufficient adult assistance and support through the work of mourning*, including faulty placement technique and adult collusion to abort the work of mourning (Palmer 1974; Aldridge and Cautley 1975).

6 / *Interactional difficulties in the foster home*, whether stemming from an inherent lack of commitment or suitability of the foster parents, from the foster parents' reactions to the attitudes and behaviours the child brings with him (Cautley and Aldridge 1973).

7 / *Too little, inadequate, and/or insufficiently systemic casework in support of the placement.* Systemic casework involves an approach to case management that takes into account the problems and position of the child, the foster parents, the natural parents, the worker and agency, as well as how these participants interact with one another.

8 / *Social factors*, such as the socio-economic status of the child and the natural family and the stigma of being a foster child: Many foster children are born with all the vulnerabilities associated with being a member of a disadvantaged natural family, such as higher rates of mental retardation (Shah, Kahan, and Krauser 1987), predisposition to poor school performance, conduct disorder, hyperactivity, and emotional disorders (Offord, Last, and Barrette 1985). In addition, foster status in itself carries a social stigma that may undermine adjustment and self-esteem within the new community.

Although Elmer (1977) suggested that lower socio-economic status has as deleterious an effect on later child development as does a history of abuse, Schneider-Rosen and colleagues (1985) have warned that, until further and better-controlled studies are available, the effects of maltreatment and of low socio-economic status must be considered independently.

These eight sets of factors interact with and accentuate one another in a circular and systemic manner. Without a clear and appropriate plan and effective intervention, foster children risk drifting at an accelerating rate into the long-term sequelae of family breakdown represented schematically in figure 2.5.

The direct results (risk of permanent detachment, persistent and diffuse rage, emotional dyscontrol, and continuing unmet needs) interact with one another to produce such characteristic sequelae as impairment in the capacity for relationships, antisocial and asocial behaviours, chronic depression and low self-esteem and (see also chapter 4), exaggerated dependency, and the tendency to compulsively, though unconsciously, evoke from the new environment a repetition of the original rejection.

Changes in Nature of Foster Care

To minimize the destructive effects of poor foster care, it is important to recognize the changing characteristics of those children coming into care and to appreciate the effects of this change on the fostering process.

Foster care today is concerned chiefly with 'special needs' children, most of whom come into care with multiple, well-established physical, mental, emotional, and behavioural problems. As a result, they considerably disrupt the life of the foster family (Wilkes 1979; Johnston 1989), forcing foster parents, whether or not they acknowledge it, to function as parent-therapists, providing specialized management, if not a prescribed treatment program, in addition to basic care. They may or may not be paid for the specialized time and services offered over and above the boarding and maintenance allowance (Steinhauer 1983b; see also chapter 1).

Whether or not they are recognized as 'specialized,' foster parents may be more a political and economic than a service issue, since only those so designated are paid for the special services they provide. Today, however, there are probably few differences among the children cared for in foster homes that have and have not been designated specialized. Therefore routine foster care, to be adequate, must usually be specialized care, as defined above (Frank 1980). Because of the difficulties presented by the care of such 'special needs' children, ongoing training, supervision, and support for foster parents are mandatory (Rosenblum 1977; Larson, Allison, and Johnston 1978; Barker, Buffe, and Zaretsky 1978; Rubenstein et al 1978; Steinhauer et al 1988, 1989). In any event, such foster parents contract to provide basic care and to cooperate with the sponsoring agency in drawing up and implementing a management plan suited to the needs of the individual child. Such a plan might include the foster parents working with the natural parents to help prepare them for their child's return home, or their preparing the child for adoption, or providing a behaviour modification program for a hyperactive child lacking impulse controls (Steinhauer 1988). Their work might also include considering the possibility of recontracting to provide adoption, subsidized adoption, or planned permanent foster care, with or without continuing access to the natural parents. Some specialized programs deliberately seek out as foster parents individuals or couples with previous training in the mental health professionals (Hazel 1981); see also chapters 10, 13, and 15).

Keys to the Preventive Use of Foster Care

How can this knowledge be used to minimize the potentially destructive effects of poorly planned long-term foster care? How can it maximize the preventive and beneficial potential that stable and accepting foster-family relationships and the systematic application of knowledge arising from child development and psychopathogenesis can provide? The remainder of this chapter will present seven keys to the prevention of psychological and social deterioration to children in foster care. These are summarized below and then discussed.

Keys to the preventive use of foster care
1 Any demand for removal deserves immediate crisis intervention.
2 Avoid colluding with family scapegoating.
3 Wherever possible, apprehend children on a planned, not an emergency, basis.
4 Plan aggressively to protect continuity with major attachment figures by:
   – systematically assessing and predicting parenting capacity;
   – protecting continuity to key attachment figures;
   – promoting multiple attachments, whenever indicated;
   – using active/systematic decision making at every stage.
5 Actively assist the work of mourning.
6 Use visits preventively.
7 Direct casework towards the optimal functioning of the foster care system, with adequate psychiatric/psychological consultation available as back-up.

KEY 1: ANY DEMAND FOR REMOVAL DESERVES CRISIS
INTERVENTION.

Any demand for removal of a child indicates a crisis for which removal is seen by someone – the community, the parents, a mental health or child welfare agency, or, occasionally, the child – as the only solution. But removal is not without its own hazards. Before removing and placing a child, one should always explore the possibility of finding other, less radical but equally effective alternatives as acceptable to family and agency, but involving less risk to the child (Steinhauer 1980a). The experience, capacity for empathy, systemic orientation, and negotiating skills of the worker, and the availability of back-up consultation when needed, are crucial in such a situation (see chapter 6).

KEY 2: AVOID COLLUDING WITH FAMILY SCAPEGOATING.

The removal of a scapegoated child or adolescent may further undermine that child's place within the family. Families who define the child as 'the' problem often see permanent elimination of the 'trouble maker' as its solution. Once rid of him, such families often close ranks, making it harder for the extruded child to return. To minimize the risk of colluding with such scapegoating, agencies should be careful, especially in the temporary placements of older children and adolescents, to emphasize to parents the role of a temporary placement in an overall plan of management, and to demand continued parental involvement directed towards the reconstitution and reintegration of the family, whenever possible (Steinhauer 1984).

At the same time, agencies should avoid organizational structures that inadvertently collude with the extrusion of such children. Agencies often further divide the families of children coming into care (Catholic Children's Aid Society of Metropolitan Toronto 1975; Rowe et al 1984; Hersov 1985). The child is assigned to a worker in the child-care department, the parents to another in a separate family service and/or protection department. All too often, these two workers do not collaborate and fail to coordinate their planning and interventions. Frequently family-service workers attenuate their work with parents once a child is safely in care, thereby exacerbating some parents' tendency to exclude their child permanently and undermining the possibility of successfully reuniting the family. These issues are more fully discussed and illustrated in chapter 6.

KEY 3: WHEREVER POSSIBLE, APPREHEND CHILDREN ON
A PLANNED, NOT AN EMERGENCY, BASIS.

Avoid an 'act now, plan later' mentality, through which a foster home is used as a place of safety in the mistaken belief that, afterwards, there will be lots of time to decide what to do next. To avoid unnecessary drift, the decision on where a child should go *after* a temporary placement must be made *before* that placement. Any placement should be part of a long-term plan, not a decision unrelated to the child's overall management. Unnecessary placements can permanently undermine children's relationships with their families. The best way to avoid a damaging drift into unnecessary and unplanned long-term care is through having a comprehensive management plan that is regularly reviewed and updated by all those involved in the child's ongoing care (Steinhauer 1983b; see also chapter 6).

Wherever possible, children should come into care on a planned, rather than an emergency, basis. Except when there is immediate risk of serious physical or sexual abuse, it is better that the child remain for a few more days, or even weeks, in a chronically inadequate family in order to allow a planned entry into care than that that child be apprehended on an emergency basis. The reasons that planned placements are so preferable to emergency ones are reviewed in chapter 6.

Littner (1970), Aldridge and Cautley (1975), and Palmer (1979) have stressed the preventive importance of adequate preparation for both children and foster parents prior to placement. The same authors have contrasted the generally accepted goal of a step-by-step introduction of child and foster parents to each other through a graduated series of pre-admission visits with an all-too-prevalent standard of practice that regularly falls far short of this ideal. Proper preparation for placement takes time. It is impossible to prepare as well for emergency placements, which, in many agencies, represent the majority of all placements (Catholic Children's Aid Society of Metropolitan Toronto 1975; Metro 1989).

Finally, there is little doubt that some unnecessary admissions to care occur because a protection worker panics or is stampeded by parental or community pressures. Such admissions undoubtedly complicate the long-term situation for both child and family, and the additional damage is often difficult, if not impossible, to undo. If workers and agencies are seriously committed to minimizing the number of children brought into care on an unplanned basis, the number of such unnecessary emergency admissions can be significantly reduced.

KEY 4: PLAN AGGRESSIVELY TO PROTECT CONTINUITY WITH
MAJOR ATTACHMENT FIGURES.

The concept of *permanency planning* has, despite the seemingly un-
challengeable virtue implied by its title, become badly confused and
distorted by accumulated rhetoric, much of it of a political and economic
nature that has at times obscured and distorted the real issues (Steinhauer 1983b). Pike and colleagues (1977) and Maluccio and Fein (1983)
have defined what should be meant by *permanency planning* as actively
clarifying and determining the intent of a given placement, and, during
a temporary placement, aggressively planning and working towards permanence (see chapters 6 and 12).

a / *Assessing and predicting parenting capacity.* For effective planning,
there is a need for clear, replicable, and researchable criteria for assessing
and, even more important, for predicting parenting capacity, when developed, these should sensitively, creatively but actively be applied to
answer, as rapidly as possible for a given case, such questions as:

What criteria can we use to decide that Mr and Mrs X are so unable to meet
their children's minimal developmental needs that their child's future development demands her removal and placement in a more adequate family setting?

Equally important, for the child in a short-term placement:

What criteria are there to allow us, in the shortest possible time, with acceptable
accuracy and without abuse of parents' rights, to decide:
1 that Mr & Mrs Y show enough evidence of being able, given help that is
   actually available, to learn to parent acceptably, so that the agency's goal
   should be that of preparing them/their child for restoration?
2 that Mr & Mrs Z, by contrast, show enough evidence of not being able, with
   the help actually available, to improve their parenting enough to ever meet
   their children's developmental needs? This being so, the agency's goal must
   be to prepare the children for an alternative other than restoration, for example, freeing them for adoption or moving them towards planned permanent
   foster care with or without continuing access to the natural parents under
   specified conditions.

Steinhauer (1983a) and Westman and Kaye (1983) have suggested guidelines that provide a rationale for long-term planning that can minimize

the drift involved either in unplanned permanent fostering or in allowing children to drift casually in and out of care. In chapter 5, the author summarizes the key issues related to assessing parenting capacity and introduces work in progress in which he and colleagues are developing guidelines for nine parameters (summarized in table 5.1). These guidelines, if used systematically, could provide and focus the necessary data and draw attention to recurrent patterns critical in assessing current parenting ability and in predicting future parenting capacity, that is, the prognosis for significant improvement in parenting in response to casework or therapy.

While not all of the guidelines apply equally to all cases, the obtaining of historical data and the structuring of a systematic assessment of parenting capacity around such guidelines will assist in identifying relevant data, in organizing them to maximize pattern recognition, and in facilitating their clear presentation in court. This organization will undermine many of the myths and decrease much of the guesswork in child-welfare cases within the family-court system.

b / *Protecting continuity to key attachment figures.* One of the more destructive effects of poor foster care is the way it allows children to lose continuity with their key attachment figures. Agencies and courts can minimize unnecessary discontinuity and help children achieve a coherent and integrated sense of identity by minimizing unnecessary moves (see chapter 11). Littner (1970) has written that each child's first placement should be the last. While this position represents an ideal rather than one that can regularly be achieved, proper planning, along with aggressively systemic casework, can decrease unnecessary breakdowns and replacements. When several placements cannot be avoided, the use of life books to capture and recall the past in concrete terms can help children develop a sense of their own history and protect their sense of the continuity of their life experience. The use of visits to key figures to re-establish continuity with important attachment figures from the past whom the child still remembers has been discussed elsewhere (Steinhauer 1977) and is summarized in chapter 7. However, one way to avoid unnecessary disruption of key attachment relationships is through the use of a 'shared parenting' or multiple-attachment model, as described in chapter 8 and summarized below.

c / *Promote multiple attachments whenever indicated.* Studies of children's longitudinal responses to marital separation (Wallerstein 1986;

Hetherington, Cox, and Cox 1986) and to being raised in day care (Belsky and Steinberg 1979) have demonstrated that children can form, hold, and benefit from several significant attachments simultaneously. Yet, surprisingly, this knowledge has remained isolated, and has been insufficiently utilized within the foster-care system.

Many adults within the foster-care system – natural parents, foster parents, child welfare workers, and mental health consultants – think of children as being a part either of one family or of another, but not of both. This 'either/or' paradigm fails to appreciate and utilize knowledge obtained through long-term studies of children whose parents have divorced and remarried – that is, that many children function quite well as members of more than one family. Practically speaking, a shared-parenting or multiple-attachment model may provide the least detrimental alternative for many children who satisfy the following conditions: there is little realistic prospect of restoration to their biological family; they are old enough to remember and retain a strong, if ambivalent, attachment to the natural parents; they have developed a personality, history, and set of problems of their own that are likely to undermine the stability of future placements and the prospects for successful adoption (Prosser 1978; Hersov 1985). Planned permanent foster care with continuing regular access to the natural parents, except when such is specifically contra-indicated as against the child's best interests, may serve for many children in care somewhat as a boarding-school might for children of wealthier families. The constructive use of such a model demands that it provide a positive choice following an active exploration of alternatives, rather than that it be one drifted into out of inertia, neglect, or passivity. To work, shared parenting requires active and systemic support from the supervising agency (Fanshel and Shinn 1978). In practice, it is all too often that workers and agencies have the hardest time breaking out of 'either/or' thinking enough to support any such solution (see also chapter 8).

d / *Use active/systematic decision making at every stage.* Finally, in order to protect, wherever possible, the continuity of key attachment relationships, all agencies should develop guidelines for the differential use of a variety of placement alternatives, including return to natural parents, freeing children for adoption, or contracting to raise children to maturity in planned permanent foster care with or without continuing access to the natural parents (i.e., shared parenting). These criteria should serve as guidelines, providing a basis for decision making on a case-by-case basis. Such decisions should include obtaining and weighing the input of all those interested in the future of the child, such as the child himself, the natural parents, the foster parents, the agency or agencies involved, and the child's therapist, if one exists (Cooper 1978; Levitt 1981; Bush and Gordon 1982). In arriving at a decision, the agency should consider both historic and systemic perspectives, utilizing guidelines like those described above as a general framework for case planning, but carefully weighing the evidence in each case to determine how best to apply these. Agencies should actively establish and carry out a long-term plan for every child. While the emphasis should remain on protecting continuity, if at all possible, the planners should be realistic in assessing the suitability of restoration or adoption for a given child, since among those children most badly damaged are those who flourished in foster families but were restored to indecisive, rejecting, and ambivalent parents (Tizard 1977; Fanshel and Shinn 1978; Maluccio et al 1980; see also chapters 6 and 12).

KEY 5: ACTIVELY ASSIST THE WORK OF MOURNING.

This involves an appreciation that 'out of sight' is not 'out of mind,' and that absent attachment figures will continue to have significant – and, possibly, increasing – emotional meaning despite physical separation. It involves recognizing that separation from major attachment figures will precipitate a process of mourning. Should this process be aborted or remain incomplete because the child has been overwhelmed by more anxiety than is tolerable at any given time, a series of serious consequences are likely to ensue, some of which will undermine subsequent attachments, thus interfering with ongoing development and inviting rejections (Littner 1960; Steinhauer 1983b).

The work of mourning, especially in the younger child, requires active and sensitive adult assistance. In actual fact, however, foster parents and child-welfare workers frequently collude to abort the mourning process, ostensibly to protect the child but, rationalizations aside, to spare themselves the pain evoked by the side-effects of the child's mourning (Steinhauer 1983b).

Some children mourn more easily and more successfully than others. Factors associated in the literature with successful mourning have included: a small-enough caseload to allow the worker to support the child through the work of mourning; post-placement visits with the lost attachment figures, which, while upsetting at the time, are correlated with better long-term adjustment (Palmer 1974; Aldridge and Cautley 1975); a committed, experienced worker (Palmer 1974); foster parents able to tolerate the child's upset and prepared to assist the child through the work of mourning at those moments when circumstances have temporarily reactivated the mourning process; an agency that is convinced of the necessity of assisting the work of mourning, and whose systemic concept of foster care supports workers in assigning and assisting foster parents who play the key role in direct work with the child; foster parents who have been trained to differentiate between transactional and transference phenomena, so that they will recognize distortions in the child's behaviour and at least consider the possibility that the child may be acting out with them angry feelings or fantasies transferred from the lost parents. While psychotherapy with foster children has been described as facilitating the completion of mourning (Kliman and Schaeffer 1984), it is the foster parents who are most likely to be available when the repressed mourning process is temporarily reactivated, for example, by feelings stirred up by an impending or cancelled visit. It is they who, given sufficient professional back-up, are most likely to be able to help the child effectively at times when he is least defended against the loss, rage, and hurt that he is struggling, at such great cost, to suppress. These issues are discussed and illustrated in chapters 7, 13, and 14.

KEY 6: USE VISITS PREVENTIVELY.

Visits with natural parents or other key attachment figures from the past can, wisely and systematically used, provide a major opportunity for preventive intervention. Lack of parental visiting, especially in the first six months after admission to care, greatly decreases the likelihood of the child returning home to the natural family (Mech 1985; Berridge and Cleaver 1987). Whether or not visits serve a preventive function will depend on the way that foster parents and social workers recognize and utilize feelings aroused before and after visits to assist the work of mourning and to help the child place in perspective the reasons for being in care. Visits with natural parents should always occur within the context of an overall management plan suited to the particular needs of a given child (see also chapter 9).

For any child in care temporarily – and the younger the child, the more important this is – regular visits should be insisted upon as long as any realistic prospect of restoration to the natural family exists. Very young children can tolerate total removal from key attachment figures for only a very limited time (Goldstein, Freud, and Solnit 1973). Deprived of their natural parents and in the absence of regular access, they will react as if the parents have been permanently lost and will begin to detach themselves from them. Unless regular visits are used to preserve the attachment to the parents, just a few weeks' separation can be enough to precipitate what could be termed an 'agency-induced abandonment.' Thus, the child would be invited to form a substitute attachment to the foster parents, from whom he would have to undergo a second – and, this time, avoidable – separation should he be returned to the biological parents who, through agency neglect, have been allowed to become psychological strangers (Steinhauer 1977).

Much of the work of mourning so crucial to the long-term ward's satisfactory attachment to foster parents and ongoing development can be catalysed by visits to the natural family. Several authors have correlated such visits to an active working through of the feelings aroused but left unresolved by separation (Aldridge and Cautley 1975; Cautley and Aldridge 1973; Palmer 1974). This result is especially likely if the foster parents, with the supervision and support of their social worker, can tolerate and utilize changes in attitude and behaviour just before and after visits to reactivate the still-incomplete mourning process.

For those children unable to be raised in their natural families but too old to repress the memory of them, visits may help them obtain what they can from parents who care but are unable to parent even minimally acceptably. Even upsetting visits or last-minute cancellations can be useful in confronting children with the reality of why they are in care. They can provide an antidote to the idealization in fantasy that so often occurs when no visiting is allowed, an idealization that frequently blocks the work of mourning and undermines successful re-attachments to parental surrogates. These issues are discussed and illustrated in chapter 9.

KEY 7: DIRECT CASEWORK TOWARDS THE OPTIMAL
FUNCTIONING OF THE FOSTER CARE SYSTEM, WITH
ADEQUATE PSYCHIATRIC / PSYCHOLOGICAL
CONSULTATION AVAILABLE AS BACK-UP.

Active systemic casework used to deal with and balance perceptions, issues, and conflicts of the child with contrasting needs and interactions among the child, the foster family, the natural family, the worker, and the agency can do much to maintain an integrated focus on the needs of the child, to further effective planning, and to coordinate the involvements of all interested parties (see also chapter 10). Failure to achieve such coordination in the interests of the child results, all too often, either in power struggles carried out in the name of the child or in insufficient or defective planning, unnecessary drift, or inappropriate involvements that result from the exclusion from the planning process of some of those occupying key roles in the child's world (Wald, Carlsmith, and Leiderman 1988; Fanshel, Finch, and Grundy 1989; discussed further in chapter 10).

Natural parents had launched a long and complicated appeal against an order of permanent wardship that was strongly contested by the agency. Both foster parents were extremely hostile to the mother, who had reportedly abused a difficult child to whom the foster parents had become extremely attached over two years in care. Both sets of parents agreed to a joint meeting with the social worker. In that meeting, resentments and suspicions on both sides were aired, freeing the natural mother to thank the foster mother for all she had done for her child. The meeting ended with each couple still determined to obtain custody but, at the same time, recognizing the psychological importance of the other to the child. Both agreed, whatever the decision, to allow the child regular access to the other in the foreseeable future.

Conclusion: The Need for Systematic, Controlled Research

Because of the multiplicity and the interdependence of the many variables involved, well-controlled prospective research in the foster-care area is extremely difficult to conduct, or even finance. As a result, more myths than facts govern decision making at present. To improve decision making and case planning, there needs to be systematic research to define criteria that can provide semi-objective guidelines as to which type of family placement is best for which child. Further research is also needed to determine to what extent damages long attributed to long-term foster care reflect, instead, the child's experiences prior to coming into care, the effects of multiple breakdown and replacements, the quality of the foster care provided, multiple changes of worker, and the failure to provide optimal services at each step along the way. Other questions needing study include how long, at different ages, separation can be tolerated without permanent detachment occurring; the indications and contra-indications of various types of family placement; when a child is an 'older' child for adoption purposes; when shared parenting protects a child's adjustment and development and when it undermines it. This list is, of course, by no means conclusive. Only through systematically studying such issues will we be able to determine the appropriate place for planned permanent foster care with and without access to natural parents, adoption, subsidized adoption, group homes, and institutional settings in the management of children needing substitute parenting to maturity. Finally, one hopes that such research may assist us in determining more effective interventions, in order to minimize the deleterious results of the cumulative effects of the multiple hazards to which these children are chronically exposed, thus improving the prognosis for the adjustment and long-term development of one of the populations of children at highest risk for emotional, behavioural, and learning disorders.

References

Adam, K.S. 1982. Loss, suicide, and attachment, In C.M. Parkes and J. Stevenson-Hinde, eds., *The Place of Attachment in Human Behavior.* New York: Basic Books

Ainsworth, M.D.S. 1967. *Infancy in Uganda: Infant Care and the Growth of Attachment.* Baltimore: Johns Hopkins University Press

– 1969. Object relations, dependency, and attachment: A theoretical review of the infant-mother relationship. *Child Development* 40: 969–1025

– 1974. Infant-mother attachment and social development: Socialization as a product of reciprocal responsiveness to signals. In M. Richards, ed., *The Integration of the Child into the Social World.* Cambridge, MA: Cambridge University Press

– 1980. Attachment and abuse. In G. Gerbner and E. Zigler, eds., *Child Abuse: An Agenda for Action.* New York: Oxford University Press

– 1982. Attachment: Retrospect and prospect. In C.M. Parkes and J. Stevenson-Hinde, eds., *The Place of Attachment in Human Behavior.* New York: Basic Books

Ainsworth, M.D.S., M.C. Blehar, E. Waters, and S. Wall. 1978. *Patterns of Attachment: A Psychological Study of the Strange Situation.* Hillsdale, NJ: Erlbaum

Aldridge, M.J., and P.W. Cautley. 1975. The importance of worker availability in the functioning of new foster homes. *J. Child Wel. Leag. Am.* 54 (January): 444–53

Allison, J., and K. Kufeldt. 1987. Fostering children – fostering families. Paper presented at 11th Western Canadian Conference on Family Practice, Banff, Alberta, May

American Academy of Pediatrics: Committee on Adoptions. 1971. Identity development in adopted children. *Pediatrics* 47 (5): 948–9

American Psychiatric Association. 1980. *Diagnostic and Statistical Manual of Mental Disorders*, 3d ed. (DSM III), ch. 6, 10, 12, 14, and 16. Washington, DC

Anglim, E.E. 1980. The politics of permanency planning for children. Paper presented at the Annual Meeting of the American Orthopsychiatric Association, Toronto, April

Anthony, E.J. 1970. The influence of maternal psychosis on children – *folie à deux*. In E.J. Anthony and T. Benedek, eds., *Parenthood: Its Psychology and Psychopathology*. Boston: Little, Brown

Anthony, E.J., and T. Benedek. 1970. *Parenthood: Its Psychology and Psychopathology*. Boston: Little, Brown

Anthony, E.J., and B.J. Cohler, eds. 1987. *The Invulnerable Child*. New York: Guilford Press

Anthony, E.J., C. Koupernik, and C. Chiland. 1978. *Vulnerable Children*. Vol. 4: *The Child in His Family*. New York: Wiley

Appathurai, C., G. Lowery, and T. Sullivan. 1986. Achieving the vision of deinstitutionalization: A role for foster care? *Child and Adolescent Social Work* 3 (1): 50–67

Arnowitz, Y. 1984. Foster home support project progress report of second year 1983–1984. Hadassah Medical Organization. Mimeograph

Aumend, S.A., and M.C. Barrett. 1984. Self-concept and attitudes toward adoption: A comparison of searching and nonsearching adult adoptees. *Child Welfare* 63: 29–59

Avery, M. 1984. The child abuse witness: Potential for secondary victimization. *Criminal Justice J.* 7: 1–48

Badgley Report. 1984. *Report of the Committee on Sexual Offences against Children*, vols. I and II. Minister of Justice and Attorney General of Canada, Ministry of National Health and Welfare

Balbernie, R. 1966. *Residential Work with Children*. Oxford: Pergamon

– 1974. Unintegration, integration and level of ego functioning as the determinants planned 'cover therapy' of unit task and of placement. *J. Assoc. Workers for Maladjusted Children* 2: 6–46

Bank, L., G.R. Patterson, and J.B. Reid. 1987. Delinquency prevention through parent training in family management. *The Behavior Analyst* 10: 75–82

Baran, A., R. Pannor, and A.D. Sorosky. 1976. Open adoption. *Social Work* 21: 97–100

– 1977. Adoptive parents and the sealed record controversy. *Social Casework* 55: 531–6

Barker, P. 1978. The 'impossible' child: Some approaches to treatment. *Can. J. Psychiat.* 23: SS1–21

Barker, P., C. Buffe, and R. Zaretsky. 1978. Providing a family alternative for the disturbed child. *Child Welfare* 57: 373–9

Barker, P., and B. Kane. 1985. The foster care research project: A comparison of two models of foster care. Part I: Design and implementation. Mimeograph

Barnum, R. 1987. Clinical experience: Understanding controversies in visitation. *J. Am. Acad. Child Adol. Psychiat.* 26 (5): 788–92

Bates, J.E. 1980. The concept of difficult temperament. *Merrill-Palmer Quart.* 26: 299–319

– 1983. Issues in the assessment of difficult temperament. A reply to Thomas, Chess and Korn. *Merrill-Palmer Quart.* 29: 89–97

Bates, J.E., C.A. Maslin, and K.A. Frankel. 1985. Attachment security, mother–child interaction, and temperament as predictors of behavior-problem ratings at age three years. In I. Bretherton and E. Waters, eds., *Growing Points of Attachment Theory and Research: Monographs of the Society for Research in Child Development* 50 (1–2). Chicago: University of Chicago Press

Bavolek, S. 1984. *Handbook for the Adult-Adolescent Parenting Inventory.* Schaumberg, IL: Family Development Associates

Belsky, J., and L.D. Steinberg. 1979. The effects of day care: A critical review. *Child Development* 49: 929–49

Benedek, E., and D. Schetky. 1985. Allegations of sexual abuse in child custody and visitation disputes. In D.H. Schetky and E.P. Benedek, eds., *Emerging Issues in Child Psychiatry and Law.* New York: Brunner/Mazel

Berliner, L., and J. Conti. 1981. Sexual abuse of children: Implications for practice. *Social Case Work* 62: 601–6

Berne, E. 1964. *Games People Play.* New York: Grove Press

Berridge D. 1985. *Children's Homes.* Oxford: Basil Blackwell

Berridge, D. and H. Cleaver. 1987. *Foster Home Breakdown.* Oxford: Basil Blackwell

Berry, S.W. 1975. Some clinical variations on a classical theme. *J. Am. Acad. Psychoanal.* 3: 151–61

Bill 77 (1987). Amendments to the Child and Family Services Act (Ontario)

Block, J.H. and J. Block. 1980. The role of ego-control and ego-resiliency in the organization of behavior. In W.A. Collins, ed., *Development of Cognition, Affect and Social Relations: The Minnesota Symposium on Child Psychology*, vol. 13. Hillsdale, NJ: Erlbaum

Block, N.M. 1981. Toward reducing recidivism in foster care. *Child Welfare* 60: 597–610

Block N., and A. Libowitz. 1983. *Recidivism in Foster Care.* New York: Child Welfare League of America

Blum, L.H. 1976. When adoptive families ask for help. *Primary Care* 3 (2): 241–9

Bohman, M. 1970. *Adopted Children and Their Families.* Stockholm: Propius

– 1972. A Study of adopted children, their background, environment and adjustment. *Acta Paediatrica Scandinavica* 61: 90–7

Bohman, M. and S. Sigvardsson. 1981. A prospective, longitudinal study of children registered for adoption: A 15-year follow-up. In S. Chess and A. Thomas, eds., *Annual Progress in Child Psychiatry and Child Development.* New York: Brunner/Mazel

Bowlby J. 1951. *Maternal Care and Mental Health.* Geneva: World Health Organization

– 1960. Grief and mourning in infancy and early childhood. *Psychoanal. Stud. Child* 15: 9–52

– 1969. *Attachment and Loss.* Vol. 1: *Attachment.* London: Hogarth

– 1973. *Attachment and Loss.* Vol. 2: *Separation, Anxiety, and Anger.* London: Hogarth

– 1979. The making and breaking of affectional bonds. *Brit. J. Psychiat.* 130: 201–10 (Part I); 421–31 (Part II)

– 1980. *Attachment and Loss.* Vol. 3: *Loss: Sadness and Depression.* New York: Basic Books

– 1982. Attachment and loss: Retrospect and prospect. *Am. J. Orthopsychiat.* 52: 664–78

Bowyer, M. 1980. Integrating adoption and fostering. *Adoption and Fostering* 99 (1): 25–9

Bradley, R.H., and B.M. Caldwell. 1976. Early home environment and changes in mental test performance in children from 6 to 36 months. *Developmental Psychology* 12: 93–7

– 1980. The relation of home environment, cognitive competence and I.Q. among males and females. *Child Development* 51: 1140–8

Brazelton, T.B., B. Koslowski, and M. Main. 1974. The origins of reciprocity: The early mother–infant interaction. In M. Lewis and L.A. Rosenbaum, eds., *The Effect of the Infant on Its Caretaker,* 49–76. New York: John Wiley

British Agencies for Adoption and Fostering. 1988. *Quarterly Journal* 1, 2, 3, and 4

Broder, E.A., and E. Hood. 1983. A guide to the assessment of child and family. In P.D. Steinhauer and Q. Rae-Grant, eds., *Psychological Problems of the Child in the Family*, New York: Basic Books

Brodzinsky, D.M., A.M. Braff. and L.M. Singer. 1981. Children's understanding of adoption: A comparison of adopted and non-adopted children. Unpublished manuscript, Rutgers University

Brown, G.W., and T. Harris. 1978. *Social Origins of Depression*. London: Tavistock.

Burke, M., and A. Dawson. 1987. Temporary care and foster parents: Motives and issues of separation and loss. *Child and Adolescent Social Work* 4 (3–4): 178–86

Burland, J.A. 1980. A psychoanalytical psychiatrist in the world of foster care. *Clinical Social Work J.* 8 (1): 51–61

Burt, M., and R. Balyeat. 1977. *A Comprehensive Emergency Services System for Neglected and Abused Children*. New York: Vantage Press

Bush, M. 1980. Institutions for dependent and neglected children: Therapeutic option of choice or last resort? *Am. J. Orthopsychiat.* 50 (2): 239–55

Bush, M., and M. Goldman. 1982. The psychological parenting and permanency principles in child welfare: A reappraisal and critique. *Am. J. Orthopsychiat.* 52 (2): 223–35

Bush, M., and A.C. Gordon. 1982. The case for involving children in child welfare decisions. *Social Work*, July: 309–14

Cadoret, R.J. 1978. Psychopathology in adopted-away offspring of biologic parents with antisocial behavior. *Arch. Gen. Psychol.* 35: 176–84

Cameron, G., and B. Bidgood. 1990. Family Builders Demonstration Project: Review of the outcome, research, and evaluation issues. Waterloo, ON: Centre for Social Welfare Studies, Faculty of Social Work, Wilfrid Laurier University, 10 July

Campbell, C., and S.W. Downs. 1987. The impact of economic incentives on foster parents. *Soc. Serv. Rev.* December: 599–609

Campos, J.J., K. Barrett, M.E. Lamb, H. Goldsmith, and C.R. Sternberg. 1983. Socioemotional development. In M.M. Haith, J.J. Campos, and P.H. Mussen, eds., *Handbook of Child Psychology*. Vol. 2: *Infancy and Developmental Psychobiology*, 783–915. New York: Wiley

Caplan, G. 1963. Types of mental health consultation. *Am. J. Orthopsychiat.* 33: 480–1

– 1970. *The Theory and Practice of Mental Health Consultation*. New York: Basic Books

– 1981. Mastery of stress: Psychosocial aspects. *Am. J. Psychiat.* 138 (4): 413–20

Carlson, V., D. Cicchetti, D. Barnett, and K. Braunwald. 1989. Disorganized/

disoriented attachment relationships in maltreated infants. *Developmental Psychology* 25 (4): 525–31

Carr, R.P. 1982. Personal communication

Catholic Children's Aid Society of Metropolitan Toronto. 1975. Some receiving home programs: Considerations and recommendations for 1975. Unpublished report

Cautley, P., and M. Aldridge. 1973. *Predictors of Success in Family Care.* Madison, WI: Dept. of Health and Social Service

Cautley, P.W., and M.B. Plane. *Facilitating Family Change: A Look at Four Agencies Working Extensively with Families.* Madison, WI: Dept. of Health and Social Services, Division of Community Services, May

Chamberlain, P. 1990. Comparative evaluations of specialized foster care for seriously disturbed delinquent youths. *Community Alternatives* 2 (2): 21–36

Chamberlain, P., and M. Weinrott. 1990. Specialized foster care: Treating seriously emotionally disturbed children. *Children Today* 19 (1): 24–7

Chandler, M.J. 1978. Role-taking, referential communication, and egocentric intrusion in mother–child interactions of children vulnerable to risk of parental psychosis. In E.J. Anthony, C. Koupernik, and C. Chiland, eds., *Vulnerable Children.* Vol. 4: *The Child in His Family.* New York: Wiley

Chappell, B. 1975. Organizing periodic review in foster care: The South Carolina story. *Child Welfare* 54: 477–86

Chimezie, A. 1975. Transracial adoption of black children. *Social Work* 20 (4): 296–301

Claburn, W.E., S. Magura, and S.P. Chizeck. 1977. Case reopening: An emerging issue in child welfare services. *Child Welfare* 56: 655–63

Clarke, A.M. 1981. Adoption studies and human development. *Adoption Fostering* 104: 17–29

Clarke-Stewart, K.A. 1973. Interactions between mothers and their young children: Characteristics and consequences. *Monographs of the Society for Research in Child Development* 38 (6–7; Serial No. 153). Chicago: University of Chicago Press

Clements, D.A. 1971. Psychological problems in adopted children. A review of the literature and some critical comments: Diss. submitted for fulfilment of the requirement for the Diploma Course in Child Psychiatry, University of Toronto, March

Clothier, F. 1939. Some aspects of the problem of adoption. *Am. J. Orthopsychiat.* 9: 598–615

– 1943. The psychology of the adopted child. *Mental Hygiene* 27: 222–30

Cohen, J.S., and A. Westhues. 1987. *How to Reduce the Risk: Healthy Func-*

tioning Families for Adoptive and Foster Children. Toronto: University of Toronto Press

Cohen, R.L., and M.A. Harnick. 1980. The susceptibility of child witnesses to suggestion. *Law and Human Behavior* 7: 59–65

Cohn, A.H. 1979. Effective treatment of child abuse and neglect. *Social Work* 24 (November): 513–19

– 1980. The pediatrician's role in the treatment of child abuse: Implications from a national evaluation study. *Pediatrics* 72 (2): 358–60

Connell, J.P. 1981. A model of the relationship among children's self-related cognitions, affects, and academic achievement. Doctoral dissertation, University of Denver

Cooley, C.H. 1902. *Human Nature and the Social Order.* New York: Charles Scribner

Cooper, J.D. 1978. *Patterns of Family Placement. Current Issues in Fostering and Adoption.* London: National Children's Bureau

Coopersmith, S. 1967. *The Antecedents of Self-esteem.* San Francisco: W.H. Freeman

Crellin, E., M.L. Pringle, D. Kellmer, and P. West. 1971. *Born Illegitimate: Social and Educational Implications.* Windsor: National Foundation of Educational Research

Crittenden, P.M. 1981. Abusing, neglecting, problematic, and adequate dyads: Differentiating by patterns of interaction. *Merrill-Palmer Quart.* 27: 201–8

– 1985. Maltreated infants: Vulnerability and resilience. *J. Child Psychol. Psychiat.* 26: 85–96

– 1987. Relationships at risk. In J. Belsky and T. Nezworski, eds., *Clinical Implications of Attachment.* Hillsdale, NJ: Erlbaum

Crockenberg, S.B. 1981. Infant irritability, mother responsiveness, and social support influences on the security of mother–infant attachment. *Child Development* 52: 857–65

Cummings, E.M. 1980. Caretaker stability and day care. *Developmental Psychology* 16: 31–7

Cunningham, L., R.J. Cadoret, R. Loftus, and J.E. Edwards. 1975. Studies of adoptees from psychiatrically disturbed biological parents: Psychiatric conditions in childhood and adolescence. *Brit. J. Psychiat.* 126: 534–49

Cutler, J.P. 1984. A study of children in foster care: Problems associated with the separation of siblings. Dissertation for DSW: Catholic University of America

Darnell, D. 1987. Report of review of foster care in Ontario, sponsored by the Ontario Association of Children's Aid Societies and the Foster Parents Association of Ontario, summarized in 'The future of foster care: Towards a redesign in '89.' *Ont. Assoc. Child. Aid Soc. J.* 32 (2): 1–20

Darnell Consulting Inc. 1988. *The Future of Foster Care.* Toronto: Ontario Association of Social Workers

Dawson, P. 1981. The psychology of eyewitness testimony: Developmental study of long term memory for film. Doctoral dissertation, New School for Social Research, New York

De Francis, V. 1969. *Protecting the Child Victims of Sex Crimes Committed by Adults.* Denver: The American Humane Association

DeJong, A. 1985. The medical evaluation of sexual abuse in children. *Hosp. Comm. Psychiat.* 36 (5): 509–12

DeLozier, P. 1982. Attachment theory and child abuse. In C.M. Parkes and J. Stevenson-Hinde, eds., *The Place of Attachment in Human Behavior.* New York: Basic Books

Derdeyn, A.P. 1977. A case for permanent foster placement of dependent, neglected and abused children. *Am. J. Orthopsychiat.* 47 (4): 604–14

Derr, D.R.F. 1983. The crisis of fostering for the foster family. Doctoral dissertation, Rutgers, October

de Young, M. 1986. A conceptual model for judging the truthfulness of a young child's allegation of sexual abuse. *Am. J. Orthopsychiat.* 56 (4): 550–9

D'Iorio M., and P. Steinhauer. 1978. Seeking out one's birth parents: Acting out a fantasy of reattachment. Presentation at conference on current issues in child psychiatry, Geneva Park, Ontario

Donaldson, M. 1978. *Children's Minds.* London: Fontana

– 1978. *Children's Thinking.* New York: Norton

Douglas, J.W.B. 1975. Early hospital admissions and later disturbances of behavior and learning. *Develop. Med. Child Neurol.* 17: 456–80

Dukette, R. 1974. Value issues in present-day adoption. *Child Welfare* 63: 233–43

Dunn, J. and C. Kendrick. 1982. Temperamental differences, family relationships and young children's response to change within the family. In R. Porter and G.M. Collins, eds., *Temperamental Differences in Infants and Young Children,* 87–100. London: Pitman

Easson, W. 1973. Special sexual problems of the adopted adolescent. *Med. Aspects of Human Sexuality,* July: 92–105

Eastman, K. 1979. The foster family in a system theory perspective. *Child Welfare* 58: 564–70

Egeland, B., and L.A. Sroufe. 1981a. Attachment and early maltreatment. *Child Development* 52: 44–52

- 1981b. Developmental sequelae of maltreatment in infancy. In R. Rizley and D. Cicchetti, eds., *Developmental Perspectives in Child Maltreatment*, 77–92. San Francisco: Jossey-Bass

Egeland, B., L.A. Sroufe, and M. Erickson. 1983. The development consequence of different patterns of maltreatment. *Child Abuse and Neglect: The International Journal* 7: 459–69

Eisenberg, L. 1961. The strategic deployment of the child psychiatrist in preventive psychiatry. *J. Child Psychol. Psychiat.* 2 (4): 229–41

- 1962. The sins of the fathers: Urban decay and social pathology. *Am. J. Orthopsychiat.* 32: 5–17

Elardo, R., R.H. Bradley, and B.M. Caldwell. 1975. The relation of infants' home environment to mental test performance from 6 to 36 months: A longitudinal analysis. *Child Development* 46: 71–6

Eldred, C.A., D. Rosenthal, P.H. Wender, S. Kety, F. Schulsinger, J. Welner, and B. Jacobsen. 1976. Some aspects of adoption in selected samples of adult adoptees. *Am. J. Orthopsychiat.* 46 (2): 279–90

Elmer, E. 1977. *Fragile Families, Troubled Children*. Pittsburgh, PA: University of Pittsburgh Press

Emlen, A., J. Lahti, G. Downs, A. McKay, and S. Downs. 1977. *Overcoming Barriers to Planning for Children in Foster Care*. Publication No. (OHDS): 78–30138. Washington, DC: Dept. of Health, Education and Welfare

Epstein, R. 1979. Children of gays. *Christopher Street*, June: 43–50

Epstein, S. 1973. The self-concept revisited or a theory of a theory. *Am. Psychologist* 28: 405–16

- 1980. The self-concept: A review and the proposal of an integrated theory of personality. In E. Staub, ed., *Personality: Basic Aspects and Current Research*, 82–131. Englewood Cliffs, NJ: Prentice-Hall

- 1981. The unity principle versus the reality and pleasure principles, or the tale of the scorpion and the frog. In M.D. Lynch, A.A. Norem-Hebeisen, and K. Gergen, eds., *Self-concept: Advances in Theory and Research*. Cambridge, MA: Ballinger

Erickson, M.F., L.A. Sroufe, and B. Egeland. 1985. The relationship between quality of attachment and behavior problems in preschool in a high-risk sample. In I. Bretherton and E. Waters, eds., *Growing Points of Attachment Theory and Research*, 147–66. Monographs of the Society for Research in Child Development 50 (1–2). Chicago: University of Chicago Press

Erikson, E.H. 1950. *Childhood and Society*. New York: Norton

- 1959. Identity and the life cycle. *Psychological Issues* 1: 18–164

- 1968. *Identity, Youth and Crisis*. New York: Norton

388 References

Evertnam, J., and V. Brazeau 1984. A treatment alternative for disturbed teens. *Perception* 7: 28–9

Faller, K.C. 1984. Is the child victim of sexual abuse telling the truth? *Child Abuse and Neglect* 8: 473–81

Fanshel, D. 1972. Far from the reservation: The transracial adoption of American Indian children. A study conducted under the auspices of the Child Welfare League of America, New York

– 1976. Status changes of children in foster care. *Child Welfare* 55: 143–71

Fanshel, D., S.J. Finch, and J.F. Grundy. 1989. Foster children in life-course perspective: The Casey Family program experience. *Child Welfare* 68: 467–78

Fanshel, D., and E.B. Shinn. 1978. *Children in Foster Care: A Longitudinal Investigation.* New York: Columbia University Press

Farran, D., and C. Ramey. 1977. Infant day care and attachment behavior toward mothers and teachers. *Child Development* 48: 1112–17

Fein, E., L. Davies, and G. Knight. 1979. Placement stability in foster care. *Social Work* 24 (March): 156–7

Fein, E., A.N. Maluccio, V.J. Hamilton, D.E. Ward. 1983. After foster care: Outcomes of permanency planning for children. *Child Welfare* 62: 485–558

Fenichel, A. 1945. *The Psychoanalytic Theory of Neurosis.* New York: W.W. Norton

Ferenczi, S. 1926. The problem of the acceptance of unpleasant ideas. In S. Ferenczi, *Further Contributions to the Theory and Technique of Psychoanalysis.* London: Institute of Psychoanalysis and Hogarth Press

Festinger, T. 1983. *No One Ever Asked Us: A Postscript to Foster Care*, 73–97. New York: Columbia University Press

Finkelhor, D. 1979. *Sexually Victimized Children*, 142–8. New York: The Free Press.

– 1984. *Child Sexual Abuse: New Theory and Research.* New York: Free Press

Finkelstein, N.E. 1980. Children in limbo. *Social Work* 25: 100–5

Fivush, R. 1984. Learning about school: The development of kindergartner's school scripts. *Child Development* 55: 1697–1709

Fodor, E.M. 1971. Resistance to social influence among adolescents as a function of moral judgment. *J. Soc. Psychol.* 85: 121–6

Frank, G. 1980. Treatment needs of children in foster care. *Am. J. Orthopsychiat.* 50: 256–63

Frankel, H. 1988. Family-centred, home-based services in child protection: A review of the research. *Soc. Serv. Rev.* March: 137–57

Freedman, A., H. Kaplan, and B. Sadock. 1976. *Comprehensive Textbook of Psychiatry.* Vol. 1, 2d ed. Baltimore, MD: Williams and Wilkins

Freeman, H. 1978. Foster home care for mentally retarded children. Can it work? *Child Welfare* 52: 113–21

Freud, A. 1946. *The Ego and the Mechanisms of Defense.* New York: International Universities Press

– 1960. Discussion of Dr. John Bowlby's paper. *Psychoanal. Stud. Child* 15: 53–62

Freud, A., and D.T. Burlingham. 1943. *War and Children.* New York: Medical Warbooks

Freud, S. 1946. Splitting of the ego in the defensive process. *Collected Papers.* New York: International Universities Press

Friedman, R. 1987. APA *Symposium of Foster Family Based Treatment.* New York: American Psychological Association

Friedrich, W.N., R.L. Beilke, and B.A. Urquiza. 1984. Behavior problems in young sexually abused boys: A comparison study. *J. Paed. Psychol.* 2 (1): 47–57

Frisk, M. 1964. Identity problems and confused conceptions of the genetic ego in adopted children during adolescence. *Acta Paed. Psychiatrica* 31: 7

Frommer, E., and G. O'Shea. 1973a. Antenatal identification of women liable to have problems in managing their infants. *Brit. J. Psychiat.* 123: 149–56

– 1973b. The importance of childhood experience in relation to problems of marriage and family building. *Brit. J. Psychiat.* 123: 161–7

Furman, E. 1974. *A Child's Parent Dies.* New Haven, CT: Yale University Press

Gabinet, L. 1983. Shared parenting: A new paradigm for the treatment of child abuse. *Child Abuse and Neglect* 7: 403–11

Galaway, B. 1978. Path: An agency operated by foster parents. *Child Welfare* 57: 667–74

Galdston, R. 1965. Observations on children who have been physically abused and their parents. *Am. J. Psychiat.* 122 (4): 440–3

Garcia-Coll, C., J. Kagan, and J.S. Reznick. 1984. Behavioral inhibition in young children. *Child Development* 55: 1005–19

Gardner, R.A. 1989. Resolving child custody disputes without adversarial proceedings. *Court Review*, Winter: 23–7

Garmezy, N. 1981. Children under stress: Perspective on antecedents and correlates of vulnerability and resistance to psychopathology. In A.I. Rabin, J. Aronoff, A.M. Barclay, and R.A. Zucker, eds., *Further Explorations in Personality.* New York: Wiley Interscience

– 1984. Stress-resistant children: The search for protective factors. In J.

Stevenson, ed., *Recent Research in Developmental Psychopathology*. Monograph supplement No. 4 to *J. Child Psychol. Psychiat.* Oxford: Pergamon Press

Gean, M., J. Gillmore, and J. Dowler. 1985. Infants and toddlers in supervised custody: A pilot study of visitation. *This Journal* 24: 608–12

Geismar, L. 1979. Home-based care to children: Harmonizing the approaches of research and practice. In S. Maybanks and M. Bryce, eds., *Home Based Services for Children and Families: Policy, Practice and Research*, 325–32. Springfield IL: Charles C. Thomas

Gelinas, D.J. 1983. The persisting negative effects of incest. *Psychiatry* 46: 312–32

Gelman, D., G. Raine, T. Jackson, S. Katz, D. Weathers, and V. Coppola. 1986. Treating teens in trouble. *Newsweek* 107 (3: 20 Jan.)

George, C., and M. Main. 1979. Social interactions of young abused children: Approach, avoidance, and aggression. *Child Development* 50: 306–18

George, V. 1970. *Foster Care: Theory and Practice*. London: Routledge and Kegan Paul

Gersten, M., W. Coster, K. Schneider-Rosen, V. Carlson, and D. Cicchetti. 1986. The socio-emotional bases of communicative functioning: Quality of attachment, language development and early maltreatment. In M. Lamb, A.L. Brown, and B. Rogoff, eds., *Advances in Developmental Psychology*, vol. 4. Hillsdale, NJ: Erlbaum

Gesell, A., and F. Ilg. 1946. *The Child from Five to Ten*. New York: Harper and Row

Gill, M.M. and C.M. Amadio. 1983. Social work and law in a foster care/adoption program. *Child Welfare* 62: 455–67

Gislason, L., and J. Call. 1982. Dog bite in infancy: Trauma and personality development. *J. Am. Acad. Child Psychiat.* 21: 203–7

Glatzer, H.T. 1955. Adoption and delinquency. *Nervous Child* 11: 52–6

Goldberg, S. 1990. Attachment in infants at risk: Theory, research, and practice. *Inf. Young Children* 2 (4): 11–20

Goldstein, J., A. Freud, and A. Solnit. 1973. *Beyond the Best Interests of the Child*. New York: The Free Press

– 1979. *Before the Best Interests of the Child*. New York: The Free Press

Golombok, S., A. Spencer, and M. Rutter. 1983. Children in lesbian and single-parent households: Psychosexual and psychiatric appraisal. *J. Child Psychol. Psychiat.* 24 (4): 551–72

Goodman, G.S., D. Hepps, and R.S. Reed. 1986. The child victim's testimony. In A. Haralambie, ed., *New Issues for Child Advocates*, 167–77. Phoenix: Arizona Association of Council for Children

Goodman, G.S., and R.S. Reed. 1986. Age differences in eyewitness testimony. *Law and Human Behavior* 10: 317–32

Goodman, G.S., L. Rudy, B.L. Bottoms, and C. Aman. 1987. Children's concerns and memory: Ecological issues in the study of children's eyewitness testimony. Unpublished mimeograph

Goodman, J.D., and R. Magno-Nora. 1975. Adoption and its influence during adolescence: A comparison of court and community referred psychiatric patients. *J. Med. Soc. New Jersey* 72 (11): 922–8

Goodwin, J., D. Sahad, and R.I. Rada. 1978. Incest hoax: False accusations, false denials. *Bull. Am. Acad. Psychiat. Law* 6: 269–76

Gray, J.D., C.A. Cutler, J.G. Dean, and C.H. Kempe. 1979. Prediction and prevention of child abuse. *Seminars in Perinatology* 3: 85–90

Green, A.H. 1986. True and false allegations of sexual abuse in child custody disputes. *J. Am. Acad. Child Psychiat.* 25 (4): 449–56

Green, R. 1979. Quoted in R. Epstein, Children of gays. *Christopher Street,* June

Greenspan, S.I. 1981. *Psychopathology and Adaptation in Infancy and Early Childhood: Principles of Clinical Diagnoses and Preventive Intervention,* 17–48. Madison: International Universities Press, Inc.

Grey, E., and R.M. Blunden. 1971. *A Survey of Adoption in Great Britain.* Home Office Research Studies. London: Her Majesty's Stationery Office

Grinnell, R.M., and S. Jung. 1981. Children placed with relatives. *Social Work Research and Abstracts* 17 (Fall): 31–2

Grisso, T. 1986. Parenting capacity – determination of child custody. In T. Grisso, ed., *Evaluating Competencies: Forensic Assessments and Instruments,* 188–267. New York: Plenum Press

Gruber, A.R. 1978. *Children in Foster Care: Destitute, Neglected, Betrayed.* New York: Human Sciences Press

Guyatt, D.E. 1980. Panel on adolescent pregnancy and motherhood. Presented at St John's, Newfoundland, 18 June. Toronto: Ontario Ministry of Community and Social Services

Haddock, M., and W. McQueen. 1983. Assessing employee potentials for abuse. *J. Clin. Psychol.* 39: 1021–9

Hall, F., and S. Pawlby. 1981. Continuity and discontinuity in the behavior of British working-class mothers and their first-born children. *Int. J. Behav. Develop.* 4: 13–36

Hall, F., S. Pawlby, and S. Wolkind. 1979. Early life experiences and later mothering behaviors: A study of mothers and their 20-week-old babies. In D. Shaffer and J. Dunn, eds., *The First Year of Life,* 153–74. New York: Wiley

Hambidge, G. 1962. Primary and secondary ego degradation. Manuscript

Hampson, R.B., and J.B. Tavormina. 1980. Feedback from the experts: A study of foster mothers. *Social Work* 25: 108–13

Hampton, R., and E. Newberger. 1985. Child abuse incidence and reporting by hospitals: Significance of severity, class and race. *Am. J. Pub. Hlth* 75 (1): 56–60

Harari, H., K. Hosey, and P. Sheedy. 1979. Role perception in a community health setting. *J. Comm. Psychol.* 1: 335–42

Harlow, H.F., M.K. Harlow, R.O. Dodsworth, and G.L. Arling. 1966. Maternal behavior of rhesus monkeys deprived of mothering and peer association in infancy. *Proc. Am. Phil. Soc.* 110 (1): 58–66

Harman, J., G. Lister, and D. Kligman. 1981. Critique of discussion paper on child advocacy: Implementing the child's right to be heard. Prepared at the request of the Legislative Review Committee, Ontario Psychiatric Association

Harris, M.B., and P.H. Turner. 1986. Gay and lesbian parents. *J. Homosexuality* 12 (2): 101–13

Harter, S. 1983. Developmental perspectives on the self-system. In P. Mussen and E.M. Hetherington, eds., *Handbook of Child Psychology.* Vol. 4: *Socialization, Personality and Social Development,* 275–385. New York: Wiley

– 1985a. Commentary: On the need for a developmental perspective in understanding child and adolescent disorders. *J. Clin. Psychol.* 3 (4): 484–99

– 1985b. Competence as a dimension of self-evaluation: Toward a comprehensive model of self-worth. In R. Leahy, ed., *The Development of Self,* 55–121. New York: Academic Press

Harter, S., and R. Barnes. 1981. Children's understanding of parental emotions: A developmental study. University of Denver. Manuscript

Harter, S., and J.P. Connell. 1984. A comparison of alternative models of the relationships between academic achievement and children's perceptions of competence, control and motivational orientation. In J. Nicholls, ed., *The Development of Achievement-Related Cognitions and Behaviors.* Greenwich, CT: J.A.I. Press

Harter, S., and R. Pike. 1981. The pictorial perceived competence scale for young children. University of Denver. Manuscript

Hartman, A. 1984. *Working with Adoptive Families beyond Placement.* New York: Child Welfare League of America

– 1987. Innovations in social work practice. State University of New York at Albany, Social Work Conference

Hausknecht, R.D. 1972. The termination of pregnancy in adolescent women. *Pediatric Clinics of North America* 19: 803–10

Hawkins, R.P., P. Meadowcraft, B.A. Trout, and W.C. Luster. 1985. Foster family–based treatment. *J. Clin. Child Psychol.* 14: 220–8

Hazel, N. 1981. *A Bridge to Independence: The Kent Family Placement Project.* Oxford: Basil Blackwell

Hazel, N., R. Cox, and P. Ashley-Mudie. 1977. *Second Report of the Special Family Project.* Maidstone, U.K.: Kent Social Services Dept.

Hegar, R.L., and J.N. Hunzeker. 1988. Moving toward empowerment-based practice in public child welfare. *Social Work*, November–December: 499–502

Heinicke, C.M., and I.J. Westheimer. 1965. *Brief Separations.* London: Longman

Helfer, R., J. Hoffmeister, and C. Schneider. 1978. *A Manual for Use of the Michigan Screening Profile of Parenting.* Boulder, CO: Test Analysis and Development Corporation

Henderson, J.O. 1972. Incest: A synthesis of data. *Can. Psychiat. Assoc. J.* 17: 299–313

Hensey, O.J., J.K. Williams, and L. Rosenbloom. 1983. Intervention in child abuse: Experience in Liverpool. *Develop. Med. Child Neurol.* 26: 606–11

Hepworth, H.P. 1980. *Foster Care and Adoption in Canada.* Ottawa: The Canadian Council on Social Development

Herman, J., and L. Hirschman. 1981. Families at risk for father–daughter incest. *Am. J. Psychiat.* 138 (7): 967–70

Herrenkohl, R.C., and E.C. Herrenkohl. 1981. Some antecedents and developmental consequences of maltreatment. In R. Rizley and D. Cicchetti, eds., *Developmental Perspectives on Child Maltreatment: New Directions for Child Development,* 11. San Francisco: Jossey Bass

Hersov, L. 1985. Adoption and fostering. In M. Rutter and L. Hersov, eds., *Child and Adolescent Psychiatry: Modern Approaches,* 2d ed., 101–17. London: Blackwell Scientific

Hetherington, E.M. 1979a. Family interaction and the social, emotional and cognitive development of children following divorce. In V. Vaughan and T. Brazelton, eds., *The Family: Setting Priorities.* New York: Science and Medicine

– 1979b. Play and social interaction in children following divorce. *J. Soc. Issues* 35 (4): 26–49

Hetherington, E.M., M. Cox, and R. Cox. 1986. Long-term effects of divorce and remarriage on the adjustment of children. In S. Chess and A. Thomas, eds., *Annual Progress in Child Psychiatry,* 407–29. New York: Brunner/Mazel

Hetherington, E.M., and B. Martin. 1979. Family interaction. In H.C. Quay and J.S. Werry, eds., *Psychopathological Disorders of Childhood*, 2d ed. London: Heinemann

Hill, M., L. Lambert, and J. Triseliotis. 1989. *Achieving Adoption with Love and Money*. London: National Children's Bureau

Hinde, R.A. 1980. Family influences. In M. Rutter, ed., *Scientific Foundations of Developmental Psychiatry*. London: Heinemann

Hinde, R.A., and L. McGinnis. 1977. Some factors influencing the effect of temporary mother–infant separation: Some experiments with rhesus monkeys. *Psychol. Med.* 7: 197–212

Hinde, R.A., Y. Spencer-Booth, and M. Bruce. 1966. Effects of six-day maternal deprivation on rhesus monkey infants. *Nature* 210: 1021–3

Hochstadt, N.J., P.K. Jaudes, D.A. Zimo, and J. Schachter. 1987. The medical and psychosocial needs of children entering foster care. *Child Abuse and Neglect* 11 (1): 53–62

Hoopes, J.L. 1982. *Prediction in Child Development: A Longitudinal Study of Adoptive and Nonadoptive Families – The Delaware Family Study*. New York: Child Welfare League of America

Hornick, J.P. 1983. A review of the foster care research project. Unpublished observation

Hoving, K.L., J. Hamm, and P. Galvin. 1969. Social influence as a function of stimulus ambiguity at three age levels. *Develop. Psychol.* 1: 631–6

Howe, G.W. 1983. The ecological approach to permanency planning: An interactionist perspective. *Child Welfare* 62: 291–301

Hudson, J., and K. Nelson. 1983. Effects of script structure on children's story recall. *Develop. Psychol.* 19 (4): 625–35

Hulsey, T.C., and R. White. 1989. Family characteristics and measures of behavior in foster and nonfoster children. *Am. J. Orthopsychiat.* 59 (4): 502–9

Humphrey, M. 1969. *The Hostage Seekers*. New York: Humanities Press

Humphrey, M.E., and C. Ounsted. 1963. Adoptive families referred for psychiatric advice I: The children. *Brit. J. Psychiat.* 109: 599–608

Ilfeld, F. Jr. 1970. Environmental theories of violence. In D. Danfield, M. Gilula, and F. Ochberg, eds., *Violence and the Struggle for Existence*. Boston: Little Brown

Jacobs, M. 1980. Foster parent training: An opportunity for skills enrichment and empowerment. *Child Welfare* 59: 615–24

Jaffe, B., and D. Fanshel. 1970. *How They Fared in Adoption: A Follow-up Study*. New York: Columbia University Press

Jaffe, P., G. Austin, A. Leschied, and L. Sas. 1987. Critical issues in the development of custody and access dispute resolution services. *Can. J. Behav. Sci.* 19 (4): 405–17

Jenkins, S., and B. Diamond. 1985. Ethnicity and foster care: Census data as predictors of placement variables. *Am. J. Orthopsychiat.* 55 (2): 267–76

Jewett, C.L. 1978. *Adopting the Older Child.* Harvard, MA: The Harvard Common Press

Johnson, A. 1949. Sanctions for superego lacunae of adolescents. In R.K. Eissler, ed., *Searchlights on Delinquency*, 225–45. New York: International Universities Press

Johnson, M.K., and M.A. Foely. 1984. Differentiating fact from fantasy: The reliability of children's memory. *J. Soc. Issues* 30 (2): 33–50

Johnston, M. 1989. How self-help discussion groups can help natural children cope with the stress of foster children in the family: Two different reports. *J. Ont. Assoc. Child. Aid Soc.* 33 (6): 2–9

Jones, D.P.H., and J.M. McGraw. 1986. Reliable and fictitious accounts of sexual abuse to children. *J. Interpersonal Violence* 2: 27–45

Jones, D.P.H., and R.D. Krugman. 1986 Can a three-year-old child bear witness to her sexual assault and attempted murder? *Child Abuse and Neglect* 10: 253–58

Jones, M.A. 1985. *A Second Chance for Families: Five Years Later.* New York: Child Welfare League of America

Jones, M.A., and G. Halper. 1981. Serving families at risk of dissolution: Public preventive services in New York City, Executive Summary. New York: Child Welfare League of America

Kadushin, A. 1970. *Adopting Older Children.* New York: Columbia University Press

– 1980. *Child Welfare Services.* New York: Macmillan

Kadushin, A., and F.W. Seidl. 1971. Adoption failure: A social work postmortem. *Social Work* 16 (3): 32–8

Kagan, J., J.S. Reznick, C. Clarke, N. Snidman, and C. Garcia-Coll. 1984. Behavioral inhibition to the unfamiliar. *Child Development* 55: 2212–25

Kagan, J., J.S. Reznick, and N. Snidman. 1987. The physiology and psychology of behavioral inhibition in children. *Child Development* 58: 1459–73

Kagan, J., J.S. Reznick, N. Snidman, J. Gibbons, and M.O. Johnson. 1988. Childhood derivatives of inhibition and lack of inhibition to the unfamiliar. *Child Development* 59: 1580–9

Kagan, M.K., and W.J. Reid. 1984. Critical factors in the adoption of emotionally disturbed youth. *Child Welfare* 65: 63–73

Kagan, R., and S. Schlosberg. 1989. *Families in Perpetual Crisis.* New York: Norton

Kaplan, H.S. 1979. Quoted in R. Epstein, Children of gays. *Christopher Street,* June: 43–50

Kashani, J., and D.P. Cantwell. 1983. Characteristics of children admitted to inpatient community mental health centre. *Arch. Gen. Psychiat.* 40: 397–400

Katz, L. 1977. Older child adoptive placement: A time of family crisis. *Child Welfare* 61: 165–71

– 1990. Effective permanency planning for children in foster care. *Social Work,* May: 220–6

Katz, M.H., R.L. Hampton, E.H. Newberger, R.T. Bowles, and J.C. Snyder. 1986. Returning children home: Clinical decision-making in cases of child abuse and neglect. *Am. J. Orthopsychiat.* 56 (2): 253–62

Katz, S.N. 1976. The changing legal status of foster parents. *Child Today* 5 (6): 11–13

Kaufman, J. and E. Zigler. 1989. The intergenerational transmission of child abuse. In D. Cicchetti and V. Carlson, eds., *Child Maltreatment: Theory and the Causes and Consequences of Child Abuse and Neglect,* 129–50. New York: Cambridge University Press

Kempe, R.S., and C.H. Kempe. 1984. *The Common Secret: Sexual Abuse of Children and Adolescents.* New York: W.H. Freeman

Kernberg, O. 1975. *Borderline Conditions and Pathological Narcissism.* New York: Jason Aronson

Kieffer, C.H. 1984. Citizen empowerment prevention. *Human Services* 3: 9–36

Kim, S.P. 1980. Behaviour symptoms in three transracially adopted Asian children: Diagnosis dilemma. *Child Welfare* 59: 213–24

King, M.A., and J. Yuille. 1987. Suggestibility and the child witness. In S.J. Ceci, M.P. Toglia, and D.F. Ross, eds., *Children's Eyewitness Memory,* 24–35. New York: Springer-Verlag

Kinney, J.M., B. Madsen, T. Fleming, and D.A. Haapala. 1977. Homebuilders: Keeping families together. *J. Consulting and Clin. Psychol.* 45 (4): 667–73

Kirgan, D.A. 1983. Meeting children's needs through placement: The placement evaluation program. *Child Welfare* 62: 157–66

Kirk, H.D. 1964. *Shared Fate: A Theory of Adoption and Mental Health.* London: The Free Press of Glencoe

Klein, M. 1946. Notes on some schizoid mechanisms. *Int. J. Psychoanal.* 27: 99–110

Klibanoff, S., and E. Klibanoff. 1973. *Let's Talk about Adoption.* Toronto: Little, Brown

Kliman, G., and M.H. Schaeffer. 1984. Summary of two psychoanalytically-based service and research projects: Preventive treatments for foster children. *J. Prev. Psychiat.* 2: 1

Knitzer, J., M. Allen, and B. McGowan. 1978. Children without homes: An examination of public responsibility to children in out-of-home care. Washington DC: Children's Defense Fund

Kohut, H. 1971. *The Analysis of Self: A Systematic Approach to the Psychoanalytic Treatment of Narcissistic Personality Disorders.* New York: International Universities Press

Kowal, K.A., and K.M. Schilling. 1985. Adoption through the eyes of adult adoptees. *Am. J. Orthopsychiat.* 55 (3): 354–61

Kraus, J. 1981. Foster children grow up: Parameters of care and adult delinquency. *Children and Youth Services Rev.* 3: 99–114

Kufeldt, K. 1982. Including natural parents in temporary foster care: An exploratory study. *Children Today* 11 (5): 14–16

Kufeldt, K., and J. Allison. 1990. Fostering children – fostering families: Community alternatives. *Int. J. Family Care* 2 (1): 11–17

Kufeldt, K., J. Armstrong, and M. Dorosh. 1991. Children's ratings of their natural and foster families. Personal communication of work in preparation

Kunkel, B.E. 1983. The alienation response of children abused in out-of-home placement. *Child Abuse and Neglect* 7: 479–84

Ladner, J.A. 1977. Mixed families: White parents and black children. *Society* 14 (6): 70–8

Lahti, J., K. Green, A. Emlen, J. Zendry, Q.D. Clarkson, M. Kuehnel, and J. Cascioto. 1978. *A Follow-up Study of the Oregon Project.* Portland, OR: Regional Research for Human Services, Portland State University

Laing, R.D. 1960. *The Divided Self.* London: Tavistock

Lamb, M.E. 1977. The development of mother–infant and father–infant attachments in the second year of life. *Develop. Psychol.* 13: 637–48

Lamb, M.E., T.J. Gaensbauer, C.M. Malkin, and L.A. Schultz. 1985. The effects of abuse and neglect on security of infant–adult attachment. *Infant Behav. Develop.* 8: 35–45

Lamb, M.E., C.P. Hwang, A. Frodi, and M. Frodi. 1982. Security of mother- and father–infant attachment and its relationship to sociability with strangers in traditional and non-traditional Swedish families. *Infant Behav. Develop.* 5: 355–67

Lambert, L., J. Essen, and J. Head. 1977. Variations in behavior ratings of children who have been in care. *J. Child Psychol. Psychiat.* 18: 335–46

Lander, H., E.J. Anthony, L. Cass, L. Franklin, and L. Bass. 1978. A measure of vulnerability to risk of parental psychosis. In E.J. Anthony, C. Kouper-nik, and C. Chiland, eds., *Vulnerable Children*, Vol. 4: *The Child in His Family*, 325–34. New York: Wiley

Larson, G., J. Allison, and E. Johnston. 1978. Alberta parent counselors: A community treatment program for disturbed youths. *Child Welfare* 57: 47–52

Law Society of Upper Canada. 1981. Minutes of Convocation, May 1981, vol. 6 (5): 217–23

Lawson, C.A. 1982. Foster Care Co-ordinator, Central Region, Ministry of Community and Social Services, Ontario. Personal communication, 27 January

Lawton, H.W., and A. Magarelli. 1980. Stress among public child welfare workers. *Catalyst* 2 (3): 57–65

Lawton, J., and S. Gross. 1964. Review of the psychiatric literature on adopted children. *Arch. Gen. Psychiat.* 11: 635–44

Lecky, P. 1945. *Self-consistency: A Theory of Personality*. New York: Island Press

LeFebvre, A. 1983. The child with physical handicaps. In P.D. Steinhauer and Q. Rae-Grant, eds., *Psychological Problems of the Child in the Family*, 2d ed., 478–508. New York: Basic Books

Leitenberg, H., J.D. Burchard, D. Healy, and E.J. Fuller. 1981. Nondelinquent children in state custody: Does type of placement matter? *Am. J. Comm. Psychol.* 9: 347–59

Lemmon, J.A. 1975. Self-concept and the foster adolescent. Doctoral dissertation, University of Illinois, *Dissertation Abstract International* 36: 313A

Lerner, R.M. 1982. Children and adolescents as producers of their own development. *Develop. Rev.* 2: 342–70

Leverette, J. 1981. Custody determination and the homosexual parent. Paper presented to Annual Conference of Family Court Clinics of Ontario

Levitt, K.L. 1981. A Canadian approach to permanency planning. *Child Welfare* 60: 109–12

Lewis, M., D.O. Lewis, S.S. Shanock, E. Klatskin, and J.R. Osborne. 1980. The undoing of residential treatment. A follow-up study of 51 adolescents. *J. Am. Acad. Child Psychiat.* 19: 160–71

Lifschitz, M., D. Berman, A. Galila, and D. Gilad. 1977. The effects of mothers' perception and social system organization on their short-term adjustment. *J. Am. Acad. Child Psychiat.* 16 (2): 272–84

Linton, M. 1982. Transformations of memory in everyday life. In U. Neisser, ed., *Memory Observed: Remembering in Natural Contexts*. New York: W.H. Freeman

Littner, N. 1960. The child's need to repeat his past. Some implications for placement. *Soc. Serv. Rev.* 34 (2): 118–48

– 1970. Separation of the child from his natural family grouping. Paper read to the annual meeting of the Ontario Association of Children's Aid Societies, May

– 1971. The importance of the natural parents to the child in placement. In *Preliminary Conference Report, First National Conference of Foster Parents*. Publication No. 72–5. Washington, DC: Dept. of Health, Education and Welfare

– 1974. The challenge to make fuller use of our knowledge about children. *Child Welfare* 53: 287–94

Loftus, E., and G. Davis. 1984. Distortions in the memory of children. *J. Soc. Issues* 40 (2): 51–67

Lynes, C. 1983. An individualized residential program. *Mental Retardation* 21: 30–6

Lyons-Ruth, K., D. Zoll, D.B. Connell, and R. Odom. 1987. Maternal depression as mediator of the effects of home-based intervention services. Paper presented at the biennial meeting of the Society for Research in Child Development, Baltimore, April

Lystad, M.H. 1975. Violence at home: A review of the literature. *Am. J. Orthopsychiat.* 45 (3): 328–45

Maas, H.S. 1960. The successful adoptive applicant. *Social Work* 5: 14–20

Maas, H.S., and R.E. Engler. 1959. *Children in Need of Parents*. New York: Columbia University Press

MacMillan, H. 1987. A protocol for a randomized controlled trial examining the efficacy of nurse home visitation in child abuse. Unpublished protocol for course MS370 (McMaster University) Design Measurement Evaluation Program

Madanes, C. 1980. The prevention of rehospitalization of adolescents and young adults. *Family Process* 37: 179–91

Madison, B., and M. Schapiro. 1970. Permanent and long-term foster care as a planned service. *Child Welfare* 49: 131–6

Main, M., and J. Cassidy. 1988. Categories of response to reunion with the parent at age six: Predictable from infant attachment classification and stable over a one-month period. *Develop. Psychol.* 24 (3): 415–26

Main, M., and E. Hesse. 1989. Adult lack of resolution of attachment-related trauma related to infant disorganized/disoriented behavior in the Ainsworth Strange Situation: Linking parental states of mind to infant behavior in a stressful situation. Manuscript

– 1990. The disorganized/disoriented pattern in infancy: Precursors and sequelae. In M. Greenberg, D. Cicchetti, and E.M. Cummings, eds., *Attachment in the Preschool Years: Theory, Research and Intervention*. Chicago: University of Chicago Press

Main, M., N. Kaplan, and J. Cassidy. 1985. Security in infancy, childhood, and adulthood: A move to the level of representation. In I. Bretherton and E. Waters, eds., *Growing Points of Attachment Theory and Research*. Monographs of the Society for Research in Child Development 50 (1–2). Chicago: University of Chicago Press

Main, M., and J. Solomon. 1986. Discovery of new, insecure–disorganized/disoriented attachment pattern. In M. Yogman and T.B. Brazelton, eds., *Affective Development in Infancy*. Norwood, NJ: Ablex

– 1990. Procedures for identifying infants as disorganized/disoriented during the Ainsworth Strange Situation. In M. Greenberg, D. Cicchetti, and E.M. Cummings, *Attachment in the Preschool Years: Theory, Research and Intervention*. Chicago: University of Chicago Press

Maluccio, A.N., and E. Fein. 1983. Permanency planning: A redefinition. *Child Welfare* 62: 195–201

Maluccio, A.N., E. Fein, J.L. Hamilton, J. Klier, and D. Ward. 1980. Beyond permanency planning. *Child Welfare* 59: 515–30

Maresca, J., D. Paulseth, and B. Rivers. 1989. *Mediation in Child Protection: A New Alternative*. Toronto: Dept. of Education, The Law Society of Upper Canada

Marin, B.C., D.L. Holmes, M. Guth, and P. Kovas. 1979. The potential of children as eyewitnesses: A comparison of children and adults on eyewitness tasks. *Law and Human Behavior* 3: 295–305

Marmor, R. 1977. Quoted in B.S. Harris, Lesbian mother–child custody: Legal and psychiatric aspects. *Bull. Am. Acad. Psychiat. and Law* 5 (1): 75–89

Marron, K. 1988. *Ritual Abuse: Canada's Most Infamous Trial on Child Abuse*. Toronto: Seal Books

Martin, S., and F. Pilon. 1986. Longitudinal outcomes of children in residential therapy: Implications for methods of treatment and policy formation. Unpublished mimeograph

Mayer, B., and M.M. Golten. 1987. *Child Protection Mediation Project Manual*. Obtainable from the authors on request to 100 Arapahoe Ave., Suite 12, Boulder, CO 80302

McCall, R.B., M.I. Appelbaum, and P.S. Hagarty. 1973. Developmental changes in mental performance. *Monographs of the Society for Research in Child Development* 38 (3, Serial No. 150)

McCord, J.A. 1983. A forty-year perspective on effects of child abuse and neglect. *Child Abuse and Neglect* 7: 265–70

McLean, P.D. 1976. Parental depression: Incompatible with effective parenting. In E.J. Mash, L.C. Handy, and L.A. Hamerlynch, eds., *Behaviour Modification Approaches to Parenting*, 209–20. New York: Brunner/Mazel

McWhinnie, A.M. 1967. *Adopted children – How They Grow Up*. New York: Humanities Press

– 1969. The adopted child in adolescence. In G. Caplan and S. Lebovici, eds., *Adolescent-Psychosocial Perspectives*, 133–42. New York: Basic Books

Mech, E.V. 1985. Parental visiting and foster placement. *Child Welfare* 64: 67–72

Meier, E.G. 1965. Current circumstances of former foster children. *Child Welfare* 44: 196

– 1966. Adults who were foster children. *Children* 13: 16–22

Melton, G.B. 1981. Children's competency to testify. *Law and Human Behavior* 5: 73–85

Menlove, F.L. 1965. Aggressive symptoms in emotionally disturbed adopted children. *Child Development* 36: 519–32

Metro. 1989. Report of representative of Children's Aid Society of Metropolitan Toronto to the 'Residential Family Resources Project: Children's Needs' Task Force of the Children's Services Division of the Ministry of Community and Social Services, Ontario

Mietus, K., and N. Fimmen. 1987. Role ambiguity among foster parents: Semi-professionals in professionalizing organizations. *J. Sociol. Social Welfare* 14: 33–41

Miller, G. 1987. Preventing out-of-home placement: Programs that work. Chairman, Select Committee on Children, Youth and Families. *Juvenile Justice Digest* 15 (15): 2–5

Miller, K., E. Fein, G. Bishop, N. Stilwell, and C. Murray. 1984. Overcoming barriers to permanency planning. *Child Welfare* 63: 45–55

Miller, L. 1980. Psychotherapy with severely deprived children: Eileen. *J. Child Psychotherapy* 6: 57–67

Millham, S., R. Bullock, K. Hosie, and M. Haak. 1986. *Lost in Care: The Problems of Maintaining Links between Children in Care and Their Families*. Aldershot, Hants; Brookfield, VT: Gower

Milner, J.S. 1980. *The Child Abuse Potential Inventory Manual*. Webster, NC: Psytec Corp.

Mineka, S., and S.J. Suomi. 1978. Social separation in monkeys. *Psychol. Bull.* 85 (6): 1376–400

Minton, B. 1979. Dimensions of information underlying children's judgements of their competence. Unpublished master's thesis, University of Denver

Money, J. 1977. Quoted in B.S. Harris, Lesbian mother–child custody: Legal and psychiatric aspects. *Bull. Am. Acad. Psychiat. and Law* 5 (1): 75–89

Monsour, A., and S. Harter. 1984. The emergence of perceived conflict between attributes within the self-concept during adolescence. Unpublished manuscript, University of Denver.

Muir, R.C., S.M. Monaghan, R.J. Gilmore, J.E. Clarkson, T.J. Crooks, and T.G. Egan. 1989. Predicting child abuse and neglect in New Zealand. *Australian and New Zealand J. Psychiat.* 23: 255–60

Murphy, H.B.M. 1964. Natural family pointers to foster care outcome. *Mental Hygiene*, July: 380–91

Mussen, T.H., J.J. Conger, and J. Kagan. 1981. *Child Development and Personality.* 5th ed. New York: Harper and Row

Nagera, H. 1970. Children's reaction to the death of important objects: A developmental approach. *Psychoanal. Stud. Child* 25: 360–400

National Commission on Children in Need of Parents. 1979. *Who Knows? Who Cares? Forgotten Children in Foster Care.* Written by J.E. Persico. New York

Neisser, U. 1979. The control of information pickup in selective looking. In A.D. Dick, ed., *Perception and Its Development: A Tribute to Eleanor Gibson.* Hillsdale, NJ: Erlbaum

Nelson, K. 1984. The transition from infant to child memory. In M. Moscouitch, ed., *Infant Memory: Its Relation to Normal and Pathological Memory in Humans and Other Animals.* New York: Plenum Press

Nelson, K., and G. Ross. 1980. The generalities and specifics of long-term memory in infants and young children. In M. Perlmutter, ed., *Children's Memory: New Directions for Child Development* (No. 10). San Francisco: Jossey Bass

Ney, P. 1989. Child mistreatment: Possible reasons for its transgenerational transmission. *Can. J. Psychiat.* 34: 594–601

Ney, P., D. Mulvihill, and R. Hanna. 1984. The effectiveness of child psychiatric inpatient care. *Can. J. Psychiat.* 29: 26–30

Nickman, S. 1986. Open adoptions – for whom? A clinician's view. *Boston Bar J.* 30: 32–5

Noshpitz, J.D., ed. 1979. *Basic Handbook of Child Psychiatry*, vol. 1. New York: Basic Books

Notes. 1985. The testimony of child victims in sex abuse prosecutions: Two legislative innovations. *Harvard Law Rev.* 98: 806–27

Nurcombe, B. 1986. The child as witness: Competency and credibility. *J. Am. Acad. Child Psychiat.* 25 (4): 473–80

Oates, R.K., A. Peacock, and D. Forrest. 1984. The development of abused children. *Develop. Med. Child Neurol.* 26: 649–56

Office of Population Censuses and Surveys Monitor. 1976. FM3 76/3. London: Her Majesty's Stationery Office

Offord, D. 1986. *Ontario Child Health Study: Summary of Initial Findings.* Toronto: Queen's Printer for Ontario

Offord, D.R., J.F. Aponte, and L.A. Cross. 1969. Presenting symptomatology of adopted children. *Arch. Gen. Psychiat.* 20: 110–16

Offord, D.R., M.H. Boyle, J.E. Fleming, H. Munroe-Blum, and N.I. Rae-Grant. 1989. Ontario child health study: Summary of selected results. *Can. J. Psychiat.* 34: 483–91

Offord, D.R., J.M. Last, and P.A. Barrette. 1985. A comparison of the school performance, emotional adjustment and skill development of poor and middle-class children. *Can. J. Pub. Hlth.* 76: 174–8

Oldershaw, L., G. Walters, and D. Hall. 1989. A behavioural approach to the classification of different types of physically abusive mothers. *Merrill-Palmer Quart.* 35: 255–79

Olds, D.L., C.R. Henderson, R. Chamberlin, and R. Tatelbaum. 1986. Preventing child abuse and neglect: A randomized trial of nurse home visitation. *Pediatrics* 78 (July): 65–78

Ontario. 1978. *Child Welfare Act of Ontario.* Ministry of Community and Social Services, Children's Services Division

Ontario Ministry of Community and Social Services. 1981. *Foster Care: Proposed Standards and Guidelines for Agencies Placing Children.* Toronto

Ordway, D.P. 1981. Parent–child incest: Proof at trial without testimony in court by victim. *Univ. of Michigan J. Law Reform* 15: 131

Orvaschel, H., S. Mednick, F. Schulsinger, and D. Rock. 1979. The children of psychiatrically disturbed parents: Differences as a function of the sex of the sick parent. *Arch. Gen. Psychiat.* 26: 691–5

Osofsky, H.J., and J.D. Osofsky. 1970. Adolescents as mothers. *Am. J. Orthopsychiat.* 40: 825–34

O'Toole, R., P. Turbett, and C. Nalepka. 1983. Theories, professional knowledge, and diagnosis of child abuse. In D. Finkelhor et al, eds., *The Dark Side of Families: Current Family Violence Research.* Beverly Hills: Sage

Palmer, S.E. 1974. Children in long-term care: The worker's contribution. *J. Ont. Assoc. Child. Aid Soc.* 17 (4): 1–14

– 1979. Predicting outcome in long-term foster care. *J. Soc. Serv. Res.* 3 (2): 201–14

– 1982. Training child placement workers in effective handling of separation. *Ont. Assoc. Child. Aid Soc. J.* 26 (10): 1–10

- 1989. Mediation in child protection cases: An alternative to the adversary system. *Child Welfare* 68: 21–31

Pannor, R., and A. Baran. 1984. Open adoption as standard practice. *Child Welfare* 63: 245–50

Pardeck J.T. 1984. Multiple placement of children in foster family care: An empirical analysis. *Social Work* 29 (6): 506–9

Pardeck, J.T., and J.A. Pardeck. 1987. Bibliotherapy for children in foster care and adoption. *Child Welfare* 66: 269–78

Parke, R.D., and C.W. Collmer. 1975. Child abuse: An interdisciplinary analysis. In E.M. Hetherington, ed., *Review of Child Development Research*, vol. 5. Chicago: University of Chicago Press

Parker, J. 1982. The rights of child witnesses: Is the court a protector or a perpetrator? *New England Law Rev.* 17: 643–717

Parker, R. 1966. *Decision in Child Care: A Study of Prediction in Fostering.* London: Allen and Unwin

Pasztor, E., and E. Burgess. 1982. Finding and keeping more foster parents. *Children Today* 11: 2–5

Patterson, G.R., J.B. Reid., R.R. Jones, and R.E. Conger. 1975. *A Social Learning Approach to Family Intervention: Aggressive Children*, vol. 1. Eugene, OR: Castalia Publishing

Pawlby, S., and F. Hall. 1980. Early and later language development of children who come from disrupted families of origin. In T. Field, S. Goldberg, D. Stern, and A. Sostek, eds., *High-Risk Infants and Children: Adult and Peer Interaction*, 61–75. New York: Academic Press

Pecora, P.J., M.W. Fraser, and D.A. Haapala. 1990. Intensive home-based family preservation services: Client outcomes and issues for program design. Revision of a paper presented at the NATO Advanced Research Workshop: State Intervention on Behalf of Children and Youth, Acquafreedda di Maratea, Italy, 23 February 1989

Perlmutter, M., and N.A. Myers. 1979. Development of recall in 2- to 4-year-old children. *Develop. Psychol.* 15 (1): 73–83

Perlmutter, M., and M. Ricks. 1979. Recall in preschool children. *J. Psychol.* 27: 423–36

Pianta, R.C., B. Egeland, and A. Hyatt. 1986. Maternal relationship history as an indicator of developmental risk. *Am. J. Orthopsychiat.* 56: 385–98

Pike, V. 1976. Permanent planning for foster children: The Oregon Project. *Children Today* 5 (6): 22–5

Pike, V., S. Downs, A. Emlen, G. Downs, and D. Case. 1977. *Permanent Planning for Children in Foster Care: A Handbook for Social Workers,*

Publication No. (OHDS) 78-30124. Washington, DC: US Dept. of Health, Education and Welfare

Pilon, F. 1988. The parent therapist program: Past, present and future. Presented at Couchiching Conference on Foster Care, sponsored by Thistletown Regional Centre, November

Price, D.W.W. 1984. Children's comprehension of recurring episodes. Unpublished doctoral dissertation, University of Denver

Price, D.W.W., and G.S. Goodman. 1985. Children's event representations for recurring episodes. Paper presented at the Society for Research in Child Development, Toronto, April

Proch, K., and J.A. Howard. 1986. Parental visiting of children in foster care. *Social Work*, May–June: 178–81

Prosser, H. 1978. *Perspectives on Foster Care: An Annotated Bibliography.* Windsor: National Foundation for Educational Research, Humanities Press

Pynos, R., and S. Eth. 1984. The child as witness to homicide. *J. Soc. Issues* 40 (2): 87–108

Quay, H.C. 1986. Residential treatment. In H.C. Quay and J. Werry, eds., *Psychopathological Disorders of Childhood*, 3d ed, 558–82. New York: John Wiley

Quinton, D., and M. Rutter. 1976. Early hospital admissions and later disturbances of behavior: An attempted replication of Douglas' findings. *Develop. Med. Child. Neurol.* 18: 447–59

– 1985. Parenting behaviors of mothers raised in care. In A.R. Nicol, ed., *Longitudinal Studies in Child Psychology and Psychiatry*, 157–201. New York: Wiley

Quinton, D., M. Rutter, and C. Liddle. 1984. Institutional rearing, parenting difficulties and marital support. *Psychol. Med.* 14: 107–24

Rae-Grant, N. 1978. But they didn't live happily ever after ... *J. Ont. Assoc. Child. Aid Soc.* 21: 3–8

Rae-Grant, N., D.R. Offord, and H. Munroe-Blum. 1989. The Ontario child health study: Implications for clinical services, research and training. *Can. J. Psychiat.* 34: 492–99

Rae-Grant, Q., and B.E. Robson. 1988. Moderating the morbidity of divorce. *Can. J. Psychiat.* 33: 443–52

Rank, O. 1914. *Myth of the Birth of the Hero.* Nervous and Mental Diseases Monograph Series, 18

Raphael, B. 1982. The young child and the death of a parent. In C.M. Parkes and J. Stevenson-Hinde, eds., *The Place of Attachment in Human Behavior.* New York: Basic Books

Regional Research Institute for Human Services. 1976. *Barriers to Planning for Children in Foster Care: A Summary*. Portland State University, School of Social Work

Reistroffer, M. 1972. Participation of foster parents in decision-making. The concept of collegiality. *Child Welfare* 51: 25–9

Report to Residential Family Resources Project Reference Group. 1989. A report to a task force appointed to recommend ways of strengthening the child welfare system. Ministry of Community and Social Services, Province of Ontario. Unpublished

Rest, E.R., and K.W. Watson. 1984. Growing up in foster care. *Child Welfare* 63: 291–306

Ricciuti, H. 1974. Fear and development of social attachments in the first year of life. In M. Lewis and L. Rosenblum, eds., *The Origins of Fear*. New York: Wiley

Rickarby, G.A. and P. Egan. 1980. Issues of preventive work with adopted adolescents. *Med. J. Australia* 1 (10): 470–2

Ricks, M.H. 1985. The social transmission of parental behavior: Attachment across generations. In I. Bretherton and E. Waters, eds., *Growing Points of Attachment Theory and Research*. Monographs of the Society for Research in Child Development 50, Nos. 1–2, Serial No. 209

Robertson, J. 1953. Some responses of young children to loss of maternal care. *Nursing Care* 49: 382–6

Robertson, J., and J. Bowlby. 1952. Responses of young children to separation from their mothers. *Courrier du Centre International de l'Enfance* 2: 131–42

Robertson, J., and J. Robertson. 1971. Young children in brief separation: A fresh look. *Psychoanal. Stud. Child* 26: 264–315

Robins, L.N. 1966. *Deviant Children Grown Up*. Baltimore: Williams and Wilkins

Robson, B. 1987. Changing family patterns: Developmental impacts on children. *J. Couns. Hum. Develop.* 19 (6): 2–12

Rogeness, G.A., S.A. Amrung, C.A. Macedo, W.R. Harris, and C. Fisher. 1986. Psychopathology in abused or neglected children. *J. Am. Acad. Child Psychol.* 25 (5): 659–65

Romig, D.A. 1978. Individual psychotherapy. In *Justice for Rehabilitation Program*, 77–85. Lexington, MA: Lexington Books

Rosenberg, M. 1979. *Conceiving the Self*. New York: Basic Books

Rosenblum, B. 1977. *Foster Homes and Adolescents: A Research Report*. Hamilton, ON: Hamilton–Wentworth Children's Aid Society

Rosenblum, L.A., and H.F. Harlow. 1963. Approach-avoidance conflict in the mother surrogate situation. *Psychological Reports* 12: 83–5

Ross, H.S., and B.D. Goldman. 1977. Establishing new social relations in infancy. In T. Alloway, P. Pliner, and L. Krames, eds., *Advances in the Study of Communication and Affect*. Vol. 3: *Attachment Behavior*. New York: Plenum

Roth, E.F. 1972. A psychodynamic model of the mother of the autistic child. *Smith College Studies in Social Work* 43 (2): 175–202

Rowe, J., H. Cain, M. Hundle, and A. Keane. 1984. *Long-Term Foster Care*. London: Batsford

Rowe, J., and L. Lambert. 1975. *Children Who Wait*. London: Association of British Adoption Agencies

Rubenstein, J.S., J.A. Aremtrout, S. Levis, and D. Herald. 1978. The parent-therapist program: Alternative care for emotionally disturbed children. *Am. J. Orthopsychiat.* 48 (4): 654–62

Runyan, D. 1985. Foster care for child maltreatment: Impact on delinquency. *Pediatrics* 75: 562–8

Russell, D.E.H. 1983. The incidence and prevalence of intrafamilial and extrafamilial sexual abuse of children. *Child Abuse and Neglect* 7: 133–46

– 1984. The prevalence and seriousness of incestuous abuse: Stepfathers vs. biological fathers. *Child Abuse and Neglect* 8: 15–22

Rutter, M. 1960. Maternal deprivation reconsidered. *J. Psychosomat. Res.* 16: 241–50

– 1971. Parent–child separation: Psychological effects on the children. *J. Child Psychol. Psychiat.* 12: 233–60

– 1972. *Maternal Deprivation Reassessed*. Harmondsworth: Penguin

– 1977. Early sources of security and competence. In J.S. Bruner and A. Garton, eds., *Human Growth and Development*. London: Oxford University Press

– 1978. Family, area and school influence in the genesis of conduct disorders. In L. Hersov, M. Berger, and D. Shaffer, eds., *Aggression and Antisocial Behavior in Childhood and Adolescence*. J. Child Psychol. Psychiat. Book series No. 1. Oxford: Pergamon

– 1979a. Attachment and the development of social relationships. In M. Rutter, ed., *Scientific Foundations of Developmental Psychiatry*. London: Heinemann Medical

– 1979b. Invulnerability or why some children are not damaged by stress. In S.J. Shamsie, ed., *New Directions in Children's Mental Health*, 53–75. New York: Spectrum

– 1979c. Maternal deprivation 1972–1978: New findings, new concepts, new approaches. *Child Development* 50: 283–305

Rutter, M., A. Cox, C. Tupling, M. Berger, and W. Yule. 1975. Attainment and adjustment in two geographical areas, I: The prevalence of psychiatric disorder. *Brit. J. Psychiat.* 126: 493–509

Rutter, M., and N. Madge. 1976. *Cycles of Disadvantage: A Review of Research.* London: Heinemann

Rutter, M., D. Quinton, and C. Liddle. 1983. Parenting in two generations: Looking backwards and forwards. In N. Madge, ed., *Families at Risk,* 60–98. London: Heinemann

Ryan, P., E.J. McFadden, and B.L. Warren. 1981. Foster families: A resource for helping parents. In A. Maluccio and P. Sinanoglu, eds., *The Challenge of Partnership: Working with Parents of Children in Foster Care.* New York: CWLA

Rzepnicki, T. 1987. Recidivism of foster children returned to their own homes: A review and new directions for research. *Soc. Serv. Rev.* 61 (1): 56–70

Sabalis, R.F., and E.A. Burch. 1980. Comparisons of psychiatric problems of adopted and non-adopted patients. *Southern Med. J.* 73 (7): 867–8

Sachdev, R. 1984. *Adoption: Current Issues and Trends.* Toronto: Butterworths

Salomon, E. 1981. Characteristics of parents of atypical and autistic children: Implications for treatment. *Smith College Studies in Social Work* 51 (2): 73–94

Santa-Barbara, J., and B. Kane. 1982a. The foster care research project: A comparison of two models of foster care service. Unpublished observation

– 1982b. The foster care research project: Follow-up report. Unpublished observation

Sants, H.J. 1964. Genealogical bewilderment in children with substitute parents. *Brit. J. Med. Psychol.* 37: 133–41

Sarbin, T.R. 1962. A preface to a psychological analysis of the self. *Psychol. Rev.* 59: 11–22

Schaefer, E. 1965. Children's reports of parental behavior: An inventory. *Child Development* 36: 417–23

Schain, R.J., D. Gardella, and J. Pon. 1982. Five year outcome of children admitted to a state mental hospital. *Hosp. Comm. Psychiat.* 33: 847–8

Schaughency, E.A., and B.B. Lahey. 1985. Mother's and fathers' perceptions of child deviance: Roles of child behavior, parental depression and marital satisfaction. *J. Consulting Clin. Psychol.* 53 (5): 718–23

Schechter, M.D. 1960. Observations of adopted children. *Arch. Gen. Psychiat.* 3: 21–32

Schechter, M.D., P.V. Carlson, J.Q. Simmons, and H.H. Work. 1964. Emotional problems in the adoptee. *Arch. Gen. Psychiat.* 10: 109–18

Schetky, D.H., R. Angell, C.V. Morrison, and W.H. Sack. 1979. Parents who fail: A Study of 51 cases of termination of parental rights. *J. Am. Acad. Child Psychol.* 8 (2): 366–83

Schmitt, B.D. 1980. The prevention of child abuse and neglect: A review of the literature with recommendations for application. *Child Abuse and Neglect* 4: 171–7

Schneider-Rosen, K., K.G. Brunwald, V. Carlson, and D. Cicchetti. 1985. Current perspectives in attachment theory: Illustration from the study of maltreated infants. In I. Bretherton and E. Waters, eds., *Growing Points of Attachment Theory and Research*, 194–210. Monographs of the Society for Research in Child Development 50 (1–2, Serial No. 209)

Schneider-Rosen, K., and D. Cicchetti. 1984. The relationship between affect and cognition in maltreated infants: Quality of attachment and the development of visual self-recognition. *Child Development* 35: 648–58

Schoenberg, C. 1974. On adoption and identity. *Child Welfare* 53: 549

Schorr, L.B. 1989. *Within Our Reach – Breaking the Cycle of Disadvantage.* New York: Anchor Books/Doubleday

Schwam, J.S., and M.K. Tuskan. 1979. The adopted child. In J.D. Noshpitz, ed., *Basic Handbook of Psychiatry*, vol. 1: 342–7. New York: Basic Books

Schwartz, I.M., P. AuClaire, and L. Harris. 1990. Family-preservation service as an alternative to the out-of-home placement of seriously emotionally disturbed adolescents: The Hennepin County experience. Centre for the Study of Youth Policy, School of Social Work, University of Michigan. Mimeograph

Schwartz, J. 1972. Effects of peer familiarity on the behavior of preschoolers in a novel situation. *J. Personality and Social Psychology* 24 (2): 276–85

Seaberg, J. 1986. Reasonable efforts: Toward implementation in permanency planning. *Child Welfare* 66: 469–79

Seay, B., B.K. Alexander, and H.F. Harlow. 1964. Maternal behavior of socially deprived rhesus monkeys. *J. Abnormal Soc. Psychol.* 69: 345–54

Seligman, L. 1979. Understanding the black foster child through assessment. *J. Non-White Concerns in Personnel and Guidance* 7: 183–91

Semancik, J. 1979. Adoption: The changing scene. *Social Thought* 5 (4): 3–61

Sgroi, S.M. 1982. *Handbook of Clinical Intervention in Child Abuse.* Lexington, MA: Lexington Books

– 1988. *Vulnerable Populations: Evaluation and Treatment of Sexually Abused Children and Adult Survivors*, vol. 1. Lexington, MA: Lexington Books

Shah, C.P., M. Kahan, and J. Krauser. 1987. The health of children in low-income families. *Can. Med. Assoc. J.* 137: 485–9

Shamsie, S.J. 1981. Antisocial adolescents: Our treatment does not work: Where do we go from here? *Can. J. Psychiat.* 26: 357–64

Sherman, E., R. Neuman, and A.W. Shyne. 1973. *Children Adrift in Foster Care: A Study of Alternative Approaches.* New York: Child Welfare League of America

Shure, M., and G. Spivack. 1978. *Problem-Solving Techniques in Child-Rearing.* San Francisco: Jossey-Bass

Siegel, E., K.E. Bauman, E.S. Schaeffer, M. Saunders, and D. Ingram. 1980. Hospital and home support during infancy: Impact on maternal attachment, child abuse and neglect, and health care utilization. *Pediatrics* 66: 183–90

Silver, L., C. Dublin, and R. Lourie. 1969. Does violence breed violence? Contributions from a study of the child abuse syndrome. *Am. J. Psychiat.* 126 (3): 152–5

Simmons, J.E., R.L. Ten Eyck, R.C. McNabb, B.S. Coleman, B. Birch, and M. Parr. 1981. Parent treatability: What is it? *J. Am. Acad. Child Psychiat.* 20: 792–809

Simon, R.S., and H. Altstein. 1981. Transracial adoption revisited. *Social Work Research and Abstracts* 17 (1): 44

Skoler, G. 1984. New hearsay exceptions for a child's statement of sexual abuse. *The John Marshall Law Review* 18: 1–48

Smith, C.R. 1984. *Adoption and Fostering: Why and How.* London: British Association of Social Work

Smith, E., and R. Guthiel. 1988. Successful foster parent recruiting: A voluntary agency effort. *Child Welfare* 67: 137–45

Smith, S.M. 1975. *The Battered Child Syndrome.* Toronto: Butterworths

Snowden, M. 1987. Adoption of the older child. Manuscript

– 1989. Permanency planning in England, Wales and the Province of Ontario. Mimeograph

Sokoloff, B. 1977. Should the adopted adolescent have access to his birth records and to his birth parents? Why? When? *Clinical Pediatrics* 16 (11): 975–7

Sorosky, A.D., A. Baran, and R. Pannor. 1975. Identity conflicts in adoptees. *Am. J. Orthopsychiat.* 45 (1): 18–27

– 1976. The effects of the sealed record in adoption. *Am. J. Psychiat.* 133 (8): 900–4

– 1977. Adoption and the adolescent: An overview. In S.C. Feinstein and P. Giovacchini, eds., *Adolescent Psychiatry*, vol. 5: 54–72. New York: Jason Aronson

Speers, R.W., and C. Lansing 1965. *Group Therapy in Childhood Psychosis.* Chapel Hill: University of North Carolina Press

Spieker, S.J., and C. Booth. 1985. Family risk typologies and patterns of insecure attachment. In J.O. Osofsky (chair), Intervention with infants at risk: Patterns of attachment. Symposium conducted at the biennial meeting of the Society for Research in Child Development, Toronto, April

Spitz, R.A. 1945. Hospitalism: An inquiry into the genesis of psychiatric conditions in early childhood. *Psychoanal. Stud. Child* 1: 53–74

Sroufe, L.A., and E. Waters. 1977. Attachment as an organizational construct. *Child Development* 48: 1184–99

Stanton, A.H., and M.S. Schwartz. 1954. *The Mental Hospital.* New York: Basic Books

Stapleton, S. 1987. Specialized foster care: Families as treatment resources. *Children Today*, March–April: 27–31

Stayton, D.J., and M.D.S. Ainsworth. 1973. Individual differences in infant responses to brief, everyday separation as related to other infant and maternal behaviors. *Develop. Psychol.* 9: 226–35

Steele, B., and C. Pollock. 1968. A psychiatric study of parents who abuse infants and small children. In R. Helfer and C. Kempe, eds., *The Battered Child.* Chicago: University of Chicago Press

Stein, J., E. Gambrill, K. Wiltse. 1978. *Children in Foster Homes: Achieving Continuity of Care.* New York: Praeger

Stein, L.M., and J.L. Hoopes. 1985. *Identity Formation in the Adopted Adolescent.* New York: Child Welfare League of America

Steinhauer, P.D. 1977. Visits of foster children with natural families. In *Hops, Steps and Jumps*, 2–3. Children's Welfare Assoc. of Victoria, Australia, June

– 1978a. The Laidlaw Foundation workshop on 'the "impossible" child': An overview. *Can. Psychiat. Assoc. J.* 23 (May, special supplement): 67–71

– 1978b. Sharing a child with his parents. Address to the United Foster Parents of Erie County, Buffalo, New York, May

– 1980a. How to succeed in the business of creating psychopaths without even trying. *Training Resources in Understanding, Supporting and Treating Abused Children*, vols. I and IV. Toronto: Ministry of Community and Social Services, Children's Services Division

– 1980b. Permanency planning: prescription for continuity or chaos? Panel presentation, American Orthopsychiatric Association annual meeting, Toronto

– 1982. The courts from the children's perspective. Paper presented at Family

Law and Social Policy Workshop Series, Faculty of Law, University of Toronto, 11 March
- 1983a. Assessing for parenting capacity. *Am. J. Orthopsychiat.* 53 (3): 468–81
- 1983b. Issues of attachment and separation: Foster care and adoption. In P.D. Steinhauer and Q. Rae-Grant, eds., *Psychological Problems of the Child in the Family*, 2d ed., 69–101. New York: Basic Books
- 1984. The management of children admitted to child welfare services in Ontario: A review and discussion of current problems and practices. *Can. J. Psychiat.* 29: 473–83
- 1985. Child development. In S.E. Greben, V. Rakoff, and G. Voineskos, eds., *A Method of Psychiatry*, 2d ed., 9–35. Philadelphia: Lea and Febiger
- 1988. The preventive utilization of foster care. *Can. J. Psychiat.* 33: 459–67
- 1990. Adoption. In B.D. Garfinkel, G.A. Carlson, and E.B. Weller, eds., *Psychiatric Disorders in Children and Adolescents*. Philadelphia: W.B. Saunders
Steinhauer, P.D., and G.W. Tisdall. 1984. The integrated use of individual and family psychotherapy. *Can. J. Psychiat.* 29: 89–97
Steinhauer, P.D., M. Johnston, J.P. Hornick, P. Barker, M. Snowden, J. Santa-Barbara, and B. Kane. 1989. The foster care research project: Clinical impressions. *Am. J. Orthopsychiat.* 59 (3): 430–41
Steinhauer, P.D., M. Johnston, M. Snowden, J. Santa-Barbara, B. Kane, P. Barker, and J.P. Hornick. 1988. The foster care research project: Summary and analysis. *Can. J. Psychiat.* 33: 509–16
Steinhauer, P.D., J. Santa-Barbara, and H. Skinner. 1984. The process model of family functioning. *Can. J. Psychiat.* 29: 77–87
Steller, M., D.C. Raskin, and J. Yuille. 1987. *Sexually Abused Children: Interview and Assessment Techniques*. Mimeograph
Stephenson, P. 1975. The emotional implications of adoption policy. *Comp. Psychiat.* 16: 363–7
Stone, L.A. 1979. Residential treatment. In Saul Harrison, ed., *Basic Handbook of Child Psychiatry*, vol. III: 231–62. New York: Basic Books
Summit, R. 1983. The child sexual abuse accommodation syndrome. *Child Abuse and Neglect* 7: 177–93
Sumner, W.G. 1959. *Folkways*. New York: Dover
Suomi, S. 1989. Presentation to Annual Meeting of Canadian Academy of Child Psychiatry, St John's, Newfoundland, September
Tator, J., and K. Wilde. 1980. Child abuse and the courts. An analysis of

selected factors in the judicial process of child abuse cases. *Can. J. Family Law* 3: 166–205

Ten Broek, E., and R.P. Barth. 1986. Learning the hard way: A pilot permanency planning program. *Child Welfare* 65: 281–94

Terr, L. 1985a. Children traumatized in small groups. In S. Eth and R. Pynoos, eds., *Post-Traumatic Stress Disorder in Children*, 45–70. Washington, DC: American Psychiatric Press

– 1985b. Remembered images in psychic trauma: One explanation for the supernatural. *Psychoanal. Stud. Child* 40: 493–533

– 1986. The child psychiatrist and the child witness: Travelling companions by necessity, if not by design. *J. Am. Acad. Child Psychiat.* 25 (4): 462–72

Terr, L., and A. Watson. 1988. The battered child rebrutalized: Ten cases of medical/legal confusion. *Am. J. Psychiat.* 124: 126–33

Tessman, L.H. 1978. *Children of Parting Parents*. New York: Jason Aronson

Thomas, A. 1981. Current trends in developmental theory. *Am. J. Orthopsychiat.* 51 (4): 580–609

Thomas, A., S. Chess, and H.G. Birch. 1968. *Temperament and Behavior Disorders in Children*. New York: New York University Press

Thorpe, R. 1980. The experience of children and parents living apart: Implications and guidelines for practice. In J. Triseliotis, ed., *New Developments in Foster Care and Adoption*. London: Routledge and Kegan Paul

Tinney, M. 1985. Role perceptions in foster parent associations in British Columbia. *Child Welfare* 64: 73–9

Tizard, B. 1977. *Adoption: A Second Chance*. London: Open Books

Tizard, B., and J. Hodges. 1978. The effect of early institutional rearing on the development of eight-year-old children. *J. Child Psychol. Psychiat.* 19: 99–118

Tizard, B., and A. Joseph. 1970. Cognitive development of young children in residential care: A study of children aged 24 months. *J. Child Psychol. Psychiat.* 11: 177–86

Tizard, B., and J. Rees. 1974. A comparison of the effects of adoption, restoration to the natural mother, and continued institutionalization on the cognitive development of four-year-old children. *Child Development* 45: 92–9

– 1975. The effect of early institutional rearing on the behavior problems and affectional relationships of four-year-old children. *J. Child Psychol. Psychiat.* 16: 61–74

Tizard, B., and J. Tizard. 1975. The social development of two-year-old children. *J. Child Psychol. Psychiat.* 16: 61–74

Tizard, J., and B. Tizard. 1971. The social development of two-year-old children in residential nurseries. In H.E. Schaffer, ed., *The Origins of Human Social Relations*. London: Academic Press

Tolpin, M. 1971. On the beginnings of a cohesive self: An application of the concept of transmuting internationalization to the study of the transitional objects and signal anxiety. In R.S. Eissler, A. Freud, M. Kris, S.L. Lustman, and A.J. Solnit, eds., *The Psychoanalytic Study of the Child*, vol. 26: 316–52. New York: Quadrangle Books

Tooley, K.M. 1978. Irreconcilable differences between parent and child: A case report of interactional pathology. *Am. J. Orthopsychiat.* 48 (4): 703–16

Toussieng, P. 1962. Thoughts regarding the etiology of psychological difficulties in adopted children. *Child Welfare* 41: 59–65

Trasler, G. 1960. *In Place of Parents*. London: Routledge and Kegan Paul

Triseliotis, J. 1970. *Evaluation of Adoption Policy and Practice*. Edinburgh: University of Edinburgh Press

– 1973. *In Search of Origins: The Experiences of Adopted People*. London: Routledge and Kegan Paul

– 1980. *New Developments in Foster Care and Adoption*. New York: Methuen

Triseliotis, J., and J. Russell. 1984. *Hard to Place – The Outcome of Adoption and Residential Care*. London: Heinemann Educational Books

Turner, J. 1984. Reuniting children in foster care with their biological parents. *Social Work* 29 (6): 501–5

Undeutsch, U. 1982. Statement reality analysis. In A. Trankell, ed., *Reconstructing the Past: The Role of Psychologists in Criminal Trials*, 27–56. Stockholm: Norstedt and Soners

Vaillant, G.E. 1975. Sociopathy as a human process: A viewpoint. *Arch. Gen. Psychiat.* 32 (Feb.): 175–83

Vaitenas, R.E. 1981. Children with special needs: Perinatal education for adoption workers. *Child Welfare* 60: 405–11

Vernon, J., and D. Fruin. 1986. *In Care: A Study of Social Work Decision-Making*. Washington, DC: National Children's Bureau, Dept. of Health and Social Security

Wadsworth, M.E.J. 1984. Early stress and associations with adult health, behavior and parenting. In *Stress and Disability in Childhood* (Colston Papers No. 14, Proceedings of the 34th Symposium of the Colston Research Society). Bristol, England: Butler and Corner

Wald, M. 1975. State intervention on behalf of 'neglected' children: A search for realistic standards. *Stanford Law Rev.* 17: 985–1040

Wald, M.S., J.M. Carlsmith, and P.H. Leiderman. 1988. *Protecting Abused and Neglected Children*. Stanford: Stanford University Press

Wallerstein, J., and S. Blakeslee. 1989. *Second Chances: Men, Women and Children a Decade after Divorce.* New York: Ticknor and Fields

Wallerstein, J.S. 1986. Children of divorce: Preliminary report of a ten-year follow-up of older children and adolescents. In S. Chess and A. Thomas, eds., *Annual Progress in Child Psychiatry and Child Development,* 430–47. New York: Brunner/Mazel

Wallerstein, J.S. and J.B. Kelly. 1982. *Surviving the Breakup: How Children and Parents Cope with Divorce.* New York: Basic Books

Ward, M. 1978. Full house: Adoption of a large sibling group. *Child Welfare* 57: 233–41

– 1981. Parental bonding in older-child adoptions. *Child Welfare* 60: 24–34

– 1984. Sibling ties in foster care and adoption planning. *Child Welfare* 63: 321–32

Wasserman, S. 1967. The abused parent of the abused child. *Children* 14 (5): 175

Watson, K.W. 1982. A bold new model for foster family care. *Public Welfare,* Spring: 14–20

Webb, D.B. 1988. Specialized foster care as an alternative therapeutic out-of-home placement model. *J. Clin. Child Psychol.* 17 (1): 34–43

Wehrspann, W., P.D. Steinhauer, and H. Klajner-Diamond. 1987. Criteria and methodology for assessing credibility of sexual abuse allegations. *Can. J. Psychiat.* 32: 615–23

Weick, K.E. 1971. Group processes, family processes and problem-solving. In J. Aldous, ed., *Family Problem Solving: A Symposium on Theoretical Methodological and Substantive Concerns.* Hinsdale IL: Dryden Press

Weidell, R.C. 1980. Unsealing sealed birth certificates in Minnesota. *Child Welfare* 59: 113–19

Weinrich, P. 1979. Cross-ethnic identification and self-rejection in a black adolescent. In G.S. Verma and C. Bagley, eds., *Race, Education and Identity,* 157–75. London: Macmillan

Weinstein, E.A. 1960. *The Self-Image of the Foster Child.* New York: Russell Sage Foundation

West, D.J., and D.P. Farrington. 1973. *Who Becomes Delinquent?* London: Heinemann Educational

– 1977. *The Delinquent Way of Life.* London: Heinemann Educational

Westhues, A., and J.S. Cohen. 1987. *How to Reduce the Risk: Healthy Functioning Families for Adoptive Foster Children.* Vol. 2: *The Research Report.* Toronto: University of Toronto Press

Westman, J.C., and D.L. Kaye. 1983. Termination of parental rights as a therapeutic option. Manuscript

White, M.S. 1981. The role of parent–child visiting in permanency planning for children. *The Social Welfare Forum*. New York: Columbia University Press

White, R.W. 1959. Motivation reconsidered: The concept of competence. *Psychol. Rev.* 66: 297–333

– 1960. Competence and the psychosexual stages of development. *Nebraska Symposium on Motivation*. Lincoln: University of Nebraska Press

– 1963. Ego and reality in psychoanalytic theory. *Psychological Issues*, Monograph 3

Whitebook, M., C. Howes, R. Darrah, and J. Friedman. 1981. Who's minding the child care workers?: A look at staff burn-out. *Children Today* 10 (1): 2–6

Wieder, H. 1977a. The family romance fantasies of adopted children. *Psychoanal. Quart.* 46 (2): 185–200

– 1977b. On being told of adoption. *Psychoanal. Quart.* 46 (1): 1–22

– 1978. On when and whether to disclose about adoption. *J. Am. Psychoanal. Assoc.* 26 (4): 793–811

Wilkes, J. 1979. The stresses of fostering. Part I: On the fostering parents. *J. Ont. Child. Aid Soc.* 22 (9): 1–8. Part II: On the fostering children. Ibid. 22 (10): 7–12

– 1989. Treatment of the limbo child. Presentation to annual meeting of Canadian Academy of Child Psychiatry, St John's, Newfoundland, September

Wiltse, K.T. 1976. Decision-making needs in foster care. *Child Today* 5 (6): 2–5

– 1978. Current issues and new directions in foster care. In *Child Welfare Strategy in the Coming Years*. DHEW Publications number (OHDS) 78-30158. Washington, DC: Government Printing Office

– 1979. Foster care in the 1970s: A decade of change. *Child Today* 8 (3): 10–14

Winnicott, D. 1960. *The Maturational Processes and the Facilitating Environment*. London: Hogarth

Winnicott, D.W. 1957. *The Child and the Outside World*. London: Tavistock

– 1976. The capacity to be alone. In the *Maturational Processes and the Facilitating Environment: Studies in the Theory of Emotional Development*. New York: International Universities Press

Winsberg, B., I. Bialer, S. Kupietz, E. Botti, and E. Balka. 1980. Home vs. hospital care of children with behavior disorders. *Arch. Gen. Psychiat.* 37: 413–18

Witmer, H.L., E. Hertzog, E.A. Weinstein, and M.E. Sullivan. 1963. *Independent Adoptions: A Follow-up Study*. New York: Russell Sage Foundation

Wolf, M.M., C.J. Braukmann, and K.A. Ramp. 1987. Serious delinquent be-

havior as part of a significantly handicapping condition: Cures and supportive environments. *J. Appl. Behav. Anal.* 20: 347–59

Wolfenstein, M. 1966. How is mourning possible? *Psychoanal. Stud. Child* 21:
93–123

Wolins, M. 1963. *Selecting Foster Parents: The Ideal and the Reality.* New
York: Columbia University Press

Wolins, M., and I. Piliavin. 1964. *Institution or Foster Family: A Century of
Debate.* New York: Child Welfare League of America

Wolkind, S., and W. DeSalis. 1982. Infant temperament, maternal mental
state and child behavioral problems. In R. Porter and G.M. Collins, eds.,
Temperamental Differences in Infants and Young Children. London: Pitman

Wolkind, S., F. Hall, and S. Pawlby. 1977. Individual differences in mothering
behavior: A combined epidemiological and observation approach. In P.J.
Graham, ed., *Epidemiological Approaches in Child Psychiatry.* London: Academic Press

Wooding, B.A. 1985. The sexually abused child. Session of workshop entitled
'Dealing with child abuse from the medical perspective.' Presented at Sev-
enth National Conference on Child Abuse and Neglect, Chicago, 11–12 November

Wright, L. 1976. The 'sick but slick' syndrome as a personality component of
parents of battered children. *J. Clin. Psychol.* 32 (1): 41–5

Yarrow, L.J. 1967. The development of focused relationships during infancy.
In J. Hellmuth, ed., *Exceptional Infant,* Vol. 1. *The Normal Infant,* 227–42.
Seattle: Special Child Publication

Yarrow, L.J., and R.P. Klein. 1980. Environmental discontinuity associated
with transition from foster to adoptive homes. *Int. J. Behav. Develop.* 3:
311–22

Yates, A. 1982. Children eroticized by incest. *Am. J. Psychiat.* 139: 482–5

Zimmerman, R.B. 1982. *Foster Care in Retrospect.* Tulane Studies in Social
Welfare XIV: 61–79. New Orleans: Tulane University

Index

- children's rights vs children's needs, 97–8, 217–18
- legal advocate, mandate of, 216–17
- universal advocacy, disadvantages of, 215–16

age: of adoption, 338–9, 351–2; at which children are able to mourn, 37–41; at which children are told about adoption, 73–4, 341–2; as a determinant of foster care or adoption, 9; influence on response to separation, 18; as influencing the response to being in limbo, 29–30

Ainsworth Strange Situation. *See* attachment, Strange Situation

Alberta Parent Counsellors Program, 287–9

antisocial/asocial behaviour, determinants of, 36–7

assessing for parenting capacity, 76–109, 371; basic developmental needs, 76–83; contribution of assessment, 93–8; contribution of history, 91–3; guidelines for (in development), 87–90; literature review, 83–7; role of in-patient assessments, 98–9

attachment: classification of, 21–3; developmental significance of, 13; effect of maltreatment on, 21–4; effect on anxiety and exploration in strange situations, 14; effect on intensity of response to separation, 19–21; effect on socialization, 14; effects of secure attachment on development, 14; effects on subsequent behaviour and competence, 23–4; protection of secure attachment in planning, 221; relation-

ship to capacity for intimacy, 14; relationship to trust, 14; role in development, 13; secure base, serving as, 13; selective, 14; Strange Situation, 20–1; strength of, 14

boundary between 'self' and 'others': effects of incomplete, on relationships, 64; idealization of absent parents, contribution to, 67–8; projection, predisposition to, 6; related to identity formation, 63–4; splitting, 64, 67

burn-out: of foster families, xviii, 188–9; role of underfunding, 227–8

child welfare worker. *See* social workers

consultation. *See* mental health consultation

court system. *See* family court system

crisis intervention: to avert placement, 120–2

defences: gradual undermining of, 152–3; when to challenge, 154

dependency, chronic, 37

depression, 36

detachment. *See* mourning

developmental delay, 87, 95

developmental needs: attachment, 13–14, 19–21, 23–4, 76–8; continuity of key relationships, 82–3; 'good-enough' parenting, 59–62, 78–80; rejection, freedom from, 81–2; socialization (transmission of values), 80–1

drift in foster care, 225–7

DATE DUE

OCT 0 7 1998			
GAYLORD			PRINTED IN U.S.A.